THE ARMCHAIR LIBRARY

THE
Armchair
TRAVELER

EDITED BY
John Thorn and
David Reuther

PRENTICE HALL PRESS

NEW YORK LONDON TORONTO SYDNEY TOKYO

Prentice Hall Press
Gulf+Western Building
One Gulf+Western Plaza
New York, New York 10023

Library of Congress Cataloging-in-Publication Data

The Armchair traveler / edited by John Thorn and David Reuther.
—1st ed.
        p.   cm.
    Includes index.
    ISBN 0-13-046194-6 : $19.95
1. Voyages and travels.   2. Authors—Journeys.   I. Thorn, John,
1947– . II. Reuther, David.
G465.A75 1988
910.4—dc 19   88-18699
CIP

Designed by Stanley S. Drate/Folio Graphics Co. Inc.

Produced by Rapid Transcript, a division of March Tenth, Inc.

Manufactured in the United States of America

10 9 8 7 6 5 4 3 2 1

FIRST EDITION

CONTENTS

INTRODUCTION

An introduction to a travel book is what customs is to travel. If you will grudgingly allow that this is a necessary business and not make too much a show of consternation, we will have you on your way in a moment. Do you have any biases to declare before boarding?

Do you believe that the age of travel is dead, and that all that's possible today is tourism? That the impulse to travel is escapist, the urge to step outside one's self and one's history; or that it is pedagogical, a necessary step to becoming an adult and a citizen of the world? That travel literature must have as its subject the journey, not the destination; or vice versa? That phrase books such as Berlitz and handbooks such as Fielding and road maps such as one might pick up at filling stations are unworthy of armchair recreation? That the traveler must set himself a course—circumnavigating Great Britain as Paul Theroux did or crossing Western Russia by car as Colin Thubron—or that he must open himself to experience by wandering aimlessly about as E. M. Forster in Alexandria, or imitating driftwood like Jonathan Raban on the Mississippi?

We're afraid you will not be able to bring any of these notions past this introduction. We will hold them here for you to gather up when you return, but we rather suspect you will not show up to claim them.

Introductions to anthologies customarily deal as much with what the book is *not* as with what it *is*. As customs agents standing between you and the journey that lies ahead, the editors assert that *The Armchair Traveler* is not just another assemblage, another roadside attraction competing for your attention. Our aim has been to provide neither an overview of travelers from Strabo to Rambo nor a global tour. The editors have elected to pass over some of the masters of travel writing—Boswell, Sterne, Dickens, Frances Trollope, Mary Kingsley—simply because they are so well represented in other collections; and we have selected lesser-known pieces to represent other masters. We offer no writers before the nineteenth century and precious few before the twentieth; we have turned aside from the copious and largely dreadful body of travel verse; and when confronted with a choice between what is historically significant and what is entertaining, we have invariably leapt to the latter. As Cecil Beaton brazenly trumpeted his book on New York, *"More incomplete than any other,"* so do we promote our book of armchair travels. Beaton's readers understood that his book would be entertaining; we trust our readers will come to the same conclusion.

A last note about our selection criteria. Beyond the obvious constraint of book length, we imposed the further restriction that no writer could be represented more than once. How else to avoid including the complete travel writings of Jan Morris or Eric Newby or Richard Halliburton? Making a virtue of necessity, we think we have presented some travel writers who may not be as familiar to you; Chiang Yee and John David Morley and (yes!) Florence Nightingale.

Bon voyage!

—JOHN THORN and DAVID REUTHER

THE
Armchair
TRAVELER

Margaret Atwood

England: A Field Guide

What makes the English so English? In a book such as this, assembled
principally for the English-speaking world, it is perhaps appropriate to
open with a mediator explaining the customs of the Old Country to
travelers from the New. Margaret Atwood is the Canadian poet and
novelist whose feminist dystopia, *The Handmaid's Tale*, was a best
seller a few years back. Her deft guide to what is OK for foreigners in
the U.K., as opposed to the requirements for natives, reminds one of
the "U" and "non-U" debate that Nancy Mitford
sparked in the 1950s.

England is a foreign country, and when you go there, you need to know
more than just what to put in your suitcase. The first thing to remember is
that you are a foreigner. North Americans are sometimes confused about this:
We speak the same language, don't we?

Not, as the English say, *quaite.*

It isn't just a matter of accent, or even vocabulary, though some of that is
bizarre enough. It's the entire attitude toward language itself that's different.

The English relish games, and England itself is one big word game. Look
and listen, and you'll find the evidence everywhere. Not only on radio and
television, but also in the pun-filled, quick-witted advertisements, and in the
House of Commons, where even the political invective is ingenious. (Would
any member of the U.S. House of Representatives call another "a supercilious
git" or "a fascist toe rag"?)

So the English love to play with their mouths, but there are rules.
Conversation, for them, isn't a matter of expressing yourself, and they find
the North American custom of letting it all hang out to be in questionable
taste, a kind of verbal mooning. They themselves talk not to reveal but to
conceal, erecting elaborate artifacts of words which distract attention from
their shy and furtive inner selves. Ask them a personal question, make a
personal remark—even a flattering one—and they stumble and freeze.

If an Englishman of the educated classes wants to charm a woman, he won't stub out his cigarette on her arm, as in Australia, do a mumble-and-flex, as in certain of the more westerly states, or confide his neuroses to her, as in large urban centers. Instead he will weaken her knees with scintillating quips and death-defying one-ups and put-downs. Or he'll go through a modest, whimsical Winnie-the-Pooh routine, after which she's supposed to say, "Silly old bear," and give him a hug. Seduction, in England, is a verbal affair and talking is a kind of ritual display, like the nests of bower birds. (On the other hand, it may not be seduction at all. He may merely be showing off. Even an Englishwoman can't always tell the difference.)

England is still very much a class society, and the English have a sixth sense built in: the class sense. They are covered with prickles, like sea urchins, and these are activated by speech. Open your mouth and you're placed, and treated accordingly. Class isn't just poor people versus rich people. Each class, each subclass of each class, has its loyalties and traditions, and a bit of contempt for those of the others. As a foreigner, however, you have a big advantage: you're classless. Your voice, for them, is white sound: it has no resonance, awakens no memories, provokes no knee-jerk responses. So you can talk to anyone, and you'll often be answered with less caution and more warmth than if you were English.

There is *done* and there is *not done*, but the details vary according to class. Oddly enough, the higher your class, the more things you may do that, at lower levels, are not done at all. You may, for instance, be rowdy and vulgar, because it's assumed you can tell the difference; anyway, background (not mere money) will get you off the hook. When the Queen ate chicken with her fingers in public, that which was previously *not done* became *done* in a twinkling. But if you are a North American, don't try rowdy and vulgar. There are two classes of Americans: plain and nice. You will wish to be considered a nice American. (For Australians, there are no such gradations, it appears.)

Un-American connotes political heresy, but what about un-English. It is eminently English to hold divergent and even eccentric opinions about politics, as about almost everything else. Un-English, then, is reserved for manner and style. But it is not a frequently used term. Not English is, however; it means foreign. Foreign means *not done*. Paradoxically, as a foreigner, you may do, within limits, almost anything. If you get it right it will be put down to lucky coincidence, and if you don't you'll be tolerated anyway, because how can you be expected to know any better?

But there are certain things that are not done whether you are foreign or not. All of them are based on the English principle of physical consideration for others. Those who violate it are known as space invaders, and are treated to those spine-congealing stares that the English do so well, or, in extreme cases, to murmurs of, "Do you *mind?*" So never light up a cigarette in the no-smoking car on the underground, do not jump queues or honk in traffic jams, or play a transistor in a park or interrupt anyone reading a newspaper. If you do, your niceness badge will be taken away.

In England, the police don't carry guns, walking is both a method of locomotion and a hobby, and even the thieves are more polite. Consequently, the English are sometimes baffled and frightened by the American preoccupation with violence. I once tried to explain to an Englishwoman that big-city American women weren't paranoid: It really *was* dangerous to walk outside by yourself after dark.

There was a pause. "I should think," she said, "one would find that undignified."

During my first visit to England many years ago, I spent some time trying to figure out how to dress. Would I really have to get myself a squashed-marshmallow hat like the Queen's; did I need white gloves? I would wander through the shops, past rows and rows of English frocks, printed with tiny flowers, in shape and pattern not unlike hot water bottle covers, and wonder who could wear them without looking like a sofa. I soon realized that the clue to the bagginess of the garments lay in the frigidity of the houses: You had to be able to get a number of things underneath.

The advent of central heating has changed things, but not everyone has it, and since it would be rather bald to ask your hostess in advance, the layered look is advisable. Festoon yourself with the shawls, cardigans, vests, scarves and other woollies which proliferate on every hand. You can always shed.

You don't have to look English, though. You aren't, and everyone will know it as soon as you begin to burble on in your artless foreign way, so you might as well wear what you like. Lapses of taste will be taken for ethnic costume.

And at dress-up time, English theatricality comes to the fore. This is the country that produced Elizabeth I, who, as you can see from her portraits, was three-quarters cloth. Artifice and historical reference still abound, for those with the nerve. Veils, feathers in unlikely places; ruffs, even. And, for men, tweed morning coats.

The hippies, with their crunchy-granola back-to-earth healthiness and blue-jean uniforms, were an American invention; but punk—urban, metallic and defiant—was English. Post-punk girls from the generation of the young unemployed, spend hours improvising their wardrobes, with scissors, colored hair spray, plastic wrap, anything they can scrounge. They're known as posers, which is itself a pun, for it also means a nearly unsolvable problem.

As you wander deeper into the thickets of English culture, stranger and stranger vistas open before you. For instance, the other side of the politeness coin is total outrageousness. England is the home of the dirty seaside postcard, the Wife of Bath, Monty Python, and those endless jokes about knickers, bottoms, loos and foreigners, all of which seem, to the English, to be equally uproarious. And what does lie behind the convention of men dressing up as women in order to make fun of both? Is nothing sacred?

The English adore de-bagging (taking the pants off) anything, especially each other; and of all things English, the sense of humor—by turns deadpan, whimsical, linguistically extravagant, or just plain silly—is perhaps the most baffling. You sometimes wonder how they managed to win the war. But don't be fooled. Underneath, they're serious. How serious? Just let your dog foul the footpath, and you'll find out soon enough.

Cecil Beaton

New York Gastronomy

Turnabout is fair play. Here we have an Englishman's observations on the domestic manners of the Americans. "More incomplete than any other book on New York"—these are the defiant first words of *Cecil Beaton's New York*, a prickly "catalogue of impressions" published in 1938. Sir Cecil stands in a long line of Britons who have been alternately (or simultaneously) fascinated and repulsed by the customs of their American cousins, from Francis Trollope to Jonathan Raban. Is fast food (the "synthetic meal," in Beaton's glorious coinage) really America's signal mark on civilization? The French would say it is the ultimate blasphemy for an Englishman to even write of food, let alone compare any nation's unfavorably to his own.

Since Oliver Cromwell's twelve years of vinegar rule, English cooking has been proverbially bad, yet nothing can be better than plain English produce well prepared. In New York the food is intrinsically tasteless, and, in order to make it appetizing, skill is essential on the part of every cook. Even before it went into the refrigerator the waterlogged lettuce-heart would have tasted of little but paper, but the cook, knowing it is up to her to make the food palatable by the concoction of sauces and tidbits, reserves her highest flight of fancy for the lettuce. Unrecognizable under its sousing of Russian dressing, it is squashed beneath half a pear on which is balanced a slice of pineapple. (Or does the pineapple come under the pear?) A pinnacle of cream-cheese coated with cayenne pepper balances on a prune, and on the summit stands a cherry or a grape. The temptation of the American cook is always to drown the sensitiveness of the palate with these highly seasoned mixtures, and the individual oyster stands no chance against the tomato ketchup.

The American has his food everywhere, but comparatively few meals are served in the home. Dining-rooms hardly exist. A city man never goes home for lunch and, rather than have a cut off the joint, will have a snack at a grill or sandwich-bar, or at the nearest Childs, with a glass of butter-, malted- or acidophulous-milk. He takes his meals fluidly, for his coffee and iced water

5

are served simultaneously with the soup. The coffee is weak. The tea, wrapped like lavender in a muslin bag, is bad and the water never hot enough. The English hide at their meals as if they were doing something immoral, but here, in broad daylight in a window, the American eats his seafood, his olives and celery and his salad course. New Yorkers were the first to eat ice-cream when it was sold by Mr. Hall in 1786, and grown men will never lose their liking for it. But of first importance to the American is the cleanliness of his food. Sugar is hermetically sealed, biscuits are done up in cellophane, sandwiches wrapped in grease-proof paper. The waiters at Childs look like dentists or operating surgeons in their white overalls. Perhaps this is why New York is one of the few cities in which white eggs are considered preferable to brown and are paid for at a premium.

At luncheon time, the counters at the drugstore fill up with customers. There are forty dishes from which to choose—"smothered chicken, grandmother style," "grilled frank on toasted roll," "tuna fish, sliced egg." Fruit pies, sandwiches, soups and sundaes appear in gastronomical disorder along the counter.

Dostoevsky describes a favorite trick that was customary in Russia. When the temperature was a sufficient number of degrees below zero, a victim was invited to lick an axe, to which his tongue became automatically frozen. So the lips of the patrons of New York drugstores appear to remain permanently attached to the rims of glasses containing the freezing streams of chocolate to which they subject their tired stomachs. Just as in Mexico food is peppered to excess, so in New York all drinks are over-iced. Ice is as much an obsession to the Americans as curry to the Indians. One cannot but feel an overt sympathy for the old man on the baby's highchair who thus for forty years must have been corroding his alimentary canal and stomach. The helpless gut suffers, unheeded and unfelt, for the momentary pleasure during which the frost passes into the throat.

Some Americans proudly announce that they have never eaten in a drugstore, and it is true that there is something innately disagreeable about perching at a counter to dispatch a meal in five minutes. One feels that time should be taken in preparing food, that a proper meal should come from a kitchen and be eaten at a table, that it should not be hastily thrown together as one watches. The activity at the gas-stove, the fusion of certain recognized ingredients served with iced water or a Coca Cola, does not seem to be cooking in the gastronomic sense. Drugstore food tends to be tasteless, but the drugstore is ideal if at any moment one is feeling vaguely hungry and wants something more than a bar of chocolate and a cigarette. The club sandwich is probably one of the best products of the "synthetic meal" mentality—the gastronomic equivalent of the skyscraper in architecture.

In Europe, where sweets, books, lunches, medicines, alarm clocks, rubber goods and cigarettes are bought at different places, the drugstore would be inappropriate. But in America, the familiar red neon sign of "Drugs Soda" in every town and village represents the centralization and "service" that makes one feel New York such an easy place to live in.

Few of America's "soda fountain clerks" have either the intention or the desire of remaining such for long. The soda fountain, feature of every American drugstore, is often merely the overture to life for these youths who despise "soda-jerking" as such. That is why so many surround themselves with an aura of intellect coupled with virility, expressed to their customers in a crackling backchat, with some knowledgeably epicurean remark thrown in here and there.

The girl on the stool beside you orders a Chocolate Milk Shake. The clerk bustles about in starched white apron and glengarry, pouring the ingredients into an aluminum mixing can, his manner efficiently scientific. The concoction is served with a glass of iced water, a paper napkin, a cellophane-wrapped biscuit, and straws. The straws sink into the brown foam and the liquid rises up them, through the rounded lips and down the avid gullet. The jerker watches intently. "Laikert?" he asks confidently. The girl goes on sucking. "Well, say something," he persists. Smiling only with her eyes, vaguely and easily, without coyness, she says, "Oh, I give it O.K." The jerker professes chagrin at her indifference and tries the intellectual touch. "Well, what's your conception?" he asks with an amiable wink at the doctor, waiting for a prescription.

"My conception is you oughta be doin' better'n joikin' if this is all you can turn out."

"Sure, we all oughta be doin' bettr'n soda-jerkin', eh, Doc?"

The Automat represents a high point in civilization. Here, *en masse* yet in pleasant conditions, people can eat well at surprisingly small cost.

England's equivalent would be a restaurant with greasy tabletops, coarse and chipped crockery, a severely limited choice of unnourishing food, almost inedible, served intermittently by defiantly tired waitresses.

The Automat has a clinical cleanliness—the tables are washed continuously, even the slots through which the nickels pass are polished many times a day. Around the marble walls are rows of dishes, an infinite variety of food, each a still-life framed in chromium.

Apple pie rests in one brilliantly lit frame, in the next a rich slice of raisin cake, in another a three-tiered sandwich, neatly wrapped in cellophane. How much more appetizing to see such food than to read smudgily printed descriptions on a pasteboard menu. An arrangement of russian salad, cole slaw, cream cheese, and saltines is yours for two nickels. Another nickel brings a cup of coffee, in black and foaming-white jets, in exactly sufficient quantities, from a golden spout; or a pot of freshly brewed tea, shooting into view on a swivel like a conjurer's trick, placed there by the unseen hand of the Trappist monk-like attendant. Returning with the booty to the table brings a feeling of pioneer satisfaction and an interest in the display of individual tastes.

The variety of food is limitless. Men in hats and mufflers gaze blindly ahead as they eat, for ten cents, strawberries in January, *leberwurst* on rye bread, a cut off the roast, huge oysters, a shrimp cocktail, or marshmallow cupcake. To be able to walk out without wasting time in further accounting or interminable waiting for bills gives a pleasant feeling of freedom.

No foreigner exiled in New York need remain at home for his national atmosphere. He is certain to find, somewhere on Manhattan, a restaurant to transport him to the gastronomical delights of home, whether he be from Canton or Bucharest, Stockholm or Marseilles. The alien has his choice of Hungarian restaurants, Turkish, Russian, Greek, Armenian, or Syrian with their *paklava* and honey sweets. In the Hindu restaurants the coffee is thickly Turkish, the bread is Bengalese, the meats are spiced and skewered, the fruits and flowers candied. He will find that the Ruby Foo, on Broadway, has the most delicious soup, made from the spittle of tubercular birds, and other equally imaginative, well-cooked foods, characteristic of the lesser-known Chinese *cuisine*. He will find German restaurants where initials are gouged into scrubbed wooden tabletops. At Luchow's, with frescoes of *The Ring*—goose-fat serving as butter—the food is as fine as any in Germany. In Swedish restaurants he will find arrays of *smorgasbord* extensive enough to hide a billiard table. He may eat Indian curries while he listens to nostalgic Indian melodies played on pear-shaped instruments, or sit in an old pew eating mutton chops and Stilton cheese at the Olde Chop House on Cedar Street, with sawdust on the floor and violins decorating the walls. Most of the English restaurants are of the "Olde Worlde" variety. Almost every nation is represented by at least one restaurant, with its native atmosphere and specialty.

The New Yorker has little taste for wine; hardly surprising, perhaps, since few wines taste well in his city. But he loves to drink for the effects of drink. Of the countless, oddly named brands of liquor that he buys, few are good. The best beer is canned, but beer is surely never the same in a can? The cocktail served before dinner is strong enough to carry him through the ice-water age to the haven of the whiskey and soda afterwards. Serious drinking is reserved, in full earnest, for the weekends. Each Saturday evening brings a run on the liquor stores. Gin is cheaper than whiskey, but it is "Gimmer-nothascotchernsodugh" that the drunkard reiterates. It is curious that no theater possesses its own bar except for soft drinks, and during the few minutes of the intervals, obscure bars down the street enjoy a brief, but inflated, popularity. No liquor is sold on a Sunday morning, even in a hotel, and when the bars are opened at one o'clock, queues have already been formed of people with hangovers, wishing to pile Pelion on Ossa.

Ludwig Bemelmans

The *Normandie*

Every veteran traveler/tourist has had the heady experience of having his class of lodgings or conveyance elevated through some inadvertence; it feels for a moment like winning a sweepstakes. This piece, taken from Bemelmans' 1942 book, *I Love You, I Love You, I Love You*, is a delight for any number of reasons: his ability to convey the humor of Chaplin in print; his "eye as innocent and malicious as a child's," in the words of one critic; and his evocation of a mode and manner of travel now quite extinct. In this last regard, it refers forward in this volume to another evocative piece on vanished ocean liners (see John Maxtone-Graham).

Every time I pass, along the West Side Highway, a spot just above Forty-Sixth Street, there comes over me the feeling that I experience at the dentist's as I wait for him to get through putting the little drill in his machine, the sorrow of saying goodbye, and the sadness of a band playing far away, all rolled into one. It's the stretch where you can look down on the *Normandie*. I am glad to report that workers are busy righting her. The superstructure is gone and on the side over the deluxe cabins are planks and lampposts. It looks as if a street stretched over the water, over the ship—a strange thing to contemplate, a fantastic scene.

I have always given more affection to the *Normandie* than to any other ship. I loved her for her gaiety, for her color, for that familiarity with all the world that was her passenger list. In her décor she leaned toward excess; there was something of the *femme fatale* about her. She assumed a seigneur's privilege of frowning on the lesser, fatter, slower, and more solid boats. Like all aristocrats, she had abominable moods. I think she was more female than all the other ships that I have known. I think that's why I loved her so.

We traveled on her once under extraordinary circumstances. We intended to spend a year in Europe. I had booked passage on her and was ready to sail when an eager young man with an extensive vocabulary came to see me. He told me that the French Line was delighted to have us cross on the *Norman-*

die, that its directors wished to make everything very comfortable for us, and that instead of giving us just an ordinary cabin, they were glad to be able to offer us a *suite de luxe.* I am not one to sleep on a hard mattress when I can have a soft one, so the young man and I bowed to each other and had three martinis each. I went to Mark Cross and bought a set of new trunks to go with the better accommodations and had my tie pressed. We also invited a lot of people to see us off.

It seemed that at the last moment all the ordinary cabins *de luxe* had been taken, and the only thing left to do with us was to put us into one of the *Suites de Grand Luxe.* We went into a palace called Trouville—private terrace, servants' dining room, feudal furniture. Everybody was satisfied, particularly with the Lalique ashtrays.

The next morning I sat in my *dodine* rocking on my private terrace and regarding the morning sun and the sea. After five minutes of the most profound rocking, and of the most profound silence, except for the rocking, I thought I would burst with rage when a man appeared on my private terrace and stood there, looking out to sea.

I shouted, "Excuse me, but I don't think we have met."

"Oh, I'm so sorry, I just came out," said the man.

"Do you happen to know that this is my private terrace *alors?*" I said to him.

"Oh, I'm so sorry. I'm just admiring the view," he said and turned away. I kept on rocking. He walked over to his own private terrace. He was introduced to me later as the banker Jules Bache.

The day after sailing, the great hall, crowded the night before with goodbye sayers, messenger boys, pickpockets and weeping relatives, was now swept clean. The runners had been taken up, the furniture put back in place. The room of silver, gold, and glass, large as a theater, floated through the ever-clean, endless ocean outside the high windows. In a corner, a steward who looked like Sacha Guitry was arranging French stamps in boxes and straightening out the writing paper. Up on the sun deck, children were riding the merry-go-round that was built inside of the first funnel. On the outside of that funnel was a small plaque. It was like the charm on a bracelet, elegant and right. On it was inscribed: *Normandie—Chantiers Penhoet, Saint Nazaire*—and the date she was built. *Chantiers* is a lovely name for a shipyard. It sounds like a song, like the name of a beautiful songbird.

There was a dark fortress of a woman on board that voyage, an old countess with a face made of Roquefort and eyes like marbles, the kind of marbles that boys call "aggies." She sat wrapped in her sables in the front row of three lines of deck chairs outside the main salon. On her lap, covered by a small hound's-tooth blanket, asthmatic and dribbly, sat a Pekingese with thyroid trouble; his eyes were completely outside of his head. Whenever my daughter Barbara passed by her chair, the old countess lifted the blanket, gave the dog, whose name was Piche, a little push, and said to him, *"Piche, regardez donc la petite fille qu'elle est mignonne!"* One day she reached out her hand, but Barbara ducked and ran all the way to the Trouville Suite nursery, where she burst into tears.

The other outstanding figure on that trip was a young widow. She was dressed in long, glamour-girl blond hair and black satin. I think she rubbed herself with a lotion every morning, and then pasted her clothes on her body; there wasn't a wrinkle in them. A doctor could have examined her as she was. Her arms were weighed down with bracelets, all of them genuine, and of course she had a silver fox jacket. An icebox full of orchids helped her bear up throughout the voyage. She appeared with fresh flowers at every meal, and she had with her a sad pale little girl, who was not allowed to play with other children. She wore a little mink coat on deck—the only junior mink I have ever seen.

The way the young widow managed her entrances into the dining-room reminded me of Easter at the Music Hall. She waited until the orchestra played Ravel's *Bolero* and then she came, surrounded by expensive vapors, heavy-lidded, the play of every muscle visible as a python's. At the first landing of the long stairs she bent down, while everyone held their breath, until she succeeded in picking up the train of her dress. Then a faultless ten inches of calf and ankle came into view and, with industrious little steps, she climbed down the rest of the stairs to the restaurant. Once seated, she smeared caviar on pieces of toast and garnished them with whites of eggs until they looked like the cards one sends to the bereaved; with this she drank champagne and looked out over the ocean. The sad little girl said nothing the whole day long.

The last night on board, the widow fell out of her role. A beautiful, exquisitely modeled, long, slim, gartered leg came dangling down from a high-held knee, out of black satin and lingerie. She danced like Jane Avril and let out a wild cowboy "Whoopee," blowing kisses to everyone.

I think the tips on that voyage amounted to more than the whole price of the passage. I have never enjoyed such service. The elevator had not only one operator but a second man who squeezed himself into the cab, pushing the first one against the wall. Then he asked the passengers for their destination and handed this information on to the operator. He also opened the door and rushed ahead to guide us to whatever room we had asked for. The service was perfect, altogether too perfect. I ran into trouble because of its perfection several times. Once, when I went to arrange for railroad tickets, the bearded man standing inside the kiosk bowed, rubbed his hands, and asked me where I wanted to go after the ship docked. I said, "First to Paris, and then to Zuerrs in the Tirol." I ordered three tickets to Zuerrs. I said to him that Zuerrs was on top of the Arlberg between—but I got no further. He stopped me, and explained, "It is I, Monsieur, who will tell you where Zuerrs is found!"

Was there ever anything more real, more certain, than the appearance of the Scilly Islands and Bishop's Rock when, at the end of the voyage, the mists began to take on a greenish tinge and slowly, out of them, came the cliffs and green hills of the English landscape?

Later, off Southampton, the *Normandie* turned into the wind, her propellers trembling as the engines idled. Baskets of Dover sole were brought on board, and a few people with ruddy complexions and sports clothes came up from the tender, to make the crossing over the Channel to France.

As we steamed slowly into Le Havre, the Sacha Guitry steward in the lounge put his stamps away and locked up the writing paper. Then came the most lenient customs inspection imaginable, and we found ourselves about to board the blue boat train for Paris. Instead of an engineer, the chef leaned out of the train, his white cap floating in the smoke of the engine.

When we arrived in Paris, we had to wait until they carried Danielle Darrieux off the train. The frugal French taxicab drivers almost threw their caps in the air when they saw her. They waved them with the greatest degree of abandon and enthusiasm, but they did not let them fly. We finally persuaded one to take us and our baggage. It was impossible to go from the Trouville suite of the *Normandie* to the old Hotel de Nice on the Boulevard Montparnasse, or even to the respectable anonymity of the Saint-Georges-et-D'Albany. So we went to my favorite hotel in Europe, the Ritz, on the Place Vendôme. This rare mansion has the quality of making one feel it has been one's home for centuries. Its elegance is effortless. It might be the residence of an archbishop or a first class *maison close.* Its chief decorative features were the woman's hats in its corridors, the garden, the porters, the waiters, the professional beauties, the young dancing men; the good and the bad made its pulses beat, its doors swing with *élan* and music. It had an imposing entrance on the Place Vendôme and a quiet one on the Rue Cambon. It had, of course, hand-churned butter, an excellent cellar and the model of maîtres d'hôtel in the person of Olivier. It also had a nice set of prices.

One day in the third month that we stayed there, I sat looking out over the elegant tops of the fat cars below in the square while on my fingers I counted the money I had left. It seemed that most of it had simply disappeared, that the year in Europe would shrink to a short vacation, and we would never see Zuerrs in the Tirol.

That afternoon, after I had counted my money three times more, and during the process it had not increased, I went over to the French Line office.

"Look here," I said to the man at the counter, "I would like to have a return passage on the *Normandie*—a cabin for three people in the third class—somewhere near the linen room; an inside cabin, all the way down near the bottom of the ship, at the minimum rate."

He took my name and disappeared. I had seen him on board several times on the way over. He came back looking extremely worried. It is hard to overdo an imitation of a Frenchman when he is excited. The young man acted like Lou Holtz telling a French joke, with gestures.

"Non, non, mais non, non, Monsieur Bemelmans—ça-ne-va-pas!" He emphasized the last syllables separately, exercising his eyebrows in double-quick time. Then he spread out a first-class cabin plan. "We have orders, Monsieur, to extend to you every courtesy. The suite in which you came over happens to be free on the return trip, and it is"—here he made a blue pencil

mark, and a princely gesture with his right hand—"hereby reserved for you again, and at the same price you paid for your passage from New York, the price of an ordinary first class cabin."

"Look," I said—while he had his hands folded and both eyes closed—"I am a writer——"

"I know," he interrupted, flashing the palms of both hands, like two searchlights, "that is just why we wish you to write something very nice—*ah, la publicité, la publicité*—is very important. That is why we are glad to be of ——"

"I am a writer," I continued, "but I do not write only about the *beau monde*. I also write about the simple life. I have found out how beautiful it is upstairs. Now I wish to go downstairs, you understand, and find out how it is down there."

He focused his attention on me by glaring at a red spot on the left side of my nose, where a French bee had stung me in the Jardin d'Acclimatation. He made a lance of his pencil, and pointing at me, he opened his mouth—but I got ahead of him.

"I now want to experience," I said, "how a man feels who has no money, or very little, and who has to eat and live in the third class."

"Ah," he replied, "Victor Hugo did not become a hunchback in order to write *Nôtre Dame de Paris*, and if Balzac had lived like Père Goriot . . ." I stopped him with an icy look, and he returned to a contemplation of my nose, folding his arms and waiting. When I had said my piece, he pushed the cabin plan so that the suite lay in front of me, and pointed at it with his pencil.

"It is all arranged," he said. "You will live in the suite, and every day someone will escort you to the third class, where you may observe life. For your repasts you will, of course, come back upstairs. Madame and the *bébé* will stay upstairs. It will mean a lot of writing and paper work, explanation and confusion, but that is what I am here for."

"Look," I began once more, "you must be very patient with me. I am a very simple person. My mind has chronic limitations. Furthermore, I belong to the ultrarealist school of writers. I want to experience the feelings of a man who is *obliged* to travel in the third class with his wife and child."

"*Enfin*," he shrugged his shoulders, "I have nothing to say." Hopelessly, he shoved the plan around and made the reservation. We sailed back in the third class later that summer.

I saw this man again, a short while ago. He was bent over another book of reservations, in a New York hotel.

"Tell me," he said, searching for the spot on my nose, "what did you find out on that trip? How was the third class?"

"Oh," I said, "I found that a glass of *vin ordinaire* is good, and the *cuisine bourgeoise* is excellent; that the vibration and the pitching are bad. But there was a sharpfaced youngster who tasted ice cream for the first time, and ate himself sick on it. There was a man at our table with a wife and child and dirty fingernails, who appeared on the Passenger List as Mr. and Mrs.

Ginsberg and Infant Condé; and at the next table was a returning missionary who brought his own savages with him in the form of three children who had to be put out of the dining room at almost every meal. There was also a beautiful girl and a young man who loved her. They were coming back from a trip, the *promenade obligatoire* through all the chateaux, cathedrals, ruins and galleries of France. They believed in themselves and in the little book in which they had the names and dates of everything. They could never let each other alone. There was a man in a sweater and cap who had left his home, his business, and a fortune of several million marks behind when he was dragged out of bed one night by the Gestapo. He still hid himself behind ventilators and sneaked along the corridors. He was a sick man when he came on board. He sat alone and ate alone, his eyes always looking down. He was still followed by ghosts. He clung to the side of the deckhouse, when he walked outside, or stood alone on the deck. He seemed to apologize for his own presence. He was afraid that it would all end and from somewhere a hand would seize him and drag him back into his misery. Slowly, he began to heal. . . . The last day, I saw him look up. He smiled.

"We also had the honor of having at our table a detective from the uniformed force of the New York Police Department. He was a wonderful man, as big as a house, with a heart of gold and a handshake that hurt for three hours. He had been on a real busman's holiday, inspected jails, police stations, crime bureaus and disorderly houses. He spoke like a radio program. He was like a book that opened at the beginning of every meal and closed again when he left the table. He lived his life more successfully than any man I have ever met. I think he was really a happy man, the happiest man I have ever known. He lacked the mechanism for being otherwise.

"This enviable functionary must be allowed to express himself. I took down his dinner conversation of Friday. Listen:

"'Well, this goil I was telling you about, Virginia di Milo, traded the love and security of a good home to become a glamor actress in Hollywood. She ran away with a rat named Max, who promised to make a star out of her. He just posed as a director. In real life, the poor goil was Goitrude Schmitt from Brooklyn.

"'I was born in Brooklyn, too, and I was raised in Brooklyn, went through kindergarten and grammar school there and right up through Adelphi Academy. My father was a Republican, but he believed in Wilson. He was like a fish out of water and I guess that's where I get my idealism from. Take Roosevelt! If something happened to that man I think I'd have a real crying spell. I feel about him the way I did about my father. He's a gentleman. My old man was kind, too, but when somebody didn't do the right thing he could slug, just like Roosevelt. . . .

"'Well, Goitrude Schmitt was dead of malnutrition in a cheap rooming house when she met her end, and the last scene was in the home of a brokenhearted mother in Brooklyn, who had come down looking for her, running through the Missing Persons Bureau, but it was too late. . . . That rat, Max, who was responsible for all this, who lured her away and brought her to a life of shame, landed in jail, and we, the detectives of this department which has brought him to justice, hope they'll throw away the key. . . .

"'Now I hope you'll understand this story and take it to heart. Don't disappear, don't be a vanishing American. Good evening.'

"There was hardly a dry eye in the room as he got up and went, with six Catholic priests, to see Betty Boop in the third class movies.

"I remember, too, half a dozen athletic young Americans who used the ship as a gymnasium, despite the purposes of its builders and all the restraining efforts of the crew. They managed to appear one night in dinner clothes, with their girls, up in the first class. . . . Oh, it was all a lot of fun on the *Normandie*, upstairs and down . . ."

"Be careful, be careful," said the clerk, beginning to breathe like a Yogi. "Don't talk about her any more, or I'll cry."

Peter Benchley

Fair Skies for the Cayman Islands

"They paved paradise and put up a parking lot." Those words from a Joni Mitchell tune sum up what has happened to the Bahamas and Hawaii and countless other sunny holiday spots. It is about to happen to the Cayman Islands, formerly a haven from the slings and arrows of civilization, now more a haven from the taxman. Increasingly, developers are eyeing the Caymans in the way the spear fishermen—cited at the end of the piece—eye the groupers: "What they don't understand is that those fish aren't just a meal. They're jobs. If we wipe them out, a whole industry will collapse." That delicate ecosystem is a model for these fair isles and fair people, as Peter Benchley attests in this 1985 article from *National Geographic*.

Our swim from shore had taken less than five minutes, but now my wife, Wendy, and I were in fifty feet of water, surrounded by animals desperately enamored of our guide, big, burly, amiable Wayne Hasson—or, at least, of the stash of ballyhoos (small, silvery, needle-nosed baitfish) he had secreted in his vest pocket. Swarms of ravenous sergeants major and schools of silvery southern sennets, frenetic yellowtail jacks, Nassau groupers. Enormous black groupers brazenly shoved me and allowed Wendy to hold them, one under each of her arms.

We settled down beside the reef, and Wayne placated the milling throng with bits of ballyhoo. And then, from their lairs deep within the reef, like performers emerging languidly from their dressing rooms, came the stars of Wayne's circus: two of the biggest green moray eels I have ever seen—Waldo, seven feet long, and his blushing bride Waldeen (anthropomorphism, I decided, is forgivable at times like this), who measured six feet.

The eels nudged Wayne, coiled around my legs, nibbled tentatively at Wendy's fingertips, never biting, never threatening, never aggressive or afraid. Wayne opened his vest pocket and handed a ballyhoo to each of us, and the eels plucked them from our fingers with surgical delicacy.

We fed the eels until they would accept no more. Then, with sinuous grace, they ambled off to their cleaning station amid the coral, where infinitesimal silvery gobies cruised over their pulsing bodies and removed parasites from their skin.

Back ashore that evening Wendy and I sat on the patio on Grand Cayman, watching the sun squash down into an orange oval, a picture-postcard Caribbean sunset. Behind us a band played calypso music, and men and women in striped slacks and pretty dresses cavorted across the floor. In the distance a small plane wheeled against the western sky—the mosquito plane on its evening patrol to subdue the island's only pests. Overhead, a Boeing 727 flew toward the Grand Cayman airport, bringing tourists—or perhaps some of the legion of wizards attracted to this unlikely world-class financial center.

"I wonder what Columbus would say," mused Wendy, gesturing vaguely at the band, the dancers, and the planes.

"He wouldn't believe a word of it," I said. But then, we wouldn't have believed it either, when we first came to the Cayman Islands eighteen years ago.

As two of a mere ten thousand hardy tourists to visit these three mountaintop islands sandwiched between Cuba and Jamaica in 1967, we watched sunsets from the shelter of a screened porch. If we ventured out in the morning or the evening, we didn't swat mosquitoes; we wiped them off, for they attacked in squadrons so thick that they smothered cattle in the fields and caused poultry to pine away and die.

Then we rented one of a handful of tiny houses on Seven Mile Beach, a band of white sand that makes up the western side of the main island, Grand Cayman. Waterfront land, useless for planting crops or grazing cattle, could then be had for $50 a running foot.

For diversion we wandered through the dusty little capital village, George Town, or went scuba diving with a young man named Bob Soto.

Now, thanks to a combination of foresight, hard work, and common sense, the congenial Caymanians have transformed their country from a backwater colony of Great Britain into a thriving tourist resort, diving mecca, banking center, and tax haven.

Office buildings sprout like tropical weeds in George Town. Twelve-foot dish antennas, aimed to pluck TV signals from orbiting satellites, are as common in backyards as poinciana trees. The downtown Burger King franchise serves some twenty-five thousand customers a month. Seven Mile Beach is packed with hotels and condominiums, and what little beachfront land remains now costs $10,000 a running foot.

The three islands—Grand Cayman, Cayman Brac, and Little Cayman—together contain only about a hundred square miles of land, and the total population (all but ten percent of whom live on Grand Cayman) is only

19,000. Yet the islands are home to 460 banks, 465 insurance companies, and more than 17,700 other companies and corporations. As one of the world's most desirable tax havens, the Cayman Islands process $350 million dollars every day—very little of which ever actually enters the colony.

More than 203,500 cruise-ship passengers visited the islands in 1984, and 148,500 other visitors came for longer stays. Many of them arrived on Cayman Airways, this colony being one of the smallest political units on the planet to own an international jet airline. There is virtually full employment, very little poverty, no visible social unrest, and almost no sentiment for independence from Great Britain.

And crime? There were no murders in 1984. Crimes against property—mostly burglary and theft—accounted for nearly half of all reported offenses. Manslaughter, attempted murder, rape, and grievous bodily harm totaled only thirteen cases.

Was there any theory as to why there is so little serious crime in the islands? Michael Rowling, Q.P.M. (Queen's Police Medal), the islands' police commissioner, believes that the small-town atmosphere is the major deterrent: Detection and harsh penalties are a strong likelihood.

But many people believe it goes beyond that. They feel they share a spirit of true community—that the islands are populated by kind, good people.

These good, kind people have come to the Cayman Islands from all over the globe, from England, Scotland, Ireland, Bermuda, the Americas, Africa, India, and Europe. They are the descendants of buccaneers, pirates, sailors, slaves, and Maroons, who scratched and fished a living from the barren soil and the bountiful sea as farmers, fishermen, seafarers, and boatbuilders. They have names like Ebanks (six columns in the telephone directory), Bodden, Kirkconnell, and Jackson. All are long-rooted and proud Caymanians.

In 1503 Christopher Columbus sailed past two of the islands. Christened Las Tortugas for turtles spied on their shores, they were known as Las Caymanas—the Caymans, possibly after iguanas mistaken for crocodilians of that name—when permanent settlers arrived two centuries later.

Despite Columbus's role in their past, many locals insist that it was Bob Soto who really discovered the islands. Thirty years ago Bob began, developed, nurtured—invented, in fact—the Cayman Islands' scuba-diving industry and thus gave the islands a focus that would attract visitors from around the world. His was the first diving operation in the Caribbean, and under new ownership it remains the largest, most diversified, and arguably one of the best not only in the Caribbean but in the world.

Leathery and weathered, with hands that could drive spikes, Bob is courtly, soft-spoken, and devoid of braggadocio. Sitting at a table with Wendy and me and his wife, Suzy, Bob pointed into the dark distance. "When they were building some new condominiums way over there," he told us, "they came upon a big stone slab in the ground. Lying on the slab were some skeletons. One had a cutlass at its side, one had a knife buried in its ribs, one had a musket-ball hole in its forehead. I asked 'em what they found under the slab. Nothing, they said, 'cause they hadn't picked it up to look. Too much trouble. They just built the condos on top if it." Bob grinned. "Suzy wants me to get a jackhammer and start to work on the floor of the condos."

Like many islanders, Bob served in the British military in World War II and then went to sea. Generations of Caymanians have gone to sea for other nations, the only way they could earn a living.

In the mid-1950s Bob returned home and started to dive. He converted a couple of old oxygen bottles, even a couple of fire extinguishers, into scuba tanks.

Quickly word about the wonders of the Cayman underwater spread throughout the small, close-knit scuba-diving fraternity: miles of virgin reefs, spectacular coral canyons, abundant wildlife unaccustomed to, and thus unafraid of, human beings, and, rarest of all, sheer coral walls descending thousands of feet into an abyss within several hundred yards of the shore.

And no sharks, apparently. I mentioned to Bob that in the dozens of dives I had made all around the islands at all seasons of the year, I had never seen a shark.

"They used to be here," he said, "thick as flies, when there was food for them. But there's been no conservation of fish or of conch or lobsters, no real effort. As the food supply dwindled, so did the sharks. I'm worried that the government won't get up and do something till it's too late. I recommended no more lobster fishing for five years, no more conch fishing for four years. But they put stupid limits on them instead—fifteen lobsters per boat, twenty conch per boat. Well, one morning they're going to wake up and there'll be *no* lobsters, *no* conch, *no* fish."

In recognition of this threat, the government is introducing new regulations to create marine parks, and the diving community is lobbying hard for them—none harder than Ron Kipp, the genial, curly-haired, former IBM branch manager to whom Bob Soto sold his diving operation in 1980.

At the moment, Ron's six boats and staff of twenty-eight handle roughly fifteen thousand divers a year, about a third of the annual total who visit the Cayman Islands.

"I think that only three things can stop this place," Ron said. "A really bad hurricane, if Fidel Castro closes the air corridor over Cuba—increasing the airfare from Florida—or the unlikely event of a really stupid act of terrorism.

"In fact," he added cheerfully, if I had to predict, I'd guess that in eight or ten years the Cayman Islands will be receiving about half a million visitors a year."

Some government officials believe, however, that Ron's rosy forecast fails to take into account the islands' scanty population.

"We have two thousand rooms here," said Eric Bergstrom, the American-born Caymanian who serves as the islands' director of tourism, "and to accommodate more people we would need many, many more rooms. The accepted ratio is one service person for each new room. Right now we're three islands of nineteen thousand people with full employment. We can't grow like that."

I suggested that labor could be imported, but Eric shook his head. The prosperity of the Cayman Islands is a magnet now for the poor, unskilled, and illiterate from Jamaica, and illegal immigrants are already burdening the economy—burdening the school and medical systems and bringing with them drugs that they sell to keep themselves in food and lodging.

"It's the old question we deal with every day," Eric had said. "How much development is enough, and what's it going to do to traditional values? We've had a tenfold increase in the number of visitors over the past few years. When do we stop?

"There's a rule of thumb that I believe in: When your ratio of visitors to locals has risen above eight to one in a small island society, you're heading for trouble. There are several examples elsewhere in the Caribbean of social upheaval and violence when the ratio rose too high. A great influx of foreigners subverts the local culture. The locals undergo a genuine culture shock. In the mind of the man in the street, outside influence is running his country and ruining his country. If we get up to the two hundred thousand level of overnight visitors, we'll see serious social problems."

After talking to Eric, I calculated that at two hundred thousand visitors, the ratio of foreigners to Caymanians would be above ten to one.

And yet the Cayman population is hardly fertile soil for the seeds of revolution. Caymanians are God-fearing (there are sixty churches, one for every 322 people), hard-working, relatively affluent, conservative, and so racially intermixed that bigotry is as rare as snowfall.

"Things good today, yah!" said a man who ought to know. Tollie McLaughlin, born in 1903, sat in the kitchen of his tidy white limestone house in the tidy town of East End. Wendy and I had driven out from East Bay, through the town of Hell, then south around Pull-and-Be-Damned Point, past Bodden Town, Breaker Point, Frank Sound. Each community was a gathering of clean pastel houses, some with picket fences, some with satellite dish antennas.

Tollie sat on an upturned crate and toyed with palm fibers with which he would repair his "wampers," sandals fashioned from old truck tires and secured to his feet with thatch cord.

His wife puttered around in the background. "He be from Irish people," she said of Tollie, whose skin was so dark that he might have been of direct

African ancestry. "I from Scotch people. But they were all pirates back then, and when they couldn't go home, they settled here."

In his fourscore years Tollie has done everything a Caymanian can do to earn a living. Until thirty-nine years ago he went to sea. "Then," he said, "I took to burnin' rock, limestone rock, to get the lime to wash [whitewash] the house. You get the grapetree wood and build a hot fire—a *hot* fire—and melt the rock, and in the end there's a white dust, and that's lime, and you use it to wash the house."

When lime went out, Tollie "took to makin' thatch rope, from the thatch tree [the silver thatch palm, whose fibers are resistant to salt water]. But that died out too, so now I catch jacks."

"Things was plenty worse back then," he said, not lamenting the passing of his several livelihoods, "and '32, she was worst of all." In 1932 the last major hurricane struck the islands. Remembering, Tollie nodded. "All was sea, all. Waves crested on the road and broke on the house, hundreds of coconut palms goin' down the road."

Tollie shook his head and smiled. "Yah. Times is good now. Good."

But during the late 1950s the islands were on a slide into the marsh of idleness and neglect. The traditional Cayman livelihoods—seafaring, making thatch rope, turtling—were in decline. Tourism was a feeble trickle, and Bob Soto had barely begun to plumb the depths of the sea.

"We took a look at our resources," says Thomas Jefferson, financial secretary of the colony, "thinking, 'How can we build Cayman? What do we have?' The conclusion was, we have no basic resources."

What the islands did have, however, were location, climate, political stability, and intelligent people—four ingredients that combined to make possible the creation of today's international tax haven.

I asked Mr. Jefferson to define the ideal tax haven. "It is a country that has no tax legislation or tax treaties on its books," he said, "but has all the services—legal, accounting, communication, transportation—to handle international financial affairs." And, he might have added, secrecy laws that ensure a depositor that all his transactions—wherever he or they may come from—will be private.

The secrecy laws have been an irritant in relations between the Cayman Islands and the United States government, which believes that the islands are a sanctuary for tax evasion and other shady dealings. "The secrecy laws provide an opportunity for laundering money," I was told by Jay Dehmlow, then a Caribbean expert in the State Department's Office of Regional Economic Policy. "Illegitimate money, from illegal enterprises."

The Cayman Islands now cooperate with U.S. investigations involving narcotics but maintain secrecy in other cases.

Regarding U.S. irritation, Mr. Jefferson protested that "in the U.S. the tax-haven issue is grossly distorted. There is nothing devious about it. For example, if the U.S. wants access to an individual's account here, all they have to do is produce proof of a crime that is an offense under the laws of the Cayman Islands. Has he committed fraud? Fine. Prove it, and you have access. But if a man is just avoiding U.S. taxes, that's not a concern of ours. After all, tax avoidance is a respected activity. It makes many a lawyer rich." He smiled wryly. "It is very important to distinguish avoidance from evasion. It is a very thin line."

Another Cayman government official who is exercised about U.S. efforts to crack the islands' secrecy laws is Jim Bodden, former head of tourism, aviation, and trade. Mr. Jim—his nickname is an honorific and a way of distinguishing from the other Boddens in the government—is a tough, white-haired ex-seaman who has become one of the colony's leading real estate developers. Mr. Jim said he keeps telling the Americans, "Don't use us to try to catch a man after he's gotten away with a crime. You catch him up there."

Before it was possible for them to become an international tax haven, the Cayman Islands had to provide a haven from those voracious mosquitoes. And on the outskirts of George Town, in an unprepossessing gray building, is the government office that is truly responsible for the country's astonishing progress—the Mosquito Research and Control Unit.

An earnest young Briton named Fred Burton took me on a tour of the laboratory. "We got our first plane in 1971," he told me. "Before then it was hard to convince people to come here—bankers or tourists—if they knew they had to carry smudge pots with them wherever they went." He stopped at a colored map showing that fully two-thirds of Grand Cayman consists of mangrove swamps. "Now," he said, "we try to contain the mosquitoes in the swamps, so we spray around the perimeters and throughout populated areas."

I wondered why they didn't try to eradicate the mosquitoes altogether. "The fear is," he explained, "that before we killed them all, some would become resistant to the spray. At the moment, things are fine. We maintain better than ninety-six percent control. But who knows? In 1973 the mosquitoes suddenly became resistant to malathion, and the next year was awful.

"Look. Nineteen seventy-four. One trap. One night: 793,103 mosquitoes." He pointed to a series of black dots indicating the locations of nearly thirty traps placed around the island to pinpoint trouble spots. "For comparison, nowadays a night of as many as fifty misquitoes in a trap is rare."

Spraying is conducted at specific times because, as Fred explained, "the black salt-marsh mosquito, which causes most of our problems, swarms only twice a day, at about fifteen minutes after sunset and again just before dawn. We have to get them while they're flying. Non-target insects, like bees, aren't flying then, so they're unaffected."

I asked whether there was any worry about environmental effects of Dibrom, an insecticide in current use, and Fred shook his head. "We use about half the amount recommended by the U. S. Environmental Protection Agency," he said, "and we don't seem to have a problem."

So far, aerial spraying is carried out only on Grand Cayman. The other islands must rely for protection on localized spraying from the backs of pickup trucks. I had heard murmurs that some out-islanders felt resentment toward the powers on Grand Cayman. The residents of Cayman Brac, for example, fewer than two thousand in number, reportedly refer to themselves as the Republic of the Brac—and I wondered whether mosquito control, or the lack of it, might be a factor.

Denise McDermott, a former Miss Cayman Brac, met me at the airport and offered to show me the island. She and her husband, Winston, ran diving operations for the three hotels on the island. As we drove along, Denise admitted that Brackers can indeed be fiercely independent.

"Sometimes we do feel like outcasts," she said. "When Brackers wanted a hospital, they darn well raised all the money and built it themselves. Here's another example: Over there [in Grand Cayman], they say the last bad hurricane was in 1932, right? Well, in 1980 we got a bad one here."

At the small Cayman Brac Museum, Will Ryan, the young caretaker-curator, showed us old farming and boatbuilding tools, old radios, a not-so-old alarm clock, and a bear trap—bought from Montgomery Ward in 1927 by a Mr. Tibbetts.

"Bear?" I asked. "On Cayman Brac?"

"No," Will laughed. "Mr. Tibbetts used it as a mantrap inside the front gate of his plantation. If his neighbor come to steal something, he reach his hand inside to open the gate, and the trap get him."

Denise's aunt, Gwendolyn Bodden, pointed out that the museum was on the site of the old post office. "Hurricane blow down the post office. When? Let's see." Mrs. Bodden calculated. "Year after my toe was cut. I on a hillside watchin' a man chop wood, and I slip and tumble down the hill, and my foot go right under the ax, and *chop!* Well, they slap it back on and it grow back. Then the post office blow down. Yessir, lots of memories here, pirate times and all."

As independent as the Brackers may feel from Grand Cayman, and as independent as all Caymanians may feel from anyone, the islanders seem unanimous in their attachment to Great Britain. Steadfastly they remain a loyal colony. Colonial status has its advantages. Four complex functions of government are handled by Great Britain: external affairs, defense, internal security, and police.

But there is genuine affection among Caymanians for Mother England, forty-five hundred miles away, to which they have been wed since 1670. During the Falkland Islands crisis, they contributed nearly one million dollars to the Mother Needs Your Help Fund—forty-nine dollars for every man, woman, and child.

"There is no real move for independence," Jim Bodden told me. "Of course, there is some agitation for change. There always is. But I don't see anything that will upset the applecart over the next twenty years."

I waited for him to knock wood, but he didn't. And, to be sure, although there are problems, they are few and thoroughly acknowledged: illegal immigration, recessions that interrupted a decade-long building boom, and a drug problem—albeit minor indeed when compared to other islands closer to mainland United States.

One of the most pressing long-term problems is the preservation of the islands' marine resources—its coral reefs and spectacularly abundant wildlife. After our dive with Wayne Hasson, I complimented him on the patience, gentleness, and understanding that has created his wonderful underwater petting zoo. Wayne grinned and said simply, "I hope it lasts."

"What do you mean?"

"One of those big black groupers had a new spear hole in him. Almost every day I have run-ins with the spear fishermen. I ask them to move, try to explain that these fish are tame, that people pay to come and feed them. They say to me, 'You keep feedin' 'em, we'll keep killin' 'em.' What they don't understand is that those fish aren't just a meal. They're jobs. If we wipe them out, a whole industry will collapse."

It was on another dive on another day that I thought of a possible reason why the alarms of the conservationists fall on many deaf ears. I dove with Harry Ward, the dive operations manager of Spanish Cove, one of the finest of the pure diving resorts in the colony. We went far from George Town, far from all human traffic, almost to Rum Point on the north side of Grand Cayman.

We descended in eighty feet of water clear as gin to coral canyons that looked like a prehistoric city on the edge of the abyssal wall. In one canyon were scores—hundreds—of huge tarpon swimming lazily in loose formation, their silver sides glinting in the dim sunlight from above. We swam easily among them, and the formation parted like a silver curtain and closed again behind us.

To the tarpon we were neither predators nor prey. Human beings were accepted members of their environment—clumsy perhaps, noisy certainly— deserving of neither fear nor aggression.

Beyond the tarpon, on a broad sand plain, big stingrays took off and flew and landed and took off again, like fighter planes practicing touch-and-go drills. Jacks followed us curiously, and the ubiquitous sergeants major hovered around in hungry hope.

I thought then, surrounded by so many wild creatures, how difficult it must be to convince a populace that the specter of scarcity looms just around the corner, how hard to make credible a warning of extinction amid such manifest plenty. How do you tell people who have known nothing but abundance from the sea that shortages can become a reality?

Tollie McLaughlin's words rang in my ears: "Yah, times is good now. Good."

And all I could do was hope that good times would remain.

Heinrich Böll

An Irish Pilgrimage

Stendhal wrote: "It is not enough for a landscape to be interesting in itself. Eventually there must be a moral and historic interest." That is the difference between sightseeing and travel, one of the many distinctions to be made between travel and its analogues. To travel with a sense of history is to make a pilgrimage, to commune with the souls of the great or with the masses of nameless people who combined in great efforts. Böll, recipient of the 1972 Nobel Prize for Literature, journeyed to Drumcliff churchyard to see if the spirit of William Butler Yeats was still palpable or if, like the wild swans at Coole, it had flown away.

As the train entered Sligo it was still raining; kisses were exchanged under umbrellas, tears were wept under umbrellas; a taxi driver was asleep over his steering wheel, his head resting on his folded arms; I woke him up; he was one of those pleasant people who wake up with a smile.

"Where to?" he asked.

"To Drumcliff churchyard."

"But nobody lives there."

"Maybe," I said, "but I'd like to go there."

"And back?"

"Yes."

"All right."

We drove through puddles, empty streets; in the twilight I looked through an open window at a piano; the music looked as if the dust on it must be an inch thick. A barber was standing in his doorway, snipping with his scissors as if he wanted to cut off threads of rain; at the entrance to a movie a girl was putting on fresh lipstick, children with prayer books under their arms ran through the rain, an old woman shouted across the street to an old man: "Howya, Paddy?" and the old man shouted back: "I'm all right—with the help of God and His most blessed Mother."

"Are you quite sure," the driver asked me, "you really want to go to Drumcliff churchyard?"

"Quite sure," I said.

The hills round about were covered with faded ferns like the wet hair of an aging red-haired woman, two grim rocks guarded the entrance to this little bay: "Benbulbin and Knocknarea," said the driver, as if he were introducing me to two distant relations he didn't much care about.

"There," said the driver, pointing to where a church tower reared up in the mist; rooks were flying round the tower, clouds of rooks, and from a distance they looked like black snowflakes. "I think," said the driver, "you must be looking for the old battlefield."

"No," I said, "I've never heard of any battle."

"In 561," he began in a guide's mild tone of voice, "a battle was fought here which was the only one ever fought in all the world on account of a copyright."

I shook my head as I looked at him.

"It's really true," he said; "the followers of St. Columba had copied a psalter belonging to St. Finian, and there was a battle between the followers of St. Finian and the followers of St. Columba. Three thousand dead—but the king decided the quarrel; he said: 'As the calf belongs to every cow, so the copy belongs to every book.' You're sure you don't want to see the battlefield?"

"No," I said, "I'm looking for a grave."

"Oh yes," he said. "Yeats, that's right—then I expect you want to go to Innisfree too."

"I don't know yet," I said; "wait here, please."

Rooks flew up from the old gravestones, circled cawing around the old church tower. Yeats' grave was wet, the stone was cold, and the lines which Yeats had had inscribed on his gravestone were as cold as the ice needles that had been shot at me from Swift's tomb: "Cast a cold eye on life, on death. Horseman, pass by!" I looked up; were the rooks enchanted swans? They cawed mockingly at me, fluttered around the church tower. The ferns lay flat on the surrounding hills, beaten down by the rain, rust-colored and withered. I felt cold.

"Drive on," I said to the driver.

"On to Innisfree then?"

"No," I said, "back to the station."

Rocks in the mist, the lonely church, encircled by fluttering rooks, and three thousand miles of water beyond Yeats' grave. Not a swan to be seen.

Anita Brookner

Hotel du Lac

The first woman to hold the post of Slade Professor at Cambridge, Anita Brookner was an internationally recognized authority on eighteenth- and nineteenth-century painting and the author of *Watteau, the Genius of the Future*. When she turned her hand to fiction, the results were even more impressive. The novel whose name this excerpt expropriates won the Booker prize for fiction in 1984, Britain's equivalent to the Prix Goncourt. About a lonely romantic novelist on holiday at an impeccably sedate hotel in Switzerland, it addresses that dreamy sense of freedom that is uniquely the province of the solitary traveler.

The Hotel du Lac (Famille Huber) was a stolid and dignified building, a house of repute, a traditional establishment, used to welcoming the prudent, the well-to-do, the retired, the self-effacing, the respected patrons of an earlier era of tourism. It had made little effort to smarten itself up for the passing trade which it had always despised. Its furnishings, although austere, were of excellent quality, its linen spotless, its service impeccable. Its reputation among knowledgeable professionals attracted apprentices of good character who had a serious interest in the hotel trade, but this was the only concession it made to a recognition of its own resources. As far as guests were concerned, it took a perverse pride in its very absence of attractions, so that any visitor mildly looking for a room would be puzzled and deflected by the sparseness of the terrace, the muted hush of the lobby, the absence of piped music, public telephones, advertisements for scenic guided tours, or notice boards directing one to the amenities of the town. There was no sauna, no hairdresser, and certainly no glass cases displaying items of jewelry; the bar was small and dark, and its austerity did not encourage people to linger. It was implied that prolonged drinking, whether for purposes of business or as a personal indulgence, was not *comme il faut*, and if thought absolutely necessary should be conducted either in the privacy of one's suite or in the more popular establishments where such leanings were not unknown.

Chambermaids were rarely encountered after ten o'clock in the morning, by which time all household noises had to be silenced; no vacuuming was heard, no carts of dirty linen were glimpsed, after that time. A discreet rustle announced the reappearance of the maids to turn down the beds and tidy the rooms once the guests had finished changing to go down to dinner. The only publicity from which the hotel could not distance itself was the word-of-mouth recommendations of patrons of long standing.

What it had to offer was a mild form of sanctuary, an assurance of privacy, and the protection and the discretion that attach themselves to blamelessness. This last quality being less than attractive to a surprising number of people, the Hotel du Lac was usually half-empty, and at this time of the year, at the end of the season, was resigned to catering for a mere handful of guests before closing its doors for the winter. The few visitors who were left from the modest number who had taken their decorous holiday in the high summer months were, however, treated with the same courtesy and deference as if they were treasured patrons of long standing, which, in some cases, they were. Naturally, no attempt was made to entertain them. Their needs were provided for and their characters perused with equal care. It was assumed that they would live up to the hotel's standards, just as the hotel would live up to theirs. And if any problems were encountered, those problems would be dealt with discreetly. In this way the hotel was known as a place which was unlikely to attract unfavorable attention, a place guaranteed to provide a restorative sojourn for those whom life had mistreated or merely fatigued. Its name and situation figured in the card indexes of those whose business it is to know such things. Certain doctors knew it, many solicitors knew it, brokers and accountants knew it. Travel agents did not know it, or had forgotten it. Those families who benefit from the periodic absence of one of their more troublesome members treasured it. And the word got round.

And of course it was an excellent hotel. And its situation on the lake was agreeable. The climate was not brilliant, but in comparison with other, similar, resorts, it was equable. The resources of the little town were not extensive, but cars could be hired, excursions could be taken, and the walking was pleasant if unexciting. The scenery, the view, the mountain, were curiously unemphatic, as if delineated in the watercolors of an earlier period. While the young of all nations hurtled off to the sun and the beaches, jamming the roads and the airports, the Hotel du Lac took a quiet pride, and sometimes it was very quiet indeed, in its isolation from the herd, knowing that it had a place in the memory of its old friends, knowing too that it would never refuse a reasonable request from a new client, provided that the new client had the sort of unwritten references required from a hotel of this distinction, and that the request had come from someone whose name was already on the Huber family's files, most of which went back to the beginning of the century.

As she descended the wide, shallow stairs Edith could hear well-behaved laughter echoing from some sort of salon where she supposed tea to be in progress, and then, as she approached, as if drawn to this sound, a sudden furious barking, high-pitched, peevish, boding ill for future peace. At the foot of the stairs crouched a very small dog, quivering with anxiety, its eyes covered by its hair. When no one came to see what was wrong, it started up again at full volume, but experimentally, like a baby. A prolonged keening, as if it were undergoing unimaginable torture, brought cries of "Kiki! Kiki! Naughty dog!", and a tall woman, of extraordinary slenderness, and with the narrow nodding head of a grebe, rushed out of the bar, collapsed at the foot of the stairs, gathered the dog into her arms, covered it with kisses, and again, with the same boneless uncoiling movement, pressed the dog to her face like a cushion, and returned to the bar. A puddle on the last step brought a momentary closing of the eyes and a quick snap of the fingers from the manager. As a boy in a white jacket wielded a cloth, impassively, as if this happened fairly often, the manager of the Hotel du Lac (Famille Huber) indicated to Edith Hope his distress that this incident should mar her arrival, and at the same time expressed dissociation from the misdemeanors of animals and, more important, from those unwise enough to harbor them. For the latter he would, of course, provide shelter, but shelter without complicity.

How interesting, thought Edith. That woman was English. And such an extraordinary shape. Probably a dancer. And she promised herself to think about this later.

The salon was more agreeable than her room would have led her to expect, furnished with a deep blue carpet, many round glass tables, comfortably traditional armchairs, and a small upright piano at which an elderly man with a made-up bow tie was playing mild selections from post-war musicals. With tea inside her, and a slice of excellent cherry cake, Edith plucked up the courage to look around. The room was sparsely populated; she supposed that most people would only come back for dinner. The pug-faced lady was eating grimly, her legs wide apart, crumbs falling unnoticed onto her lap. Two shadowy men were whispering in a far corner. A grayish couple, man and wife or brother and sister, were checking their air tickets, and the man, who had by no means finished his tea, was sent off periodically to see if the car had arrived. Although the room was bright and cheerful, its most notable feature was its air of deadly calm. Edith, recognizing the fate to which she had been consigned, sighed, but reminded herself that this was an excellent opportunity to finish *Beneath the Visiting Moon*, although it was not an opportunity that she herself had sought.

When she next raised her eyes from her book—a book from which she had absorbed not a single word—it was to find an unexpected note of glamor in the person of a lady of indeterminate age, her hair radiantly ash blonde, her nails scarlet, her dress a charming (and expensive) printed silk, beating time to the music with her hand, a smile of pleasure on her pretty face, while the waitresses, obviously attracted to such a positive presence, hovered round her, offering more cake, more tea. She bestowed a warm smile on them, and an even warmer one on the elderly pianist, who, when he got up and folded his music, came over to her and murmured something which made her laugh, then kissed her hand and left, his stiff, narrow back radiant with the appreciation he had received. Leaning back in her chair, her cup and saucer raised to her chin, this lady drank her tea with some delicacy, even with a sense of favorable presentation, and she did indeed make a delightful spectacle, devoid as she was of the anguish that attacks some people in strange places, and clearly at home in the ambience of the hotel, even if it was three-quarters empty.

Edith watched her as if under hypnosis, sorry to have missed a moment of this spectacle. Rings sparkled on the hand that brought a delicate lace handkerchief to her lips. When her tray had been taken away, Edith waited keenly to see what she would do with the hiatus between tea and dinner, so dispiriting to the unexpected or unaccompanied hotel guest. But of course this lady was not alone. "Here I am," caroled a young voice, and into the salon came a girl wearing rather tight white trousers (rather too tight, thought Edith) which outlined a bottom shaped like a large Victoria plum. "There you are, darling," cried the lady, who was, who must be, her mother. "I've just finished. Have you had tea?"

"No, but it doesn't matter," said the girl, who was, Edith saw, a rather paler version of her mother, or rather the same model as her mother but not brought to the same state of high finish.

"But my darling!" exclaimed the older lady. "You must have tea! You must be exhausted! Just ring the bell. They can make some more."

As one of the waitresses approached, they both turned on her a winning smile, begged for tea, but with an assurance that it would certainly be forthcoming, and immediately, and then lapsed into an engrossing conversation of which Edith could only hear the odd word, together with the joyous and congratulatory spasms of laughter that escaped them both from time to time. When the second tray arrived, they both turned their smiling faces to the waitress, thanked her effusively, and resumed their dialogue, although the girl lingered, as if her part in the ritual might just conceivably be prolonged, but "That will be all, dear," said the lady in the silk dress, and settled down to contemplation of her daughter.

The daughter must be about twenty-five, thought Edith, unmarried, but not worried about it. "She's in no hurry," she could imagine the mother saying, with her fine smile. "She's quite happy as she is." And the daughter would blush and bridle, thus inviting lubricious speculation on the part of the elderly gentlemen who would, Edith was sure, be in relatively constant attendance on the mother. I must stop this, she said to herself. I do not have to make up their lives for them. They are in fact doing very nicely without me. And she felt a pang of wistfulness for such a mother, so good-humored, so elegantly turned out, so insistent that her daughter should have tea, although it was nearly six o'clock. She felt a pang of wistfulness too for the daughter, so confident, so at ease with what was provided for her . . . And they were English, although not of a type with which she was familiar, and rather well-off, and having a good time. They looked as though they always did.

At last they decided to make a move, and when the mother made two attempts to lever herself out of her chair, her daughter hovering energetically beside her, as if knowing exactly when to intervene, Edith saw with some surprise that the older lady was in fact rather stiff in the joints, and that the shining impression of fairly youthful maturity, so impressive from a distance, was not prolonged when she stood up. Thoughtfully, she adjusted their ages, which she had put in the upper fifties and the middle twenties, to the upper sixties and the early thirties. But the appearance was excellent, in both cases. And she was secretly very pleased when the older lady, opposite whom she had been seated, but at some distance, turned round and gave her a mild smile of acknowledgment before she left the room.

Then there was nothing to do but go for a walk.

Through the silent garden, through an iron gate, across the busy road, and along the shore of the lake she walked in the fading light of that gray day. The silence engulfed her once she was past the town's one intersection, and it seemed as if she might walk forever, uninterrupted, with only her thoughts for company. This solitude to which she had been banished, by those who knew best, was not what she had had in mind. And this dim, veiled, discreet, but unfriendly weather: Was this to be an additional accompaniment to this time of trial, for someone who had rashly traveled without a heavy coat? The lake was utterly still; a solitary lamp gleamed above her, turning the limp leaves of a plane tree to brilliant emerald. There is no need for me to stay here if I don't want to, she decided. Nobody is actually forcing me. But I must give it a try, if only to make things easier when I get home. The place is not totally unpopulated. I do need a rest. I could perhaps give it a week. And there is a lot to find out, for someone of my benighted persuasion, although of course none of those people would fit into the sort of fiction I write. But that very long, narrow woman, that beautiful woman, with the tiresome dog. And more than that, the glamorous pair who seem so at ease here. Why are they here? But women, women, only women, and I do so love the conversation of men. Oh David, David, she thought.

Her walk along the lakeshore reminded her of nothing so much as those silent walks one takes in dreams, and in which unreason and inevitability go hand in hand. As in dreams she felt both despair and a sort of doomed curiosity, as if she must pursue this path until its purpose were revealed to her. The cast of her mind on this evening, and the aspect of the path itself, seemed to promise an unfavorable outcome: shock, betrayal, or at the very least a train missed, an important occasion attended in rags, an appearance in the dock on an unknown charge. The light, too, was that of dreams, an uncertain penumbra surrounding this odd pilgrimage, neither day nor night. In the real world through which she walked she was aware of certain physical characteristics: a perfectly straightforward gravel path flanked by two rows of trees standing in beaten earth, on one side the lake, invisible now, on the other, presumably, the town, but a town so small and so well ordered that one would never hear the screaming of brakes or the hooting of horns or the noise of voices raised in extravagant farewell. Only the modest sound of a peaceable file of evening traffic going home came faintly to her ears from somewhere beyond the trees, out of sight. Much louder was the sound of her own steps on the gravel, so loud that it seemed intrusive, and after a while she began to walk on the soft earth of the path nearest the lake. Beneath the light of an occasional lamp, she walked on uninterrupted, as if she were the only one abroad in this silent place. A perceptible chill rose from the water, which she could no longer see, and she shivered in her long cardigan. Doomed for a certain time to walk the earth, she thought, and, brooding but acquiescent, she carried on until she thought it time to be allowed to stop. Then she turned and retraced her steps.

Walking back through the twilight she saw the hotel from afar, lit up, falsely festive. I must make an effort, she decided, although she knew what a different sort of woman would have said, with a worldly sigh, "I suppose I must put in an appearance."

In the silent foyer, bright lights, a mumble from the television room, and a smell of meat. She went up to change.

At the desk, M. Huber the elder, retired but still active, benevolent and only mildly intrusive, was enjoying his favorite moment of the day. He opened the register to see who had gone and who had arrived. Business was of course very slack at this time of the year; the place was bound to be half-empty in the month before the winter closure. The German family had gone, he noted; the noise of their going had indeed penetrated to his sitting room on the fifth floor. That curious elderly couple from the Channel Islands had left after tea. The conference at Geneva might yield the odd visitor, someone who decided to stay on, perhaps, and go back after the weekend. Otherwise, only the regulars were left: the Comtesse de Bonneuil, Mme Pusey and her daughter, the woman with the dog whom he refused to name, although her husband was in the English Gotha, and as to whom his son-in-law had received certain instructions. One new arrival. Hope, Edith Johanna. An unusual name for an English lady. Perhaps not entirely English. Perhaps not entirely a lady. Recommended, of course. But in this business one never knew.

Tim Cahill

World-Class Attractions

Taking aim at the toothpaste-ribbon of kitsch that runs along Route
I-90, Cahill shoots some fish in a barrel . . . but they are the *world's
fastest fish* in what is unquestionably, indisputably, positively, *the
world's largest barrel*. The *Guinness Book of Travel* would surely give
three stars to the NoDak Holstein Hotel or the Largest Cheese Inn. This
is from the 1987 collection of Cahill's columns called,
compellingly, *Jaguars Ripped My Flesh*.

It is said that as a somewhat deflated George Armstrong Custer lay bleeding
in the Montana dirt at the Little Big Horn, he turned his glazed and dimming
eyes east and said, "At least we won't have to back through South Dakota."

These days, Custer might actually enjoy a trip through South Dakota. He
could stop at the Badlands and battle the Winnebagos for a look at Mount
Rushmore. He could hardly fail to resist those several hundred signs commanding him to visit Wall Drug (TURN WHERE YOU SEE THE 80-FOOT DINOSAUR).
Out in eastern South Dakota, in Mitchell, Custer would marvel at the "World's
Only Corn Palace," a great one-block square building decorated entirely with
colored corncobs. Although it is true that the Incas fashioned replicas of
cornstalks out of pure gold, it took South Dakotans to come up with the idea
of decorating the outside of a building with corncobs. When I was there last
Thanksgiving, birds were feeding on the colored corn face of a mammoth
astronaut.

Interstate 90 through South Dakota is, indeed, a paradise of kitsch. By
comparison, the more northerly route across the country, I-94 through North
Dakota, is bleak, barren, almost entirely lacking in roadside attractions.
Those the state does have—like Route 46, the world's straightest road, 121 miles
without a curve—seem to emphasize the drawbacks of driving through it.

Even people who love North Dakota end up damning it with faint praise. Teddy Roosevelt arrived there in 1883, at the age of twenty-five, a spindly young fellow wearing thick eyeglasses. The trip west toughened Roosevelt, and after he demolished a local bully in a fair fight, he won the fearsome nickname Old Four Eyes, which is what all the really tough guys in North Dakota are called. North Dakota, Roosevelt wrote, "has a desolate, grim beauty that has a curious fascination for me." The adjectives here tell the story: grim . . . desolate . . . curious.

Recently, I drove through North Dakota on the way to Wisconsin to visit my parents. I hadn't been in the state for more than ten years and was delighted to discover that there is now a genuine tourist attraction along I-94. Just outside the National Grasslands, I was amazed to see, in the distance, a huge cow standing on a ridge. This cow was at least five miles away, and it dwarfed all the other cows that were standing around in little groups talking about the best way to get out of North Dakota.

At eighty miles an hour, which is the only way to drive through North Dakota, you stare at that big cow for quite some time before you get to the sign saying that you have been looking at the world's largest Holstein cow. There is a turnoff and an arrow. You can drive right up to the world's largest Holstein cow. My guess, having missed the turnoff, is that the cow was fashioned from ferroconcrete. Clustered about its hooves were a cafe, a gas station, and perhaps a motel. All else was utter desolation.

I doubt if the businesses under the cow prosper. By the time you get to the sign showing you where to turn off to see the world's largest Holstein cow, you've pretty much already seen it. That brings up the question of the North Dakota mind, which my fellow Montanans do not hold in high regard.

While Montanans are ranchers, NoDaks are farmers: stolid, respectable, churchgoing folk who have difficulty mastering the mechanical intricacies of the dinner table and who can be spotted by the tiny fork-caused craters in their foreheads. Montanans tell NoDak jokes—you can always get a one-armed NoDak out of a tree simply by waving at him—and NoDaks invariably respond with polite bewilderment.

I suppose it is unfair to attribute feeblemindedness to an entire state upon the evidence of one dim-bulb roadside attraction. People from Wisconsin, where I grew up, are known to be beautiful, sexy, and wonderfully intelligent, yet the state has gone to idiotic lengths to publicize a fact that most people already know, namely that cheese is made there. I am thinking specifically of the twelve-foot-high sculpture of a rat named Igor outside the Fennimore cheese factory in Fennimore, Wisconsin. Igor has four feet, is gray with blue eyes, and has whiskers erupting from its snout. Igor appears to be gnawing a huge piece of swiss cheese.

Large as Igor's cheese may be, it is not the world's largest cheese sculpture. The world's largest cheese, indeed the alleged "Largest Cheese in the History of Mankind," is located in Neillsville, Wisconsin. The seventeen-ton cheddar is enclosed in a semitrailer with one glass side for viewing. Jane and

Michael Stern, in their book *Amazing America,* unraveled the secret of this monolithic cheese. "We peered closely at the cheese and thought it looked pretty unappetizing, like a block of compressed burlap. We looked closer at the fact sheet: 'This cheese was eaten in 1965, at a cheese convention.'" The Sterns, sticklers for accuracy, suggest a more honest appellation for the thing in the glass truck: "The Largest Piece of Cheeselike Burlap in the History of Mankind."

Out there in Neillsville, next to the truck containing the ersatz cheese, is an attraction that would astound all of North Dakota. It is "Chatty Belle, the World's Largest Talking Cow." Chatty Belle is nowhere near as large as the world's largest cow, but Chatty will, at the touch of a button, tell you about a variety of dairy products. (The NoDak Holstein is, predictably, entirely mute.)

Now, what I suggest is that North Dakota engineers—who have already built the tallest structure known to man, the 2,063-foot-high KTHI-TV tower—install a bank of Woodstock-like speakers in the world's largest Holstein, thereby wresting the locution crown from Chatty Belle as well.

The problem here is just what exactly the new world's largest talking Holstein should say. It could, perhaps, threaten tourists who refuse to turn into the cafe. This approach might work in Nevada, but NoDaks are nothing if not polite, and I imagine they wouldn't want to threaten interstate travelers. Maybe the cow should say clever things; maybe it should have a script full of aphorisms and *bons mots.* Of course, the NoDaks would have to hire a Montanan to write such a script. I could do it myself.

I'd have a photoelectric sensing device atop the rise so that even before you could say, "Hey, what's that up there on the ridge?" a great godlike voice would shake the land: "Hi, I'm Igor the Rat."

This single sentence would, in one fell swoop, establish an attraction any American family should want to see: "The Largest Talking Holstein Cow That Thinks It's a Gray Twelve-Foot-High Fiberglass Rat Outside of a Cheese Factory in Fennimore, Wisconsin, in the History of Mankind."

This is the sort of roadside attraction North Dakotans can point to with pride; then again, maybe not. It takes an awful lot of them to screw in a light bulb.

Pedro Carolino

English As She Is Spoke

Here is Berlitz gone mad, from *The New Guide of the Conversation in Portuguese and English*, 1883. A stunned Mark Twain said of Don Pedro's effort, "Many persons have believed that this book's miraculous stupidities were studied and disingenuous; but no one can read the volume through and keep that opinion. It was written in serious good faith and deep earnestness, by an honest and upright idiot who believed he knew something of the English language, and could impart his knowledge to others. . . . Nobody can add to the absurdity of this book, nobody can imitate it successfully, nobody can hope to produce its fellow; it is perfect, it must and will stand alone; Its immortality is secure."

Pâra jantár.

DIÁLOGO 14.

Vâmos jantár; êlle está prômpto.
Â sôpa está nâ mêsa.
Sênte-se âo pê dê mim. Gósta dê sôpa?
Éu cómo dê túdo.
Córte pão: equí ô têm. Não sêi sê êste cozído será bôm.
Éstas costellínhas são óptimas.
Quér feijões?

Sím, senhôr.
Trínche êste perúm. Cômo ácha éssa perdíz?
É excellênte.
Pêdro, destápa úma garráfa dê vínho dô Pôrto.

For to dine.

DIALOGUE 14.

Go to dine, the dinner is ready.
The soup is bringed.
Sit down here by me. Do you like soup?
I eat every thing.
Cut some bread; here is it, I don't know that boiled meat is good.
These cutlets are excellent.
Gentilman, will you some beans?

Yes, sir.
Cut that turkey how you like that pardridge?
It is excellent.
Peter, uncork a Porto wine bottle.

Pâra jantár.	For to dine.

Á súa saúde, senhôr.

Your health, sir.

Víva múitos ânnos.

Thank you.

Quê quér, senhôr?

Sir, what will you to?

Uma áza dê frângo.

A pullet's wing.

Pêdro léva êstes prátos, ê tráz-nos â sobremêsa.

Peter, take away, and bring the dessert.

Quér pêras ôu maçãs?

Some pears, and apples, what wilt you?

Rógo-lhe mê dê úma pêra.

I trouble you to give me a pear.

Ésta parêce-me madúra.

This seems me mellow.

Agradêço-lhe.

I thank you.

Provêmos êste liquôr, quê é bôm pâra ô estômago.

Taste us rather that liquor, it is good for the stomach.

Múito obrigádo; náda máis.

I am too much obliged to you, is done.

Pâra fallár francêz.	For to speak french.

DIÁLOGO 15.

DIALOGUE 15.

Cômo vái Vm. côm ô sêu francêz? Está já múito adiantádo?

How is the french? Are you too learned now?

Bêm pòuco; êu não sêi quási náda.

No too much, I know almost nothing.

Côm túdo, dízem quê Vm. ô fálla múito bêm.

They tell howeuver that you speak very well.

Ôs quê tál dízem estão múi enganádos.

These which tell it they mistake one's.

Certifíco-lhe quê assím m'ô dissérão.

I assure you who was told me.

Púde articulár algúmas palávras quê aprendi dê cor.

I could to tell some word's that I know by heart.

É quânto básta pâra começár â fallár.

It is what it must for to commence to speak.

Não básta quê êu coméce, é necessário quê acábe.

It is not the whole to begin, it must finish.

Fálle sêmpre, bêm ôu mál.

Speak always, right or bad.

Recêio commettêr êrros.

I apprehend, to make some faults.

Nâo tênha mêdo; â língua francêza não é diffícil.

Not apprehend you, the french language is not difficult.

Pâra fallár francêz.	**For to speak french.**

Conhêço ísso; ê quê é múito en-graçáda. Pôr felíz mê daría sê â soubésse!

Â applicação é ô único mêio d'a-prendêl-a. Quênto têmpo há quê â estúda?

Inda não há úm mêz.

Cômo sê cháma sêu méstre?

Châma-se N***

Há múito têmpo quê ô conhêço. Êlle dêu lições â algúns amígos mêus. Não díz êlle â Vm. sêr urgênte fallár francêz?

Sím, senhôr, ê múitas vêzes.

Pôis porquê ô não fálla Vm?

Côm quêm quér Vm. quê êu ô fálle?

Côm ôs quê ô fallárem côm Vm.

Êu bêm quizéra fallál-o, mâs não mê atrêvo.

Déve sêr ousádo, ê não têr ver-gônha.

I know it, and she have great deal of agreableness. Who I would be. If I was know it!

It must to study for to learn it. How long there is it what you learn it?

It is not yet a month.

How is called your master?

*It is called N***.*

I know him it is long; he has teached a many of my friends. Don't he tell you that it must to speak french?

Yes, sir, he tell me it often.

Then why you not speak french?

With which will you that I speak?

With them who shall speak you.

I would to speak too, bud I don't dare.

It must not fear; it must to be hardy.

DIÁLOGO 16.

DIALOGUE 16.

Pâra vêr â cidáde.	**For to see the town.**

António, acompânha êstes sen-hôres, ê móstra-lhés â cidáde.

Desejâmos vêr ô quê élla contêm dê curiôso.

Tênhão â bondáde dê vír comígo; hêide mostrár-lhes quânto é mer-ecedôr dê súa attenção. Êis-nos âo pé dâ cathedrál. Quérem entrár n'élla?

Vêl-â-hêmos primeiramênte pôr fóra ê depôis pôr dêntro.

Anthony, go to accompany they gentilsmen, do they see the town.

We won't to see all that is it remarquable here.

Come with me, if you please. I shall not folget nothing what can to merit your attention. Here we are near to cathedral; will you come in there?

We will first to see him in oudside, after we shall go in there for to look the interior.

DIÁLOGO 17.

Pâra sê informár d'úma pessõa.

Quêm é aquêlle sujêito quê lhê fall-
 áva há pôuco?
É úm Allemão.
Parecía-me Inglêz.
Êlle ê dâ párte dê Saxónia.

Fálla múito bêm francêz.
Aínda quê Allemão, fálla tâo bêm
italiâno, fraucêz, hespanhól ê inglêz, quê, êntre ôs Italiânos, parêce Italiâno. Fálla francêz cômo ôs
mêsmos Francêzes. Ôs Hespan-
hóes ô têem pôr Hespanhól, ê ôs
Ingelêzes pôr Ingléz.

É difícil sabêr bêm tântas línguas
divérsas.
Estêve múito têmpo n'êsses paízes.
Há múito quê Vm. ô conhêce?

Há quási dôus ânnos. Êlle tóca
hárpa, vióla, ê vários ôutros in-
strumêntos.
Folgarêi múito dê ô conhecêr.

Êu lhê darêi conhecimênto côm êlle.

Ônde móra êlle?
Aquí pérto.
Quândo quér Vm. quê vâmos vis-
itál-o?
Quândo quizér.
Irêmos á manhã pêla manhã.
Ficár-lhê-hêi múito obrigádo.

DIALOGUE 17.

To inform one'self of a person.

How is that gentilman who you did
speak by and by?
Is a German.
I did think him Englishman.
He is of the Saxony side.

He speak the french very well.
Tough he is German, he speak so
much well italyan, french, span-
ish and english, that among the
Italyans, they believe him
Italyan, he speak the frenche as
the Frenches himselves. The
Spanishesmen believe him
Spanishing, and the Englishes,
Englisman.
It is difficult to enjoy well so much
several langages.
He was longer in those countries.
How long that you know him?

There is about two years. He play
the lute, the guitar and others
several instruments.
I would be very happy to know
him?
I shall procure you their knowl-
edge.
Where he remains?
He reside hard by.
When will you to that I go to salute
him?
When it shall please you.
We will go to morrow morning.
I shall be you too much oblige.

DIÁLOGO 18.

Pâra montár â cavállo.

Eis úm cavállo quê mé parêce máo. Dême ôutro; não quéro êste. Élle não poderá andár. Ê asmático; está aguádo. Vm. não sê envergônha dê mê dár úm rossím semelhânte? Élle está desferrádo ê encravádo. É necessário mandál-o âo ferradôr. Elle manquêja; está estropeádo, ê é cégo. Ésta sélla mê ferirá. Ôs estríbos são múito comprídos, múito cúrtos. Estênda ôs estríbos, encôlha-os. Âs cílhas estão pôdres. Quê péssimo frêio! Dê-me ô mê chicóte. Áte â mála ê ô mêu capôte.

Âs súas pistólas estão carregádas?
Não. Esquecêu-me comprár pólvora ê bála. Piquêmos, vâmos máis depréssa. Núnca vi peior bêsta. Não quér andár, nêm pâra diânte, nêm pâra tráz.
Alárgue-lhe â rédea. Encúrte-lhe âs rédeas. Esporêie-o rijamênte; fáça-o andár.
Pôr máis quê ô píco, não ô pósso fazêr caminhár.
Desapêie-se; êu ô farêi avançár.
Tóme sentído não lhê atíre algúm côuce.
Élle dá côuces pêlo quê vêjo. Ólhe cômoêu ô súbe domár.

DIALOGUE 18.

For to ride a horse.

Here is a horse who have a bad looks. Give me another; I will not that. He not sall know to march, He is pursy, he is foundered. Don't you are ashamed to give me a jade as like? He is undshoed, he is with nails up, it want to lead to the farrier. He go limp, he is disable, he is blind. That saddle shall hurt me. The stirrups are too long, very shorts. Stretch out the stirrups, shorten the stirrups. The saddles girths are roted, what bat bridle? Give me my whip. Fasten the cloakbag and my cloak.

Your pistols are its loads?
No; I forgot to buy gun-powder and balls. Let us prick. Go us more fast never I was seen a so much bad beast; she will not nor to bring forward neither put back.
Strek him the bridle, hold him the reins sharters. Pique stron gly, make to marsh him.
I have pricked him enough. But I can't to make march him.
Go down, I shall make march.
Take care that he not give you a foot kick's.
Then he kicks for that I look? Sook here if I knew to tame hix.

Bruce Chatwin

In Patagonia

In Patagonia is a picturesque, sensual, exotic book about the strange, desolate vastness of an Argentina beloved of travel writers from W. H. Hudson and Charles Darwin to Paul Theroux and Chatwin. Wrote Darwin: "Why then, and the case is not peculiar to myself, have these arid wastes taken so firm a hold on my memory? Why have not the still more level, the greener and more fertile Pampas, which are serviceable to mankind, produced an equal impression? I can scarcely analyze these feelings: But it must be partly owing to the free scope given to the imagination. The plains of Patagonia are boundless. . . ." And isn't the ignorance of boundaries—territorial, social, and personal— what travel is all about?

The hotel in Río Pico was painted a pale turquoise and run by a Jewish family who lacked even the most elementary notions of profit. The rooms shambled round a courtyard with a water tower and flowerbeds edged with upturned bottles and full of fierce orange lilies. The owner was a brave and sorrowful woman in black, with heavy-lidded eyes, mourning with a Jewish mother's passion the death of her first-born son. He had been a saxophonist. He had gone to Comodoro Rivadavia and died there, of stomach cancer. She picked her teeth with a thorn and laughed at the futility of existence.

Her second son, Carlos Rubén, was an olive-skinned boy with the flickering eyes of a Semite. He ached for the outside world and would soon disappear into it. Her daughters padded over the bare scrubbed rooms in carpet slippers. She ordered a towel and a pink geranium to be put in my room.

In the morning I had a tremendous row about the bill.

"How much was the room?"

"Nothing. If you hadn't slept in it, nobody else would."

"How much was dinner?"

"Nothing. How could we know you were coming? We cooked for ourselves."

"Then how much was the wine?"

"We always give wine to visitors."

"What about the maté?"

"Nobody pays for maté."

"What can I pay for then? There's only bread and coffee left."

"I can't charge you for bread, but café au lait is a gringo drink and I shall make you pay."

Evan Connell

The Last Great Traveler

Un long desir, Anatole France called the almost sensual urge to travel, to explore, to be free of constraints—to be larger than life. *A Long Desire* is what Evan Connell called his 1979 gallery of adventurers, heroes, charlatans, and brutes. Great is what he calls Richard Halliburton, idol to generations including my own (see Halliburton's own contribution to this collection). "Certain people," Connell observes, "do not travel the way most of us travel"; no one ever traveled like Halliburton.

In 1939, when Richard Halliburton tried to cross the Pacific in a Chinese junk, I was a fourteen-year-old stamp collector. Never doubting that he would make it, I paid something like $1.50 to have him deliver a commemorative envelope. It seems to me that he was supposed to initial the envelope, or hand-cancel the stamp, or otherwise authenticate each letter he was carrying. I may be wrong, it's been a while; but I clearly remember how I felt when I heard that the junk was overdue. I felt annoyed and resentful. I wanted my commemorative envelope. And when, finally, there could be no doubt that the junk was lost at sea, I felt I had been swindled. I was nominally sorry for the people on the junk and I spent a little time wondering what happened, but I could not get over feeling peevish that my envelope was not going to arrive. In fact I thought there might be a chance the junk would be found and the cargo rescued. I remember being uncomfortable with this attitude, nevertheless it was so; Halliburton's life, I could not deny, meant less to me than a letter he was carrying.

Now, having had some years to reflect upon it, I find that still I am not proud of my reaction; but I have concluded also that I am no more inhuman than most. A trifle, perhaps, if you insist. But this isn't the point. The point is that when Halliburton vanished I realized for the first time that certain people do not travel the way most of us travel; not only do they sometimes choose odd vehicles, they take dangerous and unusual trips for incomprehensible reasons.

I don't think I wondered why he wanted to cross the Pacific in a tiny boat. He did such things. He climbed the Matterhorn and swam the Hellespont and slept beside the Taj Mahal and so on. That was Richard Halliburton. It was why everybody, boys especially, knew his name. *The Royal Road to Romance* was one of our classics, along with *Kidnapped, White Fang, The Call of the Wild,* and some unforgettable epics by Zane Grey which I have forgotten. So his trip made sense; it was altogether logical that he would set out on an utterly insane voyage across the world's largest ocean in a boat designed for sailing up and down the coast.

He himself had no doubts. In a letter to his parents dated September 10, 1938, he wrote: "Dad, if I could talk to you about the junk trip, I'm sure you would lose all your hesitation over it. Never was an expedition so carefully worked out for safety measures. I've a wonderful captain and engine and engineer . . ."

Two weeks later he wrote: "The name? I chose that long ago—the *Sea Dragon.* On the day of launching, the prettiest Chinese girl whom I can find will break a bottle of rice wine on the *Sea Dragon's* nose. And as the junk slides down the ways we'll beat gongs and shoot off firecrackers, in proper Chinese fashion, to drive away the demons of storm and shipwreck . . . We'll leave China early in January and reach Treasure Island—God willing—the middle of March."

December 12, 1938: "I have complete faith in the captain and the engineer, and feel certain that we'll arrive without the slightest mishap—except a lot of seasickness."

January 1, 1939: "I've lost none of my enthusiasm, and none of my confidence."

In a newspaper article he described how the ship was painted:

The hull is a brilliant Chinese red, edged at the rail with bands of white and gold. The "glance" of the eyes is black. On either side of the poop a Chinese artist has painted a ferocious red and yellow dragon twenty feet long, not counting the curves! Our foresail has been dyed yellow; the mizzensail, vermilion . . . On the *Sea Dragon's* stern, the central section is brilliant with a huge painting of a phoenix—the Chinese good-luck bird.

We'll be twelve aboard, all American: the captain, engineer, radioman, seven seamen including myself, a cook and a cabinboy. And because one solitary mascot would make the total thirteen, which superstitious seamen regard with horror, we're taking along *two* mascots—a pair of white Chinese kittens. This means that the *Sea Dragon* will be responsible for twelve souls and (counting the cats) thirty lives.

In late January came the shakedown cruise. He notified his parents that there were a few defects to be corrected, and that the junk sailed slowly, very deep in the water. He did not sound concerned.

Early in February the *Sea Dragon* left Hong Kong.

Two days out during a storm one of the crewmen fell down a hatch and broke an ankle. Another ruptured himself. Halliburton ordered the captain, John Welch, to return to port.

This is his account of the false start: "We turned up the coast of China, as the peak above Hongkong faded behind us, as a warm twilight came, as a huge moon rose out of the sea. The northeast monsoon, which, on nine days out of ten at this season would have been blowing a gale against us, had faded to a pleasant starboard breeze . . . The *Sea Dragon*, as we wanted it to be, as we had labored hard to make it, had turned into a fantasy of a ship, a picture of a dream-junk from some ancient Chinese painting, a poetry-ship devoid of weight and substance, gliding with bright-hued sails across a silver ocean to a magic land."

On the second day, however, things looked less poetic. Black clouds swirled overhead. Waves began to mount. The radio aerial was ripped loose. Everything not fastened down was tossed about. The messboy lay in his bunk half dead from seasickness. The auxiliary engine was turned on, but because of heavy seas it was necessary to close the hatch, with the result that fumes from the newly painted tanks and bulkheads almost suffocated everybody.

"At six o'clock on the second afternoon we caught sight of a lighthouse on the China coast. At six o'clock in the morning the same lighthouse was still in the same place. We had not gained an inch."

Bearded, exhausted, and dejected, they sailed into Hong Kong harbor on the sixth day. The injured crew members were taken to a hospital, then another collapsed with appendicitis, and the messboy resigned, calling the trip six days of terror.

Halliburton decided to add a fin keel because the *Sea Dragon* rolled heavily. He expected to have this done and new crew members signed up by the end of the week.

Two weeks later he was still in Hong Kong, exasperated but optimistic.

"Mother and Dad: One more—one last—goodbye letter. We sail, again, in a few hours—far more seaworthy than before. The delay has been heartbreaking, but worth it in added safety . . . . All our leaks have been plugged, and the hull tarred. Our fin-keel will keep us from rolling—so we'll be dry, comfortable and even-keeled . . . . So goodbye again. I'll radio you every few days, so you can enjoy and follow the voyage with me. Think of it as wonderful sport, and not as something hazardous and foolish."

On March 5, 1939, he left Hong Kong.

Eight days out he radioed: 1,200 MILES AT SEA ALLS WELL.

On March 19 he sent word that they expected to reach Midway Island by April 5 and would not be stopping at Honolulu.

This message was heard on March 24: CAPTAIN JOHN WELCH OF THE SEADRAGON TO LINER PRESIDENT COOLIDGE SOUTHERLY GALES RAIN SQUALLS LEE RAIL UNDER WATER WET BUNKS HARDTACK BULLY BEEF HAVING WONDERFUL TIME WISH YOU WERE HERE INSTEAD OF ME.

The next day Halliburton's parents were told that there had been no further radio contact. "Well," his mother said, "that's it. It's all over. It's the end."

Captain Charles Jokstad, master of the liner *President Pierce*, had inspected the *Sea Dragon* in Hong Kong at Halliburton's request. Jokstad said later, "I had the awful feeling that I would never see that young man again, and I urged him not to attempt the voyage. It is my guess that the rudder snapped off in a heavy following sea, the ship broached-to in the trough, the masts went out and she broke up—probably in minutes."

Halliburton seems to have been the last great traveler. Eventually somebody may circumnavigate the world in a canoe, but it won't be the same. Now and then an eccentric in a totally inappropriate vehicle does get across the Pacific, or the Atlantic, or survives some other formidable passage, but it reminds us more of Niagara Falls in a barrel than of that sensual urge which Anatole France called *"un long désir."*

A number of Victorian ladies were gripped by that urge. Isabella Bird Bishop. Marianne North. Fanny Bullock Workman. May French Sheldon. Kate Marsden. Mary Kingsley. Annie Taylor. To read of their adventures leaves one feeling incredulous and puny. To look at those nineteenth-century photographs—Isabella about to inspect a Chinese village, buttoned up to the neck and wearing a pith helmet, indomitable, serene, and dumpy, posing beside a tripod camera taller than herself—well, nobody who sees that picture is going to forget Isabella Bird Bishop. Or Fanny Bullock Workman high in the Himalayas, standing truculently beside an ice ax thrust into the snow, stoutly displaying a placard headlined VOTES FOR WOMEN. Kate Marsden en route to Siberia, dressed in a coat big enough for the Cardiff Giant. Mary Kingsley, looking remarkably like Dr. Livingstone, being poled across the Ogowé River in a dugout.

And those prodigious adventurers whose names we know, who couldn't rest because of that long desire. Magellan. Columbus. Marco Polo. Ibn Batuta. Hsüan-tsang. Captain Cook. There's no end to the list, of course, because gradually it descends from such legendary individuals to ourselves when, as children, obsessed by that same urge, we got permission to sleep in the backyard.

Noel Coward

Why Do the Wrong People Travel?

Photographs are to tourists what shrunken heads are to cannibals. It is collector's mania that accounts for the appeal of those six-countries-in-seven-days binges. Lots of clicking, lots of shopping, and lots of totems and luggage stickers to wow the folks back home. The dyspeptic Coward sent up his own in *Mad Dogs and Englishmen*; here he gives it to the Americans.

Travel they say improves the mind,
An irritating platitude
Which frankly, *entre nous,*
Is very far from true.
Personally I've yet to find
That longitude and latitude
Can educate those scores
Of monumental bores
Who travel in groups and herds and troupes
Of various breeds and sexes,
Till the whole world reels
To shouts and squeals
And the clicking of Rolliflexes.

Refrain 1   Why do the wrong people travel, travel, travel,
When the right people stay back home?
What compulsion compels them

And who the hell tells them
To drag their cans to Zanzibar

Instead of staying quietly in Omaha?
The Taj Mahal
And the Grand Canal
And the sunny French Riviera
Would be less oppressed
If the Middle West
Would settle for somewhere rather nearer.
Please do not think that I criticize or cavil
At a genuine urge to roam,
But why oh why do the wrong people travel
When the right people stay back home . . .

Refrain 2 Why do the wrong people travel, travel, travel,
When the right people stay back home?
What explains this mass mania
To leave Pennsylvania
And clack around like flocks of geese,
Demanding dry martinis on the Isles of Greece?
In the smallest street
Where the gourmets meet
They invariably fetch up
And it's hard to make
Them accept a steak
That isn't served rare and smeared with ketchup.
Millions of tourists are churning up the gravel
While they gaze at St. Peter's dome,
But why oh why do the wrong people travel
When the right people stay back home . . .

Refrain 3 Why do the wrong people travel, travel, travel,
When the right people stay back home?
What peculiar obsessions
Inspire those processions
Of families from Houston, Tex,
With all those cameras around their necks?
They will take a train
Or an aeroplane
For an hour on the Costa Brava,
And they'll see Pompeii
On the only day
That it's up to its ass in molten lava.
It would take years to unravel—ravel—ravel
Every impulse that makes them roam
But why oh why do the wrong people travel
When the right people stay back home?

Anita Desai

Hill Stations of the Raj

This piece gives the term *Indian summer* new meaning. Traveling
through time as well as her native India, Anita Desai evokes beautifully
the Simla that was the summer capital of the Raj, and the fading
remnants of empire. From there to the hill stations of Kasauli and
Mussoorie, Ranikhet and Naini Tal, she weaves a splendid tapestry; one
wants to leap from the armchair with her concluding words
and book passage to India immediately.

When I think of my childhood in north India, it is always summer. The
days stretch endlessly, the sun is always at its zenith, turning the sky white
with heat like a sheet of tin, the earth yellow and cracked with aridity. Dust
storms sweep in from the desert, burying whole cities under a suffocating
yellow pelt. In the garden, trees and grass shrivel and turn to straw. The
electricity wavers and dies, the taps run dry.

But then relief would come. On the fifteenth of May, schools closed for the
summer and we packed our books and clothes into tin trunks, baskets, and
bedding rolls, the woolen garments feeling coarse and scratchy to the touch,
travel fever rising in our throats till we felt sick, and then made our way
through the greasy, stifling bazaars whose entire population seemed to be
stretched out on the pavements for air, to the Victorian Gothic pile of red
brick and yellow stucco that was, and is, the Old Delhi railway station. There
we ran up and down the crowded platform, past porters, luggage trolleys,
beggars, and food stalls, searching for the carriage that had our name on the
reservation slip pasted on the door. Then we climbed in to find four green
leather bunks, a ladder for climbing into the upper ones, reading lamps and
metal holders for glasses beside each, a metal washbasin that folded against
the wall, three shutters—of wood, glass, and wire gauze—at each window, to

be pulled up and down, dim violet night lights and electric fans that buzzed like flies against the ceiling (before there was air-conditioning that brought with it not only cool air but protection from soot and grime so that clean bed linen, curtains, and carpeting became possible). A bearer in a grimy white uniform and peaked red turban brought in dinner on tin trays—invariably chicken curry and rice followed by caramel custard (now that there are refrigerators in the dining car, this is replaced by cups of ice cream)—and took our orders for breakfast, which would invariably be very strong tea, buttered toast, and omelets glistening with onions and green chilies. When he left, we prepared for bed, struggling and giggling in that confined space and wondering how some passengers managed to bathe in the closetlike bathrooms, sloshing ankle-deep in water. Finally we climbed into our bunks—not a moment too soon for our exhausted mother—certain we would not sleep for the pounding wheels and the shrill cries of vendors at passing stations—but sleep we did, hammered down into it by the rhythm of the steam train.

At six o'clock we woke to emerge onto the platform of a little toy station in the foothills. Quickly, quickly we transferred our baggage into a smaller train, or a taxi, or a bus, and began winding our way up the flanks of the mountains, rising through masses of bamboo and lantana to enter the pine forests, silvery and susurrating and resinous, then higher still, into a region where mist blew through the fir trees and sprinkled the windows with rain. Eventually it cleared, and we saw the first sloping red tin roofs, the first church steeple and the ramshackle shantytown bazaars sliding down the precipice. We rose, clutching our woolen garments with a sense of purpose because we had arrived at the hill station.

We were following a pattern laid out centuries ago by foreign invaders who came to India for its riches but could not abide its climate. The first Mogul emperor, Babur, complained on arriving: "The people are not handsome, have no idea of friendly society . . . there is no ice or cold water . . . no baths or colleges, no candles, no torches, not a single candlestick," sounding very like the memsahibs who, two centuries later, followed the British adventurers who had decided to expand the frontiers of trade into an empire. In journals, memoirs, and letters home, they deplored the dust, the incompetence of servants, and the proliferation of snakes and scorpions. Women drooped and children died. Something had to be done.

So the British loaded their families and belongings onto horses, carriages, and jampans, and climbed into the Himalayas. Here they found the cool breezes, the wild roses, the streams, waterfalls, firs, and ferns of distant England. True, the mountains towered thousands of feet into the clouds, monsoon rains drenched the hillsides, and the forests were impassable, but, with Queen Victoria's name upon their lips, they dealt with all that. Within a century, roads had been built, with the necessary bridges, tunnels, and aqueducts, and in the cleared forests little English resort towns arose, with timbered cottages, rose arbors, tea shops, theaters, churches, and cemeteries. In that farthest and remotest region, the pillars of the Raj constructed surrealistic replicas of the little coastal towns of Devon and Dorset. The hill station became a part of the Indian experience.

It could be Simla or Mussoorie, Naini Tal or Ranikhet, Darjeeling or Dharmsala. Each claims the title Queen of the Himalayas since each has a tiara of lights to crown the hilltops in the dense darkness of the Himalayan night.

Simla probably has the first claim to the title, since it was the summer capital of the British Raj and is now a state capital. There are still traces of the British but they grow increasingly faint: Viceregal Lodge still stands on top of Summerhill like a baronial castle, but as the Indian Institute of Advanced Studies, it has taken on the shabbiness of bureaucracy, the portraits of the viceroys removed from the paneled walls and metal bookracks and folding chairs shamefacedly occupying the ballroom. The Gaiety Theater on the Mall, a small gem of Regency architecture, no longer stages anything as grand as the Gilbert and Sullivan operas in which the British delighted; it now hosts "guest nites" by Bombay film stars.

This is not the elegant, somewhat decadent scene that Kipling described or Lola Montez briefly dazzled, but Simla remains a center of government: Jeeps with official number plates race busily up and down the streets, and the gray concrete and tin of government housing covers the hillsides with its dismal scab. The schools established by the British for children who could not be sent "home" are now popular with the Indian upper middle class: Boys in gray flannel play soccer on the playgrounds of Bishop Cotton School, and girls at St. Bede's College still learn music and etiquette.

Tourism has proved to be the greatest instrument of change, here as elsewhere. The rich no longer take a cottage and settle in for the summer; today the ordinary Indian middle class come up on overloaded buses from the sweltering cities of the plains, stay for a few days in cheap hotels and stroll on the Mall with transistor radios and cameras, buying spicy snacks for their children and carved walking sticks and felt caps for themselves.

To see a resort relatively untouched by the new tourism, one must take a slight detour through the pine forests on the way to Simla, to Kasauli, the smallest of the hill stations. All the essential features are to be found here—a club with a dance floor, a billiards room, tennis courts beneath gigantic, spreading deodar trees, a gray stone church, an unlovely army cantonment, and cottages called Fairhaven, The Grange, or Shrubberies. Also the first Pasteur Institute in the country, rearing its ominous gray chimneys above the town, and across the valley, the red-roofed buildings of Lawrence School, once a public school for children of army officers, now for Indian children from rich families. In summer the pine forests turn so dry that fires break out; the monsoons bring out wild dahlias and fresh grass where there were ashes.

Mussoorie has all the clamor and crowds of a summer resort. At one end, Charleville, there is a Tibetan refugee center where one can buy Tibetan rugs and embroidered coats, eat dumplings and noodle soup, and watch Tibetan orphans chant their lessons and play. At the other, Landour, there is an American mission school, Woodstock, set amid oaks and rhododendrons, where children play baseball and eat popcorn. Between the two stretches the Mall, crowded with tourists who ride on ponies, buy pink and purple woolens from the pavement stalls, eat ice cream, and play video games. Oddly enough, the sense of the mountains becomes strongest after dark when the lights of Mussoorie go on, the stars swing low out of the sky and, seven thousand feet below, the plains are sprinkled with the luminous dust of city lights beside the rivers that cross it invisibly.

Ranikhet is set deeper in the mountains, the world of the plains and cities left farther behind. One might walk for hours through forests of pine and deodar and see nothing but bands of monkeys swinging in the trees and the sweet-voiced Himalayan magpies with their long blue tails. The town is kept neat and trim and polished by the Kumaun regiment that is stationed there, and the ghosts of the British officers attend its ceremonial dinners in the mess and linger in the club, whose members sit drinking tea on verandas that look out over the gardens and tennis courts to the Trisul range, its highest peak—Nanda Devi—occasionally appearing like a white goddess. In the cavernous, coal-blackened kitchen, the cook can still rise to roast mutton with mint sauce, and the library houses popular novels of the twenties and thirties under a leaking roof. There is no fashionable promenade here, but one can take a picnic to Chaubattia, where apple trees grow in terraces and streams flow through ferns and moss. These forests were once the home of Jim Corbett, the author of "The Man-Eaters of Kumaon," and "The Man-Eating Leopard of Rudraprayag," and although tigers, an endangered species, are confined to the Corbett National Park at the foot of the hills, leopards still roam free, and goats and pet dogs have to be carefully locked up at dusk if they are not to be snatched off in the night. A three-day trek through these mountains and forests takes the more adventurous traveler to the Pindari glacier in flowering meadows below the snow range.

Nearby Naini Tal has one unique feature—a mile-long lake of glassy green water, fringed with willows, on which one can row or sail in the yachts that belong to the yacht club at one end. Across the lake is the temple of the presiding goddess of the lake, its brass bells rung continually by pilgrims. The town itself is held in a cup, climbing steeply uphill. In the season—May to July—the skating rink rings with the sound of roller skates, and ponies scamper around the lake, their tails held by panting grooms as tourists make them gallop with switches cut from willows. The streets are lined with stalls dispensing sweet, syrupy tea, fried snacks, and the plums, peaches, and pears of the region.

The town of Dharmsala, set under the craggy Dhauladhar range of mountains, seldom crossed by any but shepherds and enormous, shaggy mountain goats, has a few British touches about its upper reaches, in Macleodganj—the church and its densely overgrown cemetery, a grocery store, run by the same Parsee family for three generations, which retains posters of Bath Olivers and Chivers jams long after they have been replaced by Indian products—but is otherwise distinctive for its Tibetan population. The Dalai Lama made this his retreat on fleeing from Tibet, and the most devout of the Tibetans have remained in his vicinity so they might see him at prayer meetings or racing uphill in a jeep, pink-cheeked and owlish in large spectacles. Those who wish to study Tibetology or Buddhism or work with Tibetan refugees come to Dharmsala, but few others.

Toward the eastern end of the Himalayas, where they run into Nepal, Tibet, Sikkima, and Bhutan, there is a cluster of hill stations of a very different aspect, not only because they are approached through Calcutta, in the eastern state of Bengal, rather than Delhi, but also because their population is more Mongolian than Indian. The mountains are distinctly closer to the eastern tropics. As you emerge from the plane at Baghdora, or from the train at Siliguri a few miles away, you feel the heavily humid, steamy, sweltering air lap around you and see the dense, damp greenery of a moister land—banana groves, rice fields, straw-thatched huts on bamboo stilts and great teak forests in which elephants roam. Where the forest has been cleared, the tea gardens roll in smooth, serene miles in the shade of feathery trees, tinged blue by passing clouds. You pass the big white bungalows of the tea planters, the tin-roofed factories and the huts of the tea-garden workers as you wind uphill in the little toy train that travels at the pace of a trotting pony. You can jump out to stretch your legs, run alongside through groves of flowering creepers, lantana, and bamboo, then jump on again to climb into the higher reaches where mist swirls down from hilltops crowned with Buddhist monasteries with painted eaves and hosts of fluttering flags.

Darjeeling is as often shrouded in fog as it is bathed in sunshine. A glimpse of Mount Kanchenjunga is so rare and miraculous that one feels blessed and favored as by a goddess, which is indeed how the mountain is regarded by the hill people, Buddhist rather than Hindu, with the slanting eyes and high cheekbones of the Mongolian. There is a Tibetan refugee center where Tibetan scenes are painted on jute scrolls and Tibetan dragons woven into rugs, while the bazaar is full of chunky silver jewelry and brilliantly colored knitted woolens. The influence of the British lingers on in the Planters Club to which planters—now more often Indian than British—come from the surrounding tea gardens to relax with beer on the verandas and in the bar, and in the botanic gardens, where begonias and orchids bloom demurely in a Victorian conservatory. Government House, with its bubble of a dome, is an Occidental vision of the Orient, neither one nor the other.

A drive through the tea gardens, deodar forests, and over the frothing Tista River by a suspension bridge brings one to Kalimpong, three thousand feet lower, so that the conifers are twined with flowering bougainvillea, and mango and papaya grow alongside the wild pear and plum trees. Every third house runs a nursery of delicately scented Himalyan orchids, or Indian cacti and succulents, which are exported all over the world. The population—a mixture drawn from Nepal, Tibet, Sikkim, and Bhutan—lounges around the small bazaar that comes to life twice a week with squealing pigs, ruffled chickens, wild honey and mushrooms, fresh cheese and yak butter, loose tea leaves and medicinal herbs, brought in by farmers and their wives in colored blouses and striped aprons. Before returning to their villages they can be seen spending their earnings in soup restaurants hung with the fresh noodles that are the cottage industry of the area, playing cards and drinking the local liquor, brewed from fermented millet and drunk warm from bamboo mugs through bamboo straws.

Kalimpong's bus depot swarms with the groaning buses that can take you farther through the valley, along the racing Tista—a region known to lepidopterists the world over for its peacock-colored, slowly fanning and opulent butterflies—to Gangtok, the capital of Sikkim. Gangtok, which was once a small village that sprawled at the foot of the palace and the monastery, has grown rapidly into a bustling frontier town with hotels, restaurants, video parlors, and bars that serve the millet brew as well as sweet liqueurs made from coffee, cherries, and betel leaves. From here one can trek to the Pemeyangtse monastery for a closer look at Mount Kanchenjunga, or the Green Lakes where yaks wander in the high meadows, or to the border, where one can look through binoculars at the Chinese soldiers, who wave and shout greetings from the ice and stones of Tibet.

Edwin Asa Dix

Baedeker and His Guide Books

The Baedeker gift is practicality rather than eloquence, and as such
gave rise to modern guides such as Fielding, Fodor, and Frommer. The
public knows that behind these three exemplars of dollar-sign hard-
headedness stand three individuals (see John McPhee's profile of
Temple Fielding). But who today knows of the man behind the Baedeker guide books? This 1908 essay tells the story of a man and his idea.
During World War II the precious Baedeker files were destroyed, but
Baedeker has revived and remains a family firm.

For most travelers abroad, "Baedeker" stands for a guide book rather than a
person. What of the man behind the guide book?

Along in the early 1830s, a young fellow from Westphalia was making the
usual *"wanderjahr"* pilgrimage which the majority of Germans made and
still make as a part of their bringing-up. Poor and rich, all good Teutons
esteem a few months or a year of knocking around Europe as an almost
indispensable preliminary to their work in life. Apprentices and princes alike
rejoice in tramping the Rhine valleys or the Alpine passes with knapsacks on
their backs and a song in their hearts. It is a pleasant and wise and fruitful
custom, and Goethe's *Wilhelm Meister* is a classic record of the practice.

In the thirties the ways of travel had not been smoothed as now. There
were a few sketchy descriptive books. Such books have always existed, wherever there is travel. Even in the Middle Ages, among the earliest products of
the new and wonderful art of printing, there were in circulation treatises on
the pilgrimage to the Holy Land, which was then held to be almost a religious
duty; routes to Jerusalem and Mount Sinai were detailed, with some mention
of the inns and khans, and with warnings as to robbers and the other
dangers of the way. Later, in the sixteenth century, the tide of travel shifted to
Western Europe, attracted in part by the numerous and important book fairs
held in different centers; and about this region a little literature of travel

sprang up. Then Italy came into popularity; Goethe's trip and narrative are well known, and he may very probably have made use in his travels of such accounts as Jaegermann's *Letters on Italy,* first brought out in Weimar in 1778. Later still, especially after Napoleon was quieted and central Europe was at peace, the Rhine began to attract wanderers; the Englishman Murray compiled a handbook of the historic river, and the German Klein published a *Rhine Journey, Mayence to Cologne.* The Grand Tour, popularized in Byron's "Childe Harold," grew to be the fashion; and travelers (especially the English, who were for many years after the Napoleonic wars, the only persons rich enough to travel in any luxury), made the regular round of Paris, the Netherlands and Switzerland, posted through Italy, and perhaps sailed to Greece. This put the Rhine directly into the main course of travel.

The young fellow from Westphalia, Karl Baedeker by name, came of a long and unbroken line of printers, dating from old Diederich Baedeker, who died in Bielefeld in 1716; and he had the exact and orderly mind which should be a printer's heritage. He had served apprenticeships in Heidelberg and Berlin, and had already founded a small bookshop in Coblenz. Tramping along the Rhine, he discovered the need for a new kind of book. Murray and Klein and their like wrote eloquently of the scenery and the legends, but often omitted to advise the traveler where to stop for the night. This in a nutshell gave Karl Baedeker the germ of his idea.

He bought out Klein's copyright, and rewrote the book almost entirely. His methodical German mind evolved a precise and utilitarian system of treatment. He put the hotel first and the scenery afterward. He stated distances and times and prices. He blue-penciled many of the flowery descriptions. He sought to give facts rather than impressions. His aim was to make travel more an exact science and less a venture into the unknown. In 1839 his yellow-covered *Rhine Handbook* first appeared, and as he expected, it filled a want and met an immediate welcome. Touring industriously in person, he next wrote up Holland, and, in 1842, Germany, Austria and upper Italy. This last volume showed the riper development of his original ideas, and is not widely different in form and arrangement from the Baedekers of the present day. It had the now familiar red cover, a clear route-map, and no less than eight plans of cities. Two years later came the Switzerland, the most popular and successful of all the series.

One of the secrets of Baedeker's initial success was that he wrote for the tourist of moderate means. Previous travel books presupposed more or less dependence on lackeys and couriers, more or less subjection to fluctuating charges. Baedeker sought to make travel more independent; he was always pointing out ways of lessening cost. He was himself a sturdy and indefatigable pedestrian, and personally explored most of the routes described in his books. As an instance of his pedestrian prowess, it may be mentioned that he and a companion were the first to make the ascent of the Silberhorn in the

Bernese Alps, that gleaming snow-cone projecting from the huge shoulder of the Jungfrau. He exhibited absolute independence in judging hotels, and proved his disinterestedness by declining all advertisements. For a long while innkeepers used to send him presents, or ask his terms for favorable notices: but the presents were sent back, and the terms were not quoted. They in time discerned the utter uselessness of these overtures, and found that merit alone was the passport to praise. This simple fact has had incalculable influence in raising the standard of hotel comfort and honesty throughout Europe. To gain or lose a "star" in Baedeker may make or mar a landlord's fortune.

Karl Baedeker died in 1859, but not before he had founded a house and name which will long endure. At the time of his death he had published nine guide books. Under his equally enterprising sons Karl and Fritz and his grandson Hans, the firm has now a list of twenty-six guide books in German alone, besides the editions in French and English. In 1872 the firm moved from Coblenz to Leipzig. Of course there are now numerous co-workers and compilers, but the Baedeker system and supervision never relaxes. The firm's representatives travel incognito. Many of them are, like the founder, keen young Germans on their *wanderjahre* or pursuing their studies. For cities like Rome and Athens, scientific and historical specialists are commissioned, or members of the German Archaeological Institute. For Switzerland, picked mountaineers travel over the passes and climb the peaks. The Baedekers continue in part to travel themselves. A hotel-keeper in the Hague once told the present writer of a tall, bearded German of quiet manners, who spent several days at his hotel while exploring the city, and who, on leaving, said: "I am pleased to be able to recommend your hotel; my name is Baedeker."

The renunciation of advertising patronage makes the books slow money-makers at the first. It takes usually ten years to repay the first cost of any new volume. The forms are never stereotyped, but kept in type, subject to immediate and minute changes for each succeeding edition. An interview several years ago in *Pearson's Weekly* quoted Mr. Fritz Baedeker as ascribing much helpful information to voluntary letters from travelers themselves. "It is," he said, "the most important auxiliary that we have."

"How do you induce all these strangers to collaborate with you in the creation of your guide books?" he was asked. "You don't pay them, I suppose?"

"No, I suppose it amuses them. I can understand a sort of instinct prompting people, when they go to a place and disagree with our account of it, to sit down and send us their opinion. Besides, we invite corrections and suggestions in the preface of our books. Many Germans are good enough to take a sort of national pride in the excellence of our guide books, as if we were in some sort a national institution."

As an evidence of this sincerity in welcoming suggestions, the present writer can adduce another little personal incident.

Some years ago, he observed, in the English edition of the Switzerland, a curious and important oversight transposing the respective positions of the Upper and Lower Grindelwald Glaciers. In a letter to the Baedeker firm (who were and are entire strangers to him), he pointed out this error. At once came a most courteous reply, admitting the blunder and expressing perplexity as to how it could have occurred. Mr. Baedeker wrote that it would be promptly corrected in the then forthcoming new edition—a copy of which, in token of his appreciation, he asked permission to send when issued.

The English at first did not take kindly to Karl Baedeker's system. He was an acquired taste. They were accustomed to fine writing and to vaulting descriptions. They complained that he had no soul—only a stomach, a time-table, and a thin pocketbook. But they have long since surrendered at discretion to the value of his unfailing exactitude; and *Fliegende Blaetter* has a picture of an English paterfamilias finding the picturesque castle on the right and the foaming waterfall on the left, instead of vice versa as asserted by his infallible Baedeker, and exclaiming to his flock, "Why, this scenery is all wrong!"

Norman Douglas

The Philosophy of the Blue Grotto

Erudite yet not pedantic; cynical yet not splenetic; sensible yet not plodding—Norman Douglas was one of a kind. His famous prescription for travel writing was: "The reader of a good travel book is entitled not only to an exterior voyage, the descriptions of scenery and so forth, but to an interior, a sentimental or temperamental voyage, which takes place side by side with that outer one; . . . the ideal book of this kind offers us, indeed, a triple opportunity of exploration—abroad, into the author's brain, and into our own." The author of the travel book *Siren Land*, from which this chapter is taken, surely described his own work.

Today the north wind, the *tramontana*, is blowing. A glance out of the window suffices: The sea is deep blue, with ruffled face; mountains and villages are standing out in clear-cut sunshiny reality. And yonder goes the steamer conveying six hundred foreigners for their day's visit to Capri and its celebrated Blue Grotto. Unhappy mortals! They are packed like sheep, although they have paid untold sums for their tickets.

But—in parenthesis—if the foreigners were not constrained to travel first class and at exorbitant rates, how could the steamboat company pay its expenses? For the natives of the country are divided into two great sections: those who travel with third-class tickets, and those who travel with no tickets at all. And of these two sections the latter is by far the most numerous, comprising, as it does, everyone who claims to be a friend or patron of the company, such as: all persons connected with marine service in any part of Italy; stationmasters, engineers, signalmen, soldiers, and so forth, as "colleagues"; hotel proprietors and their families and servants, because, if there were no hotels, there would be no foreigners for the steamers to carry; village fishermen, because they can handle an oar, and their wives and sisters who cook fish which comes out of the sea; certain privileged shopkeepers who once sold a piece of soap or a cigar to a patron; greengrocers, because the captain is fond of vegetables; pastry-cooks and confectioners, because the second stoker has a large family of children—in fact, almost the entire population of the country is exempted, for one reason or another, from purchasing tickets. Eight days ago a grimy housepainter, traveling in the "foreigners'" steamer, informed me that he always voyaged gratis because he lived in the same street as the captain.

Only the poorest of the poor, those who command no respect from either captain, crew, or agents, are obliged to buy third-class fares.

On board, however, the company makes no invidious distinction between these two great sections of natives: They are all accommodated with seats in the first cabin.

And occasionally it arranges for a public example *in terrorem*. Only a short time ago I listened to a stately old gentleman protesting, with tears in his eyes, that he was a prince of the blood besides being mayor of ____. But on that day the official was obdurate. It was "tickets or stay behind." Loudly grumbling, the venerable one extracted a few sous out of his pocket for a third-class fare, and presently I found him seated at my side, explaining to a sympathetic audience that the company had lost what little reputation for honesty it ever possessed. . . .

The *tramontana* generally blows for three days, and is followed by a spell of halcyon calm. Then is the time to visit the Blue Grotto, as an English poet of the thirties has very correctly pointed out—

> The day must cloudless be to visit it,
> The brilliant skies of Italy should pour
> A flood of radiance o'er the tranquil deep,
> And zephyrs even should be hushed and still, etc.

But not in the tourist crowd, although Augustus Hare tells us that the magical effect is enhanced by the rush of boats, the general confusion, and impassioned shrieks that burst forth on all sides. Nor yet in the morning hours, whatever the guidebooks may say to the contrary, for it is only later in the day that the roof and sides of the cavern begin to clothe themselves with that quivering violet sheen due to the low position of the sun. This fairy-like bloom more than compensates for some lack of intensity in the blue of the water.

Dear Ouida! Is there really nothing to be said for the full-blooded generosity, for the passionate blend of realism and idealism of her earlier work? However that may be, it was these afternoon hours which her heroine Idalia, with her usual good taste, selected upon a memorable occasion for a visit to this "temple not built of men."

"Passion was stilled here; love was silenced; the chastened solemnity, the purity of its mysterious divinity, had no affinity with the fevered dreams and sensuous sweetness of mortal desires. . . . The boat paused in the midst of the still violet lake-like water. Where he lay at her feet he looked upwards at her through the ethereal light that floated round them, and seemed to sever them from earth. . . . Would to God I could die now!"

This was the Blue Grotto of the last generation.

"When I entered it," says Gregorovius, somewhat more articulately, "I felt myself transported into one of those fairy tales so real to childhood. The world and daylight have disappeared suddenly, and one finds oneself in the over-arching earth and in the blue twilight of electric fire. Gently the waves lap and the bubbles rise sparkling, as though flashing emeralds, ruddy rubies, and countless carbuncles were shooting up through the depths. The walls are of phantom-like blue and mysterious as the palaces of fairies. It is a glamor of strange nature and strange effects, quite marvelous, at the same time weird and familiar."

Plainly, the Blue Grotto must be one of the wonders of the world. Yet I question whether, if it were discovered today, it would attract the attention it once did. For it appeared on the crest of an immense wave of cavern and ruin worship that overswept Northern Europe—the reaction after the hard and brilliant skeptic movement of the preceding century. It was part of the return to nature; of the revolt from reason. Mankind was weary, for the moment, of straight thinking. Shelley warbled of odorous caves so tunefully that men were almost tempted to become troglodytes again; Rousseau raved of noble savages: He showed us how to discover beauty in Switzerland—the beauty of a colored photograph. Yes; and long may Switzerland with its sham honey, sham wine, sham coffee, sham cigars, and sham Wilhelm Tell—with its inhabitants whose manners and faces reflect their somber and craggy moun-tains—long may it continue to attract, and wholly absorb, the superbly virile energies of our own upper-better-middle classes! Thanks, Rousseau; thanks for not living in Italy.

Others did. Flaxen-haired dreamers, like Hans Christian Andersen, be-gan to sing the praises of the Blue Grotto to a generation reeling with emotionalism. Says Speckter, another sentimentalist: "A melancholy, dreamy effulgence irradiates all things, and in this Blue Wonder are blended Love, Art, and Nature. The Blue Grotto is the full, the over-full, nectar-goblet of Phantasy." They who wish to know to what depths of inanity this kind of talk can be carried, should read *Fiormona*.

The South Italian, constitutionally more sober and familiar with things of beauty, cannot wind himself up to this pitch of rapture over natural objects, besides being quite deficient in that pathetic fallacy which sets up a bond of communion between ourselves and the inanimate world. There are wondrous tints of earth, sky, and sea in these regions—flaring sunsets and moons of melodramatic amplitude that roll upon the hilltops or swim ex-ultingly through the ether; amber-hued gorges where the shadows sleep through the glittering days of June, and the mad summer riot of vines careering in green frenzy over olives and elms and figs; there are tremulous violet flames hovering about the sun-scorched limestone, sea mists that climb in wreathed stateliness among wet clefts, and the sulfurous gleams of a scirocco dawn when fishing boats hang like pallid spectres upon the skyline: There are a thousand joys like these, but the natives do not see them, although, to please foreigners, they sometimes pretend to.

The Blue Grotto belongs to that multitudinous class of objects whose connotation is uselessness and whose full charm is not to be perceived by the bodily eye alone. If the beauty, even of landscape, were to be perceived solely through the medium of the optic nerve, the myopic Hearn would assuredly not be the best describer of things Japanese. This is clear from the way Northerners used to write about this cave; it is not only intensely blue, but it also reminds them of things quite immaterial—of the fairies of their childhood, of the fabled blue flower of romance, of the legend of Glaucus and Elysian skies. Its beauty, therefore, lies partly in suggestion; there is something behind the blue—the mystic's spiritual associations. To a delightful Frenchman, on the other hand, its color suggested a very material object: a candle held at the back of a bowl of sulphate of copper.

The old theory that the Greeks were insensible to the romance of scenery is exploded; apart from the testimony of the anthology and other literature, a single building, like the temple of Bassæ, proves that they were a-tremble in sympathy with the milder voices of nature. And what we may call the indifferent attitude of the South Italian in such matters results, I think, from two causes: the influence of the Romans, whose chief idea of beauty was some snug villa remote from politics and bores; and of medieval movements, that destroyed certain finer emotional fibers and sundered the connection with the mythopœic lore and nature gods of olden days.

The coils of muscle about the shoulders of some stripling as he strains himself to raise a heavy limestone block; a young girl whose swelling form gives promise of fruitful maternity; a waving cornfield, a shower in May, a dish of fat roasted quails—all this is still legitimately *bello:* But mountains are mere hindrances to agriculture, unsightly protuberances upon the fair face of earth, as the pre-romantic Englishman Burnet also called them (no ancient trait of ours, this fellow-feeling with nature: The very word "romantic," as applied to scenery, occurs for the first time in Addison)*; land caves are useful for storing hay; sea caves, blue or green, for sheltering boats in rain; the sea itself, with all its choral harmonies, is merely a place where fishes are caught. The war of elemental forces, stimulating to complex modern minds, has never laid aside for them the terrible and anti-human character with which Greek poets and artists long ago invested it, and which seems to have exceeded their limit of romantic beauty because of its destructiveness to man's life or handiwork. But while the native is beginning to understand, though not to share, the Northerner's passion for storms and cliffs and solitude, he still remains hopelessly at a loss to comprehend those

*Addison in 1705, but John Evelyn in 1654.

recondite ideas of the beauty of pathological states, of suffering and disease which, creeping in from the East, have affected even us, the children of Goths. In short, it seems to me that the South Italian's notion of beauty is never dissociated from that of actual or potential well-being.

It is therefore hardly surprising that the Blue Grotto appealed so slightly to the inhabitants of Capri that they never succeeded in discovering what there was to discover in it. More than three-quarters of them, at this present moment, have not entered it. Those who have been there express no desire to behold its marvels a second time.

And are we not coming round once more to this old pre-romantic point of view? To the romanticists who flocked hitherward in such shoals that their writings and engravings still flood the market, Italy—her landscape, literature and art relics—was a teacher, *the* teacher, the very crown of life. What is Italy now? I open a catalog of travel publications and find, on three consecutive pages, a list of sixty-eight new books describing every corner of the globe, three of which deal with Italy: three out of sixty-eight, and one of them a belated translation of old de Brosses' gossip (1739).

If we now go to Italy at all, we go not to learn, but to compare. Horizons undreamed of, intellectual and geographical, have recently dawned upon us. Greece was discovered; then Egypt and Babylonia and the Sanscrit regions, and—to take only the case of antiquarians—men whose sole idea of research has been to excavate statues for decorative purposes and who, if they ventured to theorize at all, confined themselves to searching for ordered designs of Providence among disordered accidents of history—these men are not engaged in building up, out of mounds of Asiatic kitchen refuse and suchlike trash, a plan of man's early existence upon earth which their ancestors would have deemed the height of folly and blasphemy. Everything has shifted since *homo sapiens* himself shifted and ceased to be the hinge of the universe; life, once the gift of a jealous god, has become a mere series of readjustments, and "nature" the summary of our experience of them; it is hopelessly old-fashioned, nowadays, to read benevolent intentions out of, or into, a movement of things of which we ourselves, together with all the gods and devils we ever created, are only an aspect—an emanation; and which, though it displays neither good nor evil, has yet taught us an entirely new code of morality: the code of truthfulness. We are no longer men of a book, like the Turk with his Koran or the ancients who ended in being hypnotized by their Homer—things that may be a strength in early stages but that lead to ossification; if we now die of a kind of national arteriosclerosis, it will not be the fault of our teachers.

The attitude of a present-day visitor to spots like the Blue Grotto is unintelligible unless one remembers this change in the world-spirit—unintelligible often to himself. I have heard people lamenting that they cannot feel its beauties as acutely as they think they ought. And yet there is nothing to grieve ourselves about; we receive as much sensuous stimulation from the landscape as is good for us and, to atone for lack of sentimentality, we are probably interested in many things of which our grandfathers never dreamt. A sincere zest in diverse facts of life—an opening of moral pores: This is the result of the new departure. Man's field of inquiry used to be limited, while his credulity was unlimited: It is now the reverse in both cases.

Who of us nowadays writes in language like that of Speckter? Alas, we are tired of dreaming; we have become materialistic once more, like those horrid Frenchmen; we will read our Haeckel over and over again, but none of us—no, not one—visits the Blue Grotto twice. And yet it has made Capri. It has slowly but surely routed the rivals of this island, Ischia, Sorrento, and Amalfi, who are bursting with envy; it has created hotels, steamboats, and driving roads; it has stuffed the pockets of the gentle islanders with gold, transforming shoeless and hatless goatherds into high-collared Parisian cavaliers; it has altered their characters and faces, given them comfortable homes and a wondrous fine opinion of themselves. *Viva la Grotta Azzurra!* It has lately built the funicular railway; it has dappled the island with the villas of eccentric strangers; it has studded the lonely seashore with caves fancy-tinted like Joseph's coat. For hardly was the Blue Grotto discovered and the meaning of the word "blue" explained to these children of nature before other gorgeous caverns, hitherto unnoticed, claimed attention. The foreigners liked color in caves. The foreigners brought money. Color in caves is cheap. Let them have it! Therefore, in a twinkling, the two-mouthed Grotta del Turco became the Green Grotto; the venerable Grotta Ruofolo put on a roseate hue sufficient to justify the poetic title of Red Grotto, and the Grotta Monacone (*vide* the relation of Kopisach) was discovered to be white—actually quite white! The stranger had his willful way, and the metamorphosis had cost the Capriotes not a *soldo*. It was a blessed time: Every-one beamed with joy. But what will the future bring? The gentle islanders have grown rich, rich beyond the dreams of avarice, and almost turn up their noses at *soldi;* while travelers are beginning to turn up their noses at Capri caverns, whose odors, to tell the truth, are not always of violets.

If the Green and other grottos had ancient names, what was that of the Blue? It used to be called Grotta Gradola: a pleonasm, inasmuch as Gradola, or Gratula, is merely a corruption of Grottola (grottola, gruptula, grupta, crypta), and the district overhead bears the old name to this day. I know no earlier proof to show that the Italians were acquainted with the Blue Grotto than that contained in Coronelli's *Atlante Veneto,* which includes an interesting map of Capri, whereon it is marked as "Grotta Gradola." Coronelli was cosmographer to the Venetian Republic, and his work is dated 1696. In the face of a document like this, how absurd it is to say that the cave was unknown to the natives and discovered by a foreigner! It was Landor, I believe, who said that people who talk loudest are always in the right. This was exemplified only the other day when some Germans once more "discovered" a new cave above the Grotta Bianca and filled the newspapers with reports of their achievement, which consisted in using the rope left there by a previous party and effacing an inscription by which they had recorded their visit. The true facts are preserved in the *Geographical Journal.*

The poet Kopisch took a swim in the Blue Grotto in August, 1826—it was not "inaccessible," for he entered it, a few days later, in a boat—but to Andersen belongs the merit of drawing the attention of Europe to its beauties. If *The Improvisatore* had not created such a sensation—who can read it nowadays?—Kopisch would not have thought it worthwhile publishing, at a later period (in 1838), his well-known account of this exploit, which he calls a discovery, though he admits that the grotto was known to the islanders at the time. The fame of the Blue Grotto was the cause, not the result, of this publication. And another proof of Andersen's moral claim has just come to light in the recently printed diaries of the poet Platen, who spent a few days on Capri in 1827 with Kopisch, sailing all about the island, and not so much as mentioning the marvelous grotto found by his friend in the preceding year. These two romanticists—Kopisch and Andersen—beat the drum. And it strikes me as characteristic of the Northerner that he should suppose that "superstitious dread" prevented fishermen, during long centuries, from visiting this particular cave. Little they know these folk who imagine that superstitious dread plays any part in their daily lives or that supernatural beings, devils or saints, are allowed to interfere in the main objects of existence! Every nook of the shore had been searched by them from time immemorial, and Beelzebub himself could never keep a Capri fisherman out of a sea cave if there were half a franc's worth of crabs inside it.

Nor was Kopisch the first person to disport himself in this enchanted pool. Long ago, as the islanders will tell you, the Emperor Tiberius and the fair nymphs of his harem did the same, as is plainly proved by ancient masonry about the cave; indeed, seeing that nearly every sea cave on Capri bears traces of old walls, all of which were built by Tiberius for bathing purposes, it may be imagined what a clean old gentleman he must have been. The only question that remains to be solved is how he entered the cavern; volumes have been written to show that the sea level is not what it used to be in his time, and it is therefore hotly disputed whether he walked, dived, swam, drove, or flew into it. There is even something to be said for the hypothesis that he crawled on all fours. For at the back of the grotto is a mysterious and narrow passage opening westwards into the bowels of the earth, which certain sages, who have assuredly never explored it, declare to be an artificial tunnel leading from the imperial villa at Damecuta to the cool waters of the grotto. Tiberius and his frail cortège, after scrambling on their stomachs for half a league through this dank and dismal drain, certainly deserved, and perhaps needed, a bath. Let the sages decide these matters: If we do not arrive at the truth, it will not be for lack of theories. Like everyone else, I have my own views on the subject, but nothing would induce me to set them down here, for I dread controversy, and there is no more fearful wild fowl living than your historico-physico-geologist. Another of these tunnels, near at hand, is said to connect the *Palazzo a Mare* with the villa of Jupiter, about three miles distant! It is nothing but an ancient cloaca, even as that at the Blue Grotto is a natural crevice supplying in former days the water which helped to erode the cavern.

There was a confusion at one time between the Blue Grotto and a huge sea cave called the Grotta Oscura, which lay on the south side of Capri underneath the Certosa convent. This Grotta Oscura used to be one of the sights of the island, and many writers have left us descriptions of its magical twilight effects and drippings of water. The locality is now covered by earth and rocks, a landslip having taken place there in 1808 which closed it up and carried down two donkeys who happened to be grazing overhead at the critical moment, as well as a stout martello tower which the monks had built as a refuge from pirates. The hour was well chosen for this catastrophe, for the days were at hand when the corsairs ceased to threaten these shores, and when a rival cave was to become world-famous which would have eclipsed the beauties of the old. New institutions, new attractions, had made them super-fluous; they were swept away at the right moment, and no trace of them remains save the still fresh scar on the hillside which affronts the traveler's eye as he sails past under the shadow of *l' Unghia Marina.*

The shade of Tiberius, which used to haunt the Grotta Oscura, forthwith emigrated to the new cave, where it has since resided.

This is one of the many myths invented by the *Cicerones* of past days, who understood the value of quoting historical authorities and of showing pseudo-historical sites to the credulous traveler of the Grand Tours. Thus there is also a "Grotto of Polyphemus" both at Sorrento and at Capri, and at the latter place an appropriately chosen "Point of the Sirens" which, seeing that it is not mentioned in any old deeds, maps, or books of travel, must be taken to be of modern manufacture. At a certain period, Neapolitans began to take a keen interest in their Siren origin; a large literature sprang up on the subject and the name *La Sirena* has been popular ever since: Witness the ill-omened palace on the Posilipo.

On Capri the greater part of these legends are woven round the name of Tiberius. When one remembers that no serious antiquarian researches have been carried out on this island for the last hundred years, during which the science of excavating and interpreting ancient relics has been not so much revolutionized as created, one can understand the prevalence of this Cicerone archaeology. The "Villa of Jupiter" itself, which every tourist visits, is a purely modern fiction; old writers never describe it by the name; and so is the "Salto di Tiberio," where he threw objectionable people over the cliff, and the *Sellaria,* where other things occurred which are best left in the obscurity of a learned tongue. Yet to what outpourings of virtuous indignation have they not given rise on the part of our traveling forefathers, who were hugely interested in the misdeeds of Tiberius.

"May the memory of the monster vanish in the presence of this *wunderschöne Naturscene!*" exclaims the pious Stollberg, who became still more pious later on. *"Quoi!"* echoes a Frenchman, *"cette terre souillée n'est pas devenue stérile?"* An English author improves upon the Salto-legend by causing the spot to be artificially leveled "in order that the condemned might be made to take clean and flying jumps in his presence," while an Italian laments the "rocky promontory from which he was wont to cast his poor, innocent girl-victims." Such are the fruits of Cicerone archaeology.

It is a mistake, I think, to suppose that the various legends of Tiberius which now form part of the mental equipment of the Capriotes and constitute a profitable source of revenue have remained vivid in their memory ever since his day. This is the common belief: But I would hazard the statement that for more than a thousand years—before Italy began to be visited by tourists—every reminiscence of the old Roman had faded out of the popular mind. Be this as it may, from Ben Jonson onwards a long succession of imaginative writers have chosen this theme. Byron meditated a play on the subject. Some of these stories are good, but many are sad drivel—there is whispered talk of grottos and weird abominations, artless Anacapri maidens, Oriental slaves, Caligula, and other familiar figures enliven the scene, with an occasional *pas de caractère* (decidedly so) by the ladies of the ballet.

Meanwhile, it is really fitting that the inhabitants of this island, who owe to Tiberius more than to all the saints in the calendar, should put up a memorial to their benefactor. For *Timberio* is still a name to conjure with: to conjure things out of the foreigner's pockets. He is no dim memory, but a clear-cut personality who becomes more distinct and tangible in proportion as these gentle folk conceive themselves of his commercial uses. Several of the former generation knew him quite intimately, and found him most condescending and amiable—*un vero galantuomo,* one old man used to describe him. It is curious, too, to observe that the bloodthirsty aspect of the tyrant is becoming effaced, the popular mind having always a sneaking fondness for a genuine devil or Don Juan, who is never so black as he is painted. Even Timberio, everyone knows, had his little traits of gentlemanliness. He was rather too fond of a pretty face, but Lord! So are our priests and a good many others as well. And then he was a real *Signore,* not like the people who come to the island nowadays and who are worse than any Neapolitan for haggling about small change; he paid for everything just what we liked to ask, he built deuced fine cisterns, and he was the only man who could afford a carriage and pair on Capri before there were driving roads. Fine sprees in the Blue Grotto: Ha, ha! As for that Salto of his—why, if that were put into working order again, it would be the best thing possible for the place; Timberio knew what he was doing, he knew! . . . Has His Excellency perchance a cigar about him? Ah! . . . And he had electric light in his bathroom, the scoundrel! Yes, signore, it is a pity Timberio died so young—those infernal women. . . .

Gerald Durrell

Maiden Voyage

From lost luggage to ptomaine, all of us have had our travel disasters.
But if there is a model for the *Poseidon Adventure*, one hopes it is not
on the Bounding Main but only on the telly; say, "Fawlty Towers."
This delicious bit was published in 1980, with
The Picnic and Other Inimitable Stories.

However glib you are with words, your brain is inclined to falter if you try and describe the Plaza San Marco in Venice under a full daffodil-yellow summer moon. The buildings look as though they have been made out of crumbling oversweet nougat in the most beautiful shades of browns and reds and subtle autumn pinks. The moon trembles its reflection in the waters of the canals, and you can sit and watch, fascinated, for the tiny tellers, Moorish figures, which come out and strike the big bell on St. Mark's church at every quarter, so that it echoes and vibrates round the huge square.

On this particular evening, it was as ravishing as only Venice can be, spoiled only by the conglomeration of my belligerent family, clustered round two tables strewn with drinks and tiny plates of appetizers. Unfortunately, it had been my mother's idea and, as had always happened throughout her life, what she had produced as a treat had already, even at this early stage, started turning into a fiasco that was edging her slowly but relentlessly towards that pillory which all families keep for their parents.

"I wouldn't mind if you had had the decency to *tell* me in advance. I could, at least, have risked death traveling by air," said my elder brother, Larry, looking despondently at one of the many glasses that an irritatingly happy waiter had put in front of him. "But what in Heaven's name possessed you to go and book us all on a *Greek* ship for three days? I mean it's as stupid as deliberately booking on the *Titanic.*"

"I thought it would be more cheerful, and the Greeks are such good sailors," said my Mother defensively. "Anyway, it's her maiden voyage."

"You always cry wolf before you're hurt," said Margo, my sister. "I think it was a brilliant idea of Mother's."

"I must say, I agree with Larry," said Leslie, with the obvious reluctance that we all shared in agreeing with our elder brother. "We all know what Greek ships are like."

"Not *all* of them, dear," said Mother. *"Some* of them must be all right."

"Well, there's nothing we can do about it now," said Larry gloomily. "You've committed us to sail on this bloody craft which I have no doubt would have been rejected by the Ancient Mariner in his cups."

"Nonsense, Larry," said Mother. "You always exaggerate. The man at Cook's spoke very highly of it."

"He said the bar was full of life," said Margo triumphantly.

"God almighty," said Leslie.

"And to dampen our pagan spirits," agreed Larry, "the most revolting selection of Greek wines, which all taste as though they have been forced from the reluctant jugular vein of some hermaphrodite camel."

"Larry, don't be so disgusting," said Margo.

"Look," said Larry vehemently, "I have been dragged away from France on this ill-fated attempt to revisit the scenes of our youth, much against my better judgment. Already I am beginning to regret it, and we've only just got as far as Venice, for God's sake. Already I'm curdling what remains of my liver with Lacrima Christi instead of good, honest Beaujolais. Already my senses have been assaulted in every restaurant by great mounds of spaghetti, some sort of awful breeding ground for tapeworms, instead of Charolais steaks."

"Larry, I do wish you wouldn't talk like that," said my Mother. "There's no need for vulgarity."

In spite of the three bands all playing different tunes at different corners of the great square, the animated conversations of the Italians and tourists, and the sleepy crooning of the somnambulistic pigeons, it seemed that half of Venice was listening, entranced, to our purely private family row.

"It will be perfectly all right when we are on board," said Margo. "After all, we *will* be among the Greeks."

"I think that's what Larry's worried about," said Leslie gloomily.

"Well," said Mother, trying to introduce an air of false confidence into the proceedings, "we should be going. Taking one of those vaporizer things down to the docks."

We paid our bill and straggled down to the canal and climbed on board one of the motor launches which my Mother, with her masterly command of Italian, insisted on calling a vaporizer. The Italians, being less knowledge-able, called them *vaporettos.* We got into one and Venice was a splendid sight as we chugged our way down the canal, past the great houses, past the rippling reflections of the lights in the water, and even Larry had to admit that it was a slight improvement on the Blackpool illuminations. We landed eventually at the docks which, like docks everywhere, looked as though they had been designed (in an off moment) by Dante while planning his *Inferno.* We huddled in puddles of phosphorescent light that made us all look like something out of an early Hollywood horror film, and it completely destroyed the moonlight, which was by now silver as a spider's web. Our gloom was not even lightened by the sight of Mother's diminutive figure attempting to convince three rapacious Venetian porters that we did not need any help with our motley assortment of luggage. It was an argument conducted in basic English.

"We English. We no speak Italian," she cried in tones of despair, adding a strange flood of words that consisted of Hindustani, Greek, French, and German, none of which bore any relation to each other. This was my Mother's way of communication with any foreigner, be he Aborigine or Eskimo, but it failed to do more than momentarily lighten our gloom.

We stood and contemplated those bits of the Grand Canal that led out into our section of the dock, and suddenly there slid into view a ship which, even by the most landlubberish standards, could never have been mistaken for seaworthy. At some time in her career, the ship had been used as a species of reasonably sized in-shore steamer, but even in those days, when she had been, so to speak, virginal and freshly painted, she could not have been beautiful. Now, sadly lacking in any of the trappings that, in that ghastly phosphorescent light, might have made her turn into a proud ship, there was nothing. Fresh paint had not come her way for a number of years and there were large patches of rust, like unpleasant sores and scabs, all along her sides. Like a woman on excessively high-heeled shoes who has had the misfortune to lose one of the heels, she had a heavy list to starboard. Her totally unkempt air was bad enough, but the final indignity was, as she turned to come alongside the docks, thus exposed to us. It was an enormous tattered hole in her bow that would have admitted a pair of Rolls Royces side by side. This terrible defloration was made worse by the fact that no first aid of any description, of even the most primitive kind, had been attempted. The plates on her hull curved inwards where they had been crushed, like a gigantic chrysanthemum. Struck dumb, we watched her come alongside and there, above the huge hole in her bow, was her name: the *Poseidon.*

"Dear God!" breathed Larry.

"She's appalling," said Leslie, the more nautical member of our family. "Look at that list."

"But it's *our* boat," squeaked Margo. "Mother, it's our boat!"

"Nonsense, dear, it can't be," said my Mother, readjusting her spectacles and peering hopefully up at the boat as it loomed above us.

"Three days on this," said Larry. "It will be *worse* than the Ancient Mariner's experience, mark my words."

"But I do hope they are going to do something about that hole," said Mother worriedly, "before we put out to sea."

"What do you expect them to do? Stuff a blanket into it?" asked Larry.

"But surely the Captain's *noticed* it," said Mother, bewildered.

"I shouldn't think that even a Greek captain would have been totally oblivious of the fact that they have, quite recently, given something a fairly sharp tap," said Larry.

"The waves will get in," said Margo. "I don't want waves in my cabin. My dresses will all be ruined."

"I should think all the cabins are underwater by now," observed Leslie.

"Well, our snorkels and flippers will come in handy," said Larry. "*What* a novelty to have to swim down to dinner. How I shall enjoy it all."

"Well, as soon as we get on board you must go up and have a word with the Captain," said Mother. "It's just possible that he wasn't on board when it happened, and no one's told him."

"Really, Mother, you do annoy me," said Larry irritably. "What do you expect me to say to the man? 'Pardon me, Kyrie Capitano, sir, but did you know you've got death watch beetle in your bows?'"

"Larry, you always complicate things," said Mother. "You know I can't speak Greek or I'd do it."

"Tell him I don't want waves in my cabin," said Margo.

"As we are due to leave tonight, they couldn't possibly mend it anyway," said Leslie.

"Exactly," said Larry. "But Mother seems to think that I am some sort of reincarnation of Noah."

"Well, I shall have something to say about it when I get on board," said Mother belligerently, as we made our way up the gangway.

At the head of the gangway, we were met by a romantic-looking Greek steward (with eyes as soft and melting as black pansies) wearing a crumpled, off-gray colored suit with most of the buttons missing. Judging from his tarnished epaulettes, he appeared to be the Purser, and his smiling demand for passports and tickets was so redolent of garlic that mother reeled back against the rails, her query about the ship's bow stifled.

"Do you speak English?" asked Margo, gamely rallying her olfactory nerves more rapidly than Mother.

"Small," he said, bowing.

"Well, I don't want waves in my cabin," said Margo firmly. "It will ruin my clothes."

"Everything you want we give," he said. "If you want wife, I give you *my* wife. She . . . "

"No, no," said Margo, "the *waves*. You know . . . water."

"Every cabeen has having hot and cold running showers," he said with dignity. "Also there is bath or nightcloob having dancing and wine and water."

"I do wish you'd stop laughing and help us, Larry," said Mother, covering her nose with her handkerchief to repel the odor of garlic, which was so strong one got the impression it was like a shimmering cloud round the Purser's head.

Larry pulled himself together and in fluent Greek (which delighted the Purser), he elicited, in rapid succession, the information that the ship was not sinking, there were no waves in the cabins, and the Captain knew all about the accident as he had been responsible for it. Wisely, Larry did not pass on this piece of information to Mother. So, while Mother and Margo were taken in a friendly and aromatic manner down to the cabins by the Purser, the rest of us followed his instructions as to how to get to the bar.

This, when we located it, made us all speechless. It looked like the mahogany-lined lounge of one of the drearier London clubs. Great chocolate-colored leather chairs and couches cluttered the place, interspersed with formidible fumed-oak tables. Dotted about were some huge Benares brass bowls in which sprouted tattered, dusty palm trees. There was, in the midst of this funereal splendor, a minute parquet floor for dancing, flanked on one side by the small bar containing a virulent assortment of drinks, and on the other by a small raised dais surrounded by a veritable forest of potted palms, in the midst of which, enshrined like flies in amber, were three lugubrious musicians in frock coats, celluloid dickies, and cummerbunds that would have seemed dated in 1890. One played on an ancient upright piano and tuba, one played a violin with much professional posturing, and the third doubled up on the drums and trombone. As we entered, this incredible trio was playing "Roses of Picardy" to an entirely empty room.

"I can't bear it," said Larry. "This is not a ship; it's a sort of floating Cadena Cafe from Bournemouth. It'll drive us all mad."

At Larry's words, the band stopped playing and the leader's face lit up in a gold-toothed smile of welcome. He gestured at his two colleagues with his bow and they also bowed and smiled. We three could do no less, and so we swept them a courtly bow before proceeding to the bar. The band launched itself with ever-greater frenzy into "Roses of Picardy" now that it had an audience.

"Please give me," Larry asked the Barman, a small, wizened man in a dirty apron, "in one of the largest glasses you possess, an ouzo that will, I hope, paralyze me."

The Barman's walnut face lit up at the sound of a foreigner who could not only speak Greek but could be rich enough to drink so large an ouzo.

"*Amessos, kyrie,*" he said. "Will you have it with water or ice?"

"One lump of ice," Larry stipulated. "Just enough to blanch its cheeks."

"I'm sorry, *kyrie*, we have no ice," said the Barman apologetically.

Larry sighed a deep and long-suffering sigh. "It is only in Greece," he said to us in English, "that one has this sort of conversation, which gives one the feeling that one is in such close touch with Lewis Carroll that the Barman might be the Cheshire cat in disguise."

"Water, *kyrie*?" asked the Barman, sensing from Larry's tone that he was not receiving approbation but rather censure.

"Water," said Larry, in Greek, "a tiny amount."

The Barman went to the massive bottle of ouzo, as clear as gin, poured out a desperate measure, and then went to the little sink and squirted water in from the tap. Instantly, the ouzo turned the color of watered milk, and we could smell the aniseed from where we were standing.

"God, that's a strong one," said Leslie. "Let's have the same."

I agreed.

The glasses were set before us. We raised them in toast: "Well, here's to the *Poseidon* and all the fools who sail in her," said Larry, and took a great mouthful of ouzo. The next minute he spat it out in a flurry that would have done credit to a dying whale, and reeled back against the bar, clasping his throat, his eyes watering.

"Ahhh!" he roared. "The bloody fool's put bloody *hot water* in it!"

Nurtured as we had been among the Greeks, we were fairly inured to the strange behavior they indulged in, but for a Greek to put boiling water in his national drink was, we felt, carrying eccentricity too far.

"Why did you put hot water in the ouzo?" asked Leslie belligerently.

"Because we have no cold," said the Barman, surprised that Leslie should not have worked out this simple problem in logic for himself. "That is why we have no ice. This is the maiden voyage, *kyrie,* and that is why we have nothing but hot water in the bar."

"I don't believe it," said Larry despairingly. "I just don't believe it. A maiden voyage and the ship's got a bloody great hole in her bow, the Palm Court Orchestra of septuagenarians, and nothing but hot water in the bar."

At that moment Mother appeared, looking distinctly flustered. "Larry, I want to speak to you," she panted.

Larry looked at her. "What have you found? An iceberg in the bunk?" he asked.

"Well, there's a cockroach in the basin. Margo threw a bottle of eau de cologne at it, and it broke, and now the whole place smells like the hair-dresser's. I don't think it killed the cockroach either," said Mother.

"Well," said Larry. "I'm delighted you have been having fun. Have a red-hot ouzo to round off the start of this riotous voyage."

"No, I didn't come here to drink" said Mother.

"You surely didn't come to tell me about an eau de cologne—drenched cockroach?" said Larry in surprise. "Your conversation is getting worse than the Greeks for eccentricity."

"No, it's Margo," Mother hissed. "She went to the you-know-where and she's got the slot jammed."

"The 'you-know-where'? Where's that?"

"The lavatory," Mother hissed. "You know perfectly well what I mean."

"I don't know what you expect me to do," said Larry. "I'm not a plumber."

"Can't she climb out?" inquired Leslie.

"No," said Mother. "She's tried, and the hole at the top is much too small, and so is the hole at the bottom."

"But at least there are holes," Larry pointed out. "You need air in a Greek lavatory, in my experience, and we can feed her through them during the voyage."

"Don't be so stupid, Larry," said Mother. "You've got to do something."

"Try putting another coin in the slot thing," suggested Leslie. "That sometimes does it."

"I did," said Mother. "I put in a lira but it still wouldn't work."

"That's because it's a Greek lavatory and will only accept drachmas," Larry pointed out. "Why didn't you try a pound note? The rate of exchange is in its favor."

"Well, I want you to get a stewardess to get her out," said Mother. "She's been in there ages. She can't stay in there all night. Supposing she banged her elbow and fainted. You know she's always doing that."

Mother tended to look on the black side of things.

"In my experience of Greek lavatories," said Larry judiciously, "you generally faint immediately upon entering without the need to bang your elbow."

"Well, for heaven's sake, *do* something," said Mother. "Don't just stand there drinking."

Led by her, we eventually found the lavatory in question, and Leslie, striding in masterfully, rattled the door.

"Me stuck. Me English," shouted Margo from behind the door. "You find stewardess."

"I know that, you fool. It's me, Leslie," he growled.

"Go out at once. It's a ladies' lavatory," said Margo.

"Do you want to get out or not? If you do, shut up," said Leslie belligerently. He fiddled ineffectually with the door, swearing under his breath.

"I do wish you wouldn't use bad language, dear," said Mother. "Remember, you are in the 'Ladies.'"

"There should be a little knob thing on the inside which you pull," said Leslie. "A sort of bolt thing."

"I've pulled everything," said Margo indignantly. "What do you think I've been doing in here for the last hour?"

"Well, pull it again," said Leslie, "while I push."

"All right, I'm pulling," said Margo.

Leslie hunched his powerful shoulders and threw himself at the door.

"It's like a Pearl White serial," said Larry, sipping the ouzo that he had thoughtfully brought with him. "If you're not careful, we'll have another hole in the hull."

"It's no good," said Leslie panting. "It's too tough. We'll have to get a steward or something." He went off in search of someone with mechanical knowledge.

"I do wish you'd hurry," said Margo plaintively. "It's terribly oppressive in here."

"Don't faint," said Mother in alarm. "Try to regulate your breathing."

"And don't bang your elbows," Larry added.

"Oh, Larry, you do make me cross," said Mother. "Why don't you be sensible?"

"Well, shall I go and get her a hot ouzo? We can slide it in under the door," he suggested helpfully.

He was saved from Mother's ire by the arrival of Leslie, bringing in tow a small and irritated puppetlike man with a lugubrious face.

"Always the ladies is doing this," he said to Mother, shrugging expressive shoulders. "Always they are getting catched. I show you. It is easy. Why woman not learn?"

He went to the door and fiddled with it for a moment, and it flew open.

"Thank God," said Mother, as Margo appeared in the doorway. But before she could emerge into the bosom of her family, the little man held up a peremptory hand.

"Back!" he commanded masterfully. "I teaches you."

Before we could do anything intelligent, he had pushed Margo back into the lavatory and slammed the door shut.

"What's he doing?" squeaked Mother in alarm. "What's he doing, that little man? Larry, do something."

"It's all right, Mother," shouted Margo, "he's showing me how to do it."

"How to do what?" asked Mother, alarmed.

There was a long and ominous silence, eventually broken by a flood of Greek oaths.

"Margo, you come out of there at once," said Mother, considerably alarmed.

"I can't," wailed Margo. "He's locked us both in."

"Disgusting man," cried Mother, taking command. "Hit him, dear, hit him. Larry you go for the Captain."

"I mean, he can't open the door either," said Margo.

"Please to find Purser," wailed the little man. "Please finding Purser for opening door."

"Well, where do we find him?" asked Leslie.

"It's too ridiculous," said Mother. "Are you all right? Stand well away from him, dear."

"You find Purser in Purser's office, first deck," yelled the imprisoned man.

Anyone who does not know the Greek temperament or their strange ability to change a perfectly normal situation into something so complicated that it leaves the normal mind unhinged may find what followed incredible. We, knowing the Greeks, did also, so I offer no excuse for it. Leslie returned with the Purser, who not only added to the redolence of the "Ladies" with his garlic, but in quick succession complimented Larry on drinking ouzo, Leslie on his Greek accent, soothed Mother with a large carnation plucked from behind his ear, and then turned such a blast of invective on the poor little man locked up with my sister that one expected the solid steel door to melt. Then he rushed at it and pounded with his fists and kicked it several times. Then he turned to Mother and bowed.

"Madame," he said, smiling, "no alarm. Your daughter is safe with a virgin."

The remark confused Mother completely. She turned to me for explanation as Larry, knowing this sort of fracas of old, had repaired to the bar to get drinks. I said I thought he meant she would be as safe *as* a virgin.

"He can't mean *that*," she said suspiciously. "She's got two children."

I began to lose my bearings slightly, as one always seemed to do when confronted with the Greeks. I had just taken a deep breath to embark on an elaboration for my mother when I was mercifully stopped by the arrival of three fellow passengers, all large, big-bosomed, thick-legged peasant ladies, with heavy moustaches, black bombazine dresses three sizes too small, and all smelling of garlic, some sickly scent, and perspiration in equal quantities. They elbowed their way in between Mother and myself and entered the lavatory, and then, seeing the Purser still dancing with rage and pounding on the door, they all paused like massive warhorses that have scented battle. Any other nationality would have complained about the Purser's presence in this shrine to womanhood, let alone mine as a foreigner, but this is where the Greeks so delightfully differ from other peoples. They knew it was a SITUATION with capital letters, and this above all is what Greeks love. The presence of three men (if you include the invisible one closeted with Margo) in their lavatory was as nothing compared to the SITUATION. Their eyes glittered, their moustaches wiffled, and, a solid wall of eager flesh, they enveloped the Purser and demanded to know what was afoot. As usual in a SITUATION, everyone spoke at once. The temperature in the "Ladies" went up to something like seventy degrees, and the volume of sound made your head spin, like playing the noisier bits of "Ride of the Valkyries" in an iron barrel. Having grasped roughly the elements of the SITUATION from the harassed Purser, the three powerful ladies, each built on the lines of a professional wrestler, swept him out of the way with scarlet-tipped, spade-shaped hands, lifted up their skirts, and with deafening cries of "Oopah, oopah," they charged the lavatory door. Their combined weight must have amounted to some sixty stone of flesh and bone, but the door was stalwart, and the three ladies fell in a tangle of limbs on the floor. They got to their feet with some difficulty and then proceeded to argue among themselves as to the best way to break down a lavatory door. They shouted and gesticulated; one of them, the least heavy of the three, even demonstrated her idea—an ideal method—against one of the other lavatory doors which, unfortunately, was not on the latch, and so she crashed through at surprising speed and received a nasty contusion on her thigh by crashing full tilt into the lavatory pan. Although it had not proved her point, she was very good-natured about it, especially as at that moment Larry arrived, accompanied by the Barman carrying a tray of drinks. For a time we all sipped ouzo companionably and toasted each other, and asked if we were all married and how many children we had. Fresh interest in the SITUATION was aroused by the arrival of Leslie with what appeared to be the ship's carpenter for whom he had gone in search. The drinks were now forgotten as everyone's theories were retold to the carpenter, all of which he disagreed with, with the air of one who knows. Then, like a magician, he rolled up his sleeves and approached the door. Silence fell. He produced a minute screwdriver from his pocket and inserted it into a minute hole. There was a click and a gasp of admiration, and the door flew open. He stood back and spread his hands like a conjurer. The first little man and Margo emerged like survivors from the Black Hole of Calcutta. The poor little man was seized by the Purser and pounded and pummeled and shaken, while being roundly dressed down. The Carpenter, at this stage, took over. After all, he had opened the door. We listened to him with respect as he expounded and explained the cunning mechanism of locks in general and this one in particular. He drained an ouzo and waxed poetic on locks, which were his hobby, it appeared. With his little screwdriver or a hairpin or a bent nail or, indeed, a piece of plastic, one could open any lock. He, the lock expert, took the first little man and the Purser by the wrists and led them into the lavatory like lambs to the slaughter, and before we could stop them, he had slammed the door shut. My family and the three fat ladies waited with bated breath. There were strange scrapings and clickings, then a long pause. This was followed by a torrent of vituperation from the Purser and the Steward, mixed with confused excuses and explanations from the lock expert. As we furtively crept away, the three ladies were preparing to charge the door again.

So ended Day One of the maiden voyage.

Michael Frayn

The Magic Carpet Beano

Dyson the journalist parallels Frayn, who was a reporter and columnist
for the *Guardian* and *Observer* before becoming the playwright of,
among other notable comedies, *Noises Off*. The travails of a travel
writer described here—from a man who used to love airports—are a
generation and a sea change removed from those that confronted
Bemelmans on the *Normandie*. From Frayn's 1967 novel,
Towards the End of the Morning.

Dyson wandered about the Final Departure Lounge at London Airport in a
curious state of elation. The Magic Carpet Travel plane was late leaving; Dyson
and the rest of the press party should have taken off for the Trucial Riviera ten
minutes before. But he didn't mind at all. He loved airports. He would have
liked to feel blasé about them, but he didn't have the opportunity to use them
often enough. As soon as he got inside one he became elated. He seemed to
have a heightened sense of reality. Moving staircases, rubber plants, low
black leather armchairs; "Flight BE 4029 for Copenhagen and Stockholm is
departing now . . . Berlins the last call for passengers traveling on Flight LH
291 for Düsseldorf and Berlin . . ." He bought *Oggi* and *Neue Illustrierte* at
the bookstall, even though he could scarcely read a word of either Italian or
German, because being inside an airport made him feel that he could. The
Final Departure Lounge, sealed off from gross particular Britain by passport
and customs barriers, was a bright nowhere land, sterilized of nationality
and all the other ties and limitations of everyday life. Here Dyson felt like
International Airport Man—neat, sophisticated, compact; a wearer of light-
weight suits and silky blue showercoats; moving over the surface of the earth
like some free-floating spirit—from Karachi to Athens to Hong Kong, from
Honolulu to Tangier to New York—unimpeded by the traffic problems of
Karachi or the housing situation in Honolulu, not deflected from New York by

any emotional attachment in Athens, or kept from Hong Kong by business entanglement in New York. Airports and television studios—this was the way of life Dyson felt he was intended for.

He could pick out some of the other journalists in the Magic Carpet group sitting about the lounge; they were all, like himself, carrying the folder of publicity material Magic Carpet had issued them with. There was a photographer who had checked in just ahead of him. He seemed to have brought a couple of models with him—badly dressed girls with pained expressions and tragically thin legs. And the tall, cavernous man with the dark blazer and the ex-officer's moustache—wasn't he from the *Telegraph?* The red-faced young man with the thin hair falling all over the place was a humorous writer for somebody—Dyson had seen him on television. There was a man in a blue pinstripe suit, with elegantly gray curls, who freelanced food and wine, and an anxious young woman with dark eyes and three strings of beads to chew who did travel for one of the glossies; Dyson had seen them both on facilities trips before. Oh God, he thought, facilities trips! How awful they were! He could picture the holiday development at Sharjah already—new concrete hotels built too quickly, no amenities, the squalor of the local population beyond the new concrete reserves. It was only the traveling there and back which made them worthwhile at all. They could be hours late leaving for all he cared; he was quite happy to sit at London Airport all day and watch the aircraft coming and going.

Ah, the aircraft! He gazed at them through the windows of the lounge. They stood ranked on the apron, shimmering in the morning sunlight. The tangled confusion of ground equipment which surrounded them—the lorries, steps, and generators, the ordinary shoddy private cars in which the aircrew drove themselves out, the temporary sheds and stacks of building materials—only emphasized their remote and fragile perfection. They stood like swans standing—on unlikely legs, in tangled nests. Like swans they would fold their legs and beat up into the uncluttered, abstract sky. One of them moved off the stand as Dyson watched, its engines whining, the blast of air behind it crinkling the standing rainwater on the apron into a million fleeing furrows . . . And there, away across the grass a mile beyond it, one of the big jets was just starting its takeoff run. Slowly, very slowly, the great bulk gathered speed, as if the Bank of England or the National Gallery had started to walk, and was trying to run. It drew level with the airport buildings, the colossal baggage of noise it trailed swelling at great speed now, but still heavy on the ground and never in a million years capable of leaving it—a great beast charging head down at central Middlesex. Then, suddenly, it lifted its head above the runway, looked round and sniffed the air for a moment—and went straight up into the sky like spring-heeled Jack; leveled off; and vanished against the shifting clouds. Four lines of brown exhaust, rounded off at the top, hung faintly in the air where it had leapt.

Dyson turned round, moved by the performance—and there behind him, about three feet away, picking absently at a morsel of food between his front teeth and twitching his nose from time to time to ease some hidden blockage in his nasal passage, was Reg Mounce. The supraterrestrial perfection of the Final Departure Lounge faded a little.

"Well, well, well!" said Mounce, taking his finger out of his mouth, as surprised as Dyson.

"Hello," said Dyson unwelcomingly.

"What are you doing here?"

"I'm going out to the Persian Gulf," said Dyson coldly. "For the paper."

"The Magic Carpet beano?"

"Yes."

"Well, snap! Stinking snap!"

The Final Departure Lounge seemed to Dyson suddenly no more isolated from the imperfections of life than the saloon bar of the Gates of Jerusalem, and the great silver aircraft no rarer or lovelier than red London buses.

"I'm doing it for a load of crap called *Leisure and Pleasure* magazine," said Mounce. "They don't pay much, but what the hell? It's a week off from the stinking office, with nothing to do but collect a few pics from the firm, slap some sort of crap together from the handout, and get some serious drinking done."

"I see," said Dyson.

"Charge some exes up, of course. Charge a few more up to the paper. It all adds up."

"Yes."

"To tell you the truth," said Mounce confidentially, "I can do with a few days in the sun at the moment. All this business about Other Arrangements—it's been rather getting me down. I thought it might be clever to shove off for a few days and let it all blow over."

Dyson said nothing. He was swearing a solemn oath to himself that he would be absolutely ruthless about Mounce on this trip. When they went aboard the plane he would firmly find himself a seat next to the wine-and-food man, or the girl with the beads, and ignore Mounce's existence until they were back in London.

"I think it'll all just simmer down, won't it?" said Mounce.

"What?"

"All this Other Arrangements business. It'll blow over. In a month's time we'll be laughing about it. Don't you think so?"

"For God's sake—*I* don't know."

Mounce fell silent, thoughtfully trying to remove the last traces of breakfast from his teeth with his tongue. Dyson took the opportunity to move away and sit down on the other side of the lounge. He found that Mounce had followed him across the room, and had sat down in the seat beside him.

"We're twenty-five minutes late," said Mounce.

"Yes."

"These stinking trips are always late."

A small man with an archaic toothbrush moustache and a wild tangle of stand-up hair above a domed forehead came hurrying across the lounge. About half his height seemed to be forehead. He had thick spectacles, behind which his eyes darted keenly about like goldfish searching for a way out from their bowls. He had introduced himself to the party earlier, at the air terminal, as Starfield, Magic Carpet's Air Transportation Director.

"Magic Carpet group!" he cried to the room, pressing his palms together as if about to sing a tenor aria. "This is an announcement concerning the Magic Carpet party traveling to Sharjah. There is a slight delay, boys and girls, caused by the fact that the aircraft which will be taking us has burst a tire on touchdown from Amsterdam, and there will be a slight delay on account of this cause while this fact is rectified. While we are waiting, I have arranged for drinks to be served at the bar, compliments of Magic Carpet Travel, and I would ask you to rest assured, believe me, that everything humanly possible is being done to facilitate our getting away at the earliest possible moment. Thank you."

Mounce let his breath slowly out between his teeth.

"Here we go again," he said. "Bang on stinking form, as stinking usual . . ."

The Magic Carpet party got airborne eventually.

"Two hours late," said Mounce bitterly, several times, as their secondhand turbo-prop climbed through ragged cloud into the world of shining snowfields above.

"For God's sake shut up, Reg," said Dyson, gazing out of the window at the stark absolutes of white and blue.

"Yes, but two hours late! I could have mended the stinking puncture myself in that time."

They were not flying to Sharjah direct. Dyson realized he must have misread the invitation slightly. They were going to Paris first to pick up another party of journalists which had assembled there from the rest of Europe. The Continental contingent was waiting in the departure lounge at Le Bourget when the London party arrived, and had of course been waiting there for over two hours, consuming drinks supplied with the compliments of Magic Carpet. There were about thirty of them, some carrying complicated camera kits; some, as Dyson noted with approval, wearing silky blue overcoats; all of them carrying folders of Magic Carpet handout material. There were two models among the group, even worse-dressed and more pained than the English pair; they looked as if they were already preparing themselves spiritually for posing in the middle of some Arab village or Bedouin encampment wearing nothing but see-through bathing costumes and gauze yashmaks. The Paris party stared coldly at the London party, associating them with the plane's puncture and its lateness. The London party stared back no less coldly, feeling that they would be halfway to Sharjah by now but for the selfish insistence of the Paris party on being fetched along too.

Mounce, however, began to cheer up slightly. He looked round the departure lounge with some interest, and sniffed the air.

"Ah, the smell of France," he said. "Smell it the moment you arrive. Have you ever noticed that, John?"

"Yes," said Dyson. But the sight and smell of the departure lounge at Le Bourget had the opposite effect on him to Mounce. The pleasure he got from airports, it occurred to him sadly, was subject to the law of diminishing returns.

"Do you think the bar'll take sterling?" said Mounce. "Let's have a quick one before they shove us back on that snotty little plane."

"I don't think there's time. We'll be leaving again directly."

But, it turned out, they were not leaving again directly. No announcement was made about rejoining the aircraft, and Starfield seemed to have disappeared. Gradually the London party subsided into seats. A certain amount of muttering commenced within the various linguistic groups. Someone overheard, deduced, or invented the information that the Scandinavian party, which was flying down from Copenhagen to join the expedition, had landed at Orly instead of Le Bourget. Slowly the word crossed the various linguistic barriers, until even Dyson and Mounce had heard.

"Trust the Swedes," said Mounce bitterly. "Trust the Swedes to get the whole stinking thing screwed up."

"But are they *still* at Orly?" cried Dyson to the wine-and-food man.

"I expect so," said the wine-and-food man, sipping a lightly chilled Chambéry vermouth. "I expect they're waiting for us."

"*Où sont-ils?*" shouted Dyson boldly at one of the men in silky blue showercoats. The man shrugged his shoulders in a typically French way.

"Who knows?" he said, with a German accent.

"Trust the stinking Swedes," said Mounce.

Starfield came hurrying anxiously into the lounge.

"Boys and girls!" he cried, pressing his palms together. "I regret to have to inform you of the fact that we have a slight snag on our hands, owing to the fact that our Scandinavian friends are unfortunately not yet with us, the fact being that they were booked in error on to a flight arriving at Orly. As soon as they arrive we shall be departing as planned, though of course a little later than scheduled. In the meantime, there are drinks and a sandwich lunch available at the bar, compliments of Magic Carpet Travel. Thank you."

But not much more than three-quarters of an hour later, just as everyone was moving on from the free apéritifs to the free champagne with the free sandwiches, Starfield came hurrying back.

"Sorry, folks!" he said, pressing his palms together once again. "Sorry, boys and girls! There's been a bit of a misunderstanding over the plane. It seems that our Scandinavian friends are still at Orly, waiting for *us*, as a result of which I feel it would facilitate things best if we went on without them, leaving them to proceed independently by separate means of transportation and join us at the other end. Will you therefore proceed at once to the departure gate for immediate embarkation? Thank you."

Grumbling, the party picked up its folders of publicity material and shuffled towards the gate, hastily draining glasses and gnawing at ham sandwiches as it went. The language barriers began to break down slightly under the common bond of mutual discontent. "It is bad," said a Dutch photographer to Dyson, shaking his head and pursing his lips. *"Ja,"* agreed Dyson emphatically. *"Ja, ja, ja."*

As the plane rushed past the airport buildings on its takeoff run, Dyson thought he could see a number of people jumping about and waving their arms in front of the departure gate. They looked to Dyson remarkably like Scandinavian journalists. Still, they had perhaps not missed very much, because as soon as the plane was airborne Starfield came hurrying up to the front of the cabin, pressing his palms together for yet another aria.

"Our next port of call, boys and girls," he announced, "is Amsterdam."

A noise of multilingual outrage and complaint arose from the body of the plane.

"Amsterdam!" cried Dyson, unable to believe his ears. "But that's in the opposite direction to the Middle East!"

"What do you expect, John," said Mounce comfortably, from the middle of a benevolent haze of alcohol, "with a load of crap like this?"

Starfield seemed astonished at the feelings his announcement had aroused. His eyebrows climbed out from behind the shelter of his glasses and attempted the ascent of his great forehead. Dislodged by the upward progress of the eyebrows, his glasses came landsliding down his nose. He pushed them back.

"Boys and girls!" he protested. "If we want to get to Sharjah we have to go to Amsterdam first, owing to the simple fact that the plane which is taking us to Sharjah is waiting for us at Amsterdam!"

The noise of complaint continued.

"There'll be drinks at Amsterdam," appealed Starfield. "I'm radioing Schiphol Airport now to lay on full bar facilities, compliments of Magic Carpet Travel. Thank you."

He disappeared hurriedly in the direction of the flight-deck.

"Oh, *God!*" said Dyson.

"Try and be philosophical about it, John," said Mounce. "Think of the drinks. The booze is always the only good part of the spotty jaunts. The rest's always just a lot of crap, one way or another."

He was still looking on the bright side when they all filed into the transit lounge at Schiphol.

"I've always wanted to go to Amsterdam," he said, looking round with interest. "Do you know, John, the girls sit in shop windows here, just waiting for you to go along and take your pick. How about that? They sit in stinking shop windows, John—doing their stinking knitting!"

Schiphol, coming after Heathrow and Le Bourget, did not make Dyson feel like International Airport Man, free-floating in a medium entirely isolated from the world's troubles. It made him feel like a traveler on the District Line, forced by the tiresome vicissitudes of the Underground to change at Earl's Court as well as South Kensington.

The terrible claustrophobia of travel began to descend on him. He was trapped in the channels of communication, suffocating in the nothingness of neither-here-nor-there . . .

There was one particular travel poster on the wall of the lounge at Schiphol Airport which became imprinted on Dyson's memory as the evening wore on. It was of a girl in a swimming costume, frozen in the very moment of stepping off the side of a swimming pool. It irritated Dyson. She had already stepped right out into unsupported space, and was looking down at the water beneath her with a slightly anxious smile of anticipation on her face. And there, in mid-air, she remained suspended. She was there at six, when it was still generally believed that the Scandinavian party they were all waiting for was somewhere *en route* between Paris and Amsterdam. She was there at seven, when the French journalists, who were beginning to emerge as the leaders of opinion in the expedition, put the story about that the Scandinavians had by an error been flown not to Amsterdam but back to Copenhagen. At eight o'clock, when the French announced that the Scandinavians' plane had crashed, the poor girl had still not got so much as a toe into the water. The anticipation in her anxious smile was as keen as ever at nine, when the French declared that the Scandinavians had landed at Brussels and were coming on by train. It had still not faded at ten, when all the various nationalities present abandoned interest in their Scandinavian colleagues, and instead rose and mobbed Starfield as he hurried anxiously between telephone and cable office, and threatened to petition their respective governments for the revocation of all Magic Carpet's licenses and landing rights if he did not immediately arrange everyone hotels in Amsterdam for the night.

They took off soon after ten o'clock the following morning, without the Scandinavians, in another turbo-prop, larger and even more visibly secondhand than the first one. A small panel fell out of the internal trim in front of Mounce and Dyson just after takeoff, and swung back and forth on the end of a wire. Mounce, who had subsided into an early-morning liverish bitterness again, watched it sourly.

"This stinking plane's never going to get to the Middle East," he snarled. "It looks about a hundred years old."

"Oh, for God's sake!" snarled Dyson, who was also a little hung-over. "It's a jet!"

"It's got stinking straight wings, John!"

"All right—it's got straight wings! What's wrong with straight wings, for God's sake?"

"Because they mean it's just a cartload of old scrap-iron! It's obsolete!"

"Obsolete? How can it be obsolete when it's jet-propelled?"

"For God's sake, John—stinking jets have been around for a hundred stinking years. They were new when you were a kid—but that's a long stinking time ago now."

Dyson was right, though; the old plane did not break down. The loose panel swung and danced on the end of its wire, but the plane whined on across Europe unaffected.

"Anyway," said Dyson. "I don't know what you've got to worry about. I should be doing the worrying—I've got to be back in London on Friday for a television program, on which I may say my whole future career depends."

Mid-morning drinks were brought round; then pre-lunch drinks; then a sandwich lunch with lunch drinks, followed by after-lunch drinks. Everyone began to cheer up—even Starfield, who came working his way down the cabin, cheerfully saying a word here and a word there. "All right, folks? Everyone happy, boys and girls?"

"We do still reckon on getting back to London by Thursday night, do we?" Dyson asked him.

"There's a lad here worried about getting back already!" cried Starfield jovially to everyone around. He turned back to Dyson and patted his shoulder reassuringly. "Don't worry, boy," he said. "We'll get you back on time, never you fear."

After the fifth lot of drinks Mounce began to take some sort of interest in the scenery. "Rome," he said, gazing vaguely earthwards out of the window. "I'd like to take a look at Rome. Did you see *Dolce Vita*, John? Lot of crap, really. One or two quite juicy bits, though . . ."

Dyson tried to look out of the window over Mounce's shoulder, to see if they were in fact passing over Rome. But Mounce seemed to be reviewing the European scene at large. "I wouldn't mind taking a gander at Hamburg, for that matter," he said dreamily. "See some of those old judies wrestling in mud . . . Or Beirut. Old Jimmy Knowles on the *Express* was telling me about Beirut. He said it was fantastic. 'You lika leetle girl, sahib? I breenga you leetle seester for one half-dollar.' All that kind of crap."

There was a gap between after-lunch drinks and mid-afternoon drinks, however, during which Mounce began to subside a little into melancholy.

"I didn't know this stinking flight was going to take as long as this," he complained. "What time are we supposed to be getting there?"

"I don't know," said Dyson.

"It's nearly half past two already! I thought we were supposed to be traveling in a proper plane, not some snotty old wreck out of the Science Museum with straight wings. Is that the Persian Gulf down there now?"

Dyson craned over and looked out of the window. They were flying over a deep blue sea studded with islands.

"I don't think there are that many islands in the Persian Gulf," said Dyson doubtfully. "I think that must be the Aegean."

"The Aegean?" said Mounce indignantly. "The one next to Greece? Don't talk crap, John! We've been flying for hours. This is a plane, not a horse-and-cart."

More drinks were served, and more again. Just after four o'clock they began to descend. Starfield appeared at the front of the cabin and pressed his palms together.

"In just ten minutes' time, boys and girls," he began, "we shall be landing to refuel at Beirut."

He paused, as if expecting the same sort of reaction as the announcement about Amsterdam had caused. None came; everyone took the news in silence. Dyson wondered if everyone but himself and Mounce had known already that they were only just over halfway, or whether, like himself, they were too stunned to speak, or whether, like Mounce, they were too boozed to take it in. Starfield himself seemed to be slightly taken aback by the lack of response. The glasses slipped down his nose disbelievingly.

"Anyway," he said, pushing them back nervously, "drinks will be served in the transit lounge, compliments of Magic Carpet. Thank you."

Otto Friedrich

Traveling America with a Sense of History

From Fort Ticonderoga to the Plaza Hotel, from Appomattox Court-house to Bugsy Siegel's weird rose garden in Las Vegas, a traveler's perception of the present-day American scene is enriched by a knowl-edge of the past. History is the realm of ghosts, and ghosts often make the best traveling companions.

To grow up in New England is to grow up with an inescapable sense of history, a heritage that a New Englander carries with him wherever he goes. In Boston, where I was born, we paraded every April 19 to honor the patriots of 1775, and every schoolchild was supposed to memorize Longfellow's "Paul Revere's Ride": "One if by land, and two if by sea;/And I on the opposite shore will be. . . ." In Vermont, later, we acquired a farm just down the road from the estate where Rudyard Kipling had once lived, and all Brattleboro school-children had to memorize "Gunga Din" and "Recessional": "Lord God of Hosts, be with us yet,/Lest we forget—lest we forget!" In Concord, where I went to high school, we often swam in Thoreau's Walden Pond, and the parades on April 19 led out to the battlefield, where Daniel Chester French's heroic statue of the Minuteman bore Emerson's no less heroic lines: "Here once the embattled farmers stood,/And fired the shot heard round the world."

To acquire a sense of history is to acquire a sense of who one is, a sense of where one is, in time as well as place. Conversely, to lack all sense of history, to scramble continually after what is new and fashionable, is to lack all sense of identity. David McCullough, the historian, gave eloquent support to this view of the whole nation when he told last year's graduating class at Middle-bury College: "Imagine a man who professes over and over his unending love for a woman but who knows nothing of where she was born or who her parents were or where she went to school or what her life had been until he came along, and furthermore, he doesn't care to learn. What would you think of such a person?"

The highest social prestige in Concord was claimed by the survivors of those families like the Buttericks or the Wheelers who had inhabited the town since "before the fight," meaning 1775. My own ancestors had not been there then, for they had already gone West somewhat earlier, West being the Connecticut River valley and beyond, the Berkshires, the wilderness. I was thinking of them when I visited Fort Ticonderoga not too long ago and reached that majestic stone parapet where the row of black cannons stands guard over the southern tip of Lake Champlain. There are a few buildings nearby, of course, but as one gazes out over the thickly wooded hillside sloping down to the lake, one can imagine that this is the way everything once was. Here in 1758, when the stronghold was known as Fort Carillon, the Marquis de Montcalm and his thirty-six hundred men beat back a British force four times as large; here, nearly twenty years later, the British occupiers were surprised and overwhelmed by Ethan Allen and his Green Mountain Boys.

But the scene before me was all illusion. The fort was abandoned after the Revolution, and neighboring farmers made off with everything that remained in the ruins: stones, window frames—everything. There was virtually nothing left when Stephen Pell fell in love with the place and, beginning in 1908, spent the next half a century rebuilding the vanished stronghold. And if the handsome fort now boasts the world's largest collection of eighteenth-century cannons, it is partly because one of Pell's friends went roaming through the Caribbean, soliciting antique guns from Haiti, Nicaragua, the Dominican Republic.

It was long before Fort Ticonderoga was even built that my great-great-great-great-great-great-great-grandfather Benjamin Wait came wandering through these same woods in search of his kidnapped wife. Wait had been out harvesting his crops in Hatfield, Massachusetts, on September 19, 1677, when he heard shouted warnings of an Indian surprise attack. He hurried back to town to find that his house was a smoking ruin and his pregnant wife, Martha, had been taken captive. With only one companion, whose wife also had been abducted, Wait set out into the wilderness in pursuit of the retreating Indians. They hired a Mohawk to guide them to Lake George. They carried their canoe two miles overland to Lake Champlain. Then, with very little idea of where they were going, they continued paddling northward into the wilderness. According to one account, they "traveled three days without a bit of bread or any other relief but some raccoon's flesh which they had killed in an hollow tree."

In early January 1678, four months after the pregnant Martha Wait had been kidnapped, Wait and his companion found their wives and more than a dozen other captives in an Indian camp near a little Canadian town called Sorel. The Indians were not averse to a bargain with two such devoted husbands, so for two hundred pounds sterling, the colonists bought back their wives and all the other captives. One of these was Martha Wait's new baby, my great-great-great-great-great-great grandmother, whom they named Canada Wait.

The reason I know all this is that there was a time in the 1930s, during the first years of my father's exile from Nazi Germany, when both my parents became obsessed with establishing our early American ancestry. My mother, despite her Germanic married name, was determined to join the Daughters of the American Revolution. So we all wandered around Hatfield and the site of the Bloody Brook Massacre searching for traces of our past. The thing I remember most clearly is the scene of my father stopping the old blue Ford outside the weatherbeaten house of a farmer named Sanderson, who, according to my parents' researches, had to be a distant cousin, and my father asking, in his rather marked German accent, whether Mr. Sanderson knew about Benjamin Wait, their common ancestor, and the Hatfield Massacre of 1677. What? Wait? Hatfield Massacre? Sorry, mister.

My mother didn't get very much satisfaction out of her enrollment in the Daughters of the American Revolution either, because in 1939 the DAR forbade the black contralto Marian Anderson to give a concert in the DAR's Constitution Hall in Washington, D.C., so my mother felt that she had to resign her newly won membership. Do you remember that a black contralto was forbidden to give a concert in Washington, D.C., in 1939? That, too, is part of the sense of history—not just the celebration of what we enjoy celebrating on July 4 but also the remembering of what we would rather forget. And not just things that happened long ago but things that happened in rather recent times and only seem long ago.

In New York City, where I now live and work, the sense of history is constantly at war with the yearning for progress and profit. The sense of history is defended by a bureaucracy of landmark preservation; everything else supports the yearning for progress and profit. There is even a famous neo-Byzantine church on Park Avenue that is trying to have an office tower built in its own garden. The sporting institution known as Madison Square Garden keeps being torn down and rebuilt, farther and ever farther from Madison Square. For its latest and ugliest reincarnation, the builders destroyed the neoclassical splendors of Pennsylvania Station, which now survives only underground. But public places almost inevitably get torn down, if their sites are valuable, or, if not, become moribund.

And so in New York, the capital of novelty and fashionability, the sense of history survives not only in those ostentatiously preserved public ornaments like the splendid statue of General Sherman riding his horse past the Plaza Hotel but also in the lore that surrounds them. It helps to know not only who

Sherman was but also that the statue was created by Augustus Saint-Gaudens and that the angel guiding Sherman onward was modeled by a girl whom the sculptor was pursuing.

History also survives not only in the preserved establishments but in the unpreserved ones. I never walk past Broadway and Thirty-ninth Street, for example, without remembering that this was where the Metropolitan Opera used to stand, the real Met, with all those pillars, not that new place in Lincoln Center. Here it was that the wonderful baritone Leonard Warren fell dead onstage in the midst of Verdi's *La Forza del Destino.* And here it was that Sanche de Gramont won a Pulitzer Prize for scrambling across the street from the *Herald Tribune* and interviewing, under deadline pressure, witnesses to the singer's death.

Because of my profession I tend to think of such fading events in terms of the newspapers that once covered them. When I first came to New York in 1950, it still enjoyed more than a dozen major daily papers, and though most of these grimy but exciting places are now gone, I still remember being inside most of them, either working or looking for work. The *Daily News,* where I used to write half a dozen stories a day, still struggles along, but what trace is left of our great rival on East Forty-fifth Street, Hearst's *Daily Mirror?* The *Post,* where I worked on the copy desk in the ramshackle building down on West Street, took a vague sort of pride in having been founded by Alexander Hamilton, in 1801, and edited throughout much of the nineteenth century by William Cullen Bryant; but now it is losing millions over on South Street, and its fate depends on the benevolence of Rupert Murdoch. The *Times* is still strong, of course, but I miss the *Herald Tribune,* an elegant and well-written paper that was rather proud of its descent from the *Tribune* of Horace Greeley. Just the other day I went looking for Bleeck's, the tavern on West Thirty-eighth Street where the *Herald Tribune's* social life was conducted, where you might find John Lardner playing the match game with Red Smith, and I could see no sign that the place had ever existed, except in my own head.

New York is the financial capital of the United States and the capital of fashions and of crime, but it is also the capital of writing, so you can read the city in terms of Henry James' Washington Square or the customshouse where Herman Melville worked, but I like it best as the site of Scott Fitzgerald's *Tales of the Jazz Age.* Come back, now, to Saint-Gaudens' statue of General Sherman, and look over toward the Plaza Hotel, and is that fountain not enriched by the recollection that Scott and Zelda Fitzgerald once plunged into it out of sheer delight in their own triumphant youth? The ghost of Fitzgerald, if you have eyes to see it, flickers at several points in midtown Manhattan. The Racquet Club, that pseudo-Renaissance palace on Park Avenue, was where the brutally beaten Abe North, who was modeled on Ring Lardner, crawled home to die. Another character in *Tender Is the Night* disputes this disclosure: "It wasn't the Racquet Club he crawled to—it was the Harvard Club. . . . I happen to know most of the members of the Racquet Club. It *must* have been the Harvard Club."

Over on Fifty-sixth Street and Seventh Avenue is the building where Arnold Rothstein was murdered. You may remember Rothstein, who was the model for Gatsby's friend Meyer Wolfsheim, as the man who fixed the 1919 World Series. "I see you're looking at my cuff buttons . . . ," Wolfsheim said to Nick Carraway, who hadn't been. "Finest specimens of human molars." And a little south, at Fifty-fourth and Sixth, stands the Warwick Hotel, where Fitzgerald fell so disastrously off the wagon while he and the young Budd Schulberg were on their way to New Hampshire to research a film script on the Dartmouth Winter Carnival, a misadventure that Schulberg later dramatized in his novel *The Disenchanted.*

Perhaps the most historically self-conscious city in America is Washington, though its sense of history is largely limited to domestic politics and largely expressed in stone monuments. Unlike the heroine of *Born Yesterday,* I have never been overwhelmed by the Lincoln Memorial, much less the Washington Monument and Jefferson Memorial. Perhaps that is because I sympathize with the disdainful view of Henry James' Alfred Bonnycastle, the character in "Pandora" modeled on Henry Adams, whose idea of a really eclectic dinner party was to tell his wife, "Let's be vulgar and have some fun— let's invite the President."

There are many Washingtons, of course—the Reagans' mink-coated Washington, the Kennedy Camelot, the New Deal Washington of all those neoclassic office buildings—but the one I like best is Henry Adams' Washington. It was a sleepy Southern town then, not the imperial city that considers itself the command post of the Western world, and pigs rooted in the unpaved streets. The Washington Monument was still unfinished, though Mark Twain reported that it "towers out of the mud [and] has the aspect of a factory chimney with the top broken off." Twain regarded the whole city as the "grand old benevolent National Asylum for the Helpless," but Adams was more sympathetic. "One of these days this will be a very great city . . . ," he wrote to a friend. "Even now it is a beautiful one."

Adams moved into a handsome house just across Lafayette Square (then President's Square) from the White House, a building about which he still had proprietary feelings since he had first known it as the residence of his grandfather John Quincy Adams. Two weeks later Henry's wife, Clover, condescended to visit the White House and pay her respects to Mrs. Rutherford B. Hayes. She had already heard from a friend that "they suffer much from rats in the White House, who run over their bed and nibble the president's toes," but she was not prepared for "a stout, common-looking man [who] came in and came towards me and held out his hand. . . . It didn't dawn on me that it was the master of the house." One can only imagine the contempt with which Mrs. Adams probably regarded that outstretched hand and marvel that there was a time of innocence only a century ago when a well-informed woman could visit the White House and not know what its occupant looked like.

When I go to Washington, I like to stay at the Hay-Adams Hotel, the comfortable old place that stands on the site of the houses that Henry Hobson

Richardson built for Adams and John Hay. The scene is still faintly haunted by the ghost of Clover Adams; bitterly depressed after the death of her father, she took poison. I also like to go out to Rock Creek Cemetery, where Henry and Clover Adams lie buried underneath Saint-Gaudens' grieving statue. Alexander Woollcott spoke with characteristic hyperbole, but was not far wrong, when he called it the "most beautiful thing ever fashioned by the hand of man on this continent."

The Southern sense of history is scarcely less fervent than that of Boston and Washington, and as we drive south through Virginia, we constantly encounter road signs that evoke the past. I don't mean Richmond or Williamsburg so much as Chancellorsville and Fredericksburg and that wonderfully rightly named battlefield the Wilderness. I have read many stories about the New South and the Sun Belt, but to me the South is still to some extent the enemy side in the Civil War, the slave state.

My great-grandfather Alva J. Smith (Canada Wait had married a man named Joseph Smith) fought his way across this countryside as a corporal, then lieutenant, then captain, in the Fourth New York Artillery Regiment. I thought of him hauling those horse-drawn guns through these gentle hills—hardly more than a boy, really, but trained to fire those cannons against the South.

I was visiting an old friend in Columbia, South Carolina, and he wanted to show me the state capitol. We drove downtown to inspect the building, over which, as my friend observed, local patriots periodically raised the Confederate flag. Then he pointed out the scars inflicted by General Sherman's invaders, bullet holes surrounded by accusingly commemorative circles of white paint.

"A little more effort, and Sherman could have knocked the whole place down, Confederate flag and all," I said. I hate nationalism and all forms of extremism, but when I found myself in the South, I suddenly found myself becoming extremely nationalistic, meaning pro-Union, anti-Confederate, an abolitionist. Most people north of the Mason-Dixon line hardly have any feelings at all about the Civil War; only in the South do they have such feelings, and the feelings generally are based on the assumption that the South was right or at least misunderstood and ill used. My antagonism derives, I suppose, from World War II, the only other American war in which much blood was shed for an essentially moral cause, and I hate the attempts to strip away that moral element and to justify or exonerate the enemy.

"A little more effort, and Sherman could have killed all the rest of the civilians in town too," my friend said.

"Well, I think Sherman was one of the great heroes," I said, remembering that splendid statue outside the Plaza. "He would have been elected President if he'd been willing to accept it."

"He wouldn't have been elected if the South hadn't been disenfranchised," my friend retorted. "My grandmother used to get into a *rage* every time his name was mentioned."

"The liberator of Georgia." I couldn't resist firing a final shot.

"Liberator—hell!" my friend shouted. Even Southern hospitality has some limits.

Heading northward out of the Confederacy, I decided that I wanted to stop at some of the Union shrines—Harpers Ferry, Appomattox Courthouse, Gettysburg—all meticulously restored and preserved by the National Park Service. Then, when I got back to New York, I dug out a list of half-forgotten battles that my great-grandfather had recalled and written down in the quieter years when he worked as a railroad official: Rapidan campaign, Wilderness, Spotsylvania, Po River, North Anna, Cold Harbor, Deep Bottom, Strawberry Plains, White Oak Swamp, Poplar Springs Church, Dabney's Mills, Peeble's Farm, Hatcher's Run, Boydton Plank Road, Sutherland Station, Siege of Petersburg, Andrews Springs, Sailor's Creek, High Bridge, Appomattox Courthouse. Yes, it is all there.

Out West these things are forgotten, were never known. Colorado, one reads in an account of the state's history, had not a single white resident before about 1830. A proud guide in the home of the Unsinkable Molly Brown speaks of it as one of the oldest houses in Denver; it much resembles the scores of brick houses lining Commonwealth Avenue in Boston, the new houses built when the Back Bay was filled in after the Civil War.

The best thing about the West, of course, is precisely its lack of history, in the sense of history's being an encrustation of human occupation, creation, and debris. Yes, I know that Santa Fe boasts of its quaint antiquity and that the Governor's Palace dates back to 1609, a decade before anyone ever landed at Plymouth Rock, but the West I am talking about is the West of vast forests and vast plains. You can drive for miles and miles along, say, Route 14 across northern Wyoming without ever seeing any evidence (except, of course, for the highway itself) that any human being has ever set foot here. Then you come to a sign announcing the existence of some town with a name like Shawnee Fork and a population of twenty-three. And then you reach the perfection of Jenny Lake in Grand Teton National Park. If Jenny Lake were located in Switzerland, there would at least be a Benedictine monastery with a bell tolling across the meadows; if it were in New York, there would be Jenny condominiums and a Jenny marina. Here there is nothing but the incredible beauty of Jenny Lake itself, exactly as it was when God made it.

Still, the West has a peculiar kind of history all its own, not an imitation of Eastern history, as Eastern history is an imitation of European history, but—well, consider Leadville, Colorado, a small town of no distinction whatever except for the morality play that was enacted here not once but three times. Gold was discovered in 1860, in a place called California Gulch; the town that sprang up nearby was named Oro City. Within a year, five thousand prospectors had crowded in, making Oro City the largest place in the Colorado Territory. Greed was its only reason for existence and its only law. In the little town museum there are still brownish pictures of rows of miners sleeping on floors (and paying handsomely for the privilege), carousing in crowded saloons, murdering each other, and being murdered, in the ruthless struggle over gold claims.

After some $3 million worth of gold had been dug out of the mountain, the lode ran dry, and everyone decamped, and Oro City shrank to a somewhat battered village. Dust unto dust, vanity of vanities, and they that live by the sword. About ten years later somebody discovered that the slag stripped of gold still contained silver. Another explosion of greed. The new town that grew up was called Leadville (there was lead, too, of course). More miners sleeping on the barroom floors, more miners being murdered in the battles over silver claims. The silver rush proved even richer than the gold rush. By 1880, when Leadville had swollen to thirty-five thousand inhabitants, it was the largest silver-mining place in the world, with thirty producing mines, ten large smelters, nearly thirty miles of streets, and an opera house. After millions of dollars' worth of silver had been extracted—$11.5 million in 1880 alone—the price dropped sharply in 1893, there were strikes and the summoning of militia, and the town began dwindling again. Then, about 1900, somebody discovered that the hills, stripped of gold and silver, still contained molybdenum. There was reenacted the same old melodrama of greed and destruction. Is there not some lesson in all this? Hegel said that the only lesson we learn from history is that nobody learns a lesson from history.

As our westward travels finally bring us to California, we see that there are two kinds of history: old history and new history. San Francisco takes pride in its archaic cable cars and the square-rigger anchored at the pier, but though the city has its comfortable charm, I think I prefer the swaggering modernity of Los Angeles. Where else in the world could Howard Hughes' *Spruce Goose*, the gigantic wooden flying boat that never flew more than about a mile one day in 1947, be a tourist attraction? Where else could the barn that Cecil B. De Mille rented to film *The Squaw Man* in 1913 be treasured as a relic of preclassical antiquity? Where else could J. Paul Getty have created a major art museum in the form of a Roman imperial villa? Where else could a guide on a bus tour point with pride to the site of the filming of "The Beverly Hillbillies"?

For that kind of history we must eventually visit Las Vegas, where the sense of time has been totally abolished. Wander at any hour through the garish gambling casinos, which have no windows that might reveal whether it is day or night, and you can see the money-drugged customers hunched in front of the slot machines, each of them hoping to reenact the melodrama of Leadville. I asked one of the bartenders at the Rainbow Bar of the Flamingo Hilton, a middle-aged man wearing a string tie in the fashion of the Old West, whether there remained any trace of the original hotel that the notorious Bugsy Siegel had built back in the 1940s. He could suggest only that I inspect a series of photographs of the hotel in that vanished era, now framed and hung on the walls of an obscure corridor, and that I wander outside to take a look at "Bugsy Siegel's rose garden." Out in the empty darkness near the swimming pool, I eventually found the spot, a handsome array of about seventy-five rosebushes, which I suspect were no more than five or ten years old. There was a plaque, though, that claimed that every year the roses "bloom bigger and with a deeper red than the year before" because Siegel buried some of his victims here. If you wander here at midnight under a full moon, the plaque declared, you might hear the voices of those victims murmuring, "Bugsy, how do you like the roses, Bugsy?"

Now I am back home in Long Island, where it takes only a little 5-10-5 to make the roses grow. The real estate agent who sold me this 150-year-old house at the edge of the Sound gave me a handbill claiming that "among its occupants . . . have been a secretary of defense and a justice of the United States Supreme Court." I seem to remember her telling me that the secretary of defense was James Forrestal, but when I telephoned one of his sons to find out more details, the son said that he was fairly sure that his father never lived here. Such futile inquiries and such dispiriting answers are all part of the course of history. When the young Henry Luce went to Oxford and enrolled at Christ Church, his prospective tutor asked him what period he hoped to study. Modern European history, the eighteenth and nineteenth centuries, the young Luce replied. "Luce, I am bound to tell you that here at Oxford we consider that modern history ends with the Glorious Revolution of 1688," the tutor said. "After that all is mere hearsay and rumor."

Paul Fussell

From Exploration to Travel to Tourism

This provocative essay is extracted from *Abroad: British Literary Traveling Between the Wars,* Paul Fussell's provocative and profound 1980 elegy for the lost art of travel. The joy of the open road, the sentimental education of the *wanderjahr,* has given way to the pallor of the packaged experience: Jonestown as Blue Grotto. "The resemblance," Fussell observes, "between the tourist and the client of a massage parlor is closer than it would be polite to emphasize."

Because travel is hardly possible anymore, an inquiry into the nature of travel and travel writing between the wars will resemble a threnody, and I'm afraid that a consideration of the tourism that apes it will be like a satire.

Two bits of data at the outset. When you entered Manhattan by the Lincoln Tunnel twenty years ago you saw from the high west bank of the Hudson a vision that lifted your heart and in some measure redeemed the potholes and noise and lunacy and violence of the city. You saw the magic row of transatlantic liners nuzzling the island, their classy, frivolous red and black and white and green uttering their critique of the utility beige-gray of the buildings. In the row might be the *Queen Mary* or the *Queen Elizabeth* or the *Mauretania,* the *United States* or the *America* or the *Independence,* the *Rafaello* or the *Michelangelo* or the *Liberté.* These were the last attendants of the age of travel, soon to fall victim to the jet plane and the cost of oil and the cost of skilled labor.

A second bit of data, this one rather nasty. An official of the Guyanese government was recently heard to say that Jonestown might be turned into a profitable tourist attraction, "on the order of Auschwitz or Dachau." The disappearance of the ships from the Hudson, like the remark from Guyana, helps define the advanced phase of the age of tourism.

The rudimentary phase began over a century ago, in England, because England was the first country to undergo industrialization and urbanization. The tediums of industrial work made "vacations" necessary, while the unwholesomeness of England's great soot-caked cities made any place abroad, by flagrant contrast, appear almost mystically salubrious, especially in an age of rampant tuberculosis. Contributing to the rise of tourism in the nineteenth century was the bourgeois vogue of romantic primitivism. From James "Ossian" Macpherson in the late eighteenth century to D. H. Lawrence in the early twentieth, intellectuals and others discovered special virtue in primitive peoples and places. Tourism is egalitarian or it is nothing, and its egalitarianism is another index of its origins in the nineteenth century. Whether in the Butlin's Camps of the British or the National Park campsites of America or Hitler's Strength-through-Joy cruises or the current Clubs Méditerranée, where nudity and pop-beads replace clothes and cash, it is difficult to be a snob and a tourist at the same time. By going primitive in groups one becomes "equal," playing out even in 1980 a fantasy devised well over a century ago, a fantasy implying that if simple is good, sincere is even better.

It was not always thus. Before tourism there was travel, and before travel there was exploration. Each is roughly assignable to its own age in modern history: Exploration belongs to the Renaissance, travel to the bourgeois age, tourism to our proletarian moment. But there are obvious overlaps. What we recognize as tourism in its contemporary form was making inroads on travel as early as the mid-nineteenth century, when Thomas Cook got the bright idea of shipping sightseeing groups to the Continent, and though the Renaissance is over, there are still a few explorers. Tarzan's British father Lord Greystoke was exploring Africa in the twentieth century while tourists were being herded around the Place de l'Opéra.

And the terms *exploration, travel,* and *tourism* are slippery. In 1855 what we would call exploration is often called travel, as in Francis Galton's *The Art of Travel.* His title seems to promise advice about securing deck-chairs in favorable locations and hints about tipping on shipboard, but his sub-title makes his intention clear: *Shifts and Contrivances Available in Wild Countries.* Galton's advice to "travelers" is very different from the matter in a Baedeker. Indeed, his book is virtually a survival manual, with instructions on blacksmithing, making your own black powder, descending cliffs with ropes, and defending a camp against natives: "Of all European inventions, nothing so impresses and terrifies savages as fireworks, especially rockets. . . . A rocket, judiciously sent up, is very likely to frighten off an intended attack and save bloodshed." On the other hand, the word *travel* in modern usage is equally misleading, as in phrases like *travel agency* and *the travel industry,* where what the words are disguising is *tourist agency* and *the tourist industry,* the idea of a *travel industry* constituting a palpable contradiction in terms, if we understand what real travel once was.

"Explorers," according to Hugh and Pauline Massingham, "are to the ordinary traveler what the Saint is to the average church congregation." The athletic, paramilitary activity of exploration ends in knighthoods for Sir Francis Drake and Sir Aurel Stein and Sir Edmund Hillary. No traveler, and certainly no tourist, is ever knighted for his performances, although the strains he may undergo can be as memorable as the explorer's. All three make journeys, but the explorer seeks the undiscovered, the traveler that which has been discovered by the mind working in history, the tourist that which has been discovered by entrepreneurship and prepared for him by the arts of mass publicity. The genuine traveler is, or used to be, in the middle between the two extremes. If the explorer moves toward the risks of the formless and the unknown, the tourist moves toward the security of pure cliché. It is between these two poles that the traveler mediates, retaining all he can of the excitement of the unpredictable attaching to exploration, and fusing that with the pleasure of "knowing where one is" belonging to tourism.

But travel is work. Etymologically a traveler is one who suffers *travail,* a word deriving in its turn from Latin *tripalium,* a torture instrument consisting of three stakes designed to rack the body. Before the development of tourism, travel was conceived to be like study, and its fruits were considered to be the adornment of the mind and the formation of the judgment. The traveler was a student of what he sought, and he was assisted by aids like the thirty-four volumes of the Medieval Town Series, now, significantly, out of print. One by-product of real travel was something that has virtually disappeared, the travel book as a record of an inquiry and a report of the effect of the inquiry on the mind and imagination of the traveler. Lawrence's Italian journey, says Anthony Burgess, "by post-bus or cold late train or on foot are in that great laborious tradition which produced genuine travel books." And Paul Theroux, whose book *The Great Railway Bazaar* is one of the few travel books to emerge from our age of tourism, observes that "travel writing is a funny thing" because "the worst trips make the best reading, which is why Graham Greene's *The Lawless Roads* and Kinglake's *Eothen* are so superb." On the other hand, easy, passive travel results in books which offer "little more than chatting," or, like former British Prime Minister Edward Heath's *Travels*, "smug boasting." "Let the tourist be cushioned against misadventure," says Lawrence Durrell; "your true traveler will not feel that he has had his money's worth unless he brings back a few scars." (A personal note: Although I have been both traveler and tourist, it was as a traveler, not a tourist, that I once watched my wallet and passport slither down a Turkish toilet at Bodrum, and it was the arm of a traveler that reached deep, deep into that cloaca to retrieve them.) If exploration promised adventures, travel was travel because it held out high hopes of misadventures.

From the outset mass tourism attracted the class contempt of killjoys who conceived themselves independent travelers and thus superior by reason of intellect, education, curiosity, and spirit. In the mid-nineteenth century Charles Lever laments in *Blackwood's Magazine:*

> It seems that some enterprising and unscrupulous man [he means Thomas Cook] has devised the project of conducting some forty or fifty persons . . . from London to Naples and back for a fixed sum. He contracts to carry them, feed them, and amuse them. . . . When I first read the scheme . . . I caught at the hope that the speculation would break down. I imagined that the characteristic independence of Englishmen would revolt against a plan that reduces the traveler to the level of his trunk and obliterates every trace and trait of the individual. I was all wrong. As I write, the cities of Italy are deluged with droves of these creatures.

Lever's word *droves* suggests sheep or cattle and reminds us how traditional in anti-tourist fulminations animal images are. (I have used *herded,* above.) "Of all noxious animals," says Francis Kilvert in the 1870s, "the most noxious is the tourist." And if not animals, insects. The Americans descending on Amalfi in the 1920s, according to Osbert Sitwell, resemble "a swarm of very noisy transatlantic locusts," and the tourists at Levanto in the 1930s, according to his sister Edith, are "the most awful people with legs like flies who come in to lunch in bathing costume—flies, centipedes."

I am assuming that travel is now impossible and that tourism is all we have left. Travel implies variety of means and independence of arrangements. The disappearance not just of the transatlantic lovelies but of virtually all passenger ships except cruise vessels (tourism with a vengeance) and the increasing difficulty of booking hotel space if one is not on a tour measure the plight of those who aspire still to travel in the old sense. Recently I planned a trip to the Orient and the South Pacific, hoping that in places so remote and, I dreamed, backward, something like travel might still just be possible. I saw myself lolling at the rail unshaven in a dirty white linen suit as the crummy little ship approached Bora Bora or Fiji in a damp heat which made one wonder whether death by yaws or dengue fever might be an attractive alternative. Too late for such daydreams. I found that just as I was inquiring, passenger ship travel in the Pacific disappeared, in April 1978, to be precise. That month the ships of both the Matson and the Pacific Far East Lines were laid up for good, done in by the extortions of the oil-producing nations. In the same month even a small Chinese-owned "steam navigation company" running a regular service between Hong Kong and Singapore put away its toys. Formerly it had been possible to call at the remote island of Betio and Tarawa Atoll to pay respects to the ghosts of the United States and Japanese Marines, and an enterprising couple had built a small inn there. Now access to Betio and Tarawa is by air only and the plane flies on alternate Thursdays, which means you have to stay there two weeks if you go at all. No one will go there now. I did not go there but to the big places with big hotels and big airports served by big planes. I came to know what Frederic Harrison meant when he said, "We go abroad but we travel no longer." Only he wrote that in 1887. I suppose it's all a matter of degree. Perhaps the closest one could approach an experience of travel in the old sense today would be to drive in an aged automobile with doubtful tires through Roumania or Afghanistan without hotel reservations and to get by on terrible French.

One who has hotel reservations and speaks no French is a tourist. Anthropologists are fond of defining him, although in their earnestness they tend to miss his essence. Thus Valene L. Smith in *Hosts and Guests: The Anthropology of Tourism:* "A tourist is a temporarily leisured person who voluntarily visits a place away from home for the purpose of experiencing a change." But that pretty well defines a traveler too. What distinguishes the tourist is the motives, few of which are ever openly revealed: to raise social status at home and to allay social anxiety; to realize fantasies of erotic freedom; and most important, to derive secret pleasure from posing momentarily as a member of a social class superior to one's own, to play the role of a "shopper" and spender whose life becomes significant and exciting only when one is exercising power by choosing what to buy. Cant as the tourist may of the Taj Mahal and Mt. Etna at sunset, his real target today is the immense Ocean Terminal at Hong Kong, with its miles of identical horrible camera and tape-recorder shops. The fact that the tourist is best defined as a fantasist equipped temporarily with unaccustomed power is better known to the tourist industry than to anthropology. The resemblance between the tourist and the client of a massage parlor is closer than it would be polite to emphasize.

For tourist fantasies to bloom satisfactorily, certain conditions must be established. First, the tourist's mind must be entirely emptied so that a sort of hypnotism can occur. Unremitting Musak is a help here, and it is carefully provided in hotels, restaurants, elevators, tour buses, cable cars, planes, and excursion boats. The tourist is assumed to know nothing, a tradition upheld by the American magazine *Travel* (note the bogus title), which is careful to specify that London is in England and Venice in Italy. If the tourist is granted a little awareness, it is always of the most retrograde kind, like the thirties belief, which he is assumed to hold, that "transportation," its varieties and promise, is itself an appropriate subject of high regard. (Think of the 1939 New York World's Fair, with its assumption that variety, celerity, and novelty in means of transport are inherently interesting: "Getting There Is Half the Fun.") A current day-tour out of Tokyo honors this convention. The ostensible object is to convey a group of tourists to a spot where they can wonder at the grandeurs of natural scenery. In pursuit of this end, they are first placed in a "streamlined" train whose speed of 130 miles per hour is frequently called to their attention. They are then transferred to an air-conditioned "coach" which whisks them to a boat, whence, after a ten-minute ride, they are ushered into a funicular to ascend a spooky gorge, after which, back to the bus, etc. The whole day's exercise is presented as a marvel of contrivance in which the sheer variety of the conveyances supplies a large part of the attraction. Hydrofoils are popular for similar reasons, certainly not for their efficiency. Of the four I've been on in the past few years, two have broken down spectacularly, one in Manila Bay almost sinking after encountering a submerged log at sophomoric high speed.

Tourist fantasies fructify best when tourists are set down not in places but in pseudo-places, passing through subordinate pseudo-places, like airports, on the way. Places are odd and call for interpretation. They are the venue of the traveler. Pseudo-places entice by their familiarity and call for instant recognition: "We have arrived." Kermanshah, in Iran, is a place; the Costa del Sol is a pseudo-place, or Tourist Bubble, as anthropologists call it. The Algarve, in southern Portugal, is a prime pseudo-place, created largely by Temple Fielding, the American author of *Fielding's Travel Guide to Europe*. That book, first published in 1948, was to tourism what Baedeker was to travel. It did not, says John McPhee, "tell people what to see. It told them . . . what to spend, and where." Bougainville is a place; the Polynesian Cultural Center, on Oahu, is a pseudo-place. Touristically considered, Switzerland has always been a pseudoplace, but now Zermatt has been promoted to the status of its pre-eminent pseudo-place. Because it's a city that has been constructed for the purpose of being recognized as a familiar image, Washington is classic pseudo-place, resembling Disneyland in that as in other respects. One striking post-Second War phenomenon has been the transformation of numerous former small countries into pseudo-places or tourist commonwealths, whose function is simply to entice tourists and sell them things. This has happened remarkably fast. As recently as 1930 Alec Waugh could report that Martinique had no tourists because there was no accommodation for them. Now, Martinique would seem to be about nothing but tourists, like Haiti, the Dominican Republic, Barbados, Bermuda, Hong Kong, Fiji, and the Greek Islands.

Today the tourist is readied for his ultimate encounter with placelessness by passing first through the uniform airport. Only forty years ago the world's airports exhibited distinctive characteristics betokening differences in national character and style. Being in one was not precisely like being in another. In Graham Greene's novel of 1935, *England Made Me*, the character Fred Hall, we are told, "knew the airports of Europe as well as he had once known the stations on the Brighton line—shabby Le Bourget; the great scarlet rectangle of the Tempelhof as one came in from London in the dark . . . ; the white sand blowing up round the shed at Tallinn; Riga, where the Berlin to Leningrad plane came down and bright pink mineral waters were sold in a tin-roofed shed." That sort of variety would be unthinkable now, when, as Bernard Bergonzi says, airport design has become a "ubiquitous international idiom."

Moving through the airport—or increasingly, being moved, on a literal endless belt—the tourist arrives at his next non-place, the airplane interior. The vapid non-allusive cheerfulness of its décor betrays its design and manufacture as Southern Californian. Locked in this flying cigar where distance is expressed in hours instead of miles or kilometers, the tourist is in touch only with the uniform furniture and fittings and experiences the environment through which the whole non-place is proceeding only as he is obliged to fasten or loosen his seat belt. Waugh was among the first to notice "the curious fact that airplanes have added nothing to our enjoyment of height. The human eye still receives the most intense images when the observer's feet are planted on the ground or on a building. The airplane belittles all it discloses." The calculated isolation from the actual which is tourism ("We fly you above the weather") is reflected as well in the design of the last of the serious passenger liners, the QE2. Here the designers carefully eliminated the promenade deck, formerly the place where you were vouchsafed some proximity to the ocean. Now, as John Malcolm Brinnin has said, "Travelers who love the sea, delight in studying its moods, and like to walk in the sight and smell of it, were left with almost no place to go." Except the bars and fruit-machines, doubtless the intention. As the ship has been obliged to compete in the illusion of placelessness with the airport and the jet, its interior design has given over its former ambitions of alluding to such identifiable places as country estates with fireplaces and libraries, urban tea-dance parlors, and elegant conservatories full of palms, ferns, and wicker, and instead has embraced the universal placeless style, eschewing organic materials like wood and real fabric in favor of spray-painted metal and dun plastic. I don't want to sound too gloomy, but there's a relation here with other "replacements" characterizing contemporary life: the replacement of coffee-cream by ivory-colored powder, for example, or of silk and wool by nylon; or glass by lucite, bookstores by "bookstores," eloquence by jargon, fish by fish-sticks, merit by publicity, motoring by driving, and travel by tourism. A corollary of that last replacement is that ships have been replaced by cruise ships, small moveable pseudo-places making an endless transit between larger fixed pseudo-places. But even a cruise ship is preferable to a plane. It is healthier because you can exercise on it, and it is more romantic because you can copulate on it.

Safe and efficient uniform international jet service began in earnest around 1957. That's an interesting moment in the history of human passivity. It's the approximate moment when radio narrative and drama, requiring the audience to do some of the work by supplying the missing visual dimension by its own imagination, were replaced by television, which now does it all for the "viewer"—or stationary tourist, if you will. Supplying the missing dimension is exactly what real travel used to require, and it used to assume a large body of people willing to travail to earn illumination.

But ironically, the tourist is not without his own kinds of travails which the industry never prepares him for and which make tourism always something less than the ecstasy proposed. The sense that he is being swindled and patronized, or that important intelligence is being withheld from him, must trouble even the dimmest at one time or another. In addition to the incomprehensible but clearly crucial airport loudspeaker harangues, the tourist is faced by constant rhetorical and contractual challenges. He meets one the moment he accepts the standard airline baggage check and reads, "This is not the Luggage Ticket (Baggage Check) as described in Article 4 of the Warsaw Convention or the Warsaw Convention as amended by the Hague Protocol 1955." The question arises, if this baggage check is not that one, what is it? If it is not that Luggage Ticket (Baggage Check), how do you get the real one? And what does the real one say when you finally get it? Does it say, "This *is* the Luggage Ticket (Baggage Check) as described in, etc."? "On no account accept any substitute." Or "Persons accepting substitutes for the Luggage Ticket (Baggage Check) as described in Article 4 . . . will legally and morally have no recourse when their baggage is diverted (lost), and in addition will be liable to severe penalties, including immediate involuntary repatriation at their own expense."

Another cause of tourist travail is touts. The word *tout*, designating a man hounding a tourist to patronize a certain hotel or shop, dates approximately from Cook's first organized excursion to the Paris Exposition of 1855. Some tourist brochures will gingerly hint at such hazards as sharks, fetid water, and appalling food, but I've never seen one that prepared the tourist for the far greater threat of the tout.

Tour guides are touts by nature, required to lead tourists to shops where purchases result in commissions. In Kyoto recently a scholarly guide to the religious monuments, full of dignity and years, had to undergo the humiliation of finally conducting his group of tourists to a low ceramics shop. He almost wept. Tour guides are also by nature café touts: "Let's rest here a moment. I know you're tired. You can sit down and order coffee, beer, or soft drinks." And souvenir-shop touts: "This place has the best fly-whisks (postcards, scarabs, amber, coral, camera film, turquoise, pocket calculators) in town, and because you are with me you will not be cheated." All kinds of tourists are fair game for touts, but Americans seem their favorite targets, not just because of their careless ways with money and their instinctive generosity but also their non-European innocence about the viler dimensions of human nature and their desire to be liked, their impulse to say "Good morning" back instead of "Go away." It's a rare American who, asked "Where you from, Sir?" will venture "Screw you" instead of "Boise."

Touts make contemporary tourism a hell of importunity, and many of my memories of tourist trips reduce to memories of particular touts. There was the money-changing tout at Luxor so assiduous that I dared not leave the hotel for several days, and the gang of guide-touts outside Olaffson's Hotel, Port au Prince, who could be dealt with only by hiring one to fend off the others. There was the nice, friendly waiter at the best hotel in Colombo, Sri Lanka, whose kindly inquiries about one's plans cloaked his intention to make one lease his brother's car. There was the amiable student of English in Shiraz whose touching efforts at verbal self-improvement brought him gradually to the essential matter, the solicitation of a large gift. There was the sympathetic acquaintance in Srinigar whose free boat ride ended at his canalside carpet outlet. There was the civilized Assistant Manager of the

Hotel Peninsula, Hong Kong, an establishment so pretentious that it picks up its clients at the airport in Rolls-Royces, who, repulsed at the desk, finally came up to my room to tout the hotel's tours. There were the well-got-up young men of Manila who struck up conversations, innocently expressing interest in your children and place of residence, and then gradually, and in their view subtly, began to beg. Rejected there, they then touted for shops. They then turned pimps, and, that failing, whores. The Philippines is a notable tout venue, like Turkey, Iran, Mexico, Egypt, and India. All are in the grip of a developing capitalism, halfway between the primitive and the over-ripe. In London there are no touts: It's easier there to make a living without the constant fear of humiliating rebuff. On the other hand, there are none in Papua New Guinea either. It is not yet sufficiently "developed," which means it doesn't yet have a sense of a richer outside world which can be tapped. In the same way, your real native of a truly primitive place doesn't steal from tourists. Not out of primitive virtue but out of ignorance: Unlike a resident of, say, Naples, he doesn't know what incredible riches repose in tourists' luggage and handbags.

As I have said, it is hard to be a snob and a tourist at the same time. A way to combine both roles is to become an anti-tourist. Despite the suffering he undergoes, the anti-tourist is not to be confused with the traveler: His motive is not inquiry but self-protection and vanity. Dean MacCannell, author of the anthropological study *The Tourist,* remembers a resident of an island like Nantucket who remonstrated when, arriving, MacCannell offered to start the car before the ferry docked. "Only tourists do that," he was told. Abroad, the techniques practiced by anti-tourists anxious to assert their difference from all those tourists are more shifty. All involve attempts to merge into the surroundings, like speaking the language, even badly. Some dissimulations are merely mechanical, like a man's shifting his wedding ring from the left to the right hand. A useful trick is ostentatiously not carrying a camera. If asked about this deficiency by a camera-carrying tourist, one scores points by saying, "I never carry a camera. If I photograph things I find I don't really see them." Another device is staying in the most unlikely hotels, although this is risky, like the correlative technique of eschewing taxis in favor of local public transportation (the more complicated and confusing the better), which may end with the anti-tourist stranded miles out of town, cold and alone on the last tram of the night. Another risky technique is programmatically consuming the local food, no matter how nasty, and affecting to relish sheeps' eyes, fried cicadas, and shellfish taken locally, that is, from the sewagey little lagoon. Dressing with attention to local coloration used to be harder before jeans became the international costume of the pseudo-leisured. But jeans are hard for those around sixty to get away with, and the anti-tourist must be careful to prevent betrayal by jackets, trousers, shoes, and even socks and neckties (if still worn) differing subtly from the local norms.

Sedulously avoiding the standard sights is probably the best method of disguising your touristhood. In London one avoids Westminster Abbey and heads instead for the Earl of Burlington's eighteenth-century villa at Chiswick. In Venice one must walk by circuitous smelly back passages far out of one's way to avoid being seen in the Piazza San Marco. In Athens, one disdains the Acropolis in favor of the eminence preferred by the locals, the Lycabettus. Each tourist center has its interdicted zone: In Rome you avoid the Spanish Steps and the Fontana de Trevi, in Paris the Deux Magots and the whole Boul' Mich area, in Nice the Promenade des Anglais, in Egypt Giza with its excessively popular pyramids and sphinx, in Hawaii Waikiki. Avoiding Waikiki brings up the whole question of why one's gone to Hawaii at all, but that's exactly the problem.

Driving on the Continent, it's essential to avoid outright giveaways like the French TT license plate. Better to drive a car registered in the country you're touring (the more suave rental agencies know this) if you can't find one from some unlikely place like Bulgaria or Syria. Plates entirely in Arabic are currently much favored by anti-tourists, and they have the additional advantage of frustrating policemen writing tickets for illegal parking.

Perhaps the most popular way for the anti-tourist to demarcate himself from the tourists, because he can have a drink while doing it, is for him to lounge—cameraless—at a café table and with palpable contempt scrutinize the passing sheep through half-closed lids, making all movements very slowly. Here the costume providing the least danger of exposure is jeans, a thick dark-colored turtleneck, and longish hair. Any conversational gambits favored by lonely tourists, like "Where are you from?" can be deflected by vagueness. Instead of answering Des Moines or Queens, you say, "I spend a lot of time abroad" or "That's really hard to say." If hard-pressed, you simply mutter, *"Je ne parle pas Anglais,"* look at your watch, and leave.

The anti-tourist's persuasion that he is really a traveler instead of a tourist is both a symptom and a cause of what the British journalist Alan Brien has designated *tourist angst,* defined as "a gnawing suspicion that after all . . . you are still a tourist like every other tourist." As a uniquely modern form of self-contempt, *tourist angst* often issues in bizarre emotional behavior, and it is surprising that it has not yet become a classic for psychiatric study. "A student of mine in Paris," writes MacCannell, "a young man from Iran dedicated to the [student] revolution, half stammering, half shouting, said to me, 'Let's face it, we are all tourists!' Then, rising to his feet, his face contorted with . . . self-hatred, he concluded dramatically in a hiss: 'Even I am a tourist.'"

Tourist angst like this is distinctly a class signal. Only the upper elements of the middle classes suffer from it, and in summer especially it is endemic in places like Florence and Mikonos and Crete. It is rare in pseudo-places like Disneyland, where people have come just because other people have come. This is to say that the working class finds nothing shameful about tourism. It is the middle class that has read and heard just enough to sense that being a tourist is somehow offensive and scorned by an imagined upper class which it hopes to emulate and, if possible, be mistaken for. The irony is that extremes meet: The upper class, unruffled by contempt from any source, happily enrolls in Lindblad Tours or makes its way up the Nile in tight groups being lectured at by a tour guide artfully disguised as an Oxbridge archaeologist. Sometimes the anti-tourist's rage to escape the appearance of tourism propels him around a mock-full-circle, back to a simulacrum of exploration. Hence the popularity of African safaris among the upper-middle class. One tourist agency now offers package exploristic expeditions to Everest and the Sahara, and to Sinai by camel caravan, "real expeditions for the serious traveler looking for more than an adventurous vacation." Something of the acute discomfort of exploration and the uncertainty of real travel can be recovered by accepting an invitation to "Traverse Spain's Sierra Nevada on horseback ($528.00)."

But the anti-tourist deludes only himself. We are all tourists now, and there is no escape. Every year there are over 200 million of us, and when we are jetted in all directions and lodged in our pseudo-places, we constitute four times the population of France. The decisions we imagine ourselves making are shaped by the Professor of Tourism at Michigan State University and by the "Travel Administrators" now being trained at the New School in New York and by the International Union of Official Travel Organizations, whose publications indicate what it has in mind for us: *Factors Determining Selection of Sites for Tourism Development,* for example, or *Potential International Supply of Tourism Resources.* Our freedom and mobility diminish at the same time their expansion is loudly proclaimed; while more choices appear to solicit us, fewer actually do. The ships will not come back to the Hudson, and some place in Guyana will doubtless be selected as a site for tourism development. The tourist is locked in, and as MacCannell has pointed out, as a type the tourist is "one of the best models of modern man-in-general."

Graham Greene

Customs with My Aunt

In a neat follow-up to Fussell's analysis of the impulse to travel, we have here the traveler as petty criminal, flirting with the thrill of living outside the law. Henry Pulling, a retired bank manager, is persuaded by his septuagenarian Aunt Augusta to leave the comforts of Southwood and travel to exotic spots and mix with hippies, war criminals, CIA men—and truly, for the first time, come alive. This snippet is from Greene's 1969 novel, *Travels with My Aunt*.

What a lot of traveling you have done in your day, Aunt Augusta."

"I haven't reached nightfall yet," she said. "If I had a companion I would be off tomorrow, but I can no longer lift a heavy suitcase, and there is a distressing lack of porters nowadays. As you noticed at Victoria."

"We might one day," I said, "continue our seaside excursions. I remember many years ago visiting Weymouth. There was a very pleasant green statue of George III on the front."

"I have booked two couchettes a week from today on the Orient Express."

I looked at her in amazement. "Where to?" I asked.

"Istanbul, of course."

"But it takes days . . ."

"Three nights to be exact."

"If you want to go to Istanbul surely it would be easier and less expensive to fly?"

"I only take a plane," my aunt said, "when there is no alternative means of travel."

"It's really quite safe."

"It's a matter of choice, not nerves," Aunt Augusta said. "I knew Wilbur Wright very well indeed at one time. He took me for several trips. I always felt quite secure in his contraptions. But I cannot bear being spoken to all the time by irrelevant loudspeakers. One is not badgered at a railway station. An airport always reminds me of a Butlin's Camp."

"If you are thinking of me as a companion . . ."

"Of course I am, Henry."

"I'm sorry, Aunt Augusta, but a bank manager's pension is not a generous one."

"I shall naturally pay all expenses. Give me another glass of wine, Henry. It's excellent."

It was my aunt who suggested that we should fly as far as Paris. I was a little surprised after what she had just said, for there was certainly in this case an alternative means of travel. I pointed out the inconsistency. "There are reasons," Aunt Augusta said. "Cogent reasons. I know the ropes at Heathrow."

I was puzzled too at her insistence that we must go to the Kensington air terminal and take the airport bus. "It's so easy for me," I said, "to pick you up by car and drive you to Heathrow. You would find it much less tiring, Aunt Augusta."

"You would have to pay an exorbitant garage fee," she replied, and I found her sudden sense of economy unconvincing.

I arranged next day for the dahlias to be watered by my next-door neighbor, a brusque man called Major Charge. He had seen Detective-Sergeant Sparrow come to the door with the policeman, and he was bitten by curiosity. I told him it was about a motoring offense and he became sympathetic immediately. "A child murdered every week," he said, "and all they can do is prosecute motorists." I don't like lies and I felt in my conscience that I ought to defend Sergeant Sparrow who had been as good as his word and posted back the urn, registered and express.

"Sergeant Sparrow is not in homicide," I replied, "and motorists kill more people in a year than murderers."

"Only a lot of jaywalkers," Major Charge said. "Cannon fodder." However, he agreed to water the dahlias.

I picked my aunt up in the bar of the Crown and Anchor where she was having a stirrup-cup and we drove by taxi to the Kensington terminal. I noticed that she had brought two suitcases, one very large, although, when I asked her how long we were to stay in Istanbul, she had replied, "Twenty-four hours."

"It seems a short stay after such a long journey."

"The point is the journey," my aunt had replied. "I enjoy the traveling, not the sitting still."

Even Uncle Jo, I argued, had put up with each room in his house for a whole week.

"Jo was a sick man," she said, "while I am in the best of health."

Since we were traveling first-class (which seemed again an unnecessary luxury between London and Paris) we had no overweight, although the larger of her suitcases was unusually heavy. While we were sitting in the bus I suggested to my aunt that the garage fee for my car would probably have been cheaper than the difference between first and tourist fares. "The difference," she said, "is nearly wiped out by the caviar and the smoked salmon, and surely between us we can probably put away half a bottle of vodka. Not to speak of the champagne and cognac. In any case I have more important reasons for traveling by bus."

As we approached Heathrow she put her mouth close to my ear. "The luggage," she said, "is in a trailer behind."

"I know."

"I have a green suitcase and a red suitcase. Here are the tickets."

I took them, not understanding.

"When the bus stops please get out quickly and see whether the trailer is still attached. If it is still there let me know at once and I'll give you further instructions."

Something in my aunt's manner made me nervous. I said, "Of course it will be there."

"I sincerely hope not," she said. "Otherwise we shall not leave today."

I jumped out as soon as we arrived and sure enough the trailer wasn't there. "What do I do now?" I asked her.

"Nothing at all. Everything is quite in order. You may give me back the tickets and relax."

As we sat over two gins and tonics in the departure lounge a loudspeaker announced, "Passengers on Flight 378 to Nice will proceed to customs for customs inspection."

We were alone at our table and my aunt did not bother to lower her voice amid the din of passengers, glasses and loudspeakers. "That is what I wished to avoid," she said. "They have now taken to spot-checks on passengers leaving the country. They whittle away our liberties one by one. When I was a girl you could travel anywhere on the continent except Russia without a passport and you took what you liked in the way of money. Until recently they only *asked* what money you had, or at the very worst they wanted to see your wallet. If there's one thing I hate in any human being it is mistrust."

"The way you speak," I said jokingly, "I suspect we are lucky that it is not your bags which are being searched."

I could well imagine my aunt stuffing a dozen five-pound notes into the toe of her bedroom slippers. Having been a bank manager, I am perhaps over-scrupulous, though I must confess that I had an extra five-pound note folded up in my ticket pocket, but that was something I might genuinely have overlooked.

"Luck doesn't enter into my calculations," my aunt said. "Only a fool would trust to luck, and there is probably a fool now on the Nice flight who is regretting his folly. Whenever new restrictions are made, I make a very careful study of the arrangements for carrying them out." She gave a little sigh. "In the case of Heathrow I owe a great deal to Wordsworth. For a time he acted as a loader there. He left when there was some trouble about a gold consignment. Nothing was ever proved against him, but the whole affair had been too impromptu and disgusted him. He told me the story. A very large ingot was abstracted by a loader, and the loss was discovered too soon, before the men went off duty. They knew as a result that they would be searched by the police on leaving, all taxis too, and they had no idea what to do with the thing until Wordsworth suggested rolling it in tar and using it as a doorstop in the customs shed. So there it stayed for months. Every time they brought crates along to the shed, they could see their ingot propping open the door. Wordsworth said he got so maddened by the sight of it that he threw up the job. That was when he became a doorman at the Grenada Palace."

"What happened to the ingot?"

"I suppose the authorities lost interest when the diamond robberies started. Diamonds are money for jam, Henry. You see, they have special sealed sacks for valuable freight and these sacks are put into ordinary sacks, the idea being that the loaders can't spot them. The official mind is remarkably innocent. By the time you've been loading sacks a week or two, you can feel which sack contains another inside it. Then all you've got to do is to slit both coverings open and take pot luck. Like a children's bran tub at Christmas. Nobody is going to discover the slit until the plane arrives at the other end. Wordsworth knew a man who struck lucky the first time and pulled out a box with fifty gem stones."

"Surely somebody's watching?"

"Only the other loaders and they take a share. Of course occasionally a man has bad luck. Once a friend of Wordsworth's fished out a fat packet of notes, but they proved to be Pakistani. Worth about a thousand pounds if you happened to live in Karachi, but who was going to change them for him here? The poor fellow used to haunt the tarmac whenever a plane was taking off to Karachi, but he never found a safe customer. Wordsworth said he got quite embittered."

"I had no idea such things went on at Heathrow."

"My dear Henry," Aunt Augusta said, "if you had been a young man I would have advised you to become a loader. A loader's life is one of adventure with far more chance of a fortune than you ever have in a branch bank. I can imagine nothing better for a young man with ambition except perhaps illicit diamond digging. That is best practiced in Sierra Leone where Wordsworth comes from. The security guards are less sophisticated and less ruthless than in South Africa."

"Sometimes you shock me, Aunt Augusta," I said, but the statement had already almost ceased to be true. "I have never had anything stolen from my suitcase and I don't even lock it."

"That is probably your safeguard. No one is going to bother about an unlocked suitcase. Wordsworth knew a loader who had keys to every kind of suitcase. There are not many varieties, though he was baffled once by a Russian one."

The loudspeaker announced our flight and we were told to proceed at once to Gate 14 for immediate embarkation.

"For someone who doesn't like airports," I said, "you seem to know a great deal about Heathrow."

"I've always been interested in human nature," Aunt Augusta said. "Especially the more imaginative sides of it."

She ordered another two gins and tonics immediately we arrived on the plane. "There goes ten shillings towards the first-class fare," she said. "A friend of mine calculated once that on a long flight to Tahiti—it took in those days more than sixty-four hours—he recuperated nearly twenty pounds, but of course he was a hard drinker."

Again I had the impression that I was turning the pages in an American magazine in search of a contribution which I had temporarily lost. "I still don't understand," I said, "about the luggage trailer and the suitcase. Why were you so anxious that the trailer should disappear?"

"I have an impression," my aunt said, "that you are really a little shocked by trivial illegalities. When you reach my age you will be more tolerant. Years ago Paris was regarded as the vice center of the world, as Buenos Aires was before that, but Madame de Gaulle altered things there. Rome, Milan, Venice, and Naples survived a decade longer, but then the only two cities left were Macao and Havana. Macao has been cleaned up by the Chinese Chamber of Commerce and Havana by Fidel Castro. For the moment Heathrow is the Havana of the West. It won't last very long, of course, but one must admit that at the present time London Airport has a glamor which certainly puts Britain first. Have you got a little vodka for the caviar?" she asked the hostess who brought our trays. "I prefer it to champagne."

"But, Aunt Augusta, you have still not told me about the trailer."

"It's very simple," my aunt said. "If the luggage is to be loaded direct on to the aircraft, the trailer is detached outside the Queen Elizabeth building—there are always traffic holdups at this point and nothing is noticed by the passengers. If when the bus arrives at the B.E.A. or Air France entrance you find the trailer is still attached, this means that the luggage is going to be sent to the customs. Personally I have rooted objection to unknown hands, which have fiddled about in all kinds of strange luggage, some not over-clean, fiddling about in mine."

"What do you do then?"

"I reclaim my bags, saying that after all I don't require them on the voyage and wish to leave them in the cloakroom. Or I cancel my flight and try again another day." She finished her smoked salmon and went on to the caviar. "There is no such convenient system as that at Dover, or I would prefer to go by boat."

"Aunt Augusta," I said, "what are you carrying in your suitcases?"

"Only one is a little dangerous," she said, "the red. I always use the red for that purpose. Red for danger," she added with a smile.

"But what have you got in the red one?"

"A trifle," Aunt Augusta said, "something to help us in our travels. I can't really endure any longer these absurd travel allowances. Allowances! For grown people! When I was a child I received a shilling a week pocket money. If you consider the value of the pound today, that is rather more than what we are allowed to travel with annually. You haven't eaten your portion of foie gras."

"It doesn't agree with me," I said.

"Then I will take it. Steward, another glass of champagne and another vodka."

"We are just descending ma'am."

"The more reason for you to hurry, young man."

Richard Halliburton

The Enchanted Temple

For the legions of boys who read of his adventures, from *The Royal Road to Romance* in 1925 to *The Complete Book of Marvels* in 1941 (the latter being the source of this excerpt), Halliburton remains a hero. The editors of the present volume are such old boys, and in homage present one of his typically warm and engaging accounts, headed by a "Dear reader" introduction that whisks one instantly back to the dream days of youth. So, suspend adult disbelief and climb on Halliburton's magic carpet to the rose tombs of Petra.

Dear reader:

When I was a boy in school my favorite subject was geography, and my prize possession my geography book. This book was filled with pictures of the world's most wonderful cities and mountains and temples, and had big maps to show where they were. I loved that book because it carried me away to all the strange and romantic lands. I read about the Egyptian Pyramids, and India's marble towers, about the great cathedrals of France, and the ruins of ancient Babylon. The stories of such things always set me to dreaming, to yearning for the actual sight and touch of these world wonders.

Sometimes I pretended I had a magic carpet, and without bothering about tickets and money and farewells, I'd skyrocket away to New York or to Rome, to the Grand Canyon or to China, across deserts and oceans and mountains . . . then suddenly come back home when the school bell rang for recess.

I often said to myself: "I wish my father, or somebody, would take me to all these wonderful places. What good are they if you can't *see* them? If *I* ever grow up and have a son, we are going traveling together. I'll show him Gibraltar and Jerusalem, the Andes and the Alps, because I'll want my boy not only to study geography—I'd like for him to live it, too."

Well, I'm grown up now. But as yet I haven't any son or any daughter to go traveling with me. And so, in their places, may I take you? . . .

* * *

114

What was the most exciting adventure you ever had—the adventure you'll longest remember? Was it your first airplane ride, when the pilot looped-the-loop? Was it the time your automobile stalled in a snowdrift, and you had to spend the night in a deserted cabin? Or the time you walked to the summit of Pike's Peak? Or the day you met the President?

My own adventure which I'll longest remember was a visit to an enchanted city.

The city of which I speak is hidden in the mountain fastnesses of Arabia. And now that we have reached Arabia on our tour of the wonders of the Orient, I look forward with delight to visiting this enchanted place again. And *this* time I shall take you with me.

But before we set out, let me tell you an Arabian fairy tale. The tale is about the secret city and its magic spell:

Once upon a time, in the far-off ancient days, there lived in Arabia a king who wore upon his finger a magic ring. Whoever wore it (and knew the secret words that gave the ring its power) could hold enslaved the jinns who, in those days, dwelt in the land.

With the aid of these jinns the King built for himself a capital that became one of the wonders of the Arab world. He called it Petra, which means "stone."

Now in no way was Petra like other cities. It was located in the wildest mountains in the middle of a barren wilderness south of the Dead Sea. A traveler looking for Petra would not have found it, unless he knew the country well, for the chief gateway was just a crack in the mountain wall. This crack led into a deep and sunless canyon, a thousand feet deep, and this canyon led into the city.

But once the traveler had reached Petra itself, no sight could have been more wonderful. All about were beautiful palaces and noble tombs, all carved with hammer and chisel right out of the solid stone cliffs that rose on every side.

The King did not spend *all* his time building these great rock monuments. Besides being the Lord of the jinns, he was also the most dreaded robber in Arabia. Riding forth from the canyon in the rock, his robber bands would drive the passing caravans into the hidden fortress. Nor could any vengeful army pursue the robbers, for so narrow was the canyon corridor that four men could block it against four thousand. Petra became a huge fortified storehouse where dazzling piles of stolen gold and pearls and silk were guarded by the citizens.

With so much wealth and power in their hands, the people of Petra were able to conquer all the neighboring nations. To the city they dragged captive artists and sculptors from Athens. Grander and grander grew their palaces, marvelously carved by the gifted Greeks . . . all in the sandstone cliffs.

Proud as they were in life, the Petrans became prouder still in death. They spent fortunes on their own tombs. Each noble tried to plan one grander than his neighbor's. It took the strength of the jinns to hew the great rooms in the solid rock, but only the graceful hands of the Greeks could carve the columns and statues.

Soon the very gods themselves grew jealous of the splendid temple-tombs being built at Petra to bury mere mortals. They thought of a plan to subdue these bold builders . . . they would fill the soul of the King (who held the key to Petra's power) with the poison of vanity and pride. This, surely, would bring about his downfall.

And, just as the gods planned, this poison *did* destroy him. Burning with envy, he saw the tombs of his nobles rising higher and more splendid every day . . . and there was not even a *little* tomb for the King—the King whose magic ring made all these wonders possible. More and more jealous he became, until, in a violent mood, he commanded his enslaved jinns and his Greek artists to carve for him a temple-tomb such as the world had never seen—a temple that must overshadow the temples of the nobles as the moon outshines the stars.

So the King commanded, and at once he was obeyed. Roaring in anger at their hated enslavement, the jinns fell to work, hacking out tons upon tons of sandstone from the cliffs. Then the captive Greeks took their hammers and chisels and began to carve the rough rock into a sculptured temple. Slowly it took form, in one marvelous piece, massive and yet delicate, a poem in rose-red stone.

The King looked at this glowing masterpiece—and worshiped its beauty. Then, fearful lest a rival try to build a fairer monument than this, he commanded that the architect who built it be blinded.

All the people of the surrounding nations flocked to Petra to see the royal mausoleum. It became the city's crowning glory. But, just as the gods had planned, it soon proved to be the downfall of the King. The nobles, jealous, in turn, of their ruler's overtowering monument, plotted against him, and murdered him.

What madness was in this act! With the King, the power of the Petrans over the jinns departed. He alone had known how to use the ring he wore—the power that kept the jinns enslaved.

When his last heartbeat had ceased, the jinns found themselves free. No longer slaves, these terrible spirits burst the bonds that held them to their hated masters, and with a single magic word they enchanted the whole of the glorious rock city they had helped to build.

That was centuries ago. But Petra is enchanted still, unchanged in all this time. Its tombs, its monuments, the proud and lovely burial palace of the jealous King, are all still standing as on the day when the jinns, seeking revenge, cast their magic spell.

The Arab shepherds who tend their flocks in the neighborhood of Petra insist that this is a true story. And I half believe it is, because I've seen Petra with my own eyes. . . .

From Mecca, Petra is not far away—not for our airplane.

Our Mecca "pilgrimage" over, we ride our lurching camels back to Jedda, and once more climb aboard the plane. Our route this time is right up the eastern shore of the Red Sea—500 miles.

If you look at [a map], you'll note that the northern end of the Red Sea is forked. The left fork makes the Gulf of Suez (and leads to the Suez Canal). The right fork makes the Gulf of Akaba. We fly up the Akaba fork to the very end, and fifty miles on inland.

This fifty-mile stretch seems, from above, to be only a wilderness of barren mountains and rocky canyons.

But in the middle of this wilderness we'll find the magic city.

We see, presently, far below, a little oasis, surrounded by grim hills. This is our goal, for Petra lies close by. No use to hunt for Petra from our plane. Nothing can be seen of it from the air. We must go on foot.

Two Bedouins, who say they have no fear of jinns, offer themselves as guides. At dawn next morning we stand before the hidden entrance of the secret canyon corridor. Without our guides we could have passed by the canyon and never noticed it.

Following the Bedouins into the corridor, we find ourselves at the bottom of a tremendous split in the rock, overhung on either side by black precipices, hundreds of feet high, that shut out the sky and the sun. These fearsome cliffs seem only to be waiting for a human being to pass below in order to close in upon the ribbon of space and grind to bits their helpless victim.

More and more uneasy, we move deeper into this dimly lighted crack. We can stretch forth our arms and touch both walls. Bats fly about our heads. At times the daylight almost disappears. We expect, any moment, to meet demons from the lower realms, for this is a corridor not for the passage of humans but for the goblins who hide from the sunshine. We seem to be walking in a world deserted by all living things ages and ages ago.

But you can see for yourselves that it has not always been like this, for, here and there, the canyon floor is still paved with well-worn blocks of quarried stone. Along this corridor the wealth of Arabia once ebbed and flowed. Here the caravans, laden with silk and ivory, passed, musical with bells, in never-ending streams. And the followers of a king, returning from Jerusalem, once filled this living canyon with the clatter of their cavalry.

But that was before the days of the enchantment.

We creep on, for over a mile, along the bottom of the gorge. Gloomier and gloomier it grows, more overhanging, darker and more fearful.

And then we turn a corner of the canyon, and suddenly, out of the gloom, a glorious vision springs from a cliff straight ahead of us. The cliff is carved into a gleaming, rose-colored temple, towering but delicately made. And down upon the temple's face, the sun, in a blaze of light, is pouring from an opening in the rocks above.

For the first few minutes we make no effort to understand this wondrous sight. And then we realize that this great jewel must be the temple-tomb built by the Greek artists, aided by the power of the jinns, at the order of the King of ancient Petra . . . "a temple-tomb that was to overshadow the finest monuments of the nobles, a temple such as the world had never seen before." So the King had commanded, and the artists and the jinns had obeyed. . . .

If we are not too bedazzled, some of us may also judge the temple by workaday standards. It's as tall as a ten-story building, and a hundred feet broad. Inside we find a great rock hall, forty feet square and forty high. Across the front there is a row of graceful columns. And spread over everything is the most delicate and wonderful carving—garlands and flowers and goddesses— all, all in the solid rock. And in this same lovely, gleaming form, this temple has stood for nearly two thousand years—ever since the day when the jinns cast their magic spell.

We move on past the temple-tomb, and soon emerge into the great basin in which the city itself was built. The walls, all around, rise up more than a thousand feet, and are so steep that no enemy could possibly climb down. And these cliffs are lined with temples, treasuries, tombs, in endless procession, all cut from the solid rock, all huge in size and beautifully carved. The finest ones, we can be sure, are the tombs of the nobles. No wonder the King needed all his riches and power to surpass them!

There is no corner of the city we do not explore. But all the time the *supreme* tomb is in our thoughts. And so, when night comes and the desert stars shine down upon this stone wonderland, we wander back to visit again the temple of the King.

How changed it is!—yet not less beautiful. We had thought that nothing could be lovelier than its coral color glowing in the sun. We now see that there *is* something lovelier—its coral color softened by the starlight. We lean against the cliff wall opposite. Standing there in the silver shadows, before this vision of beauty, we find it easy to believe, almost, the shepherd's fairy tale of jinns and magic spells. It *must* be true—for, otherwise, what would have kept this carved stone poem from crumbling into dust a thousand years ago?

Yes, I'm sure, now that I'm here again, with you, in Petra, that the adventure I'll longest remember was my first visit to this very place. And it may be that you, too, in the years to come, when the memory of the other wonders you have seen has grown dim—that you, too, will still recall, clearly, as one of the truly magic moments of your life, the sight of the starlit temple— eternal, silent, beautiful, and alone—guarding the enchanted city.

Heinrich Harrer

The Forbidden City

In the summer of 1939, Heinrich Harrer and fellow mountain climber Peter Aufschnaiter journeyed to Nepal to plan their expedition to the top of Nanga Parbat. War broke out, and the pair were interned in an English POW camp. As Peter Fleming wrote, ". . . the foreigner tends to ride upon the high though not very reliable horse of privilege, and to view the backwoods and their denizens from above. It was otherwise with Herr Harrer. When in 1943 he made a third and successful attempt to escape from an internment camp at Dehra-Dun and headed for Tibet, he was seeing Asia from below. He traveled on foot, carried his few possessions on his back, and slept on the ground in the open." In this portion of the wonderful *Seven Years in Tibet*, Harrer, shortly to become tutor to the fourteenth Dalai Lama, approaches the Potala.

It was January 15, 1946, when we set out on our last march. From Tölung we came into the broad valley of Kyichu. We turned a corner and saw, gleaming in the distance, the golden roofs of the Potala, the winter residence of the Dalai Lama and the most famous landmark of Lhasa. This moment compensated us for much. We felt inclined to go down on our knees like the pilgrims and touch the ground with our foreheads. Since leaving Kyirong we had covered over six hundred miles with the vision of this fabulous city ever in our mind's eye. We had marched for seventy days and only rested during five. That meant a daily average of almost ten miles. Forty-five days of our journey had been spent in crossing the Changthang—days full of hardship and unceasing struggle against cold, hunger, and danger. Now all that was forgotten as we gazed at the golden pinnacles—six miles more and we had reached our goal.

We sat down near the cairns which the pilgrims put up to mark their first sight of the Holy City. Our driver, meanwhile, performed his devotions. Going on, we soon came to Shingdongka, the last village before Lhasa. The cowman refused to come any farther, but nothing could discourage us now. We went to find the bönpo and coolly informed him that we were the advance party of a powerful foreign personage on his way to Lhasa and that we had to reach the city as quickly as possible in order to find quarters for our master. The bönpo

119

swallowed our tale and gave us an ass and a driver. Years later this story used still to set people laughing at parties in Lhasa, even in the houses of ministers. The fact is the Tibetans are very proud of their organization for keeping foreigners out of the country, and they found the manner in which we had broken through the barriers not only deserving of attention but highly humorous. That was all to our advantage, for the Tibetans are a laughter-loving folk.

During the last six miles of the road we mixed with a stream of pilgrims and caravans. From time to time we passed stalls displaying all sorts of delicacies—sweets, white bread, and what not—which almost brought the tears to our eyes. But we had no money. Our last rupee belonged to our driver.

We soon began to recognize the landmarks of the town about which we had read so often. Over there must be Chagpori, the hill on which stands one of the two famous schools of medicine. And here in front of us was Drebung, the greatest monastery in the world, which houses ten thousand monks and is a city in itself, with its multitude of stone houses and hundreds of gilded pinnacles pointing upward above the shrines. Somewhat lower down lay the terraces of Nechung, another monastery, which has for centuries been the home of the greatest mystery of Tibet. Here is made manifest the presence of a protective deity, whose secret oracle guides the destinies of Tibet and is consulted by the government before any important decision is taken. We had still five miles to go and every few steps there was something fresh to look at. We passed through broad well-tended meadows surmounted by willows where the Dalai Lama pastures his horses.

For nearly an hour a long stone wall flanked our road and we were told that the summer palace of the God-King lay behind it. Next we passed the British Legation, situated just outside the town, half-hidden by willow trees. Our driver turned to go toward it thinking it must be our destination and we had some trouble in persuading him to go straight on. In fact for a moment we hesitated about going there ourselves, but the memory of the internment camp was still present in our minds and we thought that, after all, we were in Tibet and that it was the Tibetans we should ask for hospitality.

Nobody stopped us or bothered about us. We could not understand it, but finally realized that no one, not even a European, was suspect, because no one had ever come to Lhasa without a pass.

As we approached, the Potala towered ever higher before us. As yet we could see nothing of the town itself, which lay behind the hills on which the palace and the school of medicine stood. Then we saw a great gate crowned with three chorten, which spans the gap between the two hills and forms the entrance to the city. Our excitement was intense. Now we should know our fate for certain. Almost every book about Lhasa says that sentries are posted here to guard the Holy City. We approached with beating hearts. But there was nothing. No soldiers, no control post, only a few beggars holding out their hands for alms. We mingled with a group of people and walked unhindered through the gateway into the town. Our driver told us that the group of houses on our left was only a sort of suburb and so we went on through an unbuilt area coming ever nearer to the middle of the town. We spoke no word, and to this day I can find no terms to express how overwhelming were our sensations. Our minds, exhausted by hardships, could not absorb the shock of so many and such powerful impressions.

We were soon in front of the turquoise-roofed bridge and saw for the first time the spires of the Cathedral of Lhasa. The sun set and bathed the scene in an unearthly light. Shivering with cold we had to find a lodging, but in Lhasa it is not so simple to walk into a house as into a tent in the Changthang. We should probably be at once reported to the authorities. But we had to try. In the first house we found a dumb servant, who would not listen to us. Next door there was only a maid who screamed for help till her mistress came and begged us to go somewhere else. She said she would be driven out of the quarter if she received us. We did not believe that the government could be as strict as all that, but we did not want to cause her unpleasantness and so went out again. We walked through some narrow streets and found ourselves already at the other side of the town. There we came to a house much larger and finer-looking than any we had yet seen, with stables in the courtyard. We hurried in to find ourselves confronted by servants, who abused us and told us to go away. We were not to be moved and unloaded our donkey. Our driver had already been pressing us to let him go home. He had noticed that everything was not in order. We gave him money and he went off with a sigh of relief.

The servants were in despair when they saw that we had come to stay. They begged and implored us to go and pointed out that they would get into fearful trouble when their master returned. We, too, felt far from comfortable at the idea of exacting hospitality by force, but we did not move. More and more people were attracted by the din, and the scene reminded me of my departure from Kyirong. We remained deaf to all protestations. Dead-tired and half-starved, we sat on the ground by our bundles, indifferent to what might befall us. We only wanted to sit, to rest, to sleep.

The angry cries of the crowd suddenly ceased. They had seen our swollen and blistered feet, and, openhearted simple folk as they were, they felt pity for us. A woman began it. She was the one who had implored us to leave her house. Now she brought us butter tea. And now they brought us all sorts of things—tsampa, provisions, and fuel. The people wanted to atone for their inhospitable reception. We fell hungrily on the food and for the moment forgot everything else.

Suddenly we heard ourselves addressed in perfect English. We looked up, and though there was not much light to see by, we recognized that the richly clad Tibetan who had spoken to us must be a person of the highest standing. Astonished and happy we asked him if he was not, perchance, one of the four young nobles who had been sent to school at Rugby. He said he was not but that he had passed many years in India. We told him shortly what had happened to us, saying we were Germans, and begging to be taken in. He thought for a moment and then said that he could not admit us to his house without the approval of the town magistrate, but he would go to that official and ask for permission.

When he had gone the other people told us that he was an important official and was in charge of the electricity works. We did not dare to set too much store by what he had said, but nevertheless began to settle down for the night. Meanwhile we sat by the fire and talked to the people, who kept coming and going. Then a servant came to us and asked us to follow him saying that Mr. Thangme, the "Master of Electricity," invited us into his house. They called him respectfully "Kungö," equivalent to "Highness," and we followed suit.

Thangme and his young wife received us very cordially. Their five children stood around and looked at us openmouthed. Their father had good news for us. The magistrate had allowed him to take us in for one night, but future arrangements would have to be decided by the cabinet. We did not worry our heads about the future. After all we were in Lhasa and were the guests of a noble family. A nice, comfortable room was already prepared for us with a small iron stove which warmed us well. It was seven years since we had seen a stove! The fuel used was juniper wood, which smelled very good and was a real luxury, for it needed weeks of travel on the backs of yaks to bring it into Lhasa. We hardly dared, in our ragged garments, to sit on our clean carpet-covered beds. They brought us a splendid Chinese supper, and as we ate they all stood around and talked to us without ceasing. What we must have been through! They could hardly believe that we had crossed the Changthang in winter and climbed over the Nyenchenthangla range. Our knowledge of Tibetan astonished them. But how ugly and shabby we seemed to ourselves in these civilized surroundings. Our possessions, indispensable to our journey, suddenly lost all their attraction and we felt we would be glad to be rid of them.

Dead tired and confused in mind we went at last to bed, but we could not go to sleep. We had spent too many nights on the hard ground with nothing but our sheepskin cloaks and a torn blanket to cover us. Now we had soft beds and a well-warmed room, but our bodies could not quickly accustom themselves to the change and our thoughts revolved like mill wheels in our heads. All we had gone through crowded into our minds—the internment camp and the adventures and hardships of the twenty-one months since our escape. And we thought of our comrades and the unbroken monotony of their lives, for though the war had long been over the prisoners were still in captivity. But, for that matter were *we* now free?

Before we were properly awake we found a servant with sweet tea and cakes standing by our beds. Then they brought us hot water and we attacked our long beards with our razors. After shaving we looked more respectable but our long hair was a grave problem. A Moslem barber was called in to get busy on our manes. The result was somewhat exotic, but provoked lively admiration. Tibetans have no trouble with their coiffure. Either they have pigtails or shaven heads.

We did not see Thangme till noon, when he came home much relieved after a visit to the foreign minister. He brought us good news and told us we would not be handed over to the English. For the time being we might remain in Lhasa but were politely requested to stay indoors until the regent, who was in a retreat in Taglung Tra, decided about our future. We were given to understand that this was a precautionary measure made advisable by previous incidents in which fanatical monks had been involved. The government was willing to feed and clothe us.

We were highly delighted. A few days' rest was just what we needed. We attacked a mountain of old newspapers with enthusiasm, though the news we gathered was not precisely exhilarating. The whole world was still simmering and our country was going through hard times.

On the same day we received a visit from an official sent by the town magistrate. He was accompanied by six policemen, who looked dirty and untrustworthy. But our visitor was most polite and asked leave to inspect our baggage. We were astonished that he should be doing his job with such exactness. He had with him a report from Kyirong which he compared with the dates of our itinerary. We ventured to ask him if all the officials through whose districts we had passed would really be punished. "The whole matter will come before the cabinet," he said thoughtfully, "and the officials must expect to be punished." This upset us very much, and to his amusement we told him how we had dodged the district officers and how often we had deceived them. It was our turn to laugh when he then announced to us that the evening before he had been expecting a German invasion of Lhasa. It seems that everyone with whom we had spoken had rushed off to report to the magistrate. They had the impression that German troops were marching into the city!

In any case we were the talk of the town. Everyone wanted to see us and to hear the story of our adventures with his own ears, and as we were not allowed out people came to visit us. Mrs. Thangme had her hands full and prepared her best tea service to receive guests. We were initiated into the ceremonial of tea parties. Respect for guests is shown by the value and beauty of the tea service. The table stand consists of a metal mat, often of gold or silver, on which stands the Chinese teacup. I often saw marvelous Chinese tea sets many hundreds of years old.

Every day important guests came to Thangme's house. He himself was a noble of the fifth class, and since etiquette is very closely observed here, he had hitherto only received the visits of persons of equal or inferior rank. But now it was the most highly placed personages who wanted to see us. Foremost among them was the son of the celebrated Minister Tsarong and his wife. We had already read much about his father. Born in humble circumstances, he became the favorite of the thirteenth Dalai Lama, rose to a highly honorable position and acquired a great fortune by his industry and intelligence. Forty years ago the Dalai Lama was obliged to flee before the Chinese into India, and Tsarong then rendered his master valuable service. He was for many years a cabinet minister and as first favorite of the Lama had virtually the powers of a regent. Subsequently a new favorite named Khünpela dislodged Tsarong from his position of authority. He was, however, able to retain his rank and dignities. Tsarong was now in the third order of nobility and was Master of the Mint.

His son was twenty-six years old. He had been brought up in India and spoke fluent English. Conscious of his own importance he wore a golden amulet in his pigtail, as the son of a minister had the right to do.

When this young noble came to call, servants handed tea and soon the conversation became lively. The minister's son was an incredibly versatile young man with a special interest in technical matters. He asked us about the latest discoveries, and told us that he had put together his own radio receiving set and fixed a wind-driven generator on the roof of his house.

We were in the middle of a technical discussion in English, when his wife interrupted us laughingly and said she wanted to ask us some questions. Yangchenla, as she was called, was one of the beauties of Lhasa; she was well-dressed and very *soignée,* and clearly acquainted with the use of powder, rouge, and lipstick. She was not at all shy, as was obvious from the lively manner in which she questioned us in Tibetan about our journey. Now and again she broke into our explanations with swift gestures and bursts of laughter. She was particularly amused by our account of how we had imposed on the officials with our expired travel permit. She seemed to be astonished at our fluency in Tibetan, but we noticed that neither she nor even the most staid of our visitors could forbear from laughing at us from time to time. Later our friends told us that we spoke the commonest kind of peasant dialect that one could imagine. It was rather like a backwoodsman from the remotest Alpine valley talking his own lingo in a Viennese drawing room. Our visitors were immensely amused but much too polite to correct us.

By the time this young couple left us we had made friends with them. They had brought with them some very welcome gifts—linen, pullovers, and cigarettes, and they begged us to tell them frankly when we wanted anything. The minister's son promised to help us and later delivered a message from his father inviting us to go and stay with him, if the government gave us their approbation. That all sounded very consoling.

More visitors came trooping in. Our next was a general of the Tibetan Army, who was desperately anxious to learn everything possible about Rommel. He spoke with enthusiasm of the German general and said that with his smattering of English he had read everything available about him in the newspapers. In this respect Lhasa is not at all isolated. Newspapers come in from all over the world via India. There are even a few persons in the town who take in *Life*. The Indian daily papers arrive regularly a week after publication.

The procession of visitors continued. Among them were highly placed monks, who courteously brought us gifts. Some of them became my good friends later on. Then there was a representative of the Chinese Legation and after him an official belonging to the British Agency in Sikkim.

We were particularly honored by the visit of the Commander in Chief of the Tibetan Army, General Künsangtse, who insisted on seeing us before leaving for China and India on a friendly mission. He was the younger brother of the foreign minister and an unusually well-informed man. It took a load off our minds when he assured us that our request for permission to stay in Tibet would certainly be approved.

We gradually began to feel at home. Our relations with Thangme and his wife developed into a cordial friendship. We were mothered and well-fed and everyone was pleased to see that we had such good appetites. However, doubtless as reaction from hardship and overstrain, we suffered from all sorts of minor complaints. Aufschnaiter had an attack of fever and my sciatica gave me a lot of trouble. Thangme sent for the doctor of the Chinese Legation, who had studied in Berlin and Bordeaux. He examined us in approved European style and prescribed various medicines.

It is probable that no other country in the world would welcome two poor fugitives as Tibet welcomed us. Our parcel of clothes, the gift of the government, had arrived with apologies for delay caused by the fact that we were taller than the average Tibetan and there were no ready-made clothes to fit us. So our suits and shoes were made to measure. We were as pleased as children. At last we were able to throw away our lousy old rags. Our new suits, though not up to the highest sartorial standards, were decent and tidy and quite good enough for us.

In the intervals between our numerous visits we worked at our notebooks and diaries. And we soon made friends with the Thangmes' children, who usually had already gone off to school before we got up. In the evening they showed us their homework, which interested me very much as I was taking some trouble to learn the written language. Aufschnaiter had long been studying this and during our wanderings had taught me something, but it took me years to learn to write Tibetan more or less fluently. The individual letters present no difficulty, but their arrangement into syllables is no easy task. Many of the characters are taken from the ancient Indian scripts, and Tibetan writing looks more like Hindi than Chinese. Fine, durable parchment-like paper is used and Chinese ink. There are in Tibet several high-class mills, where the paper is made from juniper wood. In addition thousands of loads of paper are imported yearly from Nepal and Bhutan, where the stuff is manufactured in the same way as in Tibet. I have often watched the process of papermaking on the banks of the Kyichu River. The chief drawback of Tibetan paper is that the surface is not smooth enough, which makes writing difficult. Children are usually given wooden tablets for their exercises and use watered ink and bamboo pens. The writing can afterwards be wiped out with a wet cloth. Thangme's children often had to rub out their exercises twenty times before getting them right.

Soon we were treated like members of the family. Mrs. Thangme talked over her problems with us, and was delighted when we paid her compliments on her good looks and good taste. Once she invited us to come into her room and look at her jewels. These she kept in a great chest in which her treasures were stored either in small jewel cases or in fine silk wrappings. Her treasures were worth looking at. She had a glorious tiara of corals, turquoise, and pearls, and many rings as well as diamond earrings and some little Tibetan amulet lockets which are hung round the neck by a coral chain. Many women never take these lockets off. The amulet they contain acts as a talisman which, they believe, protects them from evil.

Our hostess was flattered by our admiration of her treasures. She told us that every man was obliged to present his wife with the jewels corresponding to his rank. Promotion in rank entailed promotion in jewelry! But to be merely rich was not enough, for wealth did not confer the right to wear costly jewels. Of course the men grumble about their wives' pretensions, for here, as in the West, every woman seeks to outshine her rivals. Mrs. Thangme, whose jewels must have been worth several thousand pounds, told us that she never went out unaccompanied by a servant, as attacks by thieves on society women were common.

Eight days passed, during which we had dutifully kept indoors. It was a great surprise to us when one day servants came bringing an invitation to visit the home of the Dalai Lama's parents, and telling us to come at once. As we felt ourselves bound by our promise not to leave the house, we consulted our host. He was horrified that we should have any misgivings; such an invitation overrode everything else. A summons from the Dalai Lama or the regent had precedence over all other considerations. No one would dare to detain us or later to call us to account. On the contrary, hesitation to comply would be a serious offense.

We were glad to learn his opinion, but then began to be nervous about the reason for our summons. Was it a good omen for our future? Anyhow we hurriedly prepared ourselves for the visit, dressing ourselves in our new clothes and Tibetan boots for the first time. We looked quite presentable. Thangme then gave us each a pair of white silk scarves and impressed on us that we must present them when we were received in audience. We had already witnessed this custom in Kyirong and had noticed that it was observed by quite simple people. When paying visits or presenting a petition to a person of higher standing, or at the great festivals, one is supposed to give presents of scarves. These scarves are found in all sort of qualities and the kind of scarf offered should be consistent with the rank of the giver.

The house of the parents of the Dalai Lama was not far away. We soon found ourselves standing before a great gate, near which the gatekeeper was already on the lookout for us. When we approached he bowed respectfully. We were led through a large garden full of vegetable plots and clusters of splendid willows till we came to the palace. We were taken up to the first floor: A door was opened and we found ourselves in the presence of the mother of the God-King, to whom we bowed in reverence. She was sitting on a small throne in a large, bright room surrounded by servants. She looked the picture of aristocratic dignity. The humble awe which the Tibetans feel for the "Holy Mother" is something strange to us, but we found the moment a solemn one.

The "Holy Mother" smiled at us and was visibly pleased when we handed her the scarves with deep obeisances, stretching out our arms to the fullest extent as Thangme had instructed us. She took them from us and handed them at once to the servants. Then with a beaming countenance she shook our hands, contrary to Tibetan custom. At that moment in came the father of the Dalai Lama, a dignified elderly man. We bowed low again and handed him scarves with due ceremony, after which he shook our hands most unaffectedly. Now and then Europeans came to the house, and the host and hostess were to some degree familiar with European customs and not a little proud of the fact.

Then we all sat down to tea. The tea we drank had a strange flavor, and was made differently from the usual Tibetan brew. We asked about it, and the question broke the ice, for it led our hosts to tell us about their former home. They had lived at Amdo as simple peasants until their son was recognized as the Incarnation of the Dalai Lama. Amdo is in China in the province of Chinghai, but its inhabitants are almost all Tibetan. They had brought their tea with them to Lhasa and now made it, not as the Tibetans do with butter, but adding milk and salt. They brought something else from their old home— the dialect they spoke. They both used a patois similar to that of the central provinces, but not the same. The fourteen-year-old brother of the Dalai Lama interpreted for them. He had come as a child to Lhasa and had quickly learned to speak pure Tibetan. He now spoke the Amdo dialect only with his parents.

While we were conversing with them we took occasion to observe our hosts. Each of them made a very good impression. Their humble origin expressed itself in an attractive simplicity, but their bearing and demeanor were aristocratic. It was a big step from a small peasant's house in a distant province to a dukedom in the capital. They now owned the palace they lived in and large properties in the country. But they seemed to have survived the sudden revolution in their lives without deterioration.

The boy whom we met, Lobsang Samten, was lively and wide awake. He was full of curiosity about us and asked us all manner of questions about our experiences. He told us that his "divine" younger brother had charged him to report on us exactly. We felt pleasantly excited by the news that the Dalai Lama was interested in us, and would have liked to learn more of him. We were told that the name Dalai Lama is not used in Tibet at all. It is a Mongolian expression meaning "Broad Ocean." Normally the Dalai Lama is referred to as the "Gyalpo Rimpoche," which means "Treasured King." His parents and brothers use another title in speaking of him. They call him "Kundün," which simply means "Presence."

The Holy Parents had in all six children. The eldest son, long before the discovery of the Dalai Lama, had been recognized as an Incarnation of Buddha and invested with the dignity of a lama in the monastery of Tagtsel. He too was styled Rimpoche, the form of address applied to all lamas. The second son, Gyalo Thündrup, was at school in China. Our young acquaintance Lobsang was destined for a monastic life. The Dalai Lama himself was now eleven years old. Besides his brothers he had two sisters. Subsequently the "Holy Mother" gave birth to another "Incarnation," Ngari Rimpoche. As the mother of three "Incarnations" she held the record for the Buddhist world.

Our visit led to cordial relations with this adaptable, clever woman, which were to continue until she fled before the invasion of the Reds to India. Our friendship had nothing to do with the transcendental worship which the "Holy Mother" received from others. But though I have a fairly skeptical attitude toward metaphysical matters, I could not but recognize the power of personality and faith with which she was invested.

It gradually became clear to us what a distinction this invitation was. One must not forget that, with the exception of his family and a few personal servants holding the rank of abbot, no one has the right to address the God-King. Nevertheless, in his isolation from the world he had deigned to take an interest in our fate. When we rose to leave we were asked if we needed anything. We thanked our hosts, but preferred modestly to ask for nothing in spite of which a line of servants marched up with sacks of meal and tsampa, a load of butter and some beautiful soft woolen blankets. "By the personal desire of the Kundün," said the "Holy Mother," smiling, and pressed into our hands a hundred-sang note. This was done so naturally and as if it was a matter of course that we felt no shame about accepting.

After many expressions of thanks and deep obeisances, we left the room in some embarrassment. As a final proof of friendliness Lobsang, on behalf of his parents, laid the scarves once more on our necks as we bowed to him. He then took us into the garden and showed us the grounds and the stables, where we saw some splendid horses from Siling and Ili, the pride of his father. In the course of conversation he let drop the suggestion that I might give him lessons in some branches of Western knowledge. That coincided with my own secret wishes. I had often thought that I could manage to keep myself by giving lessons to the children of noble families.

Loaded with gifts and escorted by servants we returned to Thangme's house. We were in high spirits and felt that now our fortunes were on the mend. Our hosts awaited us with impatient excitement. We had to tell them everything that had happened, and our next visitors were informed in detail of the honor that had been done to us. Our stocks rose considerably!

Nathaniel Hawthorne

My Visit to Niagara

Hawthorne, writing in 1835, confronts a typical traveler's dilemma:
how to visit a landmark or landscape famous throughout the world
and yet make it new, to experience it as an explorer, not as a tourist.
His ambivalence about confronting Niagara is the same any experienced traveler would feel before first setting eyes on the Grand Canyon
or Taj Mahal. But this is a feeling that must be conquered, for these
places are, after all, famous for good reason. The antitourist (see Paul
Fussell's piece) may dismiss Niagara Falls as a cliche; the tourist will
capture the image with his camera but miss the essence;
the traveler will grasp the majesty.

Never did a pilgrim approach Niagara with deeper enthusiasm than mine. I
had lingered away from it, and wandered to other scenes, because my trea-
sury of anticipated enjoyments, comprising all the wonders of the world, had
nothing else so magnificent, and I was loath to exchange the pleasures of
hope for those of memory so soon. At length, the day came. The stagecoach,
with a Frenchman and myself on the back seat, had already left Lewiston, and
in less than an hour would set us down in Manchester. I began to listen for
the roar of the cataract, and trembled with a sensation like dread, as the
moment drew nigh, when its voice of ages must roll, for the first time, on my
car. The French gentleman stretched himself from the window, and expressed
loud admiration, while, by a sudden impulse, I threw myself back and closed
my eyes. When the scene shut in, I was glad to think, that for me the whole
burst of Niagara was yet in futurity. We rolled on, and entered the village of
Manchester, bordering on the falls.

I am quite ashamed of myself here. Not that I ran, like a madman, to the
falls, and plunged into the thickest of the spray—never stopping to breathe,
till breathing was impossible; not that I committed this, or any other suitable
extravagance. On the contrary, I alighted with perfect decency and com-

posure, gave my cloak to the black waiter, pointed out my baggage, and inquired, not the nearest way to the cataract, but about the dinner hour. The interval was spent in arranging my dress. Within the last fifteen minutes, my mind had grown strangely benumbed, and my spirits apathetic with a slight depression, not decided enough to be termed sadness. My enthusiasm was in a death-like slumber. Without aspiring to immortality, as he did, I could have imitated the English traveler, who turned back from the point where he first heard the thunder of Niagara, after crossing the ocean to behold it. Many a western trader, by-the-by, has performed a similar act of heroism with more heroic simplicity, deeming it no such wonderful feat to dine at the hotel and resume his route to Buffalo or Lewiston, while the cataract was roaring unseen.

Such has often been my apathy, when objects, long sought and earnestly desired, were placed within my reach. After dinner—at which, an unwonted and perverse epicurism detained me longer than usual—I lighted a cigar and paced the piazza, minutely attentive to the aspect and business of a very ordinary village. Finally, with reluctant step, and the feeling of an intruder, I walked towards Goat Island. At the tollhouse, there were further excuses for delaying the inevitable moment. My signature was required in a huge ledger, containing similar records innumerable, many of which I read. The skin of a great sturgeon, and other fishes, beasts, and reptiles; a collection of minerals, such as lie in heaps near the falls; some Indian moccasins, and other trifles, made of deer-skin and embroidered with beads; several newspapers from Montreal, New York, and Boston; all attracted me in turn. Out of a number of twisted sticks, the manufacture of a Tuscarora Indian, I selected one of curled maple, curiously convoluted, and adorned with the carved images of a snake and a fish. Using this as my pilgrim's staff, I crossed the bridge. Above and below me were the rapids, a river of impetuous snow, with here and there a dark rock amid its whiteness, resisting all the physical fury, as any cold spirit did the moral influences of the scene. On reaching Goat Island, which separates the two great segments of the falls, I chose the right-hand path, and followed it to the edge of the American cascade. There, while the falling sheet was yet invisible, I saw the vapor that never vanishes, and the Eternal Rainbow of Niagara.

It was an afternoon of glorious sunshine, without a cloud, save those of the cataracts. I gained an insulated rock, and beheld a broad sheet of brilliant and unbroken foam, not shooting in a curved line from the top of the precipice, but falling headlong down from height to depth. A narrow stream diverged from the main branch, and hurried over the crag by a channel of its own, leaving a little pine-clad island and a streak of precipice, between itself and the larger sheet. Below arose the mist, on which was painted a dazzling sunbow, with two concentric shadows—one, almost as perfect as the original brightness; and the other, drawn faintly round the broken edge of the cloud.

Still, I had not half seen Niagara. Following the verge of the island, the path led me to the Horseshoe, where the real broad St. Lawrence, rushing along on a level with its banks, pours its whole breadth over a concave line of precipice, and thence pursues its course between lofty crags towards Ontario. A sort of bridge, two or three feet wide, stretches out along the edge of the descending sheet, and hangs upon the rising mist, as if that were the foundation of the frail structure. Here I stationed myself, in the blast of wind, which the rushing river bore along with it. The bridge was tremulous beneath me, and marked the tremor of the solid earth. I looked along the whitening rapids, and endeavored to distinguish a mass of water far above the falls, to follow it to the verge, and go down with it, in fancy, to the abyss of clouds and storm. Casting my eyes across the river, and every side, I took in the whole scene at a glance, and tried to comprehend it in one vast idea. After an hour thus spent, I left the bridge, and, by a staircase, winding almost interminably round a post, descended to the base of the precipice. From that point, my path lay over slippery stones, and among great fragments of the cliff, to the edge of the cataract, where the wind at once enveloped me in spray, and perhaps dashed the rainbow round me. Were my long desires fulfilled? And had I seen Niagara?

Oh, that I had never heard of Niagara till I beheld it. Blessed were the wanderers of old, who heard its deep roar sounding through the woods, as the summons to an unknown wonder, and approached its awful brink, in all the freshness of native feeling. Had its own mysterious voice been the first to warn me of its existence, then, indeed, I might have knelt down and worshiped. But I had come thither haunted with a vision of foam and fury, and dizzy cliffs, and an ocean tumbling down out of the sky—a scene, in short, which Nature had too much good taste and calm simplicity to realize. My mind had struggled to adapt these false conditions to the reality, and finding the effort vain, a wretched sense of disappointment weighed me down. I climbed the precipice, and threw myself on the earth—feeling that I was unworthy to look at the Great Falls, and careless about beholding them again.

All that night, as there has been and will be, for ages past and to come, a rushing sound was heard, as if a great tempest were sweeping through the air. It mingled with my dreams, and made them full of storm and whirlwind. Whenever I awoke, and heard this dread sound in the air, and the windows rattling as with a mighty blast, I could not rest again, till, looking forth, I saw how bright the stars were, and that every leaf in the garden was motionless. Never was a summer night more calm to the eye, nor a gale of autumn louder to the ear. The rushing sound proceeds from the rapids, and the rattling of the casements is but an effect of the vibration of the whole house, shaken by the jar of the cataract. The noise of the rapids draws the attention from the true voice of Niagara, which is a dull, muffled thunder, resounding between the cliffs. I spent a wakeful hour at midnight, in distinguishing its reverberations, and rejoiced to find that my former awe and enthusiasm were reviving.

Gradually, and after much contemplation, I came to know, by my own feelings, that Niagara is indeed a wonder of the world, and not the less wonderful, because time and thought must be employed in comprehending it. Casting aside all preconceived notions, and preparation to be direstruck or delighted, the beholder must stand beside it in the simplicity of his heart, suffering the mighty scene to work its own impression. Night after night, I dreamed of it, and was gladdened every morning by the consciousness of a growing capacity to enjoy it. Yet I will not pretend to the all-absorbing enthusiasm of some more fortunate spectators, nor deny, that very trifling causes would draw my eyes and thoughts from the cataract.

The last day that I was to spend at Niagara, before my departure for the far West, I sat upon the Table Rock. This celebrated station did not now, as of old, project fifty feet beyond the line of the precipice, but was shattered by the fall of an immense fragment, which lay distant on the shore below. Still, on the utmost verge of the rock, with my feet hanging over it, I felt as if suspended in the open air. Never before had my mind been in such perfect unison with the scene. There were intervals, when I was conscious of nothing but the great river, rolling calmly into the abyss, rather descending than precipitating itself, and acquiring tenfold majesty from its unhurried motion. It came like the march of Destiny. It was not taken by surprise, but seemed to have anticipated, in all its course through the broad lakes, that it must pour their collected waters down this height. The perfect foam of the river, after its descent, and the ever-varying shapes of mist, rising up, to become clouds in the sky, would be the very picture of confusion, were it merely transient, like the rage of a tempest. But when the beholder has stood awhile, and perceives no lull in the storm, and considers that the vapor and the foam are as everlasting as the rocks which produce them, all this turmoil assumes a sort of calmness. It soothes, while it awes the mind.

Leaning over the cliff, I saw the guide conducting two adventurers behind the falls. It was pleasant, from that high seat in the sunshine, to observe them struggling against the eternal storm of the lower regions, with heads bent down, now faltering, now pressing forward, and finally swallowed up in their victory. After their disappearance, a blast rushed out with an old hat, which it had swept from one of their heads. The rock, to which they were directing their unseen course is marked, at a fearful distance on the exterior of the sheet, by a jet of foam. The attempt to reach it, appears both poetical and perilous, to a looker-on, but may be accomplished without much more difficulty or hazard, than in stemming a violent northeaster. In a few moments, forth came the children of the mist. Dripping and breathless, they crept along the base of the cliff, ascended to the guide's cottage, and received, I presume, a certificate of their achievement, with three verses of sublime poetry on the back.

My contemplations were often interrupted by strangers, who came down from Forsyth's to take their first view of the falls. A short, ruddy, middle-aged gentleman, fresh from old England, peeped over the rock, and evinced his approbation by a broad grin. His spouse, a very robust lady, afforded a sweet example of maternal solicitude, being so intent on the safety of her little boy that she did not even glance at Niagara. As for the child, he gave himself wholly to the enjoyment of a stick of candy. Another traveler, a native American, and no rare character among us, produced a volume of Captain Hall's tour, and labored earnestly to adjust Niagara to the captain's description, departing, at last, without one new idea or sensation of his own. The next comer was provided, not with a printed book, but with a blank sheet of foolscap, from top to bottom of which, by means of an ever-pointed pencil, the cataract was made to thunder. In a little talk, which we had together, he awarded his approbation to the general view, but censured the position of Goat Island, observing that it should have been thrown farther to the right, so as to widen the American falls, and contract those of the Horseshoe. Next appeared two traders of Michigan, who declared that, upon the whole, the sight was worth looking at; there certainly was an immense waterpower here; but that, after all, they would go twice as far to see the noble stoneworks of Lockport, where the Grand Canal is locked down a descent of sixty feet. They were succeeded by a young fellow, in homespun cotton dress, with a staff in his hand, and a pack over his shoulders. He advanced close to the edge of the rock, where his attention, at first wavering among the different components of the scene, finally became fixed in the angle of the Horseshoe falls, which is, indeed, the central point of interest. His whole soul seemed to go forth and be transported thither, till the staff slipped from his relaxed grasp, and falling down—down—struck upon the fragment of the Table Rock.

In this manner, I spent some hours, watching the varied impression made by the cataract, on those who disturbed me, and returning to unwearied contemplation, when left alone. At length, my time came to depart. There is a grassy footpath, through the woods, along the summit of the bank, to a point whence a causeway, hewn in the side of the precipice, goes winding down to the ferry, about half a mile below the Table Rock. The sun was near setting, when I emerged from the shadow of the trees, and began the descent. The indirectness of my downward road continually changed the point of view, and shewed me, in rich and repeated succession—now, the whitening rapids and the majestic leap of the main river, which appeared more deeply massive as the light departed, now, the lovelier picture, yet still sublime, of Goat Island, with its rocks and grove, and the lesser falls, tumbling over the right bank of the St. Lawrence, like a tributary stream, now, the long vista of the river, as it eddied and whirled between the cliffs, to pass through Ontario towards the sea, and everywhere to be wondered at, for this one unrivalled scene. The golden sunshine tinged the sheet of the American cascade, and painted on its heaving spray the broken semicircle of a rainbow, Heaven's own beauty crowning earth's sublimity. My steps were slow, and I paused long at every turn of the descent, as one lingers and pauses, who discerns a brighter and brightening excellence in what he must soon behold no more. The solitude of the old wilderness now reigned over the whole vicinity of the falls. My enjoyment became the more rapturous, because no poet shared it—nor wretch, devoid of poetry, profaned it: But the spot, so famous through the world, was all my own!

Joseph Hone

No Exit

A novelist, film director, and BBC radio producer, Hone planned to follow in the footsteps of Stanley in a 2,500-mile, three-month trek across Africa from the Indian Ocean to the Atlantic. In Kinshasa, he discovered that such a journey was easier a century ago. Tourism may flourish in some parts of the Third World—packaged safaris and the like—but travel is not so easy. From *Africa of the Heart*, published in 1986.

I met Harry Jupiter on my second morning at the Memling Hotel in Kinshasa. I was late down for breakfast. The cafe terrace at the end of the lobby was crowded so I had to share a table with him. It was the luckiest meeting I had in Kinshasa—apart from Eleanor.

It was the dry season. There was no heat in the city and the terrace was set back in an almost cold shade under the roof at the back of the yellow-stained lobby. So Harry wore a pullover, a big one for he was a large man. The only unusual thing about it was that it was a cricket pullover, long-sleeved, in white wool, with the colored lines—red and green bands round the collar and waist—of some English cricket club. He was reading a French paper, not from Kinshasa, but from Brazzaville, the twin city, capital of the old French Congo on the other side of the river. A French paper and a continental breakfast: coffee and croissants. I was hoping for something more substantial.

"*Omelette au jambon,*" I asked the woman when I'd finally caught her eye and willed her over to me. The woman sighed.

"You have to mark the card up." The man opposite spoke for the first time. "You mark out what you want," he said.

The waitress got me a card and I ticked right down the list. I was hungry. I ticked the croissants, too.

"There aren't any," the man said. "I bring my own when I breakfast here. There's a good *boulangerie* right behind the hotel, on the way to the Grand Marché. You can only get croissants for breakfast up at the Intercontinental."

"Thank you."

The big man must have been in his late fifties, with a faded American accent, from the deep South, I thought, but with distinct French intonations: the r's rolled easily and he hit a fine high Norman croak on the *é* of Marché. An old French-American from New Orleans? He folded his newspaper. "I see Mitterrand is on his way out here—a shot in the arm for all the ex-French territories up north. A little of the old *mission civilisatrice.* I doubt we can expect the King of the Belgians here, though."

He took a cheroot from a small leather cigar case in front of him, offered me one. "I'll wait till I've had some food," I said. He laughed then, for the first time, a throaty, gravel-in-a-barrel laugh. "You'll be waiting half an hour for what you ordered. Have some of my coffee. You can use the other side of the cup. I'm Harry Jupiter."

I introduced myself. "Only got here yesterday. From London."

"Yes. I heard something of that. With the BBC, I think? I listen to your World Service every day. I get your magazine, too: the *Listener.*"

I was surprised.

"Oh, I have people out at the airport. You have to have—else you'd never get out of the place. Never get anything in either."

I was still surprised. "How did you spot me?"

"One of my boys did. He's a good boy, Alain. Speaks English well—I've taught him. That's one of my jobs here. Very few British people come to Kinshasa. And those that do—well, there's only two or three real flights in here a week from Europe now and I always have someone up there when they get in."

I took one of Harry's cheroots. They were small, chunky, wedge-shaped: tarry and unappetizing-looking. But they smoked well—a slow, woody, blue-whiffed smoke.

"They're from the Kivu region, way out on the eastern borders here. Though they get them in from Rwanda now. They don't make much of anything in Zaïre anymore. Gas is running out."

"Is it? I was hoping to do a lot of traveling in Zaïre."

"You were?" Harry's eyelids lifted, a sharp blue glint in the pupils. He licked his lips, as if he'd just spotted a long-odds winner in the paddock. "Travel is an interesting thing in this country," he said.

"Yes. So I've heard. I'm making for the coast first, down to Matadi and Banana Point. Then back up here and on upriver—on the big boat to Kisangani. Then I wanted to get into the Ituri forest, see something of the pygmies. And there's the Kivu region, you mentioned on the eastern border— the lakes and volcanoes. . . ."

Harry's eyes were wide open now. "I think you misunderstood me," he said. "Travel here is interesting—because you can't."

"Oh."

"Oh indeed." He laughed, the gravel barrel tilting a little in his throat.

"Well, I was going to see the tourist people here this morning."

The barrel tilted some more. "They closed down the Ministry of Tourism here two years ago, Mr. Hone. Didn't they tell you that in London?"

"No—just said I couldn't come into the country from the east; that I had to come in via Kinshasa. I was to have done the whole trip east to west, in the 'Footsteps of Stanley' sort of style. Now I'm going to have to reverse it."

"You're going to have to do a deal more than that, I fancy: You're going to have to get *out* of Kinshasa first—like a prison break. That'll be your first concern."

"Why should it be so difficult?"

The gravel barrel in his throat tilted right over now. "How were you thinking of managing it? You got a lot of native porters with tea chests, half a dozen armed askaris? There may be no other way out of here."

"No. I don't have much equipment in fact. I gave my son a compass for Christmas. He lent it back to me. I've got a map of equatorial Africa, though the scale looks a bit small to me. And I brought some tinned salmon and crackers, a bottle of lime juice, and some Johnny Walker Black Label—as well as all the usual malaria and dysentery pills."

"That's hardly enough to see you out to the suburbs here."

"But I'm going upriver by boat. I brought these as extras, a few goodies. I'd like to have gone across the continent with bearers and tea chests and old Lee-Enfield rifles. But it's not on these days."

"No, indeed. Only trouble is that nothing is on here these days. I'd revise your itinerary—or cancel it. Hang around the city here a bit. You'll have to, I guess, anyway. Apart from the transport, they don't much care for inquisitive foreigners nosing about out of town at the moment. Never have, in fact. Besides, Kinshasa is a country in itself. All you need is money to discover it."

"Well, I have a little of that. Not much, this is radio I'm doing. . . ."

Harry leaned forward, a real gleam in his eye, speaking with gravitas now. "Money is another very interesting thing here. Inflation makes it just like it was in the old Weimar Republic: You have to carry a lot of it around, in a wheelbarrow, ideally. There's no coin here at all now. It's all in old notes. Five-Zaïre notes usually. One of those used to buy you a whole night on the town. Now it won't even get you a beer."

"Oh."

"Your ham and eggs—when you get it: That'll be fifty or sixty Zaïres in this palatial establishment. Nearly fifteen dollars at the official rate."

"Is there another rate?" I asked cautiously.

Harry took a second cheroot from his little cigar case. I noticed a Star of David inlaid in silver on the leather.

"Yes," he said, sighing with gratitude. "Indeed there is another rate. None of us would be here otherwise. The Parallel Rate." He uttered the phrase with a hushed twinkle in his voice, looking cautiously over the end of his cheroot, like a comic confronting the Holy Grail.

"The parallel rate?"

"The unofficial rate. You can get three, four, five times as much for your dollar on that. Depending on the priests, if they need things from Europe for the missions; or on whether it's holiday time for the *gros Belges*. Back to Brussels on the Sunday Rocket: Well, they need the dollars then. And that's when you can move onto the parallel rate. That's when you really start to lead the life of Reilly here, Mr. Hone," Harry went on with enthusiasm. "Puts a whole different complexion on things: fresh radishes and *sole bonne femme* flown in from Brussels twice a week: a Mercedes, two chauffeurs, a dozen boys and a big villa in the old Belgian residential quarter by the river. You really start to move here—on the parallel rate. And of course you can build yourself a wall then, too."

"A wall?"

"A big wall, round your villa. You'll see when you get about town. They're all building walls furiously right now. It's the smartest thing of the season. The bigger the better."

Harry looked up just then. There was a disturbance, an excited flutter at the end of the lobby. A magnificent middle-aged African in a dazzling, multi-colored *bubus*—a sort of loose-hanging nightgown affair—was making royal progress through the hall, followed by a scatter of obsequious attendants, supplicants, and hangers-on.

"That's General N'Gongo," Harry said. "A minister, a *Commissaire* last year. But temporarily in eclipse right now. He's building a wall—the biggest in Kinshasa, I'd say."

"On the parallel rate?" I suggested.

"I wouldn't speak too loudly. In the good old days here the General—he was a sergeant then—had people like you for breakfast. And that's another thing to bear in mind here, Mr. Hone, if you're white: Keep a low profile. And don't talk French if you can help it. They might think you were Belgian, and that's not so good. The Belgians caused some trouble here, over the years, to put it mildly. Old King Leopold and his friends especially, when they had this whole country as their own private ballgame, used to chop all the black hands off everywhere upriver, if the rubber wasn't coming in quick enough. So talk English," Harry advised me firmly. "They like that. They all want to learn English. That's why I'm here. Though of course I teach American. And I tell you—they like that even *better!*"

Harry grumbled and hawked with laughter, the skin in his cheeks and jowls vibrating. His face hadn't fallen yet, but it wouldn't be long, and when it did he would be a wonderfully complete Buddha, where age would really swell and toast the half-burnt ivory of his complexion. In name a supreme God, his body was that of a demigod already: rotund, juicy, like an inverted pear about to drop, with large dewy eyes, the lids drooping a little now with the sun-struck years, so that quite soon the wry, candid gaze would be pleasantly, comfortably hooded. Although there would never be anything of the hawk in Harry's expression; no sharp queries, unease, no suspicion, no devious intent whatsoever.

Harry, as I was to discover, had learned and survived so much deception in his life, absorbed and expelled every trickery and deceit, that he was guileless now—a great balloon hanging over the city: seeing, understanding and pardoning everything. Though perhaps at ground level the image of a huge bath sponge is more appropriate: Harry absorbed and released information like water. Or like a plant—better still: He lived by osmosis, drawing in all the gossip, the life of Kinshasa, like sunlight. A balloon, a sponge, a plant—all that. And though I would probably have met him anyway, at some point in my rambles about the city, I was luckier than I knew that morning in meeting him so soon. Harry became most of my city, gave me all my entrances and exits there.

For a long time we drove round the edge of the African Cité in Kinshasa—the old native quarter in what was then Leopoldville. It was a vast area, marked simply by a huge rectangular blank space on the only map I'd seen of the city; two miles long and a mile wide, with well over a million people living there, I'd been told. Even if the crippled taxi hadn't been falling apart—splitting, tearing at the seams, tied up with string—we could never have driven through the Cité. There were no real roads, just endless mud-caked alleyways, narrow gullies that led to the mysterious interior, first among the grander breeze-block beer shops and garages that formed an outer ring to this *kasbah* before the tracks were lost in the huge mix of tacked-up buildings beyond: corrugated iron, flattened oil drums, discarded wooden pallets, circular windows framed in old tires, sacking, polyethylene, mud. The building materials stretched away to the horizon, each man his own Le Corbusier, restricted only by what seemed a regulation height—for the top of the Cité was flat, running away forever with the roofs at more or less the same level, set at little more than a man's height, flat as a warty bandaged hand. Bricks and scaffolding for a second story were things beyond the dreams of avarice in the Cité. It was gold enough to get one roof over your head here.

The beer shops were open. There was the throb of Congo reggae, taped out at 100 decibels, coming from behind each gaudy-colored pub, where local artists had dreamed up their comic strip signs in brilliant acrylic housepaint. A huge green bottle of "Primus" beer exploded above one beer hall, where the gunpowder was a woman at the center, a black, slit-skirt Marilyn Monroe kicking the glass shards. Another sign showed two Africans, with white faces and black lips like Negro minstrels in reverse, sitting under an umbrella, gold rain descending all round them, as they quaffed a bile-green beer. A third panorama showed a whole family drinking merrily round a tomb where the departed, an old grandfather and mother, were set up in effigy above it—miniaturized people who appeared as waiters waiting to pick up the empties when the party was finished round their tombstone table. I wondered if this was a funeral parlor. I asked my driver. First he shook his head; then he nodded it. A combined operation, beer shop and undertakers in one.

The really strange thing was the lack of people. There was the music and these tremendous comic strip invitations—but no people. Then, stopping at a junction, the window open, I heard a faint roar coming from all over the Cité, a bee's nest sound, a soft murmur set like a canopy over the whole rubbish-dump landscape. They were there all right, invisible, a million people under the sacks and wooden pallets, adding up the honey of their lives together in a million different ways. But I couldn't imagine how. I wanted to imagine their thoughts. But I couldn't.

When you come to the strangeness of a new city, you try and look through the buildings, into the rooms, searching the interiors, imagining the domestic intimacies, inventing the familiar as a silken thread through the labyrinth. But here, my mind reaching out over this great scrofulous, uncerous, suppurating body, I could feel nothing, sense nothing except the crazy notion that everyone in the Cité was hidden around their ancestors' tombs just then, flooded in gold rain, with Marilyn Monroe dancing on the graves, the bottles exploding while they lowered the pea-green beer.

Beyond this real Cité we came to another: Cité de la Voix de Zaïre—the new radio and TV center in bunker-style concrete built by the French a few years ago. Again, the place seemed almost totally deserted—a great skyscraper to one side, a long complex of sound stages and studios to the other. An African walked from one of the stages carrying a wheelless bicycle. Another followed with a big paintbrush. They set the bicycle down in the middle of the forecourt and the second man took his brush to it. But then—the problem: There was no paint. I was in an empty waiting room by then and I got up to look at the action, for presumably this was being filmed and I hadn't seen the cameras. There were no cameras. But the man was really painting the bicycle now, dabbing away at it. Were they rehearsing an act?—or just rehearsing the painting of the machine? I couldn't decide.

After twenty minutes I was called upstairs. I was sorry to leave, for by this time, having finished their imaginary painting, the two men had taken the bicycle to bits and were trying to reassemble it, without success. Just as I had to leave for my appointment, a third man arrived, a more severe-looking fellow, carrying a big tin of paint.

In a very grand office on the top floor of the skyscraper I met the Press Councillor, the *Citoyen Commissaire*—a tall, beautifully dressed man of the utmost sophistication, with perfect English. He wore a silk Kaunda suit in soft Windsor gray with the half-opened bud of a red rose nestling just beneath his throat. In front of him an untouched glass of fresh orange juice sat on a pile of newspapers, *The Times* and *Le Monde*. I could imagine this man's life all right, his thoughts, his domestic surroundings: a man of effortless, affable style, a welcome addition to any African reception at the Elysée Palace or 10 Downing Street; a man of the world, though not this world, I felt, for his present office was strangely mute, as the corridor outside and all the adjoining offices were: no sound of typewriters, teleprinters, telephones. And no people. The *Citoyen Commissaire* perched like a splendidly feathered rooster at the top of an empty henhouse where everything, and everyone but him, had been struck by a power failure.

I told the *Commissaire* of my hopes in Zaïre. He listened carefully. "Not a political series," I assured him. "In the 'Footsteps of Stanley'—that sort of thing. I'm going coast to coast, west-east, from the Atlantic to the Indian Ocean. Color material. . . ."

"Yes, of course. Though didn't Stanley come into Zaïre the other way round, *from* the east, downriver?"

"Yes, but I couldn't get a visa—to come the right way round—from your London Embassy. They said I had to come into Zaïre via Kinshasa."

"Of course. We still have a few problems on the eastern borders. It's not advisable—for your own safety."

"Well, here I am anyway. I thought I'd spend a few days in Kinshasa, then go down to the estuary, to Matadi, then out to Banana Point on the Atlantic. Then back up here and upriver to Kisangani on the big passenger boat—I think it's ten days on the river, you don't happen to know the times of the boats, do you?—then into the Ituri Forest. I was anxious to see something of the pygmy tribes there."

"Yes, indeed." A small secretary came into the room just then and the tall, wonderfully dressed *Commissaire* spoke to him, standing up slowly, where he seemed to go on standing up for some seconds. He signed papers. Then he turned back to me. "An excellent itinerary. Now, could you put all that down in writing for me? It's the usual paperwork thing here, I'm afraid. Bureaucracy." He gestured round the paperless room.

"Of course."

"And send it to me at once. With the heading of your BBC company, on the notepaper." The *Commissaire* lifted up the glass of orange juice—and I saw then that it was a trick glass where some oily, yellow-colored liquid had been sealed into the sides of the tumbler: an imagined glass of orange juice where the idea stood for the substance.

"Certainly. I'll send the itinerary round tomorrow morning."

I was about to leave. He held his hand up, but not to shake. "There's only one point," he said suavely. "We're holding local government elections all over Zaïre at the moment." Then he added most pleasantly, the one thing obviously following quite naturally on the other: "No foreigners are allowed out of Kinshasa for the time being."

The secretary came in then again and I heard the name "Mitterrand" exchanged in hushed tones between them. When I got downstairs and out onto the forecourt again there were the remains of three or four unpainted bicycles lying on the ground. Bicycles? I needed a boat, not a bicycle anyway.

Despite Harry and the *Commissaire* I was going up the Congo come hell or high water. And the sooner I made a start in that direction, the better. . . .

The riverboat timetable I'd finally got hold of was the most elaborate collection of promises I've ever seen. Its forty foolscap pages gave comprehensive details of every trip you could possibly take—up, down or off the Congo River. With its dozen routes and major destinations throughout the great river basin, its hundreds of stopping places and its tempting collection of symbols denoting "Deluxe Cabin," "Dog Kennels," and "First Class Restaurants"—it clearly offered the ultimate in African travel, particularly on the ONATRA company's main line—just where I wanted to go: the thousand-mile journey upstream from Kinshasa to the port of Kisangani on the great bend of the river in the heartlands of the continent.

Mbandaka, Mobeka, Lisala, Bumba, Isangi, Yangambi, Kisangani. . . . The names of the provincial capitals and smaller river stations conjured up just the sort of dramatic litany I wanted: a fabulous mix of African fact and fiction. Stanley had literally fought his way down this river just over a hundred years before: an astonishing journey in commandeered war canoes, with thirty-two ferocious pitched battles on the way, beating off an endless collection of cannibal tribes. The Belgians had taken over shortly afterward—with hippopotamus-hide whips, obscene brutalities, mass executions. Conrad had come this way a few years later—to his appointment with the evil Mr. Kurtz in the heart of darkness. André Gide and his boyfriend, Marc Allégret, had followed him. And long after that Graham Greene had followed them, taking the Bishop's boat in search of his character Querry, the stricken architect maimed by civilization, finally placing him among the genuine lepers crawling along the forest paths of the interior in *A Burnt-out Case.*

Savagery, mystery, primeval darkness—these were the real images, the real destinations hidden behind the bland facts and figures of the timetable. And now I was in Kinshasa myself, waiting to get on that boat, another traveler about to be named in this fantastic passenger list of men who had journeyed to Conrad's "dark places of the earth." Or was I about to be named?

"That will be three thousand Zaïres, first class, one-way, inclusive for the ten-day trip." The important African loomed over his huge, empty, glass-topped desk. We were in the vast ONATRA building in downtown Kinshasa: the biggest office block in the city, air-conditioned, built by the Belgians just before they ran from the country twenty-one years before. There had been an air of ponderous efficiency in the lobby and on my way along corridors to see this Great God of the riverboat company—a government monopoly with a necessary efficiency, I thought, since I was well aware that river transport is largely the only transport throughout Zaïre. Without boats everyone and everything came to a full stop in this country. I was just about to hand the money over—a stiff £300 at the official rate—when I hesitated.

"The boat still leaves Monday morning, nine o'clock?"

"No. Thursday, in fact. It's late coming downstream."

It was only my third day in Kinshasa. But already I knew enough about the crazy bureaucratic life in the city to put my money away. "I'll come back," I said. "Fix things up with you after the weekend."

I walked back up the main boulevard then—the Trente Juin: a straight two miles carved right through the heart of the city, a slummy Champs Elysées, before it curved at the top and ran out into the suburbs for another three miles. I tacked sharply away from the crippled beggars on their stumps and trolleys outside the Post Office, making for me on their pram wheels like raiders in war canoes. The sky was the usual suffocating blanket of gray above me. After only three days I was longing to be out of Kinshasa. But Harry Jupiter, when I met him at the Memling Hotel bar that lunchtime, maintained his original grave doubts about my ambitions.

"They're lying down at ONATRA," he said. "Or else they're blind. The Kisangani steamer is here right now, in port. I saw the funnel this morning."

"Maybe that's another steamer." I bought Harry a vermouth. We were in the little cocktail bar in the small corridor on the way into the restaurant. Harry didn't drink beer in the dry season.

"Listen," he said. "About the passenger boats: They don't work, they break down, they can't repair them, there's no fuel. The local boys cannibalize them, then sell the stuff as spare parts. It's all a dream—traveling upriver now. I've tried it myself."

I showed Harry the elaborate timetable then. He was amazed. "I've never seen one of these before." He looked at it carefully, handling it like a rare manuscript. "Lisala, Bumba, Basoko, Lokutu, Yangambi, Kisangani," he intoned. "Just names," he added finally. "Words, not deeds. You haven't realized that yet, have you? In Zaïre now, if they put something in writing—especially if they print it up like this—it stands for the deed. You don't actually have to *do* the thing then. It's a neat trick: timetables like this absolve them from taking any further action." Harry laughed, a generous rumble.

"Oh, I'm learning," I said. I told him about the glass of trick orange juice on the Press Councillor's desk. "Yes," he agreed. "But you're really only on chapter one."

On Monday I saw another more junior man at the ONATRA building, in the operations room this time: short, portly, officious. He was sitting in front of a huge wall plan of the whole river network, where little sliding colored buttons represented all the company's boats on stream at that moment.

"Ah yes," he said very confidently. "The Kisangani boat has been delayed—until the end of the week. Repairs. Come back tomorrow and I'll be able to tell you the position."

The next day the fat, confident executive had disappeared. Instead a thin, unconfident clerk was in his place. He looked at the wall plan for me, mystified, considering it like the Rosetta Stone. He tried to move one of the little colored buttons. But it was stuck fast. He consulted a big ledger instead.

"Kisangani?" He was equally perplexed here, thumbing nervously through the pages. But finding nothing to suit his purposes in the book, he suddenly looked up, and grasping the words out of the air, said sharply, "That boat is not leaving Kinshasa until the seventeenth." This was ten days away.

"What's the problem?"

"No problem." The clerk was affronted now. "The Kisangani boat left here yesterday. The next one isn't until the seventeenth." Triumphantly the little man closed the ledger. This boat business was obviously getting on top of these people, I thought—boats hithering and thithering up and downriver apparently at random; yesterday, today, tomorrow, the end of the week, or not at all. I produced my famous timetable then, pointing out that the Kisangani boat was supposed to leave not yesterday or on the seventeenth, but every Monday at nine o'clock.

The clerk took the timetable from me gingerly—viewing it, like Harry, with some amazement. Indeed, he was speechless, turning all the wonderful pages, pondering the remote places, the exotic destinations, the clever symbols. He'd obviously never seen this fantastic document in his life before. "Lisala, Bumba, Basoko," he chanted reverently. "Lokutu, Isangi, Yangambi. . . ." He was spellbound by the majesty of it all. I left him at it.

Harry laughed again when I met him later that morning. He rolled in the aisles. "You're certainly getting the hang of things here," he said. "And maybe you can't blame them too much for it. You see, the white man is prey in Africa now. Fair game, to be stalked. They like to play you on all sorts of hooks. It's their revenge—just as we preyed on them. They do it very politely, you think they're playing straight. But what they're actually doing is tying you up in knots—and they're *pleased* to. Remember that. It's our turn for the slavery now. We're at the sharp end and there's nothing much you can do about it. Except money. You could try hiring a private boat, or hitch a lift on a cargo barge."

I went down to the port that afternoon, noticing how the old Belgian residential quarter had been built away from the river, turning its back on it, as one would on a malign presence. No one had ever really *liked* the river here, seen it as a friend—that was the obvious, interesting thing. The waterfront quite lacked any happy life, native or European. There was just a long run of dirty wharves, crumbling warehouses, stalled cranes and endless lines of rusting or sunken ships, old paddle steamers and barges, a few bows and funnels poking up through the vast brown sheet of water, broken hulks, the remnants of a once-vibrant river transport system here which had long since disappeared. Stanley's "murderous river" had won this anti-colonial battle hands down. There were no boats at all to be seen out on the stream. The waters coursed through these narrows just as they had before Stanley discovered the place more than a hundred years before: untouched now as then.

Later that day Harry sent one of his Zaïrean boys down to the docks to inquire about cargo boats for me. The man had been promptly arrested. "As a smuggler—or what?" I asked Harry next morning.

"No. He was just the wrong tribe. Not a river tribe. He's from the Shaba region in the south. They're very fussy about who they let out on the river these days."

"*Fussy?* They don't seem to let anyone out on it."

"Yes. But maybe you're going about the whole thing the wrong way. You're asking them questions they can just give a yes or no answer to. That's fatal here. You're sort of saying, 'Does the boat leave for Kisangani today?' What you have to do is shout, 'What have you *done* with the boat for Kisangani!' You might get somewhere then."

"I see."

"Maybe I can still fix you up with something," Harry relented. "If you insist. But it'll take time. You might as well get accustomed to Kinshasa. Or maybe you could take a trip across to Brazzaville while you're waiting. Things tend to work over there. There's a little French restaurant right on the port. . . ." Harry bought me a vermouth this time—a large one—and consoled me with all the delights of Brazzaville.

Across the river you could always see Brazzaville—the chic French architecture on the city waterfront and the low white cliffs to either side, which reminded Stanley of Dover when he first came here, down the Congo river, to this western end of the Pool, just over a hundred years ago.

You could see Brazza if you leaned far enough out of my bedroom window in the Memling Hotel. And you could see it without any effort at all from most of the side windows upstairs in the Chancellery at the Embassy. You could see the other city from almost every tall building in Kinshasa, just as you could gaze at it from ground level, *en clair,* from any point along the ramparts on the southern bank, or from the port downtown, which gave straight out onto the hulks of rusting dredgers and decaying paddle steamers abandoned in the vast gray stream. Brazza was with you all the way along the riverfront, on the Avenue des Nations Unies, where the huge colonial villas and embassies looked down on the empty water, great mauve-green clumps of water hyacinth the only traffic, floating down like giant sprouting broccoli, torn out from the riverbanks all the way far up into the interior. You could see the crowded little ferry, too, morning and afternoon, plying across the mile of pewter-colored water that lay between the twin cities.

But you couldn't get to Brazzaville.

And you couldn't get up river because all the passenger boats had broken down or run aground in this dry season. You couldn't get downstream either, of course, in any sort of boat, as Stanley had discovered, for there was nothing but rapids and wicked cataracts and high falls from just below Kinshasa for 150 miles all the way until you hit open water again, on the neck of the estuary, at the port of Matadi.

There was a narrow-gauge, single-track railway from Kinshasa to Matadi, built through the tortuous Crystal Mountains by King Leopold and his murderous Belgians in the 1890s ("A black for every sleeper"), where the town guide now advertised "Train No. 50—First Class Only" leaving for the coast every morning. But I had been to the empty station at the bottom of the Boulevard Trente Juin on several mornings. It was a station in name alone: a stationary station, where once more the title sufficed for the purpose. And even if there had been trains, the fuel was running out in Zaïre anyway, which meant that cars were difficult too. Few people would drive you beyond the suburbs of Kinshasa—let alone out onto the few roads in the interior. So you couldn't move up-country that way.

You could take a local Zaïre Aero Service flight out, to one of the many airstrips in the interior which the Belgians had built so that their para-troopers could control the whole country in the old days. You could go this way, if you had the cash and the temerity to bribe and fight your way out after a week waiting for a seat at Kinshasa International. Or you could hire a small plane and fly out privately, if you were very rich. And of course there were always rumors of other escapes. A Catholic mission boat from somewhere far upstream would be in town on the nineteenth—or a little Cessna from one of the fifty-seven Protestant missions was expected in Kinshasa the day after; or there was a private cargo tug you might hitch a lift with, leaving for Kisangani, a thousand miles up on the bend of the river, next weekend. But the rumors always died at the last moment, when you were on your way down to the port with your baggage or had finally made a deal with a taxi to the airport. The rumors died and you cursed as you looked across at Brazzaville, where things apparently worked.

Davidson had told me, with deft superiority, that afternoon at the Embassy: "I go to Brazza every month or so. There are a few British over there. But it takes me my diplomatic pass and four other ministry and customs chits to get on that ferry. It might take you a lot more." He looked at me unhelpfully. "Why do you want to go there anyway?"

"I hear things work over in Brazza," I said.

"Well, comparatively speaking. It was French. Mitterrand is keen on doing well by all the francophone countries now. And they used the African franc over there, a convertible currency. So, some things work. The telephone for example."

"Locally?"

"And overseas. They've a satellite link."

"I could phone home from there, you mean?"

"You might. You'd certainly find that difficult from here." Davidson tried to smile. "But why Brazza—when you told me last time you wanted to get upriver? To Kisangani and so on."

I smiled now. "I've been trying for over two weeks to get that boat: the big passenger boat. Monday mornings at nine o'clock. That's what the timetable says. But all I get are excuses, lies—I don't know what. There's no boat."

Davidson craned his neck round, looking out of his window over the river. "I think I saw the Kisangani boat in this morning," he said. "It was late coming downstream. Think I saw the big funnel."

I stood up and rushed to the window. "I can't see it. That's the funnel of the hospital boat, isn't it?"

There was no sun on the river. There had been no sun in the city, not a moment of it, since I'd arrived. It was the dry season.

"I don't know. Why don't you go down to the port and find out?"

"I've been down. I've been living in the port. And the ONATRA building. I thought while I was waiting I might go over to Brazza. I think I need a chit from you for that—to begin with. A certificate of good conduct or something."

"I tell you it's very difficult. I can give you a chit all right. But the rest of the papers will take you up to a week or more. Why bother?"

"I hear there's a French café-restaurant on the riverfront in Brazza, run by some cantankerous old *colon*. But decent food. He does grilled *telapia* and a good *steack-frites*. The wine is drinkable, too, I'm told. And the meal doesn't cost you twenty pounds, as it does here. And there are real newspapers in Brazza, aren't there?—from France. As well as a local one. And television and real taxis. And Bic razors and lighters in the shops. And telephones. I thought if I went to Brazza for the day I might feel a little at home," I said desperately.

Jerome K. Jerome

"You Can't Beat a Sea Trip"

"We agree that we are overworked, and need a rest—A week on the rolling deep?—George suggests the river . . ." Jerome's 1889 account of three men and a dog during a rowing holiday on the Thames is his enduring contribution to travel literature. A century later, however, the canine's advocates continue to protest the abbreviated title of the book, *Three Men in a Boat.*

No," said Harris, "if you want rest and change, you can't beat a sea trip."

I objected to the sea trip strongly. A sea trip does you good when you are going to have a couple of months of it, but for a week, it is wicked.

You start on Monday with the idea implanted in your bosom that you are going to enjoy yourself. You wave an airy adieu to the boys on shore, light your biggest pipe, and swagger about the deck as if you were Captain Cook, Sir Francis Drake, and Christopher Columbus all rolled into one. On Tuesday, you wish you hadn't come. On Wednesday, Thursday, and Friday, you wish you were dead. On Saturday you are able to swallow a little beef tea, and to sit up on deck, and answer with a wan, sweet smile when kindhearted people ask how you feel now. On Sunday, you begin to walk again, and take solid food. And on Monday morning, as, with your bag and umbrella in your hand, you stand by the gunwale, waiting to step ashore, you begin to thoroughly like it.

I remember my brother-in-law going for a short sea trip once for the benefit of his health. He took a return berth from London to Liverpool; and when he got to Liverpool, the only thing he was anxious about was to sell that return ticket.

It was offered round the town at a tremendous reduction, so I am told; and was eventually sold for eighteenpence to a bilious-looking youth who had just been advised by his medical men to go to the seaside, and take exercise.

"Seaside!" said my brother-in-law, pressing the ticket affectionately into his hand: "Why, you'll have enough to last you a lifetime; and as for exercise! Why, you'll get more exercise, sitting down on that ship, than you would turning somersaults on dry land."

He himself—my brother-in-law—came back by train. He said the North-Western Railway was healthy enough for him.

Another fellow I knew went for a week's voyage round the coast, and before they started, the steward came to him to ask whether he would pay for each meal as he had it, or arrange beforehand for the whole series.

The steward recommended the latter course, as it would come so much cheaper. He said they would do him for the whole week at two-pounds-five. He said for breakfast there would be fish, followed by a grill. Lunch was at one, and consisted of four courses. Dinner at six—soup, fish, entrée, joint, poultry, salad, sweets, cheese, and dessert. And a light meat supper at ten.

My friend thought he would close on the two-pounds-five job (he is a hearty eater), and did so.

Lunch came just as they were off Sheerness. He didn't feel so hungry as he thought he should, and so contented himself with a bit of boiled beef, and some strawberries and cream. He pondered a good deal during the afternoon, and at one time it seemed to him that he had been eating nothing but boiled beef for weeks, and at other times it seemed that he must have been living on strawberries and cream for years.

Neither the beef nor the strawberries and cream seemed happy, either—seemed discontented like.

At six, they came and told him dinner was ready. The announcement aroused no enthusiasm within him, but he felt that there was some of the two-pounds-five to be worked off, and he held on to ropes and things and went down. A pleasant odor of onions and hot ham, mingled with fried fish and greens, greeted him at the bottom of the ladder; and then the steward came up with an oily smile, and said:

"What can I get you, sir?"

"Get me out of this," was the feeble reply.

And they ran him up quick, and propped him up, over to leeward, and left him.

For the next four days he lived a simple and blameless life on thin Captain's biscuits (I mean that the biscuits were thin, not the captain) and soda water; but, towards Saturday, he got uppish, and went in for weak tea and dry toast, and on Monday he was gorging himself on chicken broth. He left the ship on Tuesday, and as it steamed away from the landing-stage he gazed after it regretfully.

"There she goes," he said, "there she goes, with two pounds' worth of food on board that belongs to me, and that I haven't had."

He said that if they had given him another day he thought he could have put it straight.

So I set my face against the sea trip. Not, as I explained, upon my own account. I was never queer. But I was afraid for George. George said he should be all right, and would rather like it, but he would advise Harris and me not to think of it, as he felt sure we should both be ill. Harris said that, to himself, it was always a mystery how people managed to get sick at sea—said he thought people must do it on purpose, from affectation—said he had often wished to be, but had never been able.

Then he told us anecdotes of how he had gone across the Channel when it was so rough that the passengers had to be tied into their berths, and he and the captain were the only two living souls on board who were not ill. Sometimes it was he and the second mate who were not ill; but it was generally he and one other man. If not he and another man, then it was he by himself.

It is a curious fact, but nobody ever is seasick—on land. At sea, you come across plenty of people very bad indeed, whole boatloads of them; but I never met a man yet, on land, who had ever known at all what it was to be seasick. Where the thousands upon thousands of bad sailors that swarm in every ship hide themselves when they are on land is a mystery.

If most men were like a fellow I saw on the Yarmouth boat one day, I could account for the seeming enigma easily enough. It was just off Southend Pier, I recollect, and he was leaning out through one of the portholes in a very dangerous position. I went up to him to try and save him.

"Hi! come further in," I said, shaking him by the shoulder. "You'll be overboard."

"Oh my! I wish I was," was the only answer I could get; and there I had to leave him.

Three weeks afterwards, I met him in the coffeeroom of a Bath hotel, talking about his voyages, and explaining, with enthusiasm, how he loved the sea.

"Good sailor!" he replied in answer to a mild young man's envious query, "well I did feel a little queer *once,* I confess. It was off Cape Horn. The vessel was wrecked the next morning."

I said:

"Weren't you a little shaky by Southend Pier one day, and wanted to be thrown overboard?"

"Southend Pier!" he replied, with a puzzled expression.

"Yes; going down to Yarmouth, last Friday three weeks."

"Oh, ah—yes," he answered, brightening up; "I remember now. I did have a headache that afternoon. It was the pickles, you know. They were the most disgraceful pickles I ever tasted in a respectable boat. Did *you* have any?"

For myself, I have discovered an excellent preventive against seasickness, in balancing myself. You stand in the center of the deck, and, as the ship heaves and pitches, you move your body about, so as to keep it always straight. When the front of the ship rises, you lean forward, till the deck almost touches your nose; and when its back end gets up, you lean backwards. This is all very well for an hour or so; but you can't balance yourself for a week.

Edward Lear

The Story of the Four Little Children Who Went Round the World

The lord of the limerick and nabob of the nonsense story was also a proficient zoological draughtsman and prolific if lonely traveler. In *Journal of a Landscape Painter in Corsica* he wrote: "The night voyage . . . The slow sad hours that bring us all things ill . . . Will the daybreak ever happen? Will two o'clock ever arrive? Will the two poodles above stairs ever cease to run about the deck? Is it not disagreeable to look forward to two or three months of traveling quite alone? Would it not be delightful to travel, as J.A.S. [friend John Addington Symonds] is about to do, in company with wife and child? Does it not, as years advance, become clearer that it is very odious to be alone?" The lonely traveler, in want of family, sent four children on an inimitable trip around the world.

Once upon a time, a long while ago, there were four little people whose names were

VIOLET,   SLINGSBY,   GUY,   and LIONEL:

and they all thought they should like to see the world. So they bought a large boat to sail quite round the world by sea, and then they were to come back on the other side by land. The boat was painted blue with green spots, and the sail was yellow with red stripes; and when they set off, they only took a small Cat to steer and look after the boat, besides an elderly Quangle-Wangle, who

had to cook the dinner and make the tea; for which purposes they took a large kettle.

For the first ten days they sailed on beautifully, and found plenty to eat, as there were lots of fish, and they had only to take them out of the sea with a long spoon, when the Quangle-Wangle instantly cooked them, and the Pussy-cat was fed with the bones, with which she expressed herself pleased on the whole, so that all the party were very happy.

During the daytime, Violet chiefly occupied herself in putting saltwater into a churn, while her three brothers churned it violently, in the hope that it would turn into butter, which it seldom if ever did; and in the evening they all retired into the Teakettle, where they all managed to sleep very comfortably, while Pussy and the Quangle-Wangle managed the boat.

After a time they saw some land at a distance; and when they came to it, they found it was an island made of water quite surrounded by earth. Besides that, it was bordered by evanescent isthmuses with a great Gulfstream running about all over it, so that it was perfectly beautiful, and contained only a single tree, 503 feet high.

When they had landed, they walked about, but found to their great surprise, that the island was quite full of veal cutlets and chocolate drops, and nothing else. So they all climbed up the single high tree to discover, if possible, if there were any people; but having remained on the top of the tree for a week and not seeing anybody, they naturally concluded that there were no inhabitants, and accordingly when they came down, they loaded the boat with two thousand veal cutlets and a million of chocolate drops, and these afforded them sustenance for more than a month, during which time they pursued their voyage with the utmost delight and apathy.

After this they came to a shore where there were no less than sixty-five great red parrots with blue tails, sitting on a rail all of a row, and all fast asleep. And I am sorry to say that the Pussycat and the Quangle-Wangle crept softly and bit off the tailfeathers of all the sixty-five parrots, for which Violet reproved them both severely.

Notwithstanding which, she proceeded to insert all the feathers, two hundred and sixty in number, in her bonnet, thereby causing it to have a lovely and glittering appearance, highly prepossessing and efficacious.

The next thing that happened to them was in a narrow part of the sea, which was so entirely full of fishes that the boat could go on no farther; so they remained there about six weeks, till they had eaten nearly all the fishes, which were Soles, and all ready-cooked and covered with shrimp sauce, so that there was no trouble whatever. And as the few fishes who remained uneaten complained of the cold, as well as of the difficulty they had in getting any sleep on account of the extreme noise made by the Arctic Bears and the Tropical Turnspits which frequented the neighborhood in great numbers, Violet most amiably knitted a small woollen frock for several of the fishes, and Slingsby administered some opium drops to them, through which kindness they became quite Warm and slept soundly.

Then they came to a country which was wholly covered with immense Orange trees of a vast size, and quite full of fruit. So they all landed, taking with them the Teakettle, intending to gather some of the Oranges and place them in it. But while they were busy about this, a most dreadfully high wind rose, and blew out most of the Parrot tailfeathers from Violet's bonnet. That,

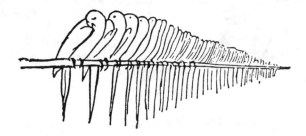

however, was nothing compared with the calamity of the Oranges falling down on their heads by millions and millions, which thumped and bumped and bumped and thumped them all so seriously that they were obliged to run as hard as they could for their lives, besides that the sound of the Oranges rattling on the Teakettle was of the most fearful and amazing nature.

Nevertheless they got safely to the boat, although considerably vexed and hurt; and the Quangle-Wangle's right foot was so knocked about, that he had to sit with his head in his slipper for at least a week.

This event made them all for a time rather melancholy, and perhaps they might never have become less so, had not Lionel with a most praiseworthy devotion and perseverance continued to stand on one leg and whistle to them in a loud and lively manner, which diverted the whole party so extremely, that

they gradually recovered their spirits, and agreed that whenever they should reach home they would subscribe toward a testimonial to Lionel, entirely made of Gingerbread and Raspberries, as an earnest token of their sincere and grateful infection.

After sailing on calmly for several more days, they came to another country, where they were much pleased and surprised to see a countless multitude of white Mice with red eyes, all sitting in a great circle, slowly eating Custard Pudding with the most satisfactory and polite demeanor.

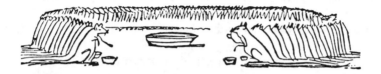

And as the four Travelers were rather hungry, being tired of eating nothing but Soles and Oranges for so long a period, they held a council as to the propriety of asking the Mice for some of their Pudding in a humble and affecting manner, by which they could hardly be otherwise than gratified. It was agreed therefore that Guy should go and ask the Mice, which he immediately did; and the result was that they gave a Walnut shell only half full of Custard diluted with water. Now, this displeased Guy, who said, "Out of such a lot of Pudding as you have got, I must say you might have spared a somewhat larger quantity!" But no sooner had he finished speaking than the Mice turned round at once, and sneezed at him in an appalling and vindictive manner (and it is impossible to imagine a more scroobious and unpleasant sound than that caused by the simultaneous sneezing of many millions of angry Mice), so that Guy rushed back to the boat, having first shied his cap into the middle of the Custard Pudding, by which means he completely spoiled the Mice's dinner.

By-and-by the Four Children came to a country where there were no houses, but only an incredibly innumerable number of large bottles without corks, and of a dazzling and sweetly susceptible blue color. Each of these blue bottles contained a Blue Bottle Fly, and all these interesting animals live continually together in the most copious and rural harmony, nor perhaps in many parts of the world is such perfect and abject happiness to be found. Violet, and Slingsby, and Guy, and Lionel, were greatly struck with this singular and instructive settlement, and having previously asked permission of the Blue Bottle Flies (which was most courteously granted), the Boat was

drawn up to the shore and they proceeded to make tea in front of the Bottles; but as they had no tea leaves, they merely placed some pebbles in the hot water, and the Quangle-Wangle played some tunes over it on an Accordion, by which of course tea was made directly, and of the very best quality.

The Four Children then entered into conversation with the Blue Bottle Flies, who discoursed in a placid and genteel manner, though with a slightly buzzing accent, chiefly owing to the fact that they each held a small clothes-brush between their teeth, which naturally occasioned a fizzy extraneous utterance.

"Why," said Violet, "would you kindly inform us, do you reside in bottles? and if in bottles at all, why not rather in green or purple, or indeed in yellow bottles?"

To which questions a very aged Blue Bottle Fly answered, "We found the bottles here all ready to live in, that is to say, our great-great-great-great-great-grandfathers did, so we occupied them at once. And when the winter comes on, we turn the bottles upside-down and consequently rarely feel the cold at all, and you know very well that this could not be the case with bottles of any other color than blue."

"Of course it could not," said Slingsby, "but if we may take the liberty of inquiring, on what do you chiefly subsist?"

"Mainly on Oyster-patties," said the Blue Bottle Fly, "and, when these are scarce, on Raspberry Vinegar and Russian leather boiled down to a jelly."

"How delicious!" said Guy.

To which Lionel added, "Huzz!" and all the Blue Bottle Flies said, "Buzz!"

At this time, an elderly Fly said it was the hour for the Evening-song to be sung; and on a signal being given, all the Blue Bottle Flies began to buzz at once in a sumptuous and sonorous manner, the melodious and mucilaginous sounds echoing all over the waters, and resounding across the tumultuous tops of the transitory Titmice upon the intervening and verdant mountains, with a serene and sickly suavity only known to the truly virtuous. The Moon was shining slobaciously from the star-bespangled sky, while her light irrigated the smooth and shiny sides and wings and backs of the Blue Bottle Flies with a peculiar and trivial splendor, while all nature cheerfully responded to the cerulaean and conspicuous circumstances.

In many long-after years, the four little Travelers looked back to that evening as one of the happiest in all their lives, and it was already past midnight, when—the Sail of the Boat having been set up by the Quangle-Wangle, the Teakettle and Churn placed in their respective positions, and the Pussycat stationed at the Helm—the Children each took a last and affectionate farewell of the Blue Bottle Flies, who walked down in a body to the water's edge to see the Travelers embark.

As a token of parting respect and esteem, Violet made a courtesy quite down to the ground, and stuck one of her few remaining Parrot tailfeathers into the back hair of the most pleasing of the Blue Bottle Flies, while Slingsby,

Guy, and Lionel offered them three small boxes, containing respectively, Black Pins, Dried Figs, and Epsom Salts: And thus they left that happy shore for ever.

Overcome by their feelings, the four little Travelers instantly jumped into the Teakettle, and fell fast asleep. But all along the shore for many hours there was distinctly heard a sound of severely suppressed sobs, and of a vague multitude of living creatures using their pocket-handkerchiefs in a subdued simultaneous snuffle—lingering sadly along the walloping waves as the boat sailed farther and farther away from the Land of the Happy Blue Bottle Flies.

Nothing particular occurred for some days after these events, except that as the Travelers were passing a low tact of sand, they perceived an unusual and gratifying spectacle, namely, a large number of Crabs and Crawfish— perhaps six or seven hundred—sitting by the waterside, and endeavoring to disentangle a vast heap of pale pink worsted, which they moistened at intervals with a fluid composed of Lavender-water and White-wine Negus.

"Can we be of any service to you, O crusty Crabbies?" said the Four Children.

"Thank you kindly," said the Crabs, consecutively. "We are trying to make some worsted Mittens, but do not know how."

On which Violet, who was perfectly acquainted with the art of mitten-making, said to the Crabs, "Do your claws unscrew, or are they fixtures?"

"They are all made to unscrew," said the Crabs, and forthwith they deposited a great pile of claws close to the boat, with which Violet uncombed all the pale pink worsted, and then made the loveliest Mittens with it you can imagine. These the Crabs, having resumed and screwed on their claws, placed cheerfully upon their wrists, and walked away rapidly on their hind-legs, warbling songs with a silvery voice and in a minor key.

After this the four little people sailed on again till they came to a vast and wide plain of astonishing dimensions, on which nothing whatever could be discovered at first; but as the Travelers walked onward, there appeared in the extreme and dim distance a single object, which on a nearer approach and on an accurately cutaneous inspection, seemed to be somebody in a large white wig sitting on an armchair made of Sponge Cakes and Oyster-shells. "It does not quite look like a human being," said Violet, doubtfully; nor could they make out what it really was, till the Quangle-Wangle (who had previously been round the world), exclaimed softly in a loud voice, "It is the Cooperative Cauliflower!"

And so in truth it was, and they soon found that what they had taken for an immense wig was reality the top of the cauliflower, and that he had no feet at all, being able to walk tolerably well with a fluctuating and graceful movement on a single cabbage stalk, an accomplishment which naturally saved him the expense of stockings and shoes.

Presently, while the whole party from the boat was gazing at him with mingled affection and disgust, he suddenly arose, and in a somewhat plumdomphious manner hurried off towards the setting sun—his steps supported by two superincumbent confidential cucumbers, and a large number of Waterwagtails proceeding in advance of him by three-and-three in a row—till he finally disappeared on the brink of the western sky in a crystal-cloud of sudorific sand.

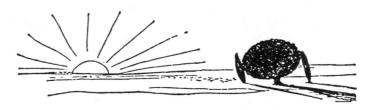

So remarkable a sight of course impressed the Four Children very deeply; and they returned immediately to their boat with a strong sense of undeveloped asthma and a great appetite.

Shortly after this the Travelers were obliged to sail directly below some high overhanging rocks, from the top of one of which, a particularly odious little boy, dressed in rose-colored knickerbockers, and with a pewter plate upon his head, threw an enormous Pumpkin at the boat, by which it was instantly upset.

But this upsetting was of no consequence, because all the party knew how to swim very well, and in fact they preferred swimming about till after the moon rose, when the water growing chilly, they sponge-taneously entered the boat. Meanwhile the Quangle-Wangle threw back the Pumpkin with immense force, so that it hit the rocks where the malicious little boy in rose-colored

knickerbockers was sitting, when, being quite full of Lucifer-matches, the Pumpkin exploded surreptitiously into a thousand bits, whereon the rocks instantly took fire, and the odious little boy became unpleasantly hotter and hotter and hotter, till his knickerbockers were turned quite green, and his nose was burnt off.

Two or three days after this had happened, they came to another place, where they found nothing at all except some wide and deep pits full of Mulberry Jam. This is the property of the tiny Yellow-nosed Apes who abound in these districts, and who store up the Mulberry Jam for their food in winter, when they mix it with pellucid pale periwinkle soup, and serve it out in Wedgwood China bowls, which grow freely all over that part of the country. Only one of the Yellow-nosed Apes was on the spot, and he was fast asleep: Yet the Four Travelers and the Quangle-Wangle and Pussy were so terrified by the violence and sanguinary sound of his snoring, that they merely took a small cupful of the Jam, and returned to re-embark in their Boat without delay.

What was their horror on seeing the boat (including the Churn and the Teakettle), in the mouth of an enormous Seeze Pyder, an aquatic and ferocious creature truly dreadful to behold, and happily only met within those excessive longitudes. In a moment the beautiful boat was bitten into fifty-five-thousand-million-hundred-billion bits, and it instantly became quite clear that Violet, Slingsby, Guy, and Lionel could no longer preliminate the voyage by sea.

The Four Travelers were therefore obliged to resolve on pursuing their wanderings by land, and very fortunately there happened to pass by at that moment, an elderly Rhinoceros, on which they seized; and all four mounting on his back, the Quangle-Wangle sitting on his horn and holding on by his ears, and the Pussycat swinging at the end of his tail, they set off, having only four small beans and three pounds of mashed potatoes to last through their whole journey.

They were, however, able to catch numbers of the chickens and turkeys, and other birds who incessantly alighted on the head of the Rhinoceros for the purpose of gathering the seeds of the rhododendron plants which grew there, and these creatures they cooked in the most translucent and satisfactory manner, by means of a fire lighted on the end of the Rhinoceros's back. A crowd of Kangaroos and Gigantic Cranes accompanied them, from feelings of curiosity and complacency, so that they were never at a loss for company, and went onward as it were in a sort of profuse and triumphant procession.

Thus, in less than eighteen weeks, they all arrived safely at home, where they were received by their admiring relatives with joy tempered with contempt; and where they finally resolved to carry out the rest of their traveling plans at some more favorable opportunity.

As for the Rhinoceros, in token of their grateful adherence, they had him killed and stuffed directly, and then set him up outside the door of their father's house as a Diaphanous Doorscraper.

William Least Heat Moon

Nameless, Tennessee

How to travel? How to see? With Fielding or Fodor in hand or, as
Forster counseled, "Wander aimlessly about"? William Least Heat
Moon's method falls somewhere in between, though much closer in
spirit to the Forster model: He does plan his movements, and he does
have a printed guide, but none of the places he visits will ever have
to fear invasion by tourist hordes. This piece comes from *Blue Highways*, a much acclaimed book published in 1982. What are blue
highways? They are the blue lines on the road map that represent the
back roads of America, where this author traveled in search
of unsung little P.O. towns like this one.

Nameless, Tennessee, was a town of maybe ninety people if you pushed it, a
dozen houses along the road, a couple of barns, same number of churches, a
general merchandise store selling Fire Chief gasoline, and a community
center with a lighted volleyball court. Behind the center was an open-roof,
rusting metal privy with PAINT ME on the door; in the hollow of a nearby oak
lay a full pint of Jack Daniel's Black Label. From the houses, the odor of coal
smoke.

Next to a red tobacco barn stood the general merchandise with a poster of
Senator Albert Gore, Jr., smiling from the window. I knocked. The door
opened partway. A tall, thin man said, "Closed up. For good," and started to
shut the door.

"Don't want to buy anything. Just a question for Mr. Thurmond Watts."

The man peered through the slight opening. He looked me over. "What
question would that be?"

"If this is Nameless, Tennessee, could he tell me how it got that name?"

The man turned back into the store and called out, "Miss Ginny! Somebody here wants to know how Nameless come to be Nameless."

Miss Ginny edged to the door and looked me and my truck over. Clearly,
she didn't approve. She said, "You know as well as I do, Thurmond. Don't keep
him on the stoop in the damp to tell him." Miss Ginny, I found out, was Mrs.
Virginia Watts, Thurmond's wife.

I stepped in and they both began telling the story, adding a detail here, the other correcting a fact there, both smiling at the foolishness of it all. It seems the hilltop settlement went for years without a name. Then one day the Post Office Department told the people if they wanted mail up on the mountain they would have to give the place a name you could properly address a letter to. The community met; there were only a handful, but they commenced debating. Some wanted patriotic names, some names from nature, one man recommended in all seriousness his own name. They couldn't agree, and they ran out of names to argue about. Finally, a fellow tired of the talk; he didn't like the mail he received anyway. "Forget the durn Post Office," he said. "This here's a nameless place if I ever seen one, so leave it be." And that's just what they did.

Watts pointed out the window. "We used to have signs on the road, but the Halloween boys keep tearin' them down."

"You think Nameless is a funny name," Miss Ginny said. "I see it plain in your eyes. Well, you take yourself up north a piece to Difficult or Defeated or Shake Rag. Now them are silly names."

The old store, lighted only by three fifty-watt bulbs, smelled of coal oil and baking bread. In the middle of the rectangular room, where the oak floor sagged a little, stood an iron stove. To the right was a wooden table with an unfinished game of checkers and a stool made from an apple-tree stump. On shelves around the walls sat earthen jugs with corncob stoppers, a few canned goods, and some of the two thousand old clocks and clockworks Thurmond Watts owned. Only one was ticking; the others he just looked at. I asked how long he'd been in the store.

"Thirty-five years, but we closed the first day of the year. We're hopin' to sell it to a churchly couple, Upright people. No athians."

"Did you build this store?"

"I built this one, but it's the third general store on the ground. I fear it'll be the last. I take no pleasure in that. Once you could come in here for a gallon of paint, a pickle, a pair of shoes, and a can of corn."

"Or horehound candy," Miss Ginny said. "Or corsets and salves. We had cough syrups and all that for the body. In season, we'd buy and sell blackberries and walnuts and chestnuts, before the blight got them. And outside, Thurmond milled corn and sharpened plows. Even shoed a horse sometimes."

"We could fix up a horse or a man or a baby," Watts said.

"Thurmond, tell him we had a doctor on the ridge in them days."

"We had a doctor on the ridge in them days. As good as any doctor a-livin'. He'd cut a crooked toenail or deliver a woman. Dead these last years."

"I got some bad ham meat one day," Miss Ginny said, "and took a vomitin'. All day, all night. Hangin' on the drop edge of yonder. I said to Thurmond, 'Thurmond, unless you want shut of me, call the doctor.'"

"I studied on it," Watts said.

"You never did. You got him right now. He come over and put three drops of iodeen in half a glass of well water. I drank it down and the vomitin' stopped with the last swallow. Would you think iodeen could do that?"

"He put Miss Ginny on one teaspoon of spirits of ammonia in well water for her nerves. Ain't nothin' works better for her to this day."

"Calms me like the hand of the Lord."

Hilda, the Wattses' daughter, came out of the backroom. "I remember him," she said. "I was just a baby. Y'all were talkin' to him, and he lifted me up on the counter and gave me a stick of Juicy Fruit and a piece of cheese."

"Knew the old medicines," Watts said. "Only drugstore he needed was a good kitchen cabinet. None of them antee-beeotics that hit you worsen your ailment. Forgotten lore now, the old medicines, because they ain't profit in iodeen."

Miss Ginny started back to the side room where she and her sister Marilyn were taking apart a duck-down mattress to make bolsters. She stopped at the window for another look at Ghost Dancing. "How do you sleep in that thing? Ain't you all cramped and cold?"

"How does the clam sleep in his shell?" Watts said in my defense.

"Thurmond, get the boy a piece of buttermilk pie afore he goes on."

"Hilda, get him some buttermilk pie." He looked at me. "You like good music?" I said I did. He cranked up an old Edison phonograph, the kind with the big morning-glory blossom for a speaker, and put on a wax cylinder. "This will be 'My Mother's Prayer,'" he said.

While I ate buttermilk pie, Watts served as disc jockey of Nameless, Tennessee. "Here's 'Mountain Rose.'" It was one of those moments that you know at the time will stay with you to the grave: the sweet pie, the gaunt man playing the old music, the coals in the stove glowing orange, the scent of kerosene and hot bread. "Here's 'Evening Rhapsody.'" The music was so heavily romantic we both laughed. I thought: It is for this I have come.

Feathered over and giggling, Miss Ginny stepped from the side room. She knew she was a sight. "Thurmond, give him some lunch. Still looks hungry."

Hilda pulled food off the woodstove in the backroom: home-butchered and canned whole-hog sausage, home-canned June apples, turnip greens, cole slaw, potatoes, stuffing, hot cornbread. All delicious.

Watts and Hilda sat and talked while I ate. "Wish you would join me."

"We've ate," Watts said. "Cain't beat a woodstove for flavorful cookin'."

He told me he was raised in a 150-year-old cabin still standing in one of the hollows. "How many's left," he said, "that grew up in a log cabin? I ain't the last surely, but I must be climbin' on the list."

Hilda cleared the table. "You Watts ladies know how to cook."

"She's in nursin' school at Tennessee Tech. I went over for one of them football games last year there at Coevul." To say *Cookeville,* you let the word collapse in upon itself so that it comes out "Coevul."

"Do you like football?" I asked.

"Don't know. I was so high up in the stadium, I never opened my eyes."

Watts went to the back and returned with a fat spiral notebook that he set on the table. His expression had changed. "Miss Ginny's *Deathbook.*"

The thing startled me. Was it something I was supposed to sign? He opened it but said nothing. There were scads of names written in a tidy hand over pages incised to crinkliness by a ballpoint. Chronologically, the names had piled up: wives, grandparents, a stillborn infant, relatives, friends close and distant. Names, names. After each, the date of *the* unknown finally known and transcribed. The last entry bore yesterday's date.

"She's wrote out twenty years' worth. Ever day she listens to the hospital report on the radio and puts the names in. Folks come by to check a date. Or they just turn through the books. Read them like a scrapbook."

Hilda said, "Like Saint Peter at the gates inscribin' the names."

Watts took my arm. "Come along." He led me to the fruit cellar under the store. As we went down, he said, "Always take a newborn baby upstairs afore you take him downstairs, otherwise you'll incline him downwards."

The cellar was dry and full of cobwebs and jar after jar of home-canned food, the bottles organized as a shopkeeper would: sausage, pumpkin, sweet pickles, tomatoes, corn relish, blackberries, peppers, squash, jellies. He held a hand out toward the dusty bottles. "Our tomorrows."

Upstairs again, he said, "Hope to sell the store to the right folk. I see now, though, it'll be somebody offen the ridge. I've studied on it, and maybe it's the end of our place." He stirred the coals. "This store could give a comfortable livin', but not likely get you rich. But just gettin' by is dice rollin' to people nowadays. I never did see my day guaranteed."

When it was time to go, Watts said, "If you find anyone along your way wants a good store—on the road to Cordell Hull Lake—tell them about us."

I said I would. Miss Ginny and Hilda and Marilyn came out to say goodbye. It was cold and drizzling again. "Weather to give a man the weary dismals," Watts grumbled. "Where you headed from here?"

"I don't know."

"Cain't get lost then."

Beryl Markham

Benghazi by Candlelight

In 1936, Beryl Markham became the first person, male or female, to fly across the Atlantic from east to west. In the ensuing years she became more famous for her flying and her flamboyant life-style than for her writing. That status reversed in 1983 when, forty-one years after its initial publication, her *West with the Night* became a surprise best seller. A neglected masterpiece, it had, however, caught the notice of Ernest Hemingway, who wrote to his editor Maxwell Perkins: "Did you read Beryl Markham's book, *West with the Night?* I knew her fairly well in Africa and never would have suspected that she could and would put pen to paper except to write in her flyer's log book. . . . But she can write rings around all of us who consider ourselves as writers." Indeed.

The Greeks of Cyrenaica called it Hesperides. Ptolemy the Third was in love with his wife, so he called it Berenice. I don't know who changed it to Benghazi, but this is not the first act of vandalism the old city has suffered. The cornerstones of Benghazi are the tombs of its founders and their conquerors, and much of its history lies still buried in hand-hewn crypts of rock.

The city lives on an ancient spit of earth between the Gulf of Sidra and a marshy waste, and the shadow it casts has changed shape through the centuries. Once the shadow was slender and small; once it was broad and tipped with the arrogant spikes of a castle; once a monastery lent its quiet contours to the cool silhouette printed each day against the sand. But now, though this castle and this monastery still stand, their shadows are dissolved in the angular blur of modern buildings. The shape of the shadow has changed and will change again because Benghazi sprawls in the path of war. Mars kicks the little city to earth and it rises again, stubbornly, and is reduced again, but not for long. It is a small city with a soul—a grubby soul, perhaps, but cities with souls seldom die.

Like all seaports of the East, Benghazi is blatant and raw; it is weary and it is wise. Once it lived on ivory brought by caravan across the desert, trading this treasure and ostrich feathers and lesser things to an appreciative world, but now it deals in duller stuff—or deals in nothing, waiting for another war to pass, knowing that in reality it has no function except to provide hostelry for armies on the march.

Blix and I landed at Benghazi minutes before night. The Italian airport there is excellent, and so are the hangars. This latter convenience was especially satisfying to me, since I knew that our plane would be whisked away from us at once and put under lock and key (which it was). But there was no satisfaction in Blix's reminder that jail awaited us.

"If they are lenient," he said, "we oughtn't to get more than five years for ignoring that last fort. It was a serious breach of etiquette."

But we got nothing. The frantic efficiency of the garrison at Amseat seemed to have burned itself out before anybody could telegraph the authorities at Benghazi that we were arriving and that our visit to each of the three forts ought to be verified. Nobody cared.

We were, of course, dragged through the usual tedious business of explaining to assorted officials just why we were there—not to say just why we were alive at all; but this had become routine for us as well as for them, and so they were stalemated.

When the order came allowing us to go to our hotel, we left the last of the Government buildings we had been filtered through, and hired a Fiat taxi whose Arab driver had lain in ambush before the official portals from the moment we had entered them. The driver knew most certainly that there was not a hotel room to be had in all of Benghazi, but he chose to break this disheartening intelligence to us gently; he drove from one hotel to another, sitting behind the wheel with a kind of anticipant leer on his face, mumbling in gulps and snatches of English that the next place would surely have rooms enough. But there were none. Mussolini's armies had outmaneuvered us; Benghazi was occupied by fifty thousand polished boots.

In the end we gave up. We were hungry and thirsty and dead tired.

"Find *any place*," said Blix, "*anywhere*, so long as it has a couple of rooms!"

"Anywhere" was the dirty fringe of Benghazi—the fringe that harbors the useless ones of twenty nations, the castoffs, the slag fallen to the side and forgotten until, out of necessity, it must sometimes be waded through or tread upon. "Anywhere" was arrived at through a webwork of pinched and broken streets, dark, swept with the odors of poverty, the trapped and stagnant smells of stagnant life. "Anywhere" was the anywhere of all cities—the refuse heap of human shards.

I sat with Blix in the back of the taxi and felt weariness turn to depression. The taxi slowed, wavered, and stopped.

We were in front of a square, mud building two stories high. A few of its windows had glass, some were spread over with rags. None was lighted. The structure had about it a mute quality; it stared at the street with the soulless expression of imbecility.

Our driver waved his arm toward the doorway which was open and had a yellow light burning somewhere behind it. "Ah!" he said, "I am lucky for you. No?"

Blix paid the fare without answering, and we went into a courtyard walled on all sides and festooned with tiers of tattered washing. The air was dead and smelled dead.

"Nice place," said Blix.

I nodded, but we were not amused. We stood there stupidly, myself in white flying overalls no longer white, and Blix in wrinkled slacks and a shirt that had lost its shape. Everything about us was alien, and so we felt alien— almost apologetic, I think.

A door opened down the yard and a woman came toward us. She had a lighted candle and she lifted it close to our faces. Her own face held the lineage of several races, none of which had given it distinction. It was just a husk with eyes. She spoke, but we understood nothing. Hers was a language neither of us had ever heard.

Blix made gestures with his hands, asking for rooms, and the woman nodded quickly enough and led us into the house and up a flight of stairs. She showed us two rooms not even separated by a door. Each contained an iron bed that cowered under a sticky blanket and had an uncovered pillow at its head. One room had a white enamel basin on the floor, and the jug to match it was on the floor of the other. Everything lay under scales of filth.

"All the diseases of the world live here," I said to Blix.

He was laconic. "So do we, until tomorrow."

He followed our hostess down the stairs in the hope of finding food and a drink while I cleaned my face with handkerchiefs until it was recognizable again. Later I followed too.

I found them both in a kind of musty cell at the rear of the house. The cell had a stove and two shelves and its walls were patrolled by cockroaches. Blix had got a tin of soup and a tin of salmon and he was prying one of these open while he talked to the tired woman and she to him. They had discovered a common language, not really familiar to either, but it served.

"We're talking Dutch," Blix told me, "and in case you haven't noticed it, this is a brothel. She runs it."

"Oh."

I looked at the woman, and then at the cockroaches on the wall, and then at Blix.

"I see," I said.

It was somehow inevitable, in the scheme of things, that this place should be a brothel and this woman the keeper of it. Inevitable, but hardly reassuring, I thought. The scheme of things was a shabby scheme.

Blix got the soup tin open and poured the contents into a pot. The brothelkeeper pressed her fragile shoulders against the wall and stood there nodding her head like a pecking bird. She was dressed in purple rags and they hung upon her in the unmistakable manner of the livery of her trade. And yet, I thought that a transformation would have been easy. Put her in an apron and soak the mask of paint from her face and she could be used as a fit subject for any artist wanting to depict the misery and despair and the loneliness of all women driven to drudgery. She might have been a seamstress, a farmhand's wife, a charwoman, a barmaid no longer maiden. She might have been anything—but of all things, why this?

Blix handed me a plate of soup and, as if it were a cue for her to retire, our hostess backed out of the room, grinning vapidly. She had long since forgotten the meaning of a smile, but the physical ability to make the gesture remained. Like the smile of a badly controlled puppet, hers was overdone, and after she had disappeared and the pad of her slippers was swallowed somewhere in the corridors of the dark house, the fixed, fragile grin still hung in front of my eyes—detached and almost tangible. It floated in the room; it had the same sad quality as the painted trinkets children win at circus booths and cherish until they are broken. I felt that the grin of the brothelkeeper would shatter if it were touched and fall to the floor in pieces.

"You're thoughtful," said Blix.

He ate some of his soup and looked thoughtful too. "Centuries ago," he said, "Benghazi was called Hesperides—'The Garden of the Gods.'"

"I know. The garden needs tending."

Blix produced a bottle of white wine that some Italian soldier had left and his successors had overlooked. We drank the wine out of enamel cups and ate the soup and the cold salmon, fighting a war of attrition against the cockroaches while the meal progressed.

The surface of our wooden table had the culinary history of the house inscribed upon it in grease. There was a candle stuck in a bottle, and a kerosene stove, and four walls, none with windows. The contrast to Shepheard's in Cairo was inescapable, but not mentioned.

Blix preferred to talk about the brothelkeeper. With the patience of a hopeful novelist, he had coaxed out of her, through the exchange of tortured Dutch, a kind of synopsis of her life. It was a life better left in synopsis—too sordid and too miserable even to afford a framework for romance.

As a child of six or seven she had been stolen from her parents and had been brought to Africa on a boat. She remembered that the boat was white on the outside and that the journey had made her sick, but could recall nothing else. She had been beaten occasionally, but not often. There had not been any great, immemorable moments of terror or suffering, nor any particular interludes of happiness that stayed in her mind. None of it was very clear, she had told Blix. She felt no resentment about anything, but lately the thought of the early period, whose dates and places she couldn't remember, had begun to prey upon her mind.

"She was about sixteen," Blix said, "before she learned she had been sold into prostitution. I've read about white slavery, but I never expected to meet a victim of it. She didn't even know it was slavery until somebody told her; she just thought life was like that."

"What does she think now?"

"She wants to get away from here, only she hasn't any money. She wants to get back to the country she was born in. She thinks it might be Holland, but she doesn't know. She says it had trees with fruit on them, and that it got cold sometimes. It's about all she knows. I think she's gone half-witted trying to remember more. It's a hell of a thing to happen to anybody—like waking up and not knowing where you spent last night, only worse. Imagine not knowing where you came from!"

"What was her original language?"

"That's a mystery too," Blix said; "she learned Dutch from a Dutch sailor and picked up Arabic, Italian, and other smatterings in one brothel or another. She mixes them all."

"Well, it's very sad, but you can't do anything about it."

"I can do a little. I'm going to give her some money."

While we were still back in Cairo, Blix had been robbed of two hundred pounds sterling in a barber shop. It was nearly all he had saved from his last safari. I judged that he had about fifty left, but I knew him to be incorrigibly philanthropic. I suppose that any man who attempted to cheat Blix out of a shilling would do it at the risk of life and limb, but if the same man asked for a shilling, he would doubtless get twenty.

"It's your money and your kind sentiment," I said, "but how do you know she's telling the truth?"

Blix stood up and shrugged. "Anybody kicked as far down the ladder as she's been kicked isn't obliged to tell the truth, but I think she told some of it. Anyway, you can't expect gospel for a few pounds."

We went upstairs and tried to get some sleep. I pulled the mattress off my bed and stretched out on the springs, fully dressed. In about ten minutes I could hear Blix snoring with magnificent resonance as he lay on the floor of his room, finding it quite as comfortable, I knew, as he had always found the forest earth that had made his bed for years.

I don't when or how he gave the woman his contribution to the crusade against the downtrodden of this world; I think he had already done it when he announced his intention to me. At least, when we prepared to leave her sad and shabby house of infamy, at 4:30 in the morning, our hostess was awake and fumbling in the kitchen.

I can't say that her face was illumined by a new hope or that her eyes shone with any more inspiring light than they had held the night before. She was dull, slovenly, and as derelict as a woman could be. But she brewed a pot of tea and swept the ever-present cockroaches from the table with an indignant gesture. And after we had drunk the tea and had gone out of the courtyard and up the street, which was still almost completely dark, the brothelkeeper stood in front of her brothel for a long time with the burning candle weeping tallow over her hands. It was the only light that we could see anywhere in the Garden of the Gods.

We crossed the Gulf of Sidra and landed first at Tripoli and then at Tunis, and then we saw green hills again and were finally at the end of the desert and at the end of Africa.

Perhaps, when we took off from the Tunis Airport, I should have circled once or twice and dipped my wings in salute, because I knew that, while Africa would be there forever, it would not ever be there quite as I remembered it nor as Blix remembered it.

Africa is never the same to anyone who leaves it and returns again. It is not a land of change, but it is a land of moods and its moods are numberless. It is not fickle, but because it has mothered not only men, but races, and cradled not only cities, but civilizations—and seen them die, and seen new ones born again—Africa can be dispassionate, indifferent, warm, or cynical, replete with the weariness of too much wisdom.

Peter Matthiessen

Manyara

Naturalist and novelist Peter Matthiessen's journey to East Africa led
to the publication of *The Tree Where Man Was Born* in 1972. In
Kenya's Lake Manyara Park, in the company of elephant expert Iain
Douglas-Hamilton and his wife, Oria, the author came closer to nature
than he will ever care to again.

I had not been in Ndala a half-hour before Iain had us in emergency. A cow-calf herd led by an old cow known as Ophelia came up the river bed to drink at a small pool at the base of the falls. The camp lies on the ascending slope of the escarpment, at the level of the falls; just below, the river levels off, flowing gradually toward Lake Manyara, and downriver a short distance, Ian has a makeshift hide or blind. From here, he thought, he could get pictures of the herd with a complex camera device of his own invention which makes double images of the subject on the same negative; using parallax, animal measurements may be made with fair accuracy without destroying the animal itself. (The animal's shoulder height is a clue to its age, and the age structure of the population—the proportion of old animals to young—is an important indication of population health: Despite the density of its elephant, Manyara at present has a healthy "pyramid" population, with many young animals at the base.) Though the device works, it is so unwieldy that another person must be present with a notebook to record the data, and that other person was me.

We descended the steep bank under the camp and made our way downriver to the hide. The herd was busy at the pool, but I disliked our position very much. The animals were cut off; their only escape was straight back down the river past the hide, which was skeletal and decrepit, utterly worthless. And here we were on open ground, a hundred yards downriver from the steep bank leading up to the camp. . . . "They'll never scent us," Iain decided, setting up his apparatus, an ill-favored thing of long arms, loose parts, and prisms. But scent us they did, before he could get one picture. Ophelia, ears flared, spun around and, in dead silence, hurried her generations down the river bed in the stiff-legged elephant run that is really a walk, keeping her own impressive bulk between man and herd. We didn't move. "I don't think she's going to charge us," Iain whispered. But the moment the herd was safely past, Ophelia swung up onto the bank, and she had dispensed with threat display. There were no flared ears, no blaring, only an oncoming cow elephant, trunk held high, less than twenty yards away.

As I started to run, I recall cursing myself for having been there in the first place; my one chance was that the elephant would seize my friend instead of me. In hopelessness, or perhaps some instinct not to turn my back on a charging animal, I faced around again almost before I had set out, and was rewarded with one of the great sights of a lifetime. Douglas-Hamilton, unwilling to drop his apparatus, and knowing that flight was useless anyway, and doubtless cross that Ophelia had failed to act as he predicted, was making a last stand. As the elephant loomed over us, filling the coarse heat of noon with her dusty bulk, he flared his arms and waved his glittering contraption in her face, at the same time bellowing, "Bugger off!" Taken aback, the dazzled Ophelia flared her ears and blared, but she had side-stepped, losing the initiative, and now, thrown off course, she swung away toward the river, trumpeting angrily over her shoulder.

From high on the bank came a great peal of laughter from Oria. Iain and I trudged up to lunch; there was very damned little to say.

Another day we took a picnic to the Endobash River, which descends in a series of waterfalls that churn up a white froth in its pools. To reach it, one must push a short ways through the bush, and Iain, who has had two bad scrapes in this region, was carrying his heavy rifle. At the river, we climbed to a high pool where we stripped and swam in the cool current. Then we sat on a hot rock ledge to dry, and drank wine with Oria's fine lunch. Afterwards, like three Sunday strollers, we walked down the river bed toward the lake. In the sun and windlessness, enclosed by leafy trees, it was intimate and peaceful, with none of that vast anonymity that subdues one in the spaces of East Africa. But we had scarcely started home when the road a quarter-mile ahead was crossed by a herd of elephants. "Endobash baddies!" Iain said, grabbing his notebook. "I'll have to have a look at those! Load up the gun!" Because we would have to approach on foot to get close to these strange elephants, he needed gun support; Oria would take the pictures. We walked quickly and quietly down the river road.

The elephants were upwind of us, and before we knew it we were right among them, so close, in fact, that we dove for cover underneath the high bush beside us when it quaked with the movements of the elephant behind. A moment later, another walked out into the open a few yards ahead. It was a large cow with odd warped tusks. "Oh hell," said Iain, "it's only Jane Eyre after all." Blithely he stepped out onto the road, hailing his old friend, and there was a moment of suspense when the cow turned toward him. Then she went off sideways, ears flapping in half-hearted threat display, and her herd came out through the wall of bush and fell into step behind her.

Iain's disappointment was matched by my own relief, and Oria, who was pregnant, felt as I did: We had gotten off easily. It was a lovely late afternoon, and whirling along the lake track in the open car, exalted by wine and wind, I reveled in the buffaloes and wading birds in the bright water of the lake edge, and the great shining purple baobab that stands on the lake shore between Endobash and Ndala. But just past the Ndala crossing there were two lionesses in an acacia, and one of them lay stretched on a low limb not ten feet above the road. Oria said, "I'll take her picture as we pass underneath," and Iain slowed the Land Rover on the bridge while she set her camera. At Manyara the tree-climbing lions are resigned to cars, and there is no danger in driving beneath one. But this animal was much closer to the road than most, and the car was wide open: Iain had removed the roof to feel closer to his elephants, and even the windshield was folded flat upon the hood. Lions accustomed to cameras and the faces in car windows see human beings in the open as a threat; when the car passed beneath her, the lioness and I scowled nervously, and I felt my shoulders hunch around my head.

Oria said she had missed the shot, and we passed beneath again, and then again, as she shot point-blank into the animal's open mouth, which was now wide open. "Once more," she said; both Oria and Iain seemed feverish with excitement. "Christ," I said, scarcely able to speak. "You people—" But already the car had been yanked around, and seeing Iain's stubborn face, I knew that any interference short of a blunt instrument would only goad him to some ultimate stupidity that might get one of us mauled. I considered jumping out, but not for long. The lioness, extremely agitated, had risen to her feet, and a man on the ground might well invite attack. Insane as it seemed, I decided I was safer in the car, which proceeded forward.

The lioness crouched, hindquarters high, pulling her forepaws back beneath her chest, and the black tuft of her heavy tail thumped on the bark. Awaiting us, she flared her teeth, and this time I saw the muscles twitch as she hitched herself to spring: Ears back, eyes flat in an intent head sunk low upon her paws, she was shifting her bony shoulders and hind feet. Apparently Iain noticed this, for when Oria murmured, "She won't jump," he snapped at her, "Don't be so bloody sure." Nevertheless he carried on—I don't think it occurred to him to stop—and a second later we were fatally committed.

The lioness hitched her hindquarters again, snarling so loudly as the threat came close that Iain, who should have shot ahead, passing beneath her, jammed on the brakes and stalled. The front of the car stopped directly under the limb, with the cat's whiskers and my whey face less than a lion's length apart; I was too paralyzed to stir. Land Rover motors spin quietly a while before they start, and while we waited for that trapped lioness to explode around our ears we listened to the scrape of claws on bark and the hiss and spitting and the heavy thump of that hard tail against the wood, and watched the twitch of the black tail tassel and the leg muscles shivering in spasms under the fly-flecked hide. The intensity, the sun, the light were terrifically exciting—I hated it, but it was terrifically exciting. I felt unbearably *aware.* I think I smelled her but I can't remember; there is only a violent memory of lion-ness in all my senses. Then Iain, gone stiff in the face, was easing the car out of there, and he backed a good long way from the taut beast before turning around and proceeding homeward through the quiet woods.

Nobody spoke. When Oria pointed out more arboreal lions, we ignored her. I felt angry and depressed—angry at having our lives risked so unreasonably, and depressed because I had permitted it to happen, as if I had lacked the courage to admit fear. At camp, I said in sour tones, "Well, you got some fantastic pictures, I'll say that much." And Iain, looking cross himself, said shortly, "I'll never use them—those were for her scrapbook. I can't stand pictures of frightened animals." Two years before a friend of Iain had given him a book of mine on travels in wild parts of South America, and now he commented that I had taken a few risks myself. But calculated risks to reach a goal were quite different from risks taken for their own sake; I was thinking of George Schaller's account of his solitary camp in the grizzly tundra of Alaska, and the care he had taken, the awareness of every step on river stones, of each swing of his ax—the disciplined courage that it took to live alone in wilderness where any mistake might be the last. What we had just done, by comparison, was merely stupid.

John Maxtone-Graham

The Only Way to Cross

Sadly, this piece is archaeological: Ocean-going passenger ships have gone the way of the dodo and the dirigible in the time-honored manner. The great floating cities, the splendor, the romance—it's hard to believe they are gone. Walter Lord, whose love of ocean liners is not limited to the *Titanic,* wrote: "If the river boats quietly faded away like a genteel lady in polite decline—if the railroads sagged into shameless decay like a Bowery bum—the Atlantic liner was taken from us like a good friend hit by a truck: swiftly, mercilessly and leaving a sudden emptiness that is only beginning to be felt." At least we can take a nostalgic ocean voyage with John Maxtone-Graham.

I have often seen friends off on ships and have as many times regretted doing so. Worse than the midday champagne hangover was a keen sense of deprivation that I was not sailing myself. Then again, for someone who had never sailed, the ship was not at her best. Tied to a pier, the cant of the decks was wrong. There was no engine tremor, and the light through the porthole had none of the brilliance it would later have at sea. The cabin seemed crowded, unbearably hot in summer, with not enough places to sit; the noise from a party next door was overwhelming and even the ministrations of the steward curiously remote.

If companies profited from visitors, stewards did not. They had just completed a laborious turnaround and were as anxious as their passengers to get to sea. In the meantime, they struggled through choked passages, fetching ice and vases, giving directions and reassuring distraught passengers about suitcases. In particularly busy seasons—westbound from Southampton in late August, for instance—it was not unusual for spaces to be double-booked through an agent's error ashore. Stewards would summon an assistant purser to make peace between two families, one ensconced in a suite and another camped furiously on suitcases in the passage. On occasions of this kind, possession was not nine-tenths and the earlier dated ticket won out. It was not uncommon for the displaced passengers, allotted whatever space could be found, to have their fares refunded.

It was and still is a tradition for visitors to ignore the first as well as the subsequent half-dozen calls ashore. On the old Cunarders, a boy in buttons paraded up and down the corridors thumping on a Chinese gong and intoning the time-honored "All ashore that's going ashore!" White Star ships used a bugle and the French a discreet little set of chimes. More recently, the ship's loudspeaker system has been substituted. But the only infallible signal was the ship's whistle, a ludicrously inadequate name for that shattering, majestic blast that rattled the cabin. Tugs whistled but liners bellowed, on a device with no appropriate name that could be heard for miles.

The *Leviathan* had three of them, one on each funnel, while her British sisters were content with two. The *Ile de France* had a trio of steam sirens with ascending scales. But the Germans outdid everyone on the *Bremen* with five. One of them was a new device called a Nautophone which was really a loudspeaker that whistled, an early model of the directional signals that ships have today. When she steamed out of Bremerhaven, she used to blow a triple blast on all five simultaneously, a jolt for those not expecting it. Steam whistles became obligatory on all Atlantic vessels after the fogbound collision of the *Arctic* in 1854; astonishingly enough, they were rare before then. On New Year's and Armistice Day, British ships tied up in port used to serenade the town for minutes on end, until the chief engineer turned off the steam. E. B. White once said: "I heard the *Queen Mary* blow one midnight and the sound carried with it the whole history of departure, longing, and loss." From the shore, the poignancy was very real, but for passengers thus summoned to sea, it was a thrilling, definitive cadence that sent visitors hastily seeking the way out.

Only after they had gone did the cabin make sense. It was a small, admirably planned space that, despite its low ceiling, seemed to grow as each day passed. Companies went to great care and expense to make them attractive. Visitors took lasting impressions away with them, and in the event of rough weather they might become sickrooms occupied for a large portion of the crossing. There was, in fact, a kind of cabin mystique that made it far more personal than temporary quarters of any other variety. Siegfried Sassoon once wrote on the *Berengaria:*

> I like it—this creaking, heaving, vibrating, white, polished box. . . .
> Mischa Elman's cabin was quite close to mine and I often heard him
> playing. . . . The memory of those evening hours has a strange serenity; the drone and thud of the turbines, the pad and patter of feet
> on the deck above, the smell of new paint, the lapping of waves on the
> side of the ship, the sunset seen through my porthole, and Elman
> practicing Bach's *Chaconne.*

Even without the splendid coincidence of a neighboring virtuoso, Sassoon's image is evocative and strangely peaceful, infinitely superior to the negative charm of most hotel rooms.

Predictably, the most lavish suites made the least successful cabins because their designers had successfully insulated them from the ocean. Bunks were replaced by brass beds and portholes, those perfect windows unique to a ship, were concealed behind conventional land-based casements. This determination to disguise honest nautical features has always seemed to me a grave error in judgment. Occupants of less pretentious accommodations, with steel ceilings, exposed pipes, proper bunks and portholes, were reminded that they were indeed on board a ship.

Portholes could be opened in those days, adding the unmistakable aroma of the sea that is sadly lacking on today's air-conditioned ships. This was best done by a steward with a port key, thus avoiding an agonizing contusion known as porthole thumb, a crunch of brass against knuckle that ship's surgeons learned to expect the first day out. Despite this occupational hazard, outside cabins were desirable, not only to passengers who craved light and air but to companies which could, in good conscience, charge more for their occupancy. The Bibby cabin, so called after the line that first implemented their design, was converted from inside to outside by addition of a narrow passage to the ship's side terminating in a single porthole. These doglegs served to reduce the dimension of legitimate outside cabins they displaced, but proved enormously popular and profitable; the *Olympic* had many of them.

On the *Aquitania*, light was admitted to a double rank of inside cabins by the ingenious provision of a platform on the inboard side of the promenade deck. It not only raised occupants of deck chairs conveniently high enough to see over the rail but also left space, within the riser, for a six-inch clerestory window into the cabin directly below. A similar window in the wall immediately behind the chair provided light for a cabin even further inside. It was a clever inspiration, unique, as far as I know, to the *Aquitania*.

Bunks began to disappear around the turn of the century, victims of the pretension of increased tonnage. One of HAPAG's boasts about their *Imperator* was that there were none in first class. They had been a necessity on small, hard-riding ships like the *Kaiser Wilhelm II*, for instance; she was christened "Rolling Billy" by those who sailed on her. During severe storms, when sleeping passengers might be flung to the floor, they served as an admirable restraint. There was also the old steward's trick of stuffing a folded blanket under the edge of the mattress away from the wall, effectively cradling the occupant. But there was a strong prejudice against bunks, particularly the upper ones which children used to fight for.

There were other design aspects common to all cabins, regardless of class or ship, that exist to the present. Bureau tops and shelves had protective rims to keep things from sliding off. Beds and bunks never ran athwartship but fore and aft. Cabin and closet doors could be secured in an open position. A thermos and accompanying glass rested in wall-hung brackets. Bathroom doors had a two-inch sill to prevent slopped-over water from reaching the carpet.

If there was a trunk in the cabin rather than the hold, it was invariably a steamer trunk, so called for the simple reason that it held clothes to be worn exclusively on board. Companies used to store these trunks in European ports free of charge against the passenger's return. This tradition remained long after the original need for special clothing had passed. Salt damp air required an especially serviceable brand of outerwear, and on earlier ships there was in addition a distinctive and presumably unwelcome smell compounded of engines, salt, tar, and bilges. A North German Lloyd brochure for 1908 advised passengers to include sachets among their clothes to keep it out. By the twenties, however, passengers on board large Atlantic liners were unaware of any smell at all, or at least any that could be termed objectionable. A frequent passenger on the *Aquitania* said that the ship smelled only of flowers, soap, and the sea.

Almost everyone who might remember nothing else about a crossing retains an uncanny sense-memory about the way something smelled or sounded. A middle-aged man of my acquaintance still finds that a freshly cut orange takes him back instantly to a cabin he had occupied as a boy on the *Majestic.* (My suspicion is that he had broken into one of those preposterous fruit baskets that were popular *bon voyage* gifts. Why people insisted on sending each other mountains of citrus, I have never discovered; I can only assume that there were those who still associated ocean crossings with scurvy). Teak decks wet with salt spray gave off a distinctive aroma. A woman who crossed only once in her life remembered the smell of fresh paint, another the particular lavender salts used by the bath steward in second class, yet another the unique pungency of a tub full of hot salt water. I remember sailing on the *Queen Mary* on my honeymoon, the first British ship I had been on since the *Georgic* seventeen years earlier; a familiar smell came flooding back, an evocative blend of tea, flowers, floor wax, and whatever stern British antiseptic had survived the war intact.

Sounds were just as familiar. Inextricably associated with those summer crossings from New York was the endless susuration of electric fans behind their marcelled wire guards, hundreds of them swinging back and forth all over the ship. There was also, often unwelcome but like no other sound, the early morning noises of an overhead deck: the scrape of holystones, the wash of the hose and the thunder of the early walkers. Or again, the *slap-slap* that grew and faded as a child in sneakers raced past the cabin along rubber-tiled passageways. Finally, there was the chorus of chattering and creaking as the vessel moved through even a moderate sea; but that was a sea sound, heard only after the harbor had been cleared.

Perhaps the best time to board was for a sailing at midnight. These were quite common in New York between the wars and had been for some time. This most romantic of departure hours was prompted by nothing more exotic than the reluctance of the French to put sleeping cars on the train between Cherbourg and Paris. To ensure that the journey would be taken in daylight, companies using the port scheduled midnight sailings from New York. The Germans had initiated the practice in 1904 for the very same reason; the crossing was thus timed to conclude off Cuxhaven at dawn. Midnight sailings from New York were features of a three-and-four-ship service, a practice with which the two *Queens* could dispense following World War II.

Yet whatever the practicalities involved, night departures achieved a mystical chic that had nothing at all to do with Cherbourg. Part of the ritual was a farewell dinner ashore, at a friend's apartment or a speakeasy, followed by a race through deserted streets to the Chelsea piers. The ship seemed incredibly romantic, floodlit and overrun with people in evening dress. Private gatherings were augmented by dancing in the lounge. This was an effort to focus the noise away from cabins where children, protesting through yawns, had been sent instantly to bed. However, the gaiety was contagious and every child was probably glued to a porthole, determined to remain awake until the moment of departure. To them, it was of no consequence that the ship's log did not acknowledge the start of a crossing until after the pilot had been dropped; their crossing began the moment the view through the porthole moved. There were some children who filled the tub and, risking a wet pillow, thrust their heads under water the better to hear the engines throbbing below.

To their parents on the boat deck above, the lights of New York glittered beyond the bow, somehow already part of another world. There was an extraordinary detached quality about being on board ship even an hour after boarding; perhaps it had to do with the height above land, exaggerated by the darkness. At any rate, it was the hardest time to tear visitors away. The almost hypnotic appeal of sailing at night proved irresistible to many. On more than one occasion, the pilot boat brought in through the dawn chill dinner-jacketed bons voyageurs. If not out-and-out stowaways, they were certainly susceptible celebrants unabashed by lack of a ticket.

Not all departures from New York were accomplished in good weather. I know of no more penetrating winds than blow up the North River in January and there were many midnights when standing on an upper deck was a test of endurance. Manhattan's famous lights could be obscured in gray murk or there might be three inches of slush underfoot. Similarly, conditioned as we are now to summer sailings, all teeth and Instamatics, it is as well to remember that many passengers who boarded then did not do so in a state of high anticipation. As Arthur Davis pointed out, some quite simply loathed the sea and everything on it. A few sailed for desperate reasons, absconding, eloping, or running away from something. There were those who remained on deck long after a face at the end of the pier had dwindled to nothing, and those who retired to their cabins for six days. They blended in with those on business, those on vacation and those with nothing else to do. Behind the neat columns of alphabetized names on any ship's passenger list lay a wealth of compelling drama. Some of it would be exchanged, relished, and forgotten before the crossing was over. Somerset Maugham remarked once that he derived inspiration for some of his best work from observations made on countless sea voyages.

The business of selecting which ship to take was a different matter for each kind of traveler. The professionals, buyers, or salesmen who had to be in London or Paris on a certain morning chose the fastest ship that sailed east as close to their deadline as possible. Although companies welcomed their patronage, they realized that convenience rather than loyalty to any particular line was involved. At the other end of the spectrum were the newcomers, on vacation and sailing for the first time. If the companies knew what dictated their often laborious choice, they did not divulge it. Recommendations from friends, the nationality of the ship, the image of glamor—there were countless reasons.

It was obvious that the large, fast ships were popular with these novices, not only because of their speed but also their prestige. Just as tourists in New York want to see only Broadway's newest and most unattainable hit, so then did passengers want a crack ship's name plastered on their suitcases when they went home. Unfortunately, this particular cachet was denied them since baggage labels never carried the ship's name in print, only the line's. But there were always postcards of the ship, dozens of them bearing an appropriate "X," to be stuffed in the library mailbox before the ship cleared the Narrows. Later, of course, there would be time for a snapshot, taken at the rail by an obliging steward. Included in the photograph was a lifebuoy, irrefutably stenciled with the ship's name.

In between these two extremes of professional and novice were the regulars who sailed annually, always on one ship or on ships of the same line. Families used to book the same cabins and stewards year after year. There was a hard core of passengers who disliked big ships, confessing intense uneasiness on such vast and impersonal vessels. They always sailed on small ones and found the slower pace and traditional appointments more to their liking than the excesses, in decor, tonnage, and shipmates, of the flagships. These intermediary vessels were delightfully conventional and as late as 1925, still carried signs advising passengers that the smoking room was reserved for gentlemen. Christopher Morley was a confirmed small-ship addict but acknowledged some boredom at the length of the slower crossing:

The Channel is opening her arms to us, the queer uneasiness returns, a whole continent of irregular verbs is waiting. And this morning, when I went on deck, I distinctly smelled England. For seven days we had the universe to ourselves but even God, I think, was restless on the eighth.

Immediately after boarding, already fitted out in plus fours and caps, knowledgeable passengers would hunt out the deck steward to reserve a deck chair. This was an errand of some urgency, for the best locations were limited. Companies used to reserve a choice half-dozen for last-minute decisions by steady clients, rather the way theatrical producers retain house seats for every performance. Eastbound, the starboard side was booked first, sheltered as it was from cold northern winds and sunny for most of the day. For Americans, it was the reverse of the old Mediterranean bromide POSH—Port Out, Starboard Home—that used to prevail for Englishmen sailing to India.

To many, the matter of sun was of less importance than the attraction of one's neighbor. For ambitious mothers, a first class ticket was a strategic weapon. It was not uncommon for women with daughters of a marriageable age to choose their ship on the basis of its passenger list. Having pored over the gossip columns for weeks in advance, these determined creatures booked only when convinced that a rich bachelor, preferably titled, would also be on board. After embarking, their first move was to bribe the chief deck steward, heavily and quite shamelessly, to obtain not only the chair location of their quarry but the privilege of engaging the one adjoining it. There was no more ideal opportunity for initiating a friendship. It is curious that people insistent elsewhere on the privacy of spatial insulation submitted quite cheerfully on deck to an intimacy reminiscent of Coney Island. With scarcely an inch separating one from a supine neighbor and bundled in rugs, two adjacent deck chairs in blustery mid-Atlantic had much of the coziness usually associated with a double bed. The impulse to reply to comments on the weather, a book, or the ship in general was almost irresistible. Professional gamblers had known and used the trick for years.

Another ritual observed as the ship cleared New York was reserving a seat in the dining room. There were some passengers who, incredibly enough, intimated to the chief steward that they would consider dining with the captain. Such gaucherie betrayed their ignorance of the tradition that a seat at the head table might be refused but never requested. The captain's table companions were selected only after exhaustive conference, sometimes necessitating careful research by company officials and other pursers of the line. Many among the famous had crossed swords ashore and to revive a feud on board was considered unfortunate. There was a dreadful flap on the *Majestic* once when a distinguished politician found himself seated at the captain's table with his ex-wife's co-respondent. Henri Villar, a fixture on French ships between the wars and dean of Atlantic pursers, was astute at avoiding precisely this kind of gaffe. He was blessed with an encyclopedic memory for names and scandals, and his diplomacy was unmatched.

Failing meals with the captain, parvenus insisted on a table nearby, again unaware that the best ones were elsewhere. Chief stewards usually assigned their new men to the middle of the room where they could be kept under observation; older and more experienced stewards were given tables to either side. The most exclusive tables apart from the captain's were those situated on the balcony (a piece of inside chic obviously restricted to those ships whose dining rooms boasted more than one floor). On the *Olympic* there was only one level, but on the *Berengaria, France, Paris,* and *Mauretania,* the smart set invariably booked upstairs in advance. To do so meant that entrances and departures could be made unobtrusively, and since the upper level was smaller, greater privacy was assured.

It is indicative that the famous were willing to have their soup a trifle colder in return for protection from unwanted attention. A first class ticket was, in effect, an invitation to a house party for a week and for arrivistes, basking in the reflected glow of celebrity was heady stuff. On larger ships, the passenger list always had its quota of important names. Short of remaining in their cabins, there was little their owners could do to maintain their privacy. Pursers were sensitive to any persecution of their eminent clients, and whenever possible discouraged the more insistent boors who could make a crossing unbearable.

Passage down New York Harbor was nearly always auspicious. Astern, the city receded, its glitter cloaked in haze. Attendant gulls breasted the cutting edge of an ocean breeze that came over the bows. The ship passed between Brooklyn and Staten Island through an opening that could only have been called the Narrows. Then a sharp turn to port, into a channel newly dredged at the turn of the century to replace the serpentine curves of the Gedney Channel farther south to Sandy Hook.

This latter had been a natural channel into New York that became increasingly difficult for large steel hulls to negotiate. So a new East Channel was dug, straight to the sea, ultimately named after John Wolf Ambrose. This was particularly appropriate for an immigrant whose success as a contractor in Brooklyn was coupled with a vital concern for New York's waterfront. Ambrose was a rare, avant garde ecologist who devoted considerable energy to discouraging the practice of harbor dumping. At the end of the channel lay a red lightship with his name lettered on both sides.

Down the ladder went the pilot, clutching the last of the mail under his arm as he stepped onto the bobbing tender. Engine revolutions, reduced for his transfer, were stepped slowly up to cruising speed, a process that would take several hours. Cargo booms were secured, hatches sealed, and sea routine begun. For the crew, this meant that double watches, mandatory while in pilotage waters, could stand down. For eastbound passengers in the twenties, sea routine meant the opening of the bar and the start of the crossing.

Mary McCarthy

Venice Observed

What is there left to say about Venice? Even Hawthorne, who struggled
to find an approach to Niagara that could be all his own, would probably throw his hands up in despair and conclude, as Mary McCarthy
has, that "the tourist Venice *is* Venice." Whether perceived as gold or
brass, Venice, that most written about, most painted, most loved of all
cities, is essentially a theme park. This passage is taken from the 1961
book of the same name, now issued in tandem
with her *Stones of Florence.*

No stones are so trite as those of Venice, that is, precisely, so well-worn. It
has been part museum, part amusement park, living off the entrance fees of
tourists, ever since the early eighteenth century, when its former sources of
revenue ran dry. The carnival that lasted half a year was not just a spon-
taneous expression of Venetian license; it was a calculated tourist attraction.
Francesco Guardi's early "views" were the postcards of that period. In the
Venetian preserve, a thick bittersweet marmalade, tourism itself became a
spicy ingredient, suited to the foreign taste; legends of dead tourists now are
boiled up daily by gondoliers and guides. Byron's desk, Gautier's palace,
Ruskin's boarding house, the room where Browning died, Barbara Hutton's
plate-glass window—these memorabilia replace the Bucintoro or Paolo
Sarpi's statue as objects of interest. The Venetian crafts have become side-
shows—glassblowing, beadstringing, lacemaking; you watch the product
made, like pink spun sugar at a circus, and bring a sample home, as a
souvenir. Venetian manufactures today lay no claim to beauty or elegance,
only to being "Venetian."

And there is no use pretending that the tourist Venice is not the real
Venice, which is possible with other cities—Rome or Florence or Naples. The

tourist Venice *is* Venice: the gondolas, the sunsets, the changing light, Florian's, Quadri's, Torcello, Harry's Bar, Murano, Burano, the pigeons, the glass beads, the *vaporetto.* Venice is a folding picture postcard of itself. And though it is true (as is sometimes said, sententiously) that nearly two hundred thousand people live their ordinary working lives in Venice, they too exist in it as tourists or guides. Nearly every Venetian is an art appreciator, a connoisseur of Venice, ready to talk of Tintoretto or to show you, at his own suggestion, the spiral staircase (said to challenge the void), to demonstrate the Venetian dialect or identify the sound of the Marangona, the bell of the Campanile, when it rings out at midnight.

A count shows the Tiepolo on the ceiling of his wife's bedroom; a dentist shows his sitting room, which was formerly a ridotto. Everything has been cataloged, with a pride that is more in the knowledge than in the thing itself. "A fake," genially says a gentleman, pointing to his Tintoretto. "Réjane's," says a houseowner, pointing to the broken-down bed in the apartment she wants to let. The vanity of displaying knowledge can outweigh commercial motives or the vanity of ownership. "Eighteenth century?" you say hopefully to an antique dealer, as you look at a set of china. "No, nineteenth," he answers with firmness, losing the sale. In my apartment, I wish everything to be Venetian, but "No," says the landlady, as I ask about a cabinet: "Florentine." We stare at a big enthroned Madonna in the bedroom—very bad. She would like me to think it a Bellini and she measures the possibility against the art knowledge she estimates me to possess. "*School* of Giovanni Bellini," she announces, nonchalantly, extricating herself from the dilemma.

A Venetian nobleman has made a study of plants peculiar to Venice and shows slides on a projector. He has a library of thirty thousand volumes, mainly devoted to Venetian history. In the public libraries, in the wintertime the same set of loungers pores over Venetian archives or illustrated books on Venetian art; they move from the Correr library, when it closes, to the heatless Merciana, where they sit huddled in their overcoats, and finally to the Querini-Stampaglia, which stays open until late at night.

The Venetians catalog everything, including themselves. "These grapes are brown," I complain to the young vegetable-dealer in Santa Maria Formosa. "What is wrong with that? *I* am brown," he replies. "I am the housemaid of the painter Vedova," says a maid, answering the telephone. "I am a Jew," begins a cross-eyed stranger who is next in line in a bakeshop. "Would you care to see the synagogue?"

Almost any Venetian, even a child, will abandon whatever he is doing in order to show you something. They do not merely give directions; they lead, or in some cases follow, to make sure you are still on the right way. Their great fear is that you miss an artistic or "typical" sight. A sacristan, who has already been tipped, will not let you leave until you have seen the last Palma Giovane. The "pope" of the Chiesa dei Greci calls up to his housekeeper to throw his black hat out the window and settles it firmly on his broad brow so that he can lead us personally to the Archaeological Museum in the Piazza San Marco; he is afraid that, if he does not see to it, we shall miss the Greek statuary there.

This is Venetian courtesy. Foreigners who have lived here a long time dismiss it with the observation: "They have nothing else to do." But idleness here is alert, on the *qui vive* for the opportunity of sightseeing; nothing delights a born Venetian so much as a free gondola ride. When the funeral gondola, a great black-and-gold ornate hearse, draws up beside a fonda-menta, it is an occasion for aesthetic pleasure. My neighborhood was es-pecially favored in this way, because across the campo was the Old Men's Home. Everyone has noticed the Venetian taste in shop displays, which extends down to the poorest bargeman, who cuts his watermelons in half and shows them, pale pink, with green rims against the green side canal, in which a pink palace with oleanders is reflected. *Che bello, che magnifico, che luce, che colore!*—they are all *professori delle Belle Arti.* And throughout the Veneto, in the old Venetian possessions, this internal tourism, this expertise, is rife. In Bassano, at the Civic Museum, I took the Mayor for the local art critic until he interrupted his discourse on the jewel-tones ("like Murano glass") in the Bassani pastorals to look at his watch and cry out: "My citizens are calling me." Near by, in a Palladian villa, a Venetian lady suspired, *"Ah, bellissima,"* on being shown a hearthstool in the shape of a lifesize stuffed leather pig. Harry's Bar has a drink called a Tiziano, made of grapefruit juice and champagne and colored pink with grenadine or bitters. "You ought to have a Tintoretto," someone remonstrated, and the proprietor regretted that he had not yet invented that drink, but he had a Bellini and a Giorgione.

When the Venetians stroll out in the evening, they do not avoid the Piazza San Marco, where the tourists are, as the Romans do with Doney's on the Via Veneto. The Venetians go to look at the tourists, and the tourists look back at them. It is all for the ear and eye, this city, but primarily for the eye. Built on water, it is an endless succession of reflections and echoes, a mirroring. Contrary to popular belief, there are no back canals where a tourist will not meet himself, with a camera, in the person of the other tourist crossing the little bridge. And no word can be spoken in this city that is not an echo of something said before. *"Mais c'est aussi cher que Paris!"* exclaims a Frenchman in a restaurant, unaware that he repeats Montaigne. The com-plaint against foreigners, voiced by a foreigner, chimes querulously through the ages, in unison with the medieval monk who found St. Mark's Square filled with "Turks, Libyans, Parthians, and other monsters of the sea." Today it is the Germans we complain of, and no doubt they complain of the Amer-icans, in the same words.

Nothing can be said here (including this statement) *that has not been said before.* One often hears the Piazza described as an open-air drawing room; the observation goes back to Napoleon, who called it "the best drawing room in Europe." A friend likens the ornamental coping of St. Mark's to sea foam, but Ruskin thought of this first: ". . . at last, as if in ecstasy, the crests of the arches break into a marbly foam, and toss themselves far into the blue sky in flashes and wreaths of sculptured spray . . ." Another friend observes that the gondolas are like hearses; I was struck by the novelty of the fancy until I found it, two days later, in Shelley: "that funereal bark." Now I find it everywhere. A young man, boarding the *vaporetto*, sighs that "Venice is so urban," a remark which at least *sounds* original and doubtless did when Proust spoke of the "always urban impression" made by Venice in the midst of the sea. And the worst of it is that nearly all these clichés are true. It is true, for example, that St. Mark's at night looks like a painted stage flat; this is a fact which everybody notices and which everybody thinks he has discovered for himself. I blush to remember the sound of my own voice, clear in its own conceit, enunciating this proposition in the Piazza, nine years ago.

"I envy you, writing about Venice," says the newcomer. "I pity you," says the old hand. One thing is certain. Sophistication, that modern kind of sophistication that begs to differ, to be paradoxical, to invert, is not a possible attitude in Venice. In time, this becomes the beauty of the place. One gives up the struggle and submits to a classic experience. One accepts the fact that what one is about to feel or say has not only been said before by Goethe or Musset but is on the tip of the tongue of the tourist from Iowa who is alighting in the Piazzetta with his wife in her furpiece and jeweled pin. Those Others, the existential enemy, are here identical with oneself. After a time in Venice, one comes to look with pity on the efforts of the newcomer to disassociate himself from the crowd. He has found a "little" church—has he?—quite off the beaten track, a real gem, with inlaid colored marbles on a soft dove gray, like a jewel box. He means Santa Maria dei Miracoli. As you name it, his face falls. It is so well known, then? Or has he the notion of counting the lions that look down from the window ledges of the palazzi? They remind him of cats. Has anybody ever noticed how many cats there are in Venice or compared them to the lions? On my table two books lie open with chapters on the Cats of Venice. My face had fallen too when I came upon them in the house of an old bookseller, for I too had dared think that I had hold of an original perception.

The cat = the lion. Venice is a kind of pun on itself, which is another way of saying that it is a mirror held up to its own shimmering image—the central conceit on which it has evolved. The Grand Canal is in the shape of a fish (or an eel, if you wish to be more literal); on the Piazzetta, St. Theodore rides the crocodile (or the fish, if you prefer). Dolphins and scallop shells carry out the theme in decoration. It becomes frozen in the state ceremonial; the Doge weds the Adriatic in a mock—i.e., a punning—marriage. The lion enters the state myth in the company of the evangelist and begets litter on litter of lions—all allusions, half jesting, half literary, to the original one: the great War Lion of the Arsenal gate whose Book ("Peace be with you") is ominously closed, the graduated lions from Greece below him, in front of the Arsenal, like the three bears in the story, the King of Beasts with uplifted tail in *trompe-l'œil* on the Scuola di San Marco, the red, roaring lions on the left of St. Mark's who play hobbyhorse for children every day, the lion of Chioggia, which Venetians say is only a cat, the doggy lion of the Porta della Carta being honored by the Doge Foscari . . . From St. Mark's Square, they spread out, in varying shapes and sizes, whiskered or clean-shaven, through Venice and her ancient territories, as far as Nauplia in the Peloponnesus. But St. Mark's lion is winged—i.e., a monster—and this produces a whole crop of monsters, basilisks, and dragons, with their attendant saints and slayers, all dear to Venetian artists. St. Jerome, thanks to his tame lion, becomes a favorite saint of the Venetians.

The twinning continues. The great pink church of the Frari is echoed on the other side of the city by the great pink church of the Dominicans, the other preaching order. And in St. Mark's shelter, near the Pietra del Bando, four small identical brothers, called the Moors, in porphyry embrace two and two, like orphans. The famous Venetian *trompe-l'œil*, marble simulating brocade or flat simulating round, is itself a sort of twinning or unending duplication, as with a repeating decimal.

Venice is a game (see how many lions you can count; E. V. Lucas found seventy-five on the Porta della Carta alone), a fantasy, a fable, a city of Methuselahs, in which mortality has almost been vanquished. Titian, according to the old writers, was carried off by the plague in his hundredth year. How many Venetian painters can you count who, like him, passed three score and ten before they were gathered to their fathers? Jacopo Bellini (seventy years), Gentile Bellini (seventy-eight), Giovanni Bellini, (eighty-six), Lorenzo Lotto (seventy-six), Tintoretto (seventy-six), Palma Il Giovane (eighty-four), Tiepolo (eighty), G. D. Tiepolo (seventy-seven), Pietro Longhi (eighty-three), Alessandro Longhi (eighty), Piazzetta (seventy-one), Canaletto (seventy-one), Guardi (eighty-one). And among the sculptors and architects, Pietro Lombardo (sixty-five), Sansovino (ninety-three), Allessandro Vittoria (eighty-three), Palladio (seventy-two), Longhena (eighty-four). This makes Venice, the nourisher of old men, appear as a dream, the Fountain of Youth which Ponce de Leon sought in the New World. It brings us back to the rationalist criticism of Venice, as a myth that ought to be exploded.

"Those Pantaloons," a French ambassador called the Venetian statesmen in the early seventeenth century, when the astuteness of their diplomacy was supposed to be the wonder of Europe. The capacity to arouse contempt and disgust in the onlooker was a natural concomitant, not only of Venice's prestige, but of the whole fairy tale she wove about herself; her Council of Ten, her mysterious three Inquisitors, her dungeons, her punishments, "swift, silent, and sure." Today, we smile a little at the fairy tale of Venetian history, at the doge under his golden umbrella, as we smile at the nuns entertaining their admirers in Guardi's picture in the Ca' Rezzonico, at the gaming tables and the masks; it is the same smile we give to the all-woman regatta, to the graduated lions, to Carpaccio's man-eating dragon. If we shiver as we pass through the Leads or as we slip our hand into the Bocca del Leone, it is a histrionic shiver, partly self-induced, like the screams that ring out from the little cars in an amusement park tunnel as they shoot past the waxworks. For us, Venetian history is a curio; those hale old doges and warriors seem to us a strange breed of sea animal who left behind them the pink, convoluted shell they grew to protect them, which is Venice.

The old historians took a different line and tended to view Venice as an allegory in which vice and reckless greed (or undemocratic government) met their just reward. They held up Venice as a cautionary example to other nations. But we cannot feel this moral indignation or this solemn awe before the Venetian spectacle. In Ravenna or Mantua, we can sense the gloom of history steal over us like a real shadow. These cities are truly sad, and they compel belief in the crimes and tragedies that were enacted in them. Venice remains a child's pageant, minute and ingenious, brightened with touches of humorous "local color," as in the pageant pictures of Gentile Bellini and Carpaccio. Or, with Tintoretto and Veronese, it swells into a bepearled myth. The sumptuous Apotheoses of the rooms of the Doge's Palace, the blues and golds and nacreous flesh tones, discredit the reality of the Turkish disasters that were befalling the Republic at the time they were painted, just as Giorgione's idylls discredit the reality of the League of Cambrai. With the eighteenth-century painters, the pneumatic goddess is deflated. The pictures of Canaletto and Guardi and Longhi take us back again into playland, with toy boats (the gondolas) and dominoes and masks and lacy shawls, while the pictures of Tiepolo with their chalky tones take us to a circus, in which everyone is a clown or a trapeze artist, in white theatrical makeup and theatrical costuming. Napoleon was at the gates, but it is hard to believe it. It was hard for the Venetians, at the time. For them, their "liberation" from the oligarchy was simply another pageant, another procession, with allegorical figures in costume before the old stage flat of St. Mark's, which was hung with garlands and draperies. At the opera that night, the fall of the Republic was celebrated by a ballet danced by the workers of the Arsenal; the patricians were there, in silks and laces and brocades, gold and silver lamés, diamonds and pearls, and, in honor of the occasion, gondoliers were admitted free.

Everything that happens in Venice has this inherent improbability, of which the gondola, floating, insubstantial, at once romantic and haunting, charming and absurd, is the symbol. "Why don't they put outboard motors on them?" an American wondered, looking on the practical side. But a dream is only practical in unexpected ways; that is, it is *resourceful*, like the Venetians. "It is another world," people say, noting chiefly the absence of the automobile. And it is another world, a palpable fiction, in which the unexpected occurs with regularity; that is why it hovers on the brink of humor.

A prominent nobleman this autumn, rushing to the sickbed of a friend, slipped getting into his motorboat and fell into the Grand Canal. All Venice laughed. But if the count had had his misadventure in Padua, on *terra ferma,* if he had fallen getting out of his car, everyone would have condoled with him. Traffic lights are not funny, but it is funny to have one in Venice over a canal intersection. The same with the Venetian fire brigade. The things of *this* world reveal their essential absurdity when they are put in the Venetian context. In the unreal realm of the canals, as in a Swiftian Lilliput, the real world, with its contrivances, appears as a vast folly.

Joe McGinniss

Top of the World

As America's last frontier, Alaska still permits adventurous travel of the sort that lured all those Victorian ladies to Africa in the last century. Alas, McGinniss's experience at the Top of the World is more accurately termed the bottom of the Barrow. In fact, it mirrors not Mary Kingsley's experience of Africa so much as Joseph Hone's: the land where nothing works. From *Going to Extremes*.

It was not as if Alaska had always been there, lurking, in my mind. I had scarcely given a thought to the place until the spring. Then, one night, a friend named Peter Herford came to dinner and we got to talking about mountains, and he said the best mountains he had ever been in—the finest mountains he had ever seen—were in Alaska. He had lived in Anchorage for a year; his first wife, in fact, had been weather lady for an Anchorage television station. He said the mountains—and the glaciers and lakes and miles and miles and miles of open tundra—started about half an hour from downtown Anchorage and just kept going, in all directions—north beyond the Arctic Circle; west to the International Date Line; further than the mind of an urban Northeasterner could comprehend.

I was by no means a mountain climber; nor, in fact, an outdoorsman of any sort. But I had hiked briefly, a few years earlier, in a small section of the Canadian Rockies, and had once walked, for a month, through the Alps. Those experiences had made a lasting impression. Now I was told, by a man who also had seen the mountains of Canada and Switzerland, that, by comparison, Alaska was a different dimension. It was, he said, a wild and raw and stimulating land; like no place else he'd ever seen. It would, he suggested, change, in some way, anyone who ventured there.

About a month later, a copy of the *National Geographic* magazine came in the mail—an issue devoted almost entirely to Alaska. The magazine was accompanied with a map which was almost wall-poster size. I am a person who likes maps. I read maps for pleasure. Sometimes, on a rainy evening, I will pick up a road map instead of a detective story. Once, after browsing through a map of Pennsylvania, I drove for hours to a town called Oil City, a place I had discovered on the map. I just wanted to see what a town called Oil City, Pennsylvania, would be like. The map of Alaska, however, was like no other map I'd ever seen.

It could not really be called a road map, because, in Alaska, there seemed to be hardly any roads. The state was more than twice as big as Texas—it was, in fact, one-fifth the size of the whole rest of the country—yet contained fewer miles of road than did Vermont. There was not even a road into Juneau, the state capital, which was accessible only by sea or air.

Juneau was also two time zones removed from Anchorage and Fairbanks, the two largest cities in the state. Alaska was so big that it contained four time zones; yet its population was smaller than that of Columbus, Ohio. There were fewer than four hundred thousand people living in the state, and half of them were in Anchorage. The rest were scattered like dots in a connect-the-dots picture in which no one had connected the dots. Alaska was so vast that if a map of it were superimposed upon an identical-scale map of the Lower Forty-eight, Alaska would extend from Canada to Mexico, north to south; and, east to west, from Savannah, Georgia, to Santa Barbara, California. If Alaska's population density, even with Anchorage included, were applied to New York City, the population of the borough of Manhattan would be fourteen.

I spent a long time looking at the map. At the place names: Dime Landing, Farewell, and Ruby. King Salmon, Talkeetna, Yakutat. And at the mountains: the Brooks Range, located entirely above the Arctic Circle, the northernmost mountain range in the world; the Wrangells, parts of which were so inaccessible that they contained peaks of ten thousand feet and more which not only had never been climbed but had not yet even been named. And at the Alaska Range itself, with Mount McKinley as its centerpiece. The highest mountain on the continent; with a vertical rise, from base to summit, that was the greatest of any mountain in the world.

And as I looked I tried to imagine all the empty space; all the darkness; all the cold. And tried to imagine the people who would choose to live in such a place. Alaska was, clearly, a land which one would have to choose. Not a place one just happened to stumble across. In this generation, except for the Natives—the Eskimos, Indians, and Aleuts, who made up 20 percent of the state's population—the adult population of Alaska was comprised almost entirely of people who had decided to leave wherever it was they had been, and whatever it was they had been doing (and, in many cases, whomever it was they had been doing it with), and start over again in a place about which, if they knew anything at all, they knew only that it would be cold and dark and lonely much of the time, and—all of the time—radically different from the place they were leaving behind.

Who were these people? What were they looking for? Or: What were they running from? And what had they found, once they arrived in a land that remained, to a degree unimaginable in any other part of the United States, unchanged by the presence of man?

I knew only two people who had moved to Alaska. I had worked with them on a newspaper in Massachusetts ten years before. One summer they had just upped and went, and I had heard nothing from them, or of them, since.

Eventually I put the map away, but the notion of Alaska lingered on. It began to grow, in fact, and spread: through the spring and into early summer. What was it like up there? What would it be like to be there? I had spent most of the previous couple of years cooped up inside a stuffy little workroom in New Jersey, writing a book that had turned out to be mostly about the inside of my head. I was hungry for something different: something big, something fresh, something new. Like Alaska.

I imagined it as a vast and primal wilderness: an immovable object of sorts; frozen in time. But under attack now—under sudden and vicious assault—by the irresistible forces of big business, modern technology, and greed.

The pipeline, it seemed, was changing the state in ways that would never be undone. Not just physical changes, though they, in places, were severe; but changes in the psychological climate; deep scars cut not just across the tundra, but across Alaska's very soul. The pipeline's advocates had claimed it would be merely a piece of string across a football field; its detractors feared it would be a knife slash across the "Mona Lisa." Whatever it was, it was there now; would soon be complete. The Americanization of Alaska had begun.

It had become a cliché, perhaps, to say that Alaska was America's last frontier; but, if so, it was a cliché that contained a certain irreducible level of truth. For always, in America, there had been an edge; a farthest reach; a place to which one could travel in order to live a different and a simpler sort of life. To escape pressure and progress and crowds. To start anew, perhaps; building on inner resources.

After Alaska, there would no longer be any such place. It began to seem important to me to go there while at least some of its original qualities remained intact. Before it became just another place you went to get rich quick.

I decided that I would travel to Alaska in the fall. That I would remain there through the winter, and through the summer that would follow. That I would wander, as freely as possible, across the land. In order to experience, and, perhaps, to some degree record, what I suspected might indeed be the last days of the last frontier America would ever have.

*   *   *

On Sunday afternoon, Tom and I flew from Prudhoe Bay to Barrow in a twin-engine Atlantic Richfield plane. We flew two hundred miles west, along the empty Arctic coast, in total darkness. The sun had set on November 18 and would not reappear until January 23. There was nothing to see out the window: no lights, no signs of habitation, no signs of life. In the winter darkness it was not even possible to distinguish the coastline. From the Brooks Range to the northern horizon and beyond, there was nothing but flatness and emptiness; ice and snow; darkness and cold.

Barrow was all alone; set apart; as far out on the edge as a place could be. Lying 330 miles above the Arctic Circle, it was Alaska's—and America's—northernmost settlement. With a population of 3,000, 90 percent of which was Eskimo, it was also the largest Eskimo community in the world.

"On Barrow's left," began a description in a Federal Writers Project book about Alaska, "is Siberia; on its right Arctic Canada and Greenland. Facing it are Leningrad, Stockholm, Oslo and London—on the other side of the Polar Mediterranean, the last of the Northern Hemisphere's great inland seas to await the coming of industrial civilization."

From Anchorage, Barrow had seemed even more foreign and remote than Anchorage had from New York City. Very few Alaskans had ever been there, and talking to Anchorage residents about Barrow was the equivalent of asking a citizen of Rio de Janeiro about some obscure river village up the Amazon. As nearly as I could determine, not even the two Anchorage newspapers had ever sent a reporter to Barrow. It was just too far away, too expensive to get to, and, from the perspective of Anchorage—which was the perspective of half the population of the state—there simply did not seem any reason to go.

From the perspective of Prudhoe Bay, however, a trip to Barrow was the essence of high adventure: a journey from the twenty-first century to the nineteenth; from illusion to reality; from the antiseptic soullessness of the ARCO and British Petroleum base camps to an authentic Arctic Eskimo whaling village, which might even turn out to be—who could tell?—the real Alaska that Alaskans did not seem to believe in any more.

We landed at 6 P.M. Our pilot said goodbye, then flew back to Prudhoe Bay for lobster dinner. We dragged our bags through the snow to the Federal Aviation Administration cabin at the far end of the airfield. A warm front had moved into Barrow: The temperature was only 6 below. Barrow claimed to have a taxi service, and, from the FAA building, Tom called a cab. We waited half an hour, then a genuine American-made automobile arrived, driven by a slender young Eskimo man who would not look at us, or speak to us, or help us load our bags into the trunk. Tom explained that racial tensions in Barrow were pretty high. The Eskimos were not fond of whites; especially now, with white money and white technology disrupting the quiet, self-sufficient life that the Eskimos had lived for centuries. For five dollars, however, the driver did agree to drive us six blocks, to the only place where an overnight visitor to Barrow could stay—the Top of the World Motel.

This was the new Top of the World. It had opened in June, replacing the old Top of the World, which had been closed by the state board of health, and which, subsequently, had burned down. The Top of the World was not, strictly speaking, a motel. For a motel you needed motorists, and there wasn't a motorist—or even a highway that was open to the public—within five hundred miles of the Top of the World.

It was a modular wooden building, at the edge of the sea, up on stilts so the water would not wash it away. The sea was frozen now, of course, and there were big chunks of ice on the beach. We climbed a flight of wooden steps and entered the lobby. There was a smell of unflushed toilets as soon as we opened the door. The lobby was filled with Eskimos. Eskimos of all ages, slumped on chairs and on the floor; some sleeping, some just staring into space. In one corner there was a cluster of teenagers, smoking cigarettes and giggling, as if they were waiting on a subway platform for a train. At the far end of the lobby, by the desk, there was a stuffed polar bear, rearing up on its hind legs, inside a glass case. The bear had been shot on the beach, outside the motel, two years before.

A young white woman, sleepy and sullen, was behind the desk. She said yes they had rooms. Sixty-one eighty for a single, pay in advance.

She locked the money in a box inside a safe. Then she told us there was no running water. There had not been running water for three days. The water was obtained from a freshwater lake and was delivered to the motel in a truck. The truck engine had been broken for three days, she said, and the only mechanic in town had been too drunk to fix it, and he was still drunk, and was acting as if he planned to stay drunk until spring. There would not be water until someone could be found to fix the truck. This might mean flying a mechanic up from Fairbanks. If the ice fog in Fairbanks should ever lift.

"Does this mean we can't use the toilet?"

"Oh, you can use it. Just don't expect it to flush."

She gave us more bad news when we asked how to get to the bar. The bar had been shut down since August, closed by the state police. Too many fistfights and knifings. The Eskimos of Barrow, apparently, did not handle their liquor very well.

We asked how to get to the restaurant.

The restaurant, she told us, was closed for the night.

"But it's only ten after six."

"That's right. The restaurant closes at six."

"Closes at six? What do you mean, closes at six? Who ever heard of a restaurant closing at six?"

She shrugged. "Mike wants it closed. Too much of a hassle keeping it open."

The girl left the counter and went back into an office where we could see a tall man with red hair and a red beard reading a paperback book. She closed the door. We were left standing in the lobby.

I went around behind the counter and knocked on the door. The man with the red beard came out. This was Mike.

"How come the restaurant closes at six?"

"Because I feel like closing it at six."

"Is there any other restaurant in town that might be open?"

"Nope. There's no other restaurant in town."

"Well, how about a grocery store, where we might get some food and something to drink?"

"Brower's store, across the street, but that's closed until tomorrow morning."

"Do you mean to tell me that there is no way to get anything to eat, or anything to drink in this town—not even a goddamned glass of water—until tomorrow?"

"That's right," he said. And he smiled, and stepped back into his office, and closed the door. The top of the world. The end of the line.

Tom and I took a walk through the town, to get our minds off our hunger and our thirst and to get away from the smell of the motel. There were Eskimos roaring up and down the streets on snow machines, and barking dogs running in packs. The houses of Barrow seemed to be mostly wooden shacks. Outside the shacks there were big piles of dog shit, frozen to the snow. And frozen whale meat, and caribou meat, cut into chunks. The town was only six blocks long, with the airfield at one end and the frozen Arctic Ocean at the other. There did not seem to be stores of any kind, and I saw no other white people on the streets.

We went back to the motel and shared a pack of wintergreen Life Savers that I found at the bottom of my duffel bag, and an old bag of peanuts left over from a Wien flight. After we ate them we went to bed. My room was overheated and the toilet smell was very strong. I lay in bed with the windows wide open, listening to the buzzing of the snow machines and to the incessant barking of the dogs.

In the morning we went to Brower's store. It had bright electric lights and long rows of nearly empty shelves. Eskimos in heavy parkas trudged slowly up and down the aisles. There were no drinks in the store, no soda, no juices, no milk. And very little food. Because of the ice fog in Fairbanks, no food had reached Barrow for a week. I finally found a dented six-pack of baby food orange juice, a can of sardines, and a package of cheese. They cost twice what they would have in Anchorage.

We walked back to the motel. The restaurant was closed and chained shut. There were about a dozen Eskimos in the lobby. Sprawling, leaning, smoking, dozing. Monday morning in Barrow, Alaska, in December. Nowhere to go, nothing to do. Life in the caboose of the world.

It was just about noon: maximum daylight, which was a dusky, late-twilight sort of thing. Eskimo kids wandering the streets. Hanging out, hanging around, nothing to do. Twenty below and darkness at noon. The only kind of winter they'd ever known. A lot of them in school, but a lot, apparently, not bothering to go.

Everyone in Barrow seemed to have a snow machine. At least one, maybe two. The people would roar up and down the streets on them, and would leave the motors running while they went inside to shop or to visit, and the machines would send fumes and racket into the air. Besides the one or two working snow machines for each adult, there seemed to be three or four already broken. Discarded machines, which cluttered yards, porches, vacant lots, and even the tundra at the edge of the town. If a machine of any kind broke down in Barrow, it was thrown away, not repaired. Though, more often than not, the owner didn't even bother to throw it away. He would just let it sit there where it died. And buy a new one. Plenty of government money, and oil money, for that. The old machines would sit there for years, for decades, scarcely changing. Abandoned, broken cars would sit in front of houses, their interiors stuffed with plastic bags containing garbage. I peeked at the odometer of one: It registered only 2,000 miles.

I kept walking past all the houses and past the Top of the World Motel and right out onto the ice on the ocean. I walked maybe half a mile out. It was hard to judge distance, staring straight ahead, plenty warm in my parka, looking at the darkness to the north.

The ice was chunky and rough, full of big bumps and ridges. I picked my way among them, hoping I would not meet a polar bear. One had been seen a couple of days earlier, crossing the Point Barrow road.

I walked slowly around the bigger chunks of ice. As if by walking slowly I was somehow giving myself a better chance against a bear. I reached a large flat chunk of ice which rose about four feet above the surface. It was rough enough on the sides for my boots to catch hold and I was able to climb up on top.

From this vantage point, I looked slowly in all directions. No bears. Nothing moving. Nothing alive, out on the ice. To the north, the emptiness; the void. To the south, the edge of the continent. The edge of life in North America. From the mayor, from the electric typewriters in the municipal office building, from the talk of closed-circuit TV, it was only a fifteen-minute walk to reach this.

The day was dull gray, with a slightly brighter light to the south. From half a mile out, the racket of the snow machines seemed more the distant buzzing of a chainsaw. Smoke was rising from dozens of chimneys: the skyline of Barrow.

I could see occasional headlights as trucks passed along the shore road that led out to Browerville, a smaller cluster of houses across a lagoon from the main part of the town. The road then went five miles north to Point Barrow. At Point Barrow there was a DEW line station, and the Naval Arctic Research Laboratory, where a few scientists studied aspects of Arctic biology and charted the movements of polar ice. This was the edge. The ragged edge.

But from half a mile out there seemed a warmth, a feeling of life to the shacks all jammed together like that. I would turn and face north: toward the void. The absence of life. The choppy ice extending another thousand miles, to the North Pole, and beyond.

Then I would turn and face Barrow. There was now a faint trace of color, a thin orange rim to the far south. With smoke and traces of ice fog mingling at the edge of the town.

From that distance, half a mile out, Barrow was, for the first time, almost appealing. It was the edge, but, from this perspective, for the first time, it semed not the end but the beginning.

It was as if I had walked off the edge of the earth and were now floating free, in the void, staring back. The smells and noise and the shabbiness receded, and Barrow became a still life: the dawn of man.

Patrick F. McManus

But Where's the Park, Papa?

National parks in the United States have become famous as places to avoid, at least in the summer. Only certified masochists are any longer permitted in Yellowstone Park or Yosemite in July and August, although Glacier Park and Grand Teton are not yet so choosy. McManus, a columnist and oracle for *Field and Stream*, wrote this a decade ago.

On one of the doggier of last summer's dog days, my family and I simmered grimly in our own juices as we toiled along, a bit of the flotsam in a sluggish river of traffic. Our rate of speed was somewhere between a creep and an ooze. Heat waves pulsed in a blue sea of exhaust fumes. Blood boiled and nerves twitched. Red-faced, sweating policemen would occasionally appear and gesture angrily at the drivers to speed it up or slow it down. At least one of the drivers felt like gesturing back.

We were on one of those self-imposed exiles from the amenities of civilized life popularly referred to as vacations. I was in my usual vacation mood, which is something less than festive. My kids were diligently attempting to perfect the art of whining, while my mother expressed her growing concern and disbelief at the scarcity of restrooms along this particular stretch of highway. Whenever the speed of the traffic slowed to the ooze stage, my wife took the opportunity to spoon tranquilizers into my mouth from a cereal bowl, all the while urging me not to enlarge the children's vocabulary too far beyond their years. Mother, in her increasing anxiety, already had them up to about age forty-seven.

"Hey," one of the kids paused in mid-whine to complain. "You said you was gonna take us to a national park!"

"Clam up!" I counseled him, drawing upon my vast store of child psychology. "This *is* a national park!"

To keep the children amused until we found a park campsite, my wife invented one of those games which start with the idea of increasing the youngsters' awareness of their environment and end with them beating each other with tire irons in the back seat. As I recall, this particular game resulted in a final score of three, six, and eight points. Each kid got one point for every square foot of ground he spotted first that didn't have any litter on it.

I can recall a time when tourists visiting national parks appeared to be folks indulging themselves in a bit of wholesome outdoor enjoyment. Now they seem to have a sense of desperation about them, like people who have fled their homes nine minutes before the arrival of Genghis Khan. Most of them no longer have any hope of seeing unspoiled wilderness, but they have heard rumors that the parks are places where the ground is still unpaved. Of course, if they want to see this ground they have to ask the crowd of people standing on it to jump into the air in unison.

The individuals I really feel sorry for are the serious practitioners of littering. Some of these poor souls have hauled their litter a thousand miles or more under the impression they would have the opportunity of tossing it out into a pristine wilderness, only to discover that they have been preceded by a vast multitude of casual wrapper-droppers. (The Park Service does make a heroic effort to keep the litter cleared from along the highways but is handicapped because its rotary plows don't work well on paper and beverage bottles.)

Since there are many people who get the bends and have to be put into decompression chambers if they get more than thirty minutes from a shopping center, the parks, at least the one we were in, provide the usual cluster of supermarkets and variety stores. Here it was possible to buy plastic animals at a price that suggested they were driven on the hoof all the way from Hong Kong. I refused to buy my youngsters any of these souvenirs. I told them they should find something that was truly representative of the park, and they did. Each of them picked up and brought home a really nice piece of litter.

I find the rangers to be about the most enjoyable thing in the national parks anymore. I always make a point to take my children by the ranger station to watch the rangers climb the walls. In recent years the rangers have been going on R-and-R in such places as New York and Los Angeles in order to get away from the crowds and noise and to get a breath of fresh air. By the end of the peak season they have facial twitches so bad they have to wear neck braces to guard against whiplash.

The park bears aren't what they used to be either. Most of the bears you see along the roads look as if they've spent the past five years squatted in a chair before a television set drinking beer and eating corn chips. Half of them should be in intensive care units. They have forgotten what it is that a bear is supposed to do. If panhandling along the roads were outlawed, they would probably hustle pool for a living. A dose of pure air would drop them like a shot through the heart from a .44 Magnum. Any bear that wanders more than a mile from the road has to carry a scuba tank on his back filled with carbon monoxide. As far as spectacle goes, the bears just don't have it anymore. I'd rather drive my kids across town to watch their Uncle Harry nurse a hangover. Now there's a spectacle!

Camping in a national park is an invigorating experience. My seventy-year-old mother went off looking for a restroom among the sea of tents, cabins, and campers. After about an hour of unsuccessful searching, she was loping along looking for a path that led off into the wilderness and came upon a wild-eyed man loping in the opposite direction.

"Sir," she said as they passed, "could you tell me where I can find a restroom?"

"I don't know, lady," he shouted over his shoulder. "I've been here for three days and haven't found one yet!"

Some parks still have excellent fishing in them if you can find it, but on the easily accessible streams you would have better luck digging for clams in Montana. There are of course the tame fish planted by the park service, and these can be caught with a bent pin on the end of a clothesline with bubble gum for bait. The sight of a live insect or even a dry fly makes them nauseous. Catching one of them is almost as exciting as changing the water in the goldfish bowl. After being dumped into one of the park streams the fish quickly adjust to their new environment, however, and within a week or two are consuming vast quantities of soggy hot dog buns and cigarette butts. (Scientists estimate that eating one of these fish is equivalent to eating two loaves of bread and four packs of cigarettes.) If anti-littering eventually catches on, a lot of fish will be up alongside the highways with the bears. They'll be begging smokes from tourists.

Many people are under the mistaken impression that transistor radios come from Japan, but that is not the case. Transistor radios breed in national parks and from there move out to infest the rest of the country. Their mating cries at night are among the most hideous sounds on earth, approximately on the order of those of catamounts with arthritis. The offspring are pro-digious in number. During the day you can see hundreds of youngsters carrying the baby transistor radios around the park. I proposed to a park ranger that a season be opened on the adults of the species with an eye to limiting the population growth. He said he himself was all for it but the park regulations forbid hunting of any kind.

The site on which we finally pitched our tent was in the middle of a vast caldron of writhing humanity. This made it easy to meet interesting people. Several times I chatted with the fellow next door about his hobby of pumping the exhaust from his car into our tent. The fellows on the other side of us were members of a rock band. For a long time I thought they were just pounding dents out of their bus, but it turned out they were practicing. Their rendition of "A Truck Full of Empty Milk Cans Crashing into a Burglar Alarm Factory" was kind of catchy, but the rest of their stuff was much too loud for my taste. People would also drop into our tent at all hours. They would look about for a second or two, a puzzled expression on their face, then leave. Then we discovered that the trail to the restroom passed under our tent. This discovery made Mother noticeably happy and she vanished like a shot up the trail.

I decided that the best thing to do was to give up on tenting and try to get into one of the park tourist cabins. After mortgaging our home and indenturing two of the children for fourteen years, we managed to scrape together sufficient rent for two nights. The architecture of the cabin was about halfway between Neoshack and Neolithic. Frank Lloyd Wright would have loved it because it blended so naturally into its surroundings—a superb replica of a hobo jungle.

The only good thing about the cabin was that the roof didn't leak all the time we were there. Of course if it had rained, there's no telling what might have happened. It is doubtful that the seine net used for roofing would have kept us dry, but I figured we could always set up the tent inside the cabin.

Our days at the park were filled with the delights of viewing the marvelous phenomena. There was the spring hot enough to boil an egg in, and someone was running a scientific experiment to see if it would do the same thing for an old newspaper and a half-eaten hamburger. Reflection Lake was truly beautiful, with the scraggly spruce trees around its edges so sharply defined in the glass on the lake bottom that you could make out the hatchet marks on them. The Painted Rocks were interesting in their own way, especially where park employees had managed to remove some of the paint. The kids seemed to enjoy the ancient hieroglyphics to be found everywhere: "Fred & Edith Jones, Peanut Grove, Calif.—1968," etc. Then there were the antics of the wildlife. Once we were fortunate enough to observe two mature male *Homo sapiens* locking horns in a territorial dispute over a parking spot.

Just when I finally found a way to amuse myself in the park, my wife insisted that we leave. She was afraid I would get arrested for trying to poach transistor radios with rocks. Also, while attempting to photograph a bald woodpecker, she flushed a covey of young people deeply engrossed in their own particular study of nature. (If the truth were known, she was probably more flushed than they.) Anyway, she said the only vistas she wanted to see for some time to come were the insides of the four walls of our mortgaged house. We hit the road for home the next day.

Next summer I think I'll skip the national parks and take my family to a place I know up in the Rockies. It doesn't have all the conveniences and accommodations of a national park, of course. The bears aren't especially friendly (but if you do see one, he doesn't look as if he recently escaped from an iron lung). If you have the sudden urge to buy a plastic animal, you just have to grit your teeth and bear it. The scenery isn't all that spectacular, unless you get a little excited over invisible air. The place doesn't have even a geyser, but when I get there it will at least have an old geezer. Some people like to watch him sit on a log and smoke his pipe, in particular a certain middle-aged woman and four ignorant kids. If you need more spectacle than that, you can always go to a national park.

John McPhee

A Guide to Fielding's Europe

Simplex, complex, duplex, Rolex—all are rolled into Temple Fielding, whom some call simply Templex (no doubt out of earshot). As the man behind *Fielding's Guide to Europe* (and the rest of God's creation), he has done for tourism what Baedeker did for travel, and millions are grateful to him. Some are not. This excerpt comes from McPhee's delicious *New Yorker* profile titled "Templex."

Temple Hornaday Fielding was thirty-two—a freelance writer married to a literary agent and living in New York City—when he went to Europe in 1946 to collect information for the first of the guidebooks that were to make him the most widely consulted travel writer in history. His book, *Fielding's Travel Guide to Europe*, did not tell people what to see. It told them—in earnest dedication to the comforts and pleasures of the traveling creature—what to spend, and where. Fielding was soon operating virtually without competition as counselor to the millions of American tourists who have traversed Europe in the postwar years, and his closest competitors became, as they have remained, scarcely visible behind him. Therefore, it has been Temple Fielding who, in large part, has directed the great flow of American tourist dollars to Western Europe. For some twenty years, he has sprayed money in whatever direction he has chosen, and, needless to say, he is looked upon as a kind of national hero in any number of European countries. He has been decorated frequently, and as he approaches an airport in the course of one of his long annual trips, he slides into his lapel the colors of the highest order he has yet received from the country upon which he is about to descend. He is feared as well, for his disapproval can shrink a business and his wrath can kill one. But he does not hunt things down so much as he hunts them up. He wants to praise. He wants to find things that he can recommend. And when he finds them, he leaves new fortunes behind him. Towns and whole regions—Zermatt, for example, and the Algarve coast of Portugal—have grown rich on booms traceable to his words, and all over Europe there are storekeepers, restaurateurs, and even artists who owe their extraordinary prosperity to him. In Paris not long ago, four little American girls went with their mother and father to a glove shop that is recommended in Fielding's book. This was in the off-season, but the place was stuffed with large North American ladies, and more were pressing in at its doorway. The little girls were determined to get the gloves they had come for, which were on display in the shop window, so they pressed in, too, with their mother, until they had all disappeared from view. Their father wandered off. In another store, where one middle-aged Frenchwoman was quietly shopping, he saw gloves identical to the ones that his children were fighting for a few doors away. Some years ago, Fielding met an English painter who had ample talent but no money, and who traveled around on a bicycle—the only vehicle he owned. Fielding admired the painter's work very much. He said so in the *Travel Guide.* And now the painter—who will readily say that he owes everything to Fielding—goes around in an automobile that cost him $25,000.

In his younger days, Fielding slept with some frequency in pensions and cheap hotels, but he is now fifty-three and he has slept in his last fleabag. He stays in the most expensive hotel suites in Europe, and not long ago, characteristically, he blew $1,700 in five days at the Bristol in Paris. In some other ways, he has not evolved as much as one might expect. Since 1951, he has been a year-round European resident, yet he speaks no language but English. His home for nearly all of that time has been in Formentor, on Mallorca, but, in the words of a Spaniard who is one of Fielding's closest friends, Fielding "cannot make a Spanish sentence." The Spaniard repeats, "Not one sentence. He cannot say three words. It is not given to him. I have been with Temple at times when he has gotten up to try to give a speech of thanks to a group of Spanish people. When this happens, I look at my shoes. I stare at the floor. I die." Except during scenes like this one, Fielding speaks in English wherever he is, and he would do so by choice if he had a choice to make, for he tries to keep himself at all times in the position of the usual American tourist facing European situations and unable to speak the languages of the Continent. He speaks very slowly, syllabically, precisely, and he explains that this is the result of a professional lifetime of trying to make himself understood to Europeans. . . .

When Fielding is in Dublin, he stays in one of four suites on the top of the Gresham Hotel, and they are his favorite hotel rooms in the world. He glows like an ember when he describes these rooms. Each suite has a kitchen, a sitting room, two baths, and a bedroom. Peat burns all day in the fireplaces. Each sitting room has a fully stocked bar, and a chambermaid takes notes on what is consumed. Floor-to-ceiling windows look out on a terrace, beyond which the city and the River Liffey are spread to view. One has one's private butler there. The mattresses are "good Irish ones." The flowers are fresh, and the cost, in Fielding's view, is virtually nothing—$87 a day. In the way that some tourists go from cathedral to cathedral, Fielding goes from hotel to hotel. His interest is obviously supra-professional. He says that he can remember the details of every hotel room he has ever stayed in. A hotel room is a work of such artistic consequence to him that he visibly shudders when he remembers some of the failures he has slept in, and he says, "Thank God we've reached the point where we don't have to stay in horrible, sickening, grimy dumps any longer." When he is in Venice, he stays in Room 110 at the Gritti Palace. "The door is here—there's a round table here," he says, recreating the room in space. "The fabulous thing is the overall Venetian taste—the deep golds, the rich colors. One really feels that one is in old Venice, fine Venice, Venice in its glory. Yet the Gritti is modern as hell in its comforts. It's damned expensive." The room at the Gritti is one of three coequal favorites that he places just after the suites in Dublin, the others being the penthouse of the Bristol in Paris and 471–473 at the Palace Hotel in Madrid. The Bristol penthouse is a duplex with a private internal elevator that lifts the paying guest—he is paying NF 1,150 per day—to either of two Louis XV bedrooms or takes him down to the writing room, the paneled library, the sitting room, and the dining room, which seats twelve. All this agrees with Fielding, but is not as close to home as the flowing rooms and high ceilings of 471–473 at the Palace Hotel in Madrid. "Sheer comfort," Fielding says. "I just love that place." He has stayed in 471–473 for nearly a year in accumulated time. When distractions have slowed his work in Formentor, he has gone to the Palace to write, and has remained in 471–473 for more than a week without once coming out. Fielding thinks the Ritz in Lisbon is the finest modern hotel in the world. He is awed by the virtuosity of the Negresco in Nice, which has 250 rooms, each different in décor from all the others. He has a special fondness for the Love Nest, a downy suite in the Dolder Grand in Zurich. And he greatly admires the "client attention" at the Savoy in London, where the staff outnumbers the clients by three to one, and where files are kept on clients' tastes and preferences. "Clients" is the Savoy word. There are no "guests" there. In the early days of Fielding's clienthood, he once asked for guava jelly, and the Savoy kept giving it to him until he was thoroughly sick of it. Finally, after nine years, he developed enough courage to ask the Savoy not to give him guava any more.

Fielding last went to the Eiffel Tower sixteen years ago, and he wouldn't have gone then if it had not been for a business luncheon in the tower restaurant. Once every ten years, he will surprise himself and go to Westminster Abbey, but he is not a sightseer. He explains, "When we started, we worked through national tourist offices, and we were dragged by the earlobes through every goddamned gallery, tomb, cathedral, castle, and stoa. We had such a tremendous overdose that now I just loathe sightseeing. When a city builds a new TV complex that is really spectacular, or when a new cathedral is built, like the one at Coventry, we go see it, but the tombs and the statues and so on—to hell with them." He prefers to absorb culture in optimum comfort, and he reads books in bed by the hundred each year. He does go with some frequency to the major art museums of Europe. His taste in museums has wide dimensions. On visits to London, he almost always has a fresh look at the waxen forms at Madame Tussaud's. "I enjoy them," he says. "Maybe it's ghoulish, but it's fun." Fielding publishes a *Selective Shopping Guide to Europe,* but his contribution to it is prose alone. "I hate shopping," he says simply. "When we're traveling, Nancy does 99.999 percent of the shopping." Although his reports on nightclubs are the result of tireless visits, he despises nightclubs, too. Thus, for the most part, Fielding's Europe narrows down to hotels and restaurants, and when he is in a favored example of the one or the other, he is in the Europe he knows and likes best. Fielding's Switzerland, for example, consists not only of the Love Nest in the Dolder Grand but also of Bündnerfleisch and rösti potatoes. His Germany is primarily sausage. His Belgium is a coiled green eel. His France is, in his own words, "fresh crevettes with a Chevalier-Montrachet 1947, pheasant en papillote with wild rice, mashed turnips, romaine salad, a Romanée-Conti 1937, ice-cold melon, a Port du Salut, a Delmain Cognac—about 1928—and espresso without caffeine." Experts who have scanned this menu say that Fielding may not show much confidence in his choice of wines but that he more than redresses the balance by slipping turnips into a meal like that one—surely the mark of an experienced fork who has been through all the phases of gourmandise and now encounters himself coming the other way. As rarefied as his buds may be, however, Fielding's taste remains American, and more often than not he likes to secure his day with a dry martini. When this has presented a problem, he has overcome it. Some years ago, martinis of any quality were insignificantly available in Europe, but now there are good ones from Finnmark to Andalusia, and it is possible that Fielding will be remembered as Johnny Martiniseed, the man who ingratiated himself with several thousand European bartenders and then—almost always getting behind the bar himself—taught them how to make his favorite drink.

By and large, Fielding's Europe is peopled by American tourists, and if the fabric of his Europe were to be pulled away from Europe as a whole, a great deal would remain. "We have led people into certain byways," he will say, "but in general we try to follow tourist patterns." In the current *Guide,* Fielding has written fifteen hundred words on Marseilles and four thousand on Torremolinos, a coastal village in southern Spain that has had a fad as a resort in recent years. The *Guide* has a chapter on each of twenty-five countries and also has separate chapters on Mallorca, the Greek islands, and the French Riviera. Fielding is exhaustive on the places he covers and unconcerned with other places. "A place that's a hundred percent French or ninety-nine percent Italian may be great, but an American just wouldn't be happy there, so we leave it out of the book," he once said to me. "We won't go to Trieste this year. It's not too popular with Americans." It is no strain on him to scratch out ten thousand square miles of southern Italy ("There's nothing between Salerno and Reggio—just a waste") or a similar chunk of Germany ("The area between Düsseldorf and Hamburg is not important"). He has never been to Sardinia or Corsica. In his England, there is practically nothing between London and York. He describes Spain as "an insipid picture in a million-dollar frame," and with the exception of Madrid and the tourist triangle in Andalusia—Granada, Cordoba, Seville—his Spain is predominantly coastal. He dislikes some European tourists, and where they go he goes lightly, if at all. The upper Adriatic coast of Italy is a badlands for guidesters, he pointed out to me, because so many Germans go there in summer that even the signs along the road are in German. "Germans are O.K. in ones or twos," he said, "but they are terrible in groups. You can spot a German group a mile away, and hear them farther than that."

Fielding thinks that the most commendable traveler in Europe is the Englishman, who as a rule is knowledgeable and well-mannered. Fielding has been told by his hotelier friends that English people will accept absolutely anything that is served to them, and no matter how dismal things get they will not complain. Apart from this unmatchable type, the American, in Fielding's view, is the best tourist in Europe. The day of the incandescent creature in the Hawaiian shirt may not have ended, but the American rube, once the only traveling boor on the Continent, now has peers from many nations. European tourists are all over Europe each summer, and one has to hunt for gauche Americans among the competition. Meanwhile, the ungauche Americans—or most Americans who take vacations in Europe—generally stand out in the other direction. "The Americans come right after the English," Fielding told me. "They're the most open. They're quiet. They don't complain. They are mannerly. They're honest. They tip well. They're generous of themselves. They dress well, or most of them do. One idiosyncrasy that astonishes Europeans is that Americans write letters of appreciation for extra kindnesses. In a hotel, if they're not satisfied they just pay and move out. The image of the American tourist has completely changed among hoteliers over here. Of course, there are some Americans who are loathsome. Some of them put their cowboy boots up on restaurant tables. Some of them try to haggle in Fortnum & Mason." Fielding's book is full of schoolmarmish warnings about sloppy dress and gross manners. He has done a great deal to improve the image he now applauds, and he wants to keep it that way. Once when I was with him in a Spanish city, he ran after a taxicab, stopped it, stuck his head into it, and bawled out three Americans whom he had seen being rude to an elderly Spanish woman a few moments before. Recently, he received a number of letters in which tourists complained about some of the fine hotels of Europe. Comfort may be important to Fielding, but never at the expense of atmosphere. He inserted a thousand-word sermon in his book telling his readers that what they were complaining about was, among other things, precisely what Europe had to offer them. When Europeans deride Americans in Fielding's presence, they sometimes have a scene on their hands. "We won't tolerate anti-American talk," he said. "We used to be polite about it, but no longer. We flip on this, Nancy and I both."

Fielding said that the most frequent criticism of his book is that "we shoot for the snob reader," and he added, "Possibly there is a great deal of justice in it." But he doesn't follow the strawberries. In *The Rich Man's Guide to Europe,* Charles Graves uses that expression to describe the high-snob itinerary—being at Baden-Baden for Race Week, seeing the polo at Cannes— and what is hypertypically nibbled along the way. One knows when to be in Saint-Moritz or Deauville and when not to be. One tries to be in Gstaad in February for the Gala at the Palace Hotel—if one is one again after New Year's Eve in the Hôtel de Paris in Monaco. One tries, but Fielding does not. These are not the scenes he is trying to make, and he says of each of them, "Once, once is enough." Fielding does not make a strong impression at such events anyway. "The minute Temple puts on a dinner jacket, he is the most boring man on earth," a close friend of Fielding said to me one evening. "He is a very small little person inside, incredibly shy." There are hierarchies in snobland, and the criticism that is aimed at Fielding usually refers to nothing more than that he writes at length and with particular affection about expensive hotels and restaurants. Fielding has no single category of reader in mind when he writes, and last spring, for travelers on low budgets, he published a *Super-Economy Guide to Europe,* which sold a hundred thousand copies in paperback in its first month. Nonetheless, there is a personage farther up the money scale who makes frequent appearances in Fielding's consciousness as he writes. Fielding described him to me as "the banker in the small town who is a big shot, has security and respect in his community, and to whom Europe is a jungle." For this man—"who wants to get a smile, a good table, be well received"—Fielding has created Temple Fielding's Epicure Club of Europe. Members pay fifteen and a half dollars for a set of thirty cards, each of which serves as an introduction to a different European restaurant, all of them being first-rank and well-chosen places, such as Lasserre in Paris and Horcher's in Madrid. Fielding is selling prefabricated prestige, and it works. When a card carrier walks into one of the restaurants, he is treated even better than he would be in a restaurant within sight of his bank. He and his partner are seated in a prime location. So many waiters surround the table that it seems as if one of them is about to call a play. A round of "complimentary" cocktails is served. And the maître d' goes out of his mind. Maxim's, of Paris, which has held three stars in the *Guide Michelin* for a great many years, used to be a part of the Epicure Club, but Fielding dropped it for not meeting his standards.

When Fielding talks about a restaurant or a hotel, he frequently displays an intimate knowledge of the personalities and personal histories of the chef, the headwaiters, the boss—the whole staff—and even their wives, naming them all by first names. A high percentage of his friends are hoteliers and restaurateurs. He goes on vacations with them. They visit him at his home. Among the people he refers to in casual conversation, none are more recurrent than his friends who run hotels and restaurants. "A good maître d' is always on patrol, snapping," Fielding will say. He should know. On more than one occasion, Americans entering the Bali in Amsterdam have been greeted by a friendly middle-aged maître d' who surprises them with his flawless English and answers their inevitable questions by saying, "I was in America once. Now I am here." He shows them to the best table he can give them. He makes discreet suggestions. He is always on patrol—snapping. Fielding does this, he says, because he wants to see how Americans look from a maître d's point of view. The owner and real maître d' at the Bali is a pal of his named Max Elfring. Fielding envies Max a little, for Max has all that restaurant to himself. Fielding wants to see, as well, how it feels to be Max.

His regard for hoteliers can amount to something like hero worship. "You can never fool a hotelier—no matter what—if he's good," Fielding told me. He described the steps of a hotelier's typical career as if he almost wished that he himself had followed it. "In their apprenticeship, they go through the patisserie, the cold kitchen, the hot kitchen, the spirits section, and on into room service," he said. "They're waiters. They go into engineering. They become assistant concierges. The dream, after they have moved around, is to get into reception. From there it's a straight line to *chef de réception*, assistant manager, and manager." Fielding won't say this in so many words, but he obviously thinks that the best hotelier in the world is Alfonso Font Yllan, managing director of both the Ritz and the Palace in Madrid. Fielding and Font have been friends since 1946. Remembering Fielding when he first met him, Font once told me, "His line was not yet drawn. He was very plain, but he knew what he wanted. He liked wines. Good food. I thought that unusual in an American." Now, when Fielding sequesters himself in the Palace to work, Font appears most evenings at seven, pours a drink, and sits down to talk for an hour. Font's Palace is the largest hotel in Europe, and his Ritz is one of the most exclusive. He has said to Fielding many times, "You run a hotel like your own house, where you have friends." Fielding has taken this precept and reversed it. He runs his home as if it were a hotel, and, considered as a hotel, it is surely without parallel in Europe.

When a guest awakens at Fielding's home, he presses a button and a pretty chambermaid appears with a breakfast menu that is decorated with a sketch of a sunrise over the bay below the house. On the chambermaid's uniform, as on the uniforms of other members of the staff, are the words "Villa Fielding." The menu offers three kinds of fruit juice, eight kinds of cereal (including Rice Krispies, Corn Flakes, Shredded Wheat, and Grape Nuts), eggs in eleven styles, ham, bacon, sausages, dried beef, butifarra, creamed chicken on toast, liver and bacon, kidney and bacon, four kinds of fish, pancakes with Vermont maple syrup, eighteen kinds of baked goods, champagne, coffee, tea, hot chocolate, gaseosa, beer, assorted jams and jellies, Skippy peanut butter, three cheeses, and eight kinds of fruit. (At lunchtime, the resident chef, Rafael Pons, appears wearing a tall white hat and carrying a menu that is headlined "Rafael Recommends.") There is only one guest room at Villa Fielding, an outside double, with view—looking down a pine-covered hillside and across the mottling blues and greens of the Bay of Formentor to the cliffs of the Cabo del Pinar. Close to hand, for the guest's convenience, are Alka Seltzer, Bufferin, Mercurochrome, Band Aids, Noxzema, a bug bomb, sleeping masks, and a fever thermometer. On the back of the bathroom door is a permanent notice:

> The small jar on the washbasin contains a special detergent to remove suntan oil from the body.
> Tap water saline, drink from carafe at bedside table.
> We always leave both windows wide open while showering in the sunken tub in order to enjoy the lovely view of the sea. No one would ever watch you, so please have no trepidations about this possibility.
> You will find a continental-style peignoir for your after-bath toweling.

Built of white stucco on a steep hillside, Villa Fielding is landscaped with a blaze of bougainvillaea, and plastic ivy climbs the columns of its sweeping terrace. Flags fly from a cantilevered flagstaff, selected from a large collection according to the nationalities of guests who may be there. Because of the declivity of the hill, the house has, in effect, two ground floors. Fielding's office, like the guest room, is on the lower level. The office is small and crowded. He works at a U-shaped table. The walls are covered with certificates—the first Equator Certificate ever issued by Ethiopian Airlines, a "Hangover Chart" from the late Shepheard's Hotel in Cairo—and the place is full of little doodads of the sort that public relations men are forever giving to travel writers. Fielding seems to be touched by these gifts and to see them as gestures of personal affection. The calendar he uses is Pan American's, because his name is printed in large blue letters across the bottom of it. "Since it is personalized, I use this one," he told me.

At cocktail time, Fielding tends bar along with his assistant manager, Martín Cifre, who also acts as bellhop, butler, and chauffeur, and who has his own office in the building. The bar is in the living room, which is decorated with still lifes and nudes by the English painter Michael Huggins, and among dozens of souvenirs there is a handprint pressed by the Fieldings' son into solid gold. (Their son, Dodge, is their only child, and is now a junior at Hamilton College.) From a mass of bottles concentrated on the living room floor, a visitor can choose any of some 120 different drinks from all over the world. Fielding has Irish moonshine, "non-poisonous Italian wood alcohol," 136-proof Spanish absinthe. Of the absinthe, he told me, "It is genuine absinthe, with the wormwood elixirs in it. It's not a beverage, it's a narcotic. We never drink it. It's for friends." For dinner, the Fieldings might serve turkey, cranberry sauce, and corn on the cob. Their meals are, like their flags and their liquors, intended to make their guests feel at home. They offer steamer clams for New Englanders, haggis for Scots, couscous for Moroccans, tortillas for Mexicans, bamboo sprouts and water chestnuts for Orientals, raclette for the Swiss, and, for Southern Americans, hominy grits, turnip greens, black-eyed peas, and White Rose yams. The cost of importing all this into Spanish Mallorca is very large, and Fielding hungrily pays thousands of dollars in duty to the postal authorities each year. He brings in kerupuk from Indonesia, truffles from the Périgord, and cornmeal from Louisa, Virginia. The Fieldings like Mallorquin food, too. Mrs. Fielding once said to me, "We try to live off the ground here as much as we can."

After dinner, over a frozen blue liqueur, the Fieldings sometimes flatter their guests with a Danish custom they have adopted that they call the Skål Ceremony. Going around the table, Fielding addresses each guest in turn, delivering a deep analysis of the guest's first name, giving its origin and etymology, and citing all the *other* great people who have shared the name. If a guest happens to be called Paul, for example, Fielding will solemnly mention that his name was Paulus in Latin and Paulos in Greek, and he will liken the guest, if the comparisons seem at all appropriate, to Paul Gallico, Paul Tillich, Paul Scofield, Paul Gauguin, John Paul Jones, St. Paul, and Pope Paul, always with full explanations of the similarities involved. As Paul turns slowly into a pillar of crimson, Fielding finishes the address by lifting his glass and skåling him. Fielding will do absolutely anything to make a guest feel very special and very much at home. Once when Alfonso Font checked in at Villa Fielding, he found that Fielding had equipped the guest room with ashtrays, stationery, blotting paper, glassware, bedspreads, bath mats, towels, and soap from Font's Palace Hotel. Fielding's friend MacKinlay Kantor wrote a part of *Andersonville* at Villa Fielding, and when Kantor returned a year or so later he found that his bed had been fondly enclosed with barbed wire.

John David Morley

Pictures from the Water Trade

> Take a stroll on the seedy side of Tokyo with John David Morley
> ("Boon") as he introduces us to *Mizu-shobai* (the water trade), which
> *The Kojien* defines as "the vulgar term for any precarious form of trade
> yielding an income entirely dependent on the patronage of its custom-
> ers; for example, entertainment provided by geishas, bars, cabarets,
> and so on." But Morley's eye is sharp not only for the sensual detail but
> also for curiosities by and large, such as the rituals of rooftop golfers
> and the chant of the clam criers. Irresistible stuff.

The old lady's chopsticks. The rooms in which Boon spent most of the next two years had something it would have been hard to find anywhere else in the Tokyo Metropolitan area—a view. From his window he could watch the industrial barges plying up and down the Sumida River, and a couple of hundred yards beyond lay a second river, the Arakawa, which was the boundary between Tokyo and Saitama prefecture. The view across these two rivers stretched uninterrupted for a couple of miles.

On the slender finger of land dividing the Sumidagawa and the Arakawa enterprising businessmen had laid out a golf course and a driving range, but it was on a tiny piece of fenced-off wasteland directly beneath Boon's window that the beginners living on the housing estate practiced their first erratic swings. Boon knew some of these men by sight, and in the course of the next months he was able to follow their progress from this patch of wasteland to the driving range across the river and finally to the golf course itself. One dedicated group laid down a simple, if occasionally hazardous, procedure for graduation to the awesome professionals across the river—the ability to drive a ball over to the opposite bank.

What surprised Boon about these would-be golfers was their equipment: It was superb. Men who had never hit a golf ball in their lives swaggered out

214

to the miserable little piece of turf kitted out as if embarking on the most gruelling international tournament; cap, shoes, pants, gloves, and a cartload of new clubs were indispensable for any beginner who really meant business.

Golf was only one outlet for this spirit of grim professionalism. The same kind of thing was true of tennis. On the asphalt enclosure between the two wings of the block where he lived couples would periodically stride out in immaculate whites, sternly challenge a section of wall, claim victory after half an hour or so, and retire to a flat on the tenth floor. Where the tennis players rallied by day, other, more sinister practitioners appeared at night. Sometimes Boon would arrive home in the early hours of the morning to find a solitary white figure repeatedly springing up and kicking the wall. This might continue for ten or twenty minutes, in absolute silence. Naturally the man was dressed in the loose judo blouse and breeches, and sometimes he would be barefoot, even in winter.

All these sportsmen lived in a society in which uniforms held an honored place. The training began very early. When Boon first saw three- and four-year-old children trundling around inside the wire pen of the housing estate kindergarten all dressed in the same mauve smocks and wearing the same yellow plastic hats he was horrified, but he soon became so used to seeing uniforms that they ceased to bother him. And as he learned more about the country he was able to see the point about uniforms in a more subtle perspective, revising the facile conclusions which he, like many foreigners, had immediately drawn.

One afternoon, when he strolled out to see how his golfers were getting on, Boon was distracted by the sight of a middle-aged man kneeling on the bank of the river fishing a kite out of the reeds. No sooner had the man retrieved his kite, however, than he turned his back on it and ran as fast as he could in the opposite direction. After a hundred yards or so he stopped, his back still turned to the kite, raised both arms and began tugging gently, very much as if he were pulling two invisible lavatory chains. The kite at Boon's feet remained inert. He was about to step forward to help get it airborne when he caught sight of three other kites, dipping and bobbing several hundred feet above him. The two renegade kites having been coaxed up on a buoyant airstream, the man hurried back to the river to attend to the fourth.

Boon thought about helping him and decided not, for it was obvious that the man's pleasure in the sport lay in flying his four kites simultaneously and single-handed. After several abortive starts and a great deal of rushing back and forth on the part of the kite flier the watery, long-tailed paper frame staggered into the air and soared cleanly up to join the others. The man sat down by his anchor on the grass, lit a cigarette, and gazed up at his flock of kites with an expression of grudging satisfaction.

In Boon's experience this kite flier was someone rather unusual in Japanese life: He played. Kite-flying cost next to nothing, required no membership in a club, no special equipment, headgear, gloves, shoes, or anything of that kind. It could claim tradition, but certainly not social status. It was something done solely for its own sake. Most activities usually had to be *for* something, however woolly, like improving one's mind or one's powers of concentration.

Golf players and their kind were legion in Japan, the overwhelming majority. Recreational activities almost had to become indistinguishable from work in order to qualify as pleasure. Grit your teeth and enjoy yourself. The ordeal of pleasure in Japanese society was compounded by another difficulty which had nothing to do with personal attitudes—the lack of space for recreational facilities, and inadequate access to such as were available. For the urban Japanese (that is, most Japanese), who did not have a golf course or tennis courts on their doorstep, the attention to stylish appearance and the wholesale purchase of classy equipment sustained a world of make-believe. The men standing in tiered decks on top of an office building in central Tokyo, driving their quota of golf balls into a net not more than ten yards away, could not have found it easy to imagine they were teeing up at a country club, but perhaps it was a little bit easier, particularly for those who had never played and quite possibly never would play on a real golf course, if the outfit they wore and the clubs they used were, at least, "the real thing," the best that money could buy.

These rooftop cages and their solemn devotees presented a sight that Boon found both sad and ludicrous. There was little to be said for taking one's exercise on top of a building, let alone underneath it, but in Tokyo it had to be either the one or the other. Every day for a year Boon walked over a vast subterranean sporting facility without even being aware of its existence. The golf cages and underground sports palaces were one aspect of a modern civilization which Boon rejected as monstrous for as long as he remained unaware of the desperate congestion that made it inevitable.

There were many things he found offensive but which he learned to accept because they were necessary, and equally a number of things that were unacceptable because they were offensive without being necessary. The worst of these was noise. Hour by hour and day after day columns of vans and cars, loudspeakers blaring, circled the estate laying a cordon of noise from which there was no escape. Occasionally there were political announcements, but on the whole they dealt with the price of fish and vegetables or some forthcoming attraction in a local hall, always couched in the most effusive courtesy language; a futile palliative, for the damage had already been done. Most Japanese had become resigned to this violation of their peace and assured Boon that he would soon get used to it, but he didn't. In fact it became steadily worse. The first jarring notes of the tinny melodies that were always churned out before these announcements were enough to drive him to fury.

Later, when he moved out into the country, these raiders on wheels duly followed him. Here they were more or less tolerable, however, because there were fewer of them and they offered more variety, including the traditional chants of itinerant fishmongers who had long since vanished from central Tokyo. *Shijimi'asari, a'sári!* Boon had to practice this difficult chant (advertising clams) several times in the bath before being able to reproduce it convincingly. The rise and fall of the little ditty reminded him of the responses he had sung as a boy, and it occurred to him that the texts as well were perfectly compatible.

O Lord, open thou our lips:
And our mouth shall show forth thy praise.

He was sure that the clam crier would have been gratified to learn this, but unfortunately the point was too subtle for him to be able to communicate.

On one occasion, only an hour or so after the ancient fish crier had passed through the village, a van with loudhailer drove up and down the street warning the inhabitants that it was about to rain and that on no account should anybody go out without suitable protection. By this time Boon was sufficiently familiar with the indulgent, paternalistic attitudes of public corporations to be only mildly surprised by this curious announcement, but when he attempted to go out for a walk later in the afternoon—naturally without an umbrella—he was pounced on by his watchful landlady and scolded for his foolhardiness. He had only partly understood the announcement; it was not just rain but *acid* rain, borne on clouds from a nearby chemical plant.

If the Japanese had become immune to noise sources outside the building, the sensitivity to noise inside the building, where the culprit was easily identifiable, could sometimes lead to extreme violence. Boon read a terrifying newspaper article about an event on another housing estate which he would not have believed if he hadn't happened to know someone who lived there and who could confirm it for him.

Arriving home one evening and finding himself increasingly irritated by the yapping of a dog in the next apartment, a man had apparently gone over and rung his neighbor's bell, forced his way into the apartment, and hurled the offending animal from a balcony on the seventh floor. Shortly afterwards the owner of the dog himself arrived back and was told by his distraught wife of what had happened. Seized with rage, he in turn rushed over to the neighbor and without more ado threw *him* over the balcony. People in Tokyo were generally phlegmatic and very long-suffering, but when occasionally the pressure of their cramped living conditions became too much for them and the lid blew off, outbursts of such violence were not altogether surprising.

One of Boon's greatest pleasures during the first months of his stay was that whenever he went out for a stroll he would discover something novel and arresting; the longer he stayed the more he lost the capacity for this pleasure, the things that had once delighted him would seem dowdy and commonplace, or he failed even to notice them at all. Washing-lines, for instance, he often stopped and inspected with wondering curiosity. Happi-coats and *yukata*, which he had often enough seen people wearing on warm autumn evenings, only revealed their true form when hung out on a washing-line to dry. The broad-sleeved cotton gowns hung on balconies or in gardens like great birds with spread wings, pinned back and captive, struggling faintly against the breeze.

The men who had tamed these splendid birds and nonchalantly wore them on Saturday morning shopping excursions, clacking up and down the aisles of the supermarket with the short, slightly feminine steps characteristic of *geta* (clogs), never seemed in the least self-conscious, or their appearance incongruous. The *geta* added a few inches to their height, of course, and the swathe of the *yukata* made them look broader; but, as Boon discovered when he tried it out himself, an element of *gaki-daisho,* a robust, cock-of-the-walk swagger, was as inalienable from the man's *geta* as a quality of subdued grace from the woman's *kimono.* Whenever the Japanese male discarded his crumpled suit, in which he easily looked puny and downtrodden, and slipped on a broad-sleeved robe, he underwent a truly Phoenix-like transformation: Out of the ashes of urban man rose an exotic creature of proud plumage, not just impressive, but even majestic. . . .

Straight sex could be had instantly, on demand, for cash and by the hour, at any respectable Turkish baths. Boon was genuinely not interested in a commodity so easily available, and he was too poor in any case. Certainty of pleasure intimidated him. He preferred it to steal up on him unawares.

Second only to the Turkish baths were the so-called Pink Cabarets, where delivery was as prompt if not as complete. These places resembled the *séparées* of cheap hostess bars in Europe. Boon went along once in the company of a group of colleagues shortly before he left the country.

With echoes of the former pleasure quarters in Yoshiwara, pink cabarets tended to be confined to a few parts of the city where they came not singly but by the street. The Japanese were enthusiasts who did not do things by halves, least of all in their pursuit of pleasure. The house touts who vied belligerently outside the dark entrances gave such explicit and graphic accounts of what awaited the customer inside that for Boon's taste, at least, the entertainment was over before it had begun. He would have found it very difficult to decide whose recommendation to follow, but fortunately his companions knew exactly where to go.

Entrance was by flashlight, the five of them treading cautiously in Indian file, with one hand on the shoulder of the man in front. Submissive and slightly anxious, they were herded in more like prisoners than customers, thus making it a lot easier for the cashier inside the door to extract considerable sums of money from each man as he passed without inconvenience of protest. Singly or in pairs they were shown to tables which Boon heard the sleek usher in the dark behind him refer to by numbers. Boon was Six, his friends, from whom he had been separated, Nine and Ten. The numbers traveled like a password back into the gloomy interior and elicited whispering female echoes. Five minutes passed, and Boon began to wonder if rather than pay he should not have been paid to sit there alone in the dark. At last more whispering. Two or three rustles approached.

Someone wearing a *kimono* sat down beside him.

"*Konban wa.*"

"Hello, are you number six?"

"What? Oh, yes . . ."

Laughter.

"Six is my table. My name's Michiko."

Common enough name. Boon wondered what her real name was. He thought about the five minutes he had been kept waiting and hazarded a guess.

"I suppose you'd gone to the toilet . . . "

Michiko gasped.

"How d'you know that!"

"My name is Sherlock Holmes," replied Boon in impeccable Japanese.

Rustling consternation in the dark. Michiko got down to business.

"Aren't you going to give me a kiss?"

"Where are you?"

"Here."

Boon aimed his head. The first part of him that struck Michiko's face must have been his beard, which after a couple of years of unimpeded growth was approaching biblical dimensions. Michiko gave a squeak of astonishment.

"What are you doing?"

"I was hoping to kiss you," replied Boon abashed.

"But what's that?"

"My beard."

"Beard? Is it real?"

"Of course it's real."

But Michiko's suspicions were now thoroughly aroused. In the reddish glow of a flashlight she held inside her sleeve she briefly inspected Boon's face.

"But you're not Japanese."

"I never said I was."

"Are you a half?"

"Certainly not. I'm whole. I'm English."

The furtive show of light at table number six elicited jubilant, bawdy comment from tables nine and ten. Gales of laughter. Boon spoke out firmly in the dark to quash imputations. Michiko took his hand and inserted it encouragingly between her breasts. He fondled her, she gave an audible sigh of relief to find that her client, though not Japanese, was normal, and deftly began to open his trousers. Not entirely at his ease, Boon was in favor of making a private arrangement and pursuing the matter after business hours, but Michiko rejected this suggestion as improper.

At this delicate moment the usher's bodiless voice oozed out of the dark and substantiated a request for ¥8,000. Boon said no. The request was repeated at tables nine and ten, where the absolute silence was momentarily broken by the thick crackle of ¥10,000 notes. He wondered without envy what they were getting for their money. "Whatever you like," he heard them gleefully urge him, but Boon's knees were wedged under the impossibly small table, and even had he felt carnal he was not an acrobat.

Back in the street, where they were deposited after quarter of an hour, there was a great deal of hitching up of trousers and conspiratorial merriment. His friends were entirely relaxed and unself-conscious. An experience which in Europe would have been shabby in Japan did not seem so, redeemed by a naturalness which Boon, though he came close to it, could never quite share. He went away with other things on his mind: pounds of flesh turned over per night, manhandling, womanhandling: How did the girls do it? Well, a lot of them no doubt welcomed the opportunity of a living made possible by pink cabarets, where they remained nameless, unseen, and, however impersonally, desired. Michiko had seen Boon's face, but he also had seen hers: She was an extremely ugly girl.

In the straight cabarets she would not have been employed. It did not matter if the girls in straight cabarets were stupid, indeed, it was an advantage, but they had to pass a minimum standard of attractiveness. The prettiest girls naturally made the most money, and they graduated from school to establishments on the Ginza as unquestioningly as the cleverest students were dispatched to Tokyo University. The also-ran were distributed more or less evenly over the rest of Tokyo.

Boon's own preferences would have led him to give cabarets a wide berth, because they were usually ripoffs and rather soulless, but in the interests of completeness a knowledge of cabarets was indispensable to his studies, and so he sampled quite a few. Rather tiresomely, the less he wanted to visit them the more the opportunities seemed to be thrown at him. His reluctant career was eventually crowned by the paradox of being *commissioned* by a Tokyo radio station to do a report on cabarets, actually paid to endure an enforced pleasure. If the things he wanted in Japan had come to him as effortlessly as those he did not Boon would have been a very happy man.

The first visit to a cabaret was in the company of Sugama and co-regional friends. In his early innocence, the invitation to a cabaret had aroused in Boon visions of the plangent Liza Minelli—pneumatic girls and acerbic political wit; he was quickly undeceived. Between the bosoms of the entertainers and those they entertained there was no such thing as a stage, in fact not any distance at all. In cabarets one practiced the art of the clinch, either in cubbies with motionless feet, or in a lumbering shuffle over the dance floor.

Under discreet but all-revealing purple lights hands were allowed in laps when stationary, when active with willful intent they were not. On the six inches of stockinged flesh between hemline and knee more assiduous clients could span a hand grope for chords, but these efforts were misplaced. In cabarets it was not the knee or thigh that came into its own, but the breast.

Boon, an ardent if still bashful student, watched with astonishment how Sugama's friends sat down with the hostesses they had been assigned and almost at once reached out for their breasts as nonchalantly as they helped themselves to the fruit on the table. Sugama was not much of a fruit-eater himself, so he was willing to handle Boon's questions instead. Boon admitted cautious surprise: Were then these vegetarian devotions the dietary concomitants of some religion hitherto unknown to him? Religion, answered Sugama, in the conventional sense, no; an archaic instinct of adoration, yes. Witness his friend Kato to Boon's left. Married, with three children, he had long since vacated the suckling place who was himself most sorely in need of maternal nourishment. Boon looked to his left. The hands of the meager Kato were cupped like a chalice. With greedy reverence he squeezed, snuffed, and pawed his companion in search of a surrogate fuel, not actual, but also not fruitless. Still, persisted Boon, again facing Sugama, the promptness with which his friends fastened themselves to the breasts of strange women had rather taken him aback. Sugama told him to look more closely. Did Kato's actions display sexual intent? Were his gropings lecherous? Were they not rather the gropings of a spent animal toward a haven of safety? Boon granted that the latter seemed to be the case. Quite so, said Sugama, and that was why they caused no offense, however forward, however importunate their behavior might seem to Boon. The women might be strangers, but their breasts ah!—their breasts were familiar. For the breast was the sacred if unacknowledged fount of all the nutritious gentleness that flowed through Japanese life.

Consider, said Sugama, getting into his stride, the word *chichi.* He and Boon leaned forward over the table, inadvertently drawing into the conversation their two hostesses, who for better or worse remained firmly attached. It means "father," said Boon. Sugama chided his fatuity and the two girls laughed, pointing at each other's vacant breasts. It is an androgynous word, ventured Boon. No, said Sugama, a homonym: *chichi* could mean either breast or father, and when it referred to breast the word was written with a Chinese character meaning milk. The breast was milk or the vessel of milk, not primarily sensual or even aesthetic, but utilitarian—his friend Kato's behavior was the best example. Nowadays they were concerned not just with size but with bare adequacy of supply; there were not enough breasts to go round. To satisfy demand on the home market reinforcements had to be imported from foreign parts. Boon's girl was Taiwanese, his own from Korea. The two hostesses became uneasy at this turn to the conversation, for although their breasts were welcome as tourist attractions their misappropriation for any professional purpose had not been sanctioned by the director of immigrations. The upshot of Sugama's breast theory, Boon concluded facetiously, was that the term *mizu-shobai* was a patent misnomer. And they drank a toast to the water trade, which all agreed should thereafter be known as the milk trade.

Boon now turned to his Taiwanese girl and things started to come on very nicely. He was just wondering how an evening that had begun without preliminaries could appropriately end, when Sugama and his friends got up as one man and headed for the door. They will have arranged a party, he surmised gratefully, picked up his coat, and followed them outside. But no, suddenly the evening seemed to be over. Hurriedly they took leave of one another, climbed one by one into separate taxis and drove straight home to their waiting wives. Boon couldn't understand this at all.

It was the rule, however. The fruit sampled in cabarets was merely an *hors-d'oeuvre*, by and large the water trade as a whole supplied appetizers but not the full course. Dinners warmed by professional caterers were usually eaten in the privacy of the home. This was not just the practice of raffish individuals but of millions of ordinary married men.

Jan Morris

Very Strange Feeling: A Chinese Journey

Is she the best of contemporary travel writers? While there are others of comparable stature, Morris is surely the peer of anyone you'd care to mention. Called the "Flaubert of the jet set" by Alistair Cooke, she has written many notable books, including *Stones of Empire*, *Places*, *Travels*, *Destinations*, and the 1984 *Journeys*, from which this piece on China is taken. In an epilogue to that volume, she remarked: "For better or worse this is my fifth book of collected travel essays, and with it I bring to fulfillment a jejune ambition—to have seen and described, before I died, the whole of the urban world. Beijing and Shanghai were my last great cities. I may go upstream now, or strike into the mountains."

And in the distance, through the porthole, there stood China.

Of course wherever you are in the world, China stands *figuratively* there, a dim tremendous presence somewhere across the horizon, sending out its coded messages, exerting its ancient magnetism over the continents. I had been prowling and loitering around it for years, often touched on the shoulder by its long, long reach—watching the Chinese-Americans shadow-box in San Francisco, say, or being dragged screaming and kicking to the Chinese opera somewhere, or interviewing renegade patriots in Taiwan, or debating whether to go to the fish-and-chip shop or the Cantonese take-away in Dublin. It had seemed to me always the land of the grand simplicities, pursuing its own mighty way through history, impassive, impervious, where everything was more absolute than it was elsewhere, and the human condition majestically overrode all obstacles and reversions. I had wondered and marveled at it for half a lifetime: and here I was at last on my way to meet it face to face, on a less than spanking Chinese steamship, rust-streaked, off-white, red flag at the stern, steaming steadily northward through the blue-green China Sea.

My fellow passengers assiduously prepared me for the encounter. They showed me how best to suck the goodness out of the smoked black carp at dinner. They taught me to count up to ten in Mandarin. They drew my attention to an article in *China Pictorial* about the propagation of stink-bugs in Gandong Province. Mrs. Wang, returning from a visit to her sister in Taiwan, vividly evoked for me her hysterectomy by acupuncture ("When they slit me open, oh, it hurt very bad, but after it was very *strange* feeling, very *strange* . . ."). The Bureaucrat, returning from an official mission to Hong Kong, thoroughly explained to me the Four Principles of Chinese Government policy.

Around us the sea was like a Chinese geography lesson, too. It was never empty. Sometimes apparently abandoned sampans wallowed in the swell, sometimes flotillas of trawlers threshed about the place. Red-flagged buoys mysteriously bobbed, miles from anywhere, gray tankers loomed by high in the water. Islands appeared, islands like pimples in the sea, like long knobbly snakes, islands with lighthouses on them or radio masts, or white villas. And always to the west stood the hills of China, rolling sometimes, sheer sometimes, and once or twice molded into the conical dome-shapes that I had hitherto supposed to be the invention of Chinese calligraphers. Ah, but I must go far inland, the Bureaucrat told me on our third day at sea, I must go to Guangxi in the south, to see such mountains properly—mountains like no others, said he, the Peak of Solitary Beauty, the Hill of the Scholar's Servant— "But look" (he interrupted himself)—"you notice?—the water is turning yellow. We are approaching the mouth of the Yangtze!"

So we were. In the small hours that night, when I looked out of my porthole again, I found we were sailing through an endless parade of ships, gloomily illuminated in the darkness: And when at crack of dawn I went on deck to a drizzly morning, still we were passing them, up a scummy river now, lined with ships, thick with ships, barges, and tugs, and container ships, and a warship or two, and country craft of shambled wood so fibrous and stringy-looking that it seemed to me the Chinese, who eat anything, might well make a dish of them. Hooting all the way we wedged a passage up the Huangpu, narrowly avoiding ferryboats, sending sampans scurrying for safety, until after thirty miles of ships, and docks, and grimy warehouses, and factories, we saw before us a waterfront façade of high towers and office buildings, red and shabby in the rain. It was my China landfall: It was the city of Shanghai.

"Moonlight Serenade!" demanded the elderly American tourists in the bar of the Peace Hotel. "Play it again!" The band obliged—half a dozen well-worn Chinese musicians, a lady at the piano, an aged violinist, an excellent trumpeter: Glenn Miller lived again in Shanghai, and the old thump and blare rose to a deafening climax and a smashing roll of drums. The Americans tapped their feet and shook their hands about, exclaiming things like "Swing it!" The band's eyes, I noticed, wandered here and there, as though they had played the piece once too often.

They have been playing it, after all, since they and the song were young. Their musical memories, like their personal experiences, reached back through Cultural Revolution, and Great Leap Forward, and People's Revolution, and Kuomingtang, and Japanese Co-Prosperity Zone, back through all the permutations of Chinese affairs to the days of cosmopolitan Shanghai—those terrible but glamorous times when European merchants lived like princes here, Chinese gangsters fought and thrived, the poor died in their hundreds on the sidewalks, and the Great World House of Pleasure offered not only singsong girls and gambling tables, but magicians, fireworks, strip shows, storytellers, mah-jong schools, marriage brokers, freak shows, massage parlors, porn photographers, a dozen dance platforms, and a bureau for the writing of love letters.

No wonder the musicians looked world-weary. The Great World is the Shanghai Youth Palace now, the past of its former prostitutes being known only, we are primly told, to their Revolutionary Committee leaders. The band plays on all the same, and in many other ways too I was taken aback to find Old Shanghai surviving despite it all. The Race Club building, it is true, has been transformed into the Shanghai Public Library, and the racetrack itself is partly the People's Square, and partly the People's Park, but nearly everything else still stands. The pompous headquarters of the merchant houses still line the Bund, along the waterfront, surveying the tumultuous commerce that once made them rich. The Customs House still rings out the hours with a Westminster chime. The celebrated Long Bar of the Shanghai Club, which used to serve the best martinis at the longest bar in Asia, is propped up now by eaters of noodles with lemonade at the Dongfeng Hotel. The Peace Hotel itself is only the transmogrified Cathay, where Noel Coward wrote *Private Lives*, with its old red carpets still in place, 135 different drinks still on its bar list, and the Big Band sound ringing nightly through the foyer.

Even the streets of Shanghai, where the poor die no longer, seemed unexpectedly like home. There are virtually no private cars in this city of eleven million people, but I scarcely noticed their absence, so vigorously jostled and tooted the taxis, the articulated buses, and the myriad bicycles: If there were few bright flowered clothes to be seen along the boulevards, only open-neck shirts and workaday slacks, there were still fewer of the baggy trousers, blue jerkins, and Mao caps that I had foreseen. The theme music from *Bonanza* sounded through Department Store No. 10; there were cream cakes at Xilailin, formerly Reisling's Tea Rooms; the Xinya Restaurant still ushered its foreigners, as it had for a hundred years, into the discreet curtained cubicles of its second floor. On my first morning in Shanghai I ate an ice cream in the People's Park (admission 2 *feng*), and what with its shady trees and winding paths, the old men playing checkers at its concrete tables, the students at their books, the health buffs at their calisthenics, the miscellaneous mediators, and the tall buildings looking through its leaves above, I thought it, but for an absence of muggers and barouches, remarkably like Central Park.

Mrs. Wang had invited me to lunch at her apartment, and this was no culture shock, either. True, we ate eggs-in-aspic, a kind of pickled small turnip, and strips of a glutinous substance which suggested to me jellified sea-water, but nevertheless hers was a home that would not seem unduly exotic in, say, Cleveland. It was the bourgeois home *par excellence.* It had the statutory upright piano, with music open on the stand, the sixteen-inch color TV on the sideboard, a picture of two kittens playing with a ball of wool, a bookshelf of paperbacks, and a daily help. It had a daughter who had come over to help cook lunch, and a husband away at the office who sent his regards. "We are very lucky," said kind Mrs. Wang. "We have a certain social status."

So this was *China?* I had to pinch myself. The Dictatorship of the People (Principle of Government number three, I remembered) does not visibly discipline Shanghai. Occasionally bespectacled soldiers of the People's Revolutionary Army trundle through town on rattly motorbikes with sidecars, and outside the Municipal Headquarters (*né* Hong Kong and Shanghai Bank) two fairly weedy-looking troopers stand on sheepish sentry-go. Otherwise Authority is inconspicuous. The traffic flows in cheerful dishevelment over the intersections, ineffectually chivvied along over loudspeakers by policemen smoking cigarettes in their little white kiosks. Jaywalkers proliferate, and in the crinkled backstreets of the old quarter there seems no ideological restraint upon the free-enterprise peddlers and stallholders, with their buckets of peaches, their plastic bags of orange juice, eels squirming in their own froth, and compounds of doomed ducks.

Nobody seemed shy of me. Everyone wanted to talk. A factory worker I met in the park took me off without a second thought to his nearby apartment (two dark rooms almost entirely occupied by cooking utensils and bicycles), and the only hazard of the Shanghai street, I discovered, was the student who wished to practice his English. Stand just for a moment on the Bund, watching the ships go by, or counting the flitting sea bats in the evening, and you are hemmed in, pressed against the balustrade, squeezed out of breath, by young men wanting to know if the word "intend" can legitimately be followed by a gerund. Go and lick an ice cream in the park, and like magic there will materialize out of the trees Mr. Lu and a troop of elderly friends, all of whom remember with affection their English lessons with Miss Metcalfe at the Mission School, but none of whom has ever been *quite* sure about the propriety of the split infinitive.

Well! So this was the policy of the Open Door, which is bringing modernity to China, and has made foreigners and all their ways respectable. It seemed remarkably liberating. I often talked politics with people I met, and their answers sounded uninhibited enough. The Cultural Revolution, that hideous upheaval of the 1960s! A terrible mistake, a tragedy. The future of

China? Nobody knew for sure what kind of country this was going to be. Communism versus Capitalism? There was good and bad in both. Would they like to go to America? Of course, but they would probably come home again. What a kind face Chou en-Lai had! Yes, he had a lovely face, he was a good kind man, the father of his people. Did they like the face of Mao Zedong?

Ah, but there was a hush when I asked this question. They thought for a moment. Then—"We don't know," was the mumbled answer, and suddenly I realized that they had not been frank with me at all. Not a reply had they given, but was sanctioned by the political orthodoxy of the moment. Did they like the *face* of Chairman Mao? He was a great man, they knew, he had fallen into error in his later years, it had been admitted, but nobody it seems had ever told them whether to like his *face.* My perceptions shifted there and then, and where I had fancied frankness, now I began to sense evasions, veils, or obliquities everywhere. This was, I reminded myself, the very birthplace and hotbed of the Gang of Four, that clique of xenophobic zealots—it was from an agreeable half-timbered villa near the Zoo, Frenchified in a bowered garden, that their murderous frenzies were first let loose. A decade ago I might have had a very different greeting in Shanghai, and Mrs. W. would probably have been banished to one of the remoter onion-growing communes for giving me lunch.

No, perhaps it was not so home-like, after all. On the Bund one evening a man with the droopy shadow of a moustache pushed his way through the crowd and confronted me with a kind of dossier. Would I go through this examination paper for him, and correct his mistakes? But I had done my grammatical duty, I considered, for that afternoon, and I wanted to go and look at the silks in Department Store No. 10. "No," said I. "I won't."

At that a theatrical scowl crossed the student's face, screwing up his eyes and turning down the corners of his mouth. He looked, with that suggestion of whiskers round his chin, like a Chinese villain in a bad old movie, with a gong to clash him in. I circumvented him nevertheless, and ah yes, I thought in my newfound understanding, if the Gang of Four were still around you would have me up against a wall by now, with a placard around my neck, and a mob there to jeer me, not to consult me about participles!

As it was, I hasten to add, every single soul in Shanghai was kind to me, and as a matter of fact my conscience pricked me, and I went back and corrected his damned papers after all. The Open Door really is open in this city, and Foreign Guests are enthusiastically welcomed, from package tourists shepherded by guides in and out of Friendship Stores to bearded language students scooting about on bicycles. Backpackers labor through town in search of dormitories: Peripatetic writers hang over the girders of Waibaidu Bridge watching the barges pass below.

Of these categories, the peripatetic writer seems the hardest for the

Chinese mind to accommodate. "What is your *field?*" Mr. Lu asked me. I answered him with a quotation from the Psalms, to the effect that my business was simply to grin like a dog and run about the city. "You are a veterinary writer?" he inquired. Other people urged me to contact the Writers' Association, or at least to visit the new quarters on the northeast of the city, "where many intellectuals live," so that we could discuss common literary problems. Just running about the city did not satisfy them. It could not be productive.

One night I went to the acrobats, as every Shanghai visitor must, and realized with a jerk—I choose the word deliberately—what the sense of role means in China. There have been professional acrobats in this country for more than two thousand years, and in Shanghai they have an air-conditioned circular theater, elaborately equipped with trapdoors, pulleys, and chromium trapezes, for their daily performances of the all-but-incredible. They were astonishing, of course. They leapt and bounced around like chunks of rubber, they hurled plates across the stage faster than the eye could see, they balanced vast pyramids of crockery on tops of poles while standing on one foot on each other's heads, they were yanked to appalling standstills after falling headlong out of the roof.

"It is interesting to think," said my companion, "that in the Old China acrobats were like gypsies, of very low status. Now they are honored performers. They have their role in society." They were slotted, in short, and as I watched them it seemed to me that they not only had acrobats' limbs, and muscles, and eyes, but acrobats' thoughts, too, acrobats' emotions, specifically acrobatic libidos, and I fancied that if you stripped away their masks of acrobat makeup, there would only be other masks below, left behind from previous performances.

And it dawned on me that all those homely shuffling Shanghai crowds could be slotted too, if you had the key, into their inescapable roles. They were not really, as I had thought at first, at all like crowds of Third Avenue or Oxford Street. Every single citizen out there had his allotted place in the order of things, immutable: Not a layabout loitered on those sidewalks, not an actor resting, not a busker, hardly a worker out of a job. What is your field? I am a Housewife. I am a Retired Worker. I am a Peasant. I am an Acrobat. I am a Student, and would be much obliged, please, if you would explain to me in simple language the meaning of the following English sentence. . . .

I did see one beggar in Shanghai, on the pavement opposite the former Park Hotel (famous once for its Sky Terrace, whose roof rolled back above the dance floor). He seemed to have broken his leg, and sat all bowed and bandaged, sobbing, while an associate held up an X-ray of the fracture. I am a Beggar, it seemed to say! The passersby looked horrified, but whether by the mendicant himself, or by the nature of his injuries, I was unable to determine, the Shanghai dialect not being my field.

I went to the Yu Garden from a sense of duty—it is a National Protected Treasure, even though it was built in pure self-indulgence by an official of the

Ming Dynasty, who caused its Rockery Hill to be constructed out of boulders brought from thousands of miles away and stuck together with rice glue. I was ensnared there, however, by the children. There must have been a hundred of them outside the Hall for the Viewing of Rockery Hill, all three or four years old, some of them tied together with string to prevent them straying off into the Hall for Watching Swimming Fish, and I wasted a good half-hour playing with them. What adorable merry faces! What speed of mood and response, mock-terror, sham-apprehension, sheer hilarity! I stayed with them until they were led off two by two, a long crocodile of black-haired roly-poly imps, towards the Hall of Jade Magnificence.

There is nowhere like Shanghai for infant-watching, but in the end, among all the increasingly puzzling and deceptive inhabitants of this city, it was the children who baffled me most. They have a particular fondness for foreigners, and will pick one out from miles away, across a crowded square, clean through the Tower of Lasting Clearness, to wiggle an introductory finger. They have no apparent vices. They never cry, they don't know how to suck a thumb, and though their trousers are conveniently supplied with open slits in their seats, I am sure they never dirty themselves anyway.

How I wished I could get inside their little heads, and experience the sensations of a People's Revolutionary childhood! Do they never fret, these infants of the Middle Kingdom? Is that sweet equanimity of theirs force-fed or innate, ethnic or indoctrinated? Could it really be that this society is bringing into being a race that needs no diapers? The children in the Yu Garden waved and made funny faces at me as they stumped away, but they left me uneasy all the same.

So next day I went to one of the notorious Children's Palaces, after-school centers where children can either have fun, or be coached in particular aptitudes. I say notorious, because for years these places have been shown off to visiting foreigners, so that they long ago acquired the taint of propaganda. Certainly through my particular Palace a constant succession of tourist groups was passing, led by the hand by selected infants in somewhat sickly intimacy, and in the course of the afternoon the children presented a musical show, mostly of the Folk-Dance-from-Shanxi-Province kind, which did seem short on innocent spontaneity, and long on ingratiation.

But what disturbed me more than the stage management was the utter oblivion of the children themselves to the peering, staring, bulb-flashing tourists led all among them, room by room, by those minuscule trusties (who have an unnerving habit, by the way, of calling their charges *Auntie*). With an uncanny disregard they continued their ping-pong or their video games, pedaled their stationary bicycles, made their model ships, practiced their flutes, repeated once again that last crescendo in the Harvest-Song-of-the-Yugur-Minority, or sat glued to the pages of strip-cartoon books, turning their pages with what seemed to me an unnatural rapidity. Their eyes never once flickered in our direction. Their attention never wavered. They simply pursued their activities with an inexorable concentration, never idle, never squabbling, just turning those pages, batting those balls, pedaling those pedals, twanging those strings, or piping those Chinese flutes.

I was bemused by them. Were they really reading at all? Were they even playing, in our sense of the verb? Search me! I can only report one odd little episode, which sent me away from the Children's Palace peculiarly uncomfortable, and came to color my whole memory of Shanghai. Early in a performance of "Jingle Bells" by an orchestra of children under the age of five, the virtuoso lead xylophonist happened to get herself a full tone out of key. She never appeared to notice; nor did any of the other performers, all dimples, winsome smiles, and bobbing heads up there on the stage. On they went in fearful discord, tinkle-tinkle, clang-clang, simpering smugly to the end.

The airline magazine on CAAC Flight 1502, Shanghai to Beijing, was six months old (and reported the self-criticism of a Chinese women's volleyball team defeated by Americans in 1982—"They were desperate with fiery eyes, whereas we were passive and vulnerable to attack"). It was like flying in a dentist's waiting room, I thought. Also the seats in the 707 seemed to be a job lot from older, dismembered aircraft, some of them reclining, some of them rigid, while people smoked unrestrictedly in the nonsmoking section, and our inflight refreshment was a mug of lukewarm coffee brought by a less than winning stewardess. I was not surprised by all this. I was lucky, I knew, that there were no wicker chairs in the middle of the aisle, to take care of overbooking, and at least we were not called upon, as passengers on other flights have been, to advance *en masse* upon reactionary hijackers, bombarding them with lemonade bottles.

The enigmas were mounting. Why, I wondered, were the Chinese modernizing themselves with such remarkable ineptitude? Did they not invent the wheelbarrow a thousand years before the West? Had they not, for that matter, split the atom and sent rockets into space? Were they not brilliantly quick on the uptake, acute of observation, subtle of inference? The broadminded Deng Xiaoping is boss man of China these days, and he is dedicated to technical progress of any derivation—as he once said in a famous phrase, what does it matter whether a cat is black or white, so long at it catches mice? China simmers all over with innovation and technology from the West: Yet still the coffee's cold on Flight 1502.

The bricklaying of contemporary China would shame a backyard amateur in Arkansas. The architecture is ghastly. In the newest and grandest buildings cement is cracked, taps don't work, escalators are out of order. *Respect Hygiene,* proclaim the street posters, but the public lavatories are vile, and they have to put spittoons in the tombs of the Ming Emperors. Western architects, I am told, often despair to find air-conditioning connected to heating ducts, or fire escapes mounted upside-down, and though it is true that the Chinese-made elevators in my Shanghai hotel were the *politest* I have ever used, with buttons marked Please Open and Please Close, still I felt that all the courtesy in the world would not much avail us if we ever got stuck halfway.

Why? What happened to the skills and sensibilities that built the Great Wall, molded the exquisite dragon-eaves, dug out the lovely lakes of *chinoiserie*? Feudalism stifled them, the official spokesmen say. Isolation atrophied them, the historians maintain. Maoism supressed them, say the pragmatists. Communism killed them, that's what, say the tourists knowingly. But perhaps it goes deeper than that: Perhaps the Chinese, deprived of their ancient magics, observing that nothing lasts, come Ming come Mao, have no faith in mere materialism, and put no trust in efficiency. *Feng shui*, the ancient Chinese geomancy which envisaged a mystic meaning to the form of everything, is banned from the People's Republic; and dear God, it shows, it shows.

Never mind: With an incomprehensible splutter over the public address system, and a bit of a struggle among those who could not get their tables to click back into their sockets, we landed safely enough in Beijing.

The first thing that struck me about this prodigious capital, which commands the destinies of a quarter of the earth's inhabitants, was the nature of its light. It was a continental light, a light of steppes or prairies, and it seemed to be tinged with green. At first I thought of it as metallic, but later it seemed to me more like concrete: arched in a vast bowl over the capital, a sky of greenish concrete!

And concrete too was the dominant substance of the city down below: stacks of concrete, yards of concrete, parks paved with concrete, their trees ignominiously sunk in sockets of soil, vast highways like concrete glaciers across the city, and everywhere around the flat skyline the looming shapes of highrise blocks, their grim squareness broken only by the outlines of cranes lifting final concrete slabs to their summits. No need for rice glue, I concluded, in Beijing.

I was staying on the outskirts of the city, almost in the country. There the concrete was interrupted often by fields of vegetables, and the traffic that passed in the morning was half-rural—mulecarts all among the buses, juddering tractors sometimes. Most of the drivers looked half-dead with fatigue, so early had they awoken in the communes, I supppose, and the traffic itself seemed to rumble by in monotonous exhaustion. I went one morning to the Lugou Bridge, which used to be the city limit for foreigners, and standing there amongst its 282 sculpted lions, all different, above its green-rushed river, watched those tired reinforcements laboring into the city: on the next bridge upstream, big black puffing freight trains, wailing their whistles and snorting; on the next bridge to the south, bumper to bumper an unbroken line of ugly brown trailer-trucks; across the old structure beside me, past the ancient stele eulogizing Morning Moonlight on Lugou Bridge, half a million bicyclists, half-awake, half-asleep, lifeless on their way to work.

Somewhere over there, I knew, was the source and fulcrum of the Chinese presence—the Inner City of Beijing, which used to be Peking, which used to be Peiping, which was Kubla Khan's Dadu—the home of Deng Xiaoping, the home of Chairman Mao, the home of the Manchu Emperors, and the Mings and the Hans before them. I approached it warily. Like the supplicants of old China, kept waiting for a year or two before granted audience with the Son of Heaven, I hung around the fringes of the place, waiting for a summons.

I grinned a lot, and ran (but not too energetically, for the temperature was around 95° Fahrenheit). If Shanghai felt at first unexpectedly familiar, Beijing seemed almost unimaginably abroad. Everything was different here. The faces were different, the eyes were different, the manners were colder and more aloof. Nobody wanted help with gerunds. Though as it happened people were more attractively dressed than they had been in Shanghai, far more girls in skirts and blouses, even a few young men in suits and ties, still they were infinitely more alien to me. The children, their heads often shaved or close-clipped, their cheekbones high, did not respond so blithely. A sort of grave and massive contemplation greeted me wherever I went, as though through each pair of thoughtful eyes all the billion Chinese people, Jilin to Yunnan, were inspecting me as I passed.

Beneath that great green sky, treading those interminable concrete pavements, I felt awfully far from home: And when I followed the immemorial tourist route, and took a car to the Great Wall at Badaling, there on the sun-blazed masonry, looking out across those vast northern plains and purpled mountains, I felt I was breaking some strange and lifelong dream. The Wall has been reconstructed around Badaling Gate, and is overrun there by tourists of all nationalities, milling among the cars and buses below, having their pictures taken, riding the resident camel, eating little peaches, and drinking Kekou Kele, "Tasty and Happy"—Coke, that is. It is easy to escape them, though. You make the fearfully steep ascent away from the gate towards the watchtower to the west ("We certainly are thankful to you, Mr. Kung," I heard a sweating American businessman unconvincingly gasp, as he dragged himself, temples pulsing, up those formidable steps, "for making this trip possible—isn't this a *great* trip, you guys?").

Once at the tower, you find that beyond it the wall is reconstructed no farther, but degenerates instantly into crumbled stone and brickwork, rambling away over the undulating ridges with nobody there at all. I walked a long way along it, out into the empty countryside, all silent but for the wind, all lifeless but for the hairy caterpillars which crossed and recrossed the uneven stonework beneath my feet. But lo, when in the middle of nowhere I sat down upon the parapet to think about my rather lonely situation, out of that wilderness four or five wispy figures emerged, and opening paper bags and wrappings of sackcloth, asked if I wished to buy some antique bells or back-scratchers. Yet again, China had topsy-turvied me. I had fallen among old acquaintances, and when one by one they took turns to look through my binoculars, well, said I to myself, what's so strange about the great Wall of China, anyway?

Looked at from the east, Beijing is not remote at all—only a hundred miles from the sea, only three hours or so by air from Tokyo. It is only when you come to it out of the west, or more pertinently out of the Western sensibility, that it remains so romantically distant. On a Monday afternoon I went down to the gigantic railway station, twin-towered and green-roofed (escalator out of order) to see the arrival of the Trans-Siberian Express from Moscow. This was a dramatic occasion. Hundreds of us had come to meet the train, for hours beforehand we waited in the cavernous International Travelers' Waiting Room, and when the bell rang, the great doors were opened and we burst on to the platform, an air of headiest expectancy prevailed. We stood on one leg, so to speak, we stood on the other—we looked at our watches again, we sat down, we got up—we gave the children another bottle of Kekou Kele to keep them quiet—and there, slowly round the curve into the station, very, very grandly appeared the Trans-Siberian.

With a triumphant blast of its whistle it came majestically to Beijing, the three engineers in their cab sitting there like a trio of admirals on a flagship bridge, and the waiting people clapped, and cheered, and waved newspapers, as the doors opened and from Mongolia or Siberia, Omsk or Moscow itself, their travel-worn loved ones fell home into China. One coach was full of a Western travel group: And these voyagers as they emerged glazed and haggard on the platform, looking wonderingly around them, reminded me of the long-lost pilots returning to earth out of the space ship, in the closing sequences of *Close Encounters.*

There is not much left of Old Peking, except for Protected Treasures. The city walls have been torn down, most of the fortress gates have vanished, the clutter of medievalism which so entranced the old travelers has been swept away as though it never were. Across the face of the central city has been laid the cruel thoroughfare called Changan, down which the trolley-buses trundle and the bikes chaotically swarm. Here and there though, all the same, I felt a powerful tug of organic continuity, in this city of two thousand years.

I felt it for instance at the Summer Palace of the last of the Manchu Empresses, which is now a public park, but is still everyone's idea of a Chinese imperial retreat, with its pagodas and its towering temples, its ornamental bridges among the waterlilies, its myriad boats upon the limpid lake, its covered way, decorated with a thousand scenes of Chinese legend, from which it is said no pair of lovers can emerge unbetrothed, and its ridiculous Marble Paddle-Steamer forever moored beside the quay (the Empress built the place with money intended for the reconstruction of the Chinese navy, and commissioned this nautical folly, they say, as a slap in the face of the outraged Fleet).

I sensed the constancy of things ominously when, lifting my head unawares as I walked up Qianmen Street, I saw the vast glowering shape of the Qianmen Gate blocking the thoroughfare in front, for all the world as though it were still the portentous gateway, as it used to be, into the Inner City beyond. I sensed it delectably beside the lonely neglected pagoda of Balizhuang, twittered about by martins out on the western outskirts, at whose feet the women of the local commune worked crouching in their straw hats among the beanpoles, chitter-chattering half-hidden like so many swallows themselves. I felt it pungently in the traditional pharmacy called The Shared Benevolence Hall, founded in 1669, which is a treasurehouse of arcane specifics, stack upon stack of mysterious powders, brown bottles of roots and seeds, phials of restorative nuts, seahorses, antlers, extract of deertail, heart of monkey. . . .

In the early mornings I used to go wandering through the *hutongs*, the crooked quarters of small courtyard houses which survive here and there off the huge new highways. A curious hush pervades these parts. No motor traffic goes along the alleyways, high walls conceal the jumbled yards. Only by peering through half-open gates can you glimpse the tangled, crowded life within, meshed in laundry and potted plants, here a man in no shirt eating porridge from a tin bowl, there an old woman smoking her first cigarette of the day, or a girl in a spotless white blouse extracting her bicycle from the rubble. A faint haze of smoke hangs in the air, and from the public lavatory, smelling violently of mingled excrement and disinfectant, heavy breathing and a vigorous swishing of brooms show that some unprivileged comrade is fulfilling early-morning labor norms. Nobody ever took much notice of me, wandering these quiet lanes as the sun came up: Only a fairly hooded eye focused on me now and then, when a woman emerged to empty her slops down a drain, or a bicycle bell chivvied me out of the way.

And once very early I strayed over a bridge to a leafy path beside a moat. I was led there by a curious cacophony of shouts, singing and twanged instruments, and I found it to be the most hauntingly timeless place of all. It was a place of self-fulfillment. Resolutely facing a high stone rampart above the moat, like Jews at the Wailing Wall, all along the path men and women were rehearsing their own particular accomplishments privately in the dawn. As we sing in the evening tub, so the people of Beijing go to that wall. Here was a man, his face a few inches from the masonry, declaiming some heroic soliloquy. Here a woman was practicing an astonishing range of arpeggios, shrill soprano to resonant baritone. A splendid bass was singing a romantic ballad, a poet seemed to be trying out a lyric, an old man with a bicycle was plucking the strings of an antique lute. I thought of joining in, so universal did these impulses seem, sending To Be or Not To Be reverberating down that wall, or perhaps reciting some of my own purpler passages: But I restrained myself, as a Foreign Guest, and just whistled my way home to breakfast.

*   *   *

I must have walked a hundred miles! and gropingly I circled towards the center of things—to what the old Chinese would have called the center of *all* things. The measured and muffled restraint of this city was like a fog in the sunshine. Gentle, unpushing, polite, its people kept me always wondering, and I missed the flash of underlife that gives most great cities their clarity. I missed scamps, drunks, whores, hagglers, ticket touts offering me seats (which Heaven forfend) for the Chinese opera. I saw no Dostoevsky brooding over his minced shrimps, no tragic rebel sticking up wall posters. All seemed in bland order. I had been told to look out, in the dizzily Westernized new Jianguo Hotel, for Party officials in expensive suits taking luncheon with their mistresses: But all I saw were security guards from the American Embassy, eating Weight-Watchers' Salad.

How bored this quarter of the earth must be! Even the procreation of the urban Chinese is limited, if not by law, at least by powerful persuasion. They must not gamble, there is nowhere to dance, it is miles on a bike to a cinema, and if they turn the TV on, what do they get but improving documentaries, English lessons, historical dramas of suitable import, or Chinese opera. Their one emotional release seems to be eating, which they do with a gusto in which all their passions are surely sublimated. The grander restaurants of Beijing generally have two sections, one for bigwigs and foreigners, the other for the masses: But though the downstairs rooms are usually rough and ready, with linoleum tableclothes and creaky old electric fans, an equal riotous festivity attends them all.

No wonder the Chinese are such hypochondriacs. They live so strangely, I was coming to feel, in a condition of such crossed uncertainty and brain-wash, that psychotic illness must be rampant. I went to one restaurant devoted to the cult of Dinetotherapy, sponsored by another three-hundred-year-old herb store, and was not surprised to find it prospering mightily. When I told the waiter I was suffering from headaches and general debility, he prescribed Sautéed Chicken with Fruit of Chinese Wolfberry, followed by Giant Prawns Steamed in Ginger. They worked a treat: I walked out feeling terrific.

But not all the prawns in China can cure the stresses of history, and the real malaise of Beijing, I came to think, was its domination by an ideology so all-pervading, so arbitrary, in many ways so honorable, but apparently so inconstant, which can change the very way the nation thinks from one year to another. Today it is liberal and welcoming, Chinese tradition is honored, people are free to wear what they like, consort with foreigners if they will, sell their ducks in a free market, and even build themselves houses with the profits. Yesterday it was puritanically narrow, the revolutionary condition was permanent, aliens were devils, Mao caps and floppy trousers were *de rigueur,* angry activists with stepladders and paintbrushes went all down that covered way at the Summer Palace, expunging pictures of unprogressive myth. And tomorrow, when another generation succeeds to domination, everything may be different again, and all the values so painstakingly absorbed into the public consciousness may have to be ripped out of mind once more.

There is a blankness to this despotism. What is it? Who is it? Is it the people we see on the TV news, smiling benevolently at visiting delegates, or is it scoundrels out of sight? Is it noble at heart, or rotten? Is it genial Deng Xiaoping, or some up-and-coming tyrant we have never heard of? If you climb to the top of Jingshan, Coal Hill, the ornamental mount on which the last of the Ming Emperors hanged himself from a locust tree, you may look down upon a string of pleasure lakes. Their northern waters, within the Behai Park, are alive always with pleasure craft, and their lakeside walks are always crowded. The southern lakes look dead and sterile. No rowing-boats skim their surfaces. No lovers take each other's photographs. The buildings on their banks, contained within high walls, look rich but tightly shuttered, and only occasionally do you glimpse a big black car snaking its way down to Changan.

This is where that despotism resides. Behind those walls, beside those silent lakes, the condition of the Chinese is decided, whether by cynical opportunists shacked up with girls and Japanese electronics, or by somber philosophers bent over their calligraphy. The compound is called Zhongnanhai, and if it all looks numb from Jingshan, it must really be full of gigantic thrust and calculation. Its main entrance is to the south, with tilted eaves and two great guardian lions. The red flag flies bravely on a mast outside, and within the gate an inner wall—the "spirit wall" of old China—is inscribed with the cabalistic text "Serve the People." You cannot see past it, though. Two armed sentries stand there, with two more watchful over their shoulders. They look distinctly unwelcoming, even to Foreign Guests, as they stare motionless and expressionless into the street: And sure enough, when I asked them if I could take a stroll inside Zhongnanhai, they seemed to think not.

But anyway Zhongnanhai is only authority for the moment—only a few years ago it was the private preserve of Mao's widow Jiang Qing, chief witch of the Gang of Four, and now locked up forever. Power in Beijing runs much deeper than that, is endemic to the very existence of the city: When the summons came to me at last, I knew better where to go.

From the top of Jingshan a dead straight axis runs from north to south—or as the Chinese always say, from south to north—through the center of the city. This is the line of Chinese power. It is like one of those energy-leys the visionaries profess to find in Europe, conveying the earth force century after century from mountain to megalith. From the pavilion on the hill it runs steeply down to the entrance of Jingshan Park (posters of criminals, placards around their necks, stuck up for the public example) and over a wide highway, and across that moat where the singers sing at dawn, and through a great flowery gateway, the Gate of Inspired Military Genius, into the Forbidden City of the Emperors.

This is only a museum now, but it retains the numen of absolute command—a walled city in itself, a matchless assembly of palaces, temples, gardens, and gazebos for the exaltation of one single man, the only Son of Heaven, the chieftain of China. Marvelous objects litter our path through this fabulous enclave, grimacing lions of gilded bronze, huge sculpted tortoises, incense burners, ancient crinkled rocks. Now the way opens into a noble courtyard, speckled with green grass, now it narrows into a staircase, or passes through some tall gilded hall, or pauses upon a belvedere, or crosses a running stream. Here is the Palace of Heavenly Purity, and here the Palace of Earthly Tranquility, and here the Hall of Supreme Harmony itself, where surrounded by gold and vermilion, seated on an immense carved throne amidst dimmed lights and incense, the Emperor looked down contemptuously upon the representatives of the rest of humanity, groveling on the floor below.

But wait! The line goes on. Down the monumental steps—through the Meridian Gate, where the Emperor, reviewing parades of prisoners, decided there and then which should be decapitated—under that Gate of Heavenly Peace, Tiananmen, which every good Chinese would wish to see before he dies—and suddenly the prospect opens into a plaza a hundred times, a thousand times as big as anything the Manchus knew. It is the forum of the new China, Tiananmen Square, the greatest square on earth, where an army could be massed, where all the kites in the world could fly, where a million people can gather to cheer their leaders upon the gateway balcony, and stare with curious awe at the twenty thousand Elders massed in their grandstands upon the northern side.

Nothing, not even in Beijing, is quite so utterly concrete as Tiananmen Square. Across it Changan runs mercilessly east and west, on each side of it are monstrous buildings in the Revolutionary Heroic manner, all columns and swollen symmetry—the Museum of History on the east, on the west the Great Hall of the People, which was built by twenty-five thousand laborers in ten months, and is bigger than all the buildings of the Forbidden City put together. In the center of the Square towers the obelisk of the People's Heroes Monument; at the southern end, immense but squat, there stands the four-square Mausoleum of Mao Zedong, looking back in vindication past obelisk and Great Hall to the gate from which, on October 1, 1949, Mao himself, the Great Helmsman, proclaimed the new Heaven and the new Earth. Morose sentries stand guard at each corner of this tomb, wearing sandals or baseball shoes, there are gigantic sculpted panels of peasants resurgent, soldiers victorious, and inside, behind a towering effigy of himself, Mao lies in a crystal coffin embalmed, he hopes, for all the ages.

But wait again! The line ends not with Mao Zedong! Past the mausoleum, through the Qianmen Gate, straight as a die the power-force flows through the Outer City to the Temple of Heaven in the south. Three times a year, in old Peking, the Emperor journeyed to this holy place to communicate with his only superiors, the gods themselves. All windows were shuttered for his passing, and the city was plunged in silence: And though we ourselves can take a No. 116 bus down there (try not to hang on to the safety bars—they leave your hands all brown), still a mighty suggestion of celestial collusion awaits us there as it awaited him. After sundry rites and sacrifices in the temple complex it was his duty to ascend the Circular Mound, built in arcane configurations of the number nine, there to seal the intimate association between this city and the ultimate source of all authority, Destiny itself.

We will do the same. Up those terraces we go, to the wide round platform at the top, and on the slab in the very center we will stand like the Son of Heaven before us, and speak aloud to the gods. "All Power is Illusion!" we may impertinently choose to cry: And instantly, by some eerie manipulation of the acoustics, we find ourselves surrounded by the sound of it—*Power, Power, Power, Illusion, Illusion!*—embracing us within the echo of our own thoughts, and making us feel that we really do stand at the bottom of a cylinder reaching directly, from that stone on the mound in Beijing, China, to the Emperor or Chairman of all things.

Dazzled, bewildered, profoundly affected, all at once, I retreated from the Chinese presence. Some of those caterpillars on the Great Wall, I had noticed, never make it to the other side, but settle in crannies among the paving: And from there if all goes well, I suppose, they turn themselves into butterflies, and flutter away into the empyrean from the very substance of China. I felt rather like them when the time came for me to leave, for I took the advice the Bureaucrat had given me, and floated my way out through those humped green mountains of Guangxi, away in the humid south.

My two cities of China had left me hazed with conflicting emotions and contradictory conclusions, and like a sleepwalker I wandered back towards the coast. I bicycled down dusty lanes through fecund communes, where laboring girls waved and laughed beneath their comical hats, as in propaganda posters. I clambered precipitous hillocks to take jasmine tea in faery huts. I joined the great daily migration of the tourists down the Li River, stretched out flat in the front of the boat, eating lychees all the way, drifting through a fantasy of bulbous mountains, and green, green paddy-fields, and dragonflies, and ferrymen, and riverside villages clouded in the song of crickets, and cormorant fishermen squatting on bamboo rafts, and junks punted upstream by women bent agonizingly double at their poles, and geese in the shallows, and peasants high on rock tracks, and water buffalos snuffling, and old river steamers panting and thumping, while the lychees got steadily squashier in the sun, and the sad man beside me, erect in the prow, bared his chest in the breeze and sailed through those legendary landscapes singing the proud songs of his revolutionary youth.

And so I came out of the heart of China back to the sea once more. I had found no absolutes after all. I had found nothing immutable. I had met a people as confused as any other. I had seen marvelous things and miserable, I had eaten pickled turnip with Mrs. Wang and been sent packing by the sentries of Zhongnanhai. I had been cured of headache by Chinese Wolfberry. I had successfully evaded the Chinese opera. I had bought a bamboo goat, and beaten Mr. Lu at checkers in the park. I had visited the grand simplicities of my imagination, and found them grand indeed, but muddled. I had reached that mighty presence at last, and it was smiling nervously.

Out on the Pearl River, surrounded by black sampans, the ship lay waiting.

Eric Newby

In and Out of a Pyramid

The author of A Short Walk in the Hindu Kush and Slowly Down the Ganges brings his characteristic erudition and good humor to the great mysteries of the Great Pyramid. There may be no royal road to learning—or to the innermost and uppermost parts of a pyramid—but a little bakshish wouldn't hurt. From On the Shores of the Mediterranean, 1984.

As no one at the El Nil Hotel, one of the less expensive caravanserais, seemed to have any idea what time rosy-fingered dawn occurs over Cairo in mid-January, we settled for a 4:45 A.M. departure to get us to the Pyramids in time to witness it.

At 4:15 A.M., rather like a *corps-de-ballet* all taking off on the same foot, everything began to happen at once. The alarm clock went off. The telephone waking system jangled into action, operated by the night porter who a few seconds later—we were five floors up—was thundering on the door with what sounded like an obsidian sledgehammer, announcing, "Your limousine, Mister!" I opened it a couple of inches to tell him that we had got his message and would he kindly desist, and a chambermaid the shape of a scarab beetle slipped in through this chink and began dusting my hat. She was followed by three humble but dogged-looking men, the sort I imagined who had been forced to build the Pyramids. They began shutting our bags, apparently under the impression that we had already had enough of Cairo and were on our way to the exit, although we had not checked in until midnight, having come straight from a party that was probably still going on. In the face of all this, still dressed in pajamas, I felt my reason going.

"*Ma fish bakshish,*" ("There is no baksheesh.") "Try again Monday," I said, the last bit in English, when we were finally ready to go.

240

"Mas es-Salama!" "Go with safety," they said, hoping that I would be preserved that long, raising some sickly grins.

Take plenty of baksheesh, ladies and gentlemen, when visiting Egypt under your own steam, unprotected by couriers. Wonderful how it softens the hardest Muslim or Coptic heart, better than any nutcrackers. And do not begrudge it; most people, even those quite far up the social scale, are poorer than it is possible for most of us to imagine.

Then in the limousine, an immense, black, air-conditioned Mercedes, we howled up the road to the Pyramids, the six-mile-long, dead straight Shari el-Ahram, built by the Khedive Ismail for the visit of the Empress Eugènie of France on the occasion of the opening of the Suez Canal in 1869. Then, having traversed it at more than a mile a minute, we climbed onto the escarpment on which the Pyramids would have long since been descried if it hadn't still been pitch black night with a sandstorm in progress.

After a bit we stopped and the driver, a distinguished-looking Egyptian of fifty-odd on whom constant intercourse with the limousine-using classes had conferred the manners of a Firbankean cardinal, assisted us out of the vehicle by the elbows as if we were antiques.

"Good place, Sir," he said.

"Good place for what?" Apart from a small segment of flying sand, illuminated by the headlights, one could see nothing. The only thing it seemed adapted for was a witches' coven.

"Good place for seeing Pyramids," he said, gently, as if humoring a couple of loonies, which I suppose, thinking about it in retrospect, was what we were. "From up there," pointing into the murk. "Up there, where there are weruins, broken buildings in the desert, Sir."

"Is it safe?" I asked. "I mean for my wife and I to be here alone? It's horribly dark."

"Safe, Sir, safe? What is safe?"

"I mean are there any bad people?"

"No bad peoples, all good peoples here," he said, raising his hands in an expansive gesture, as if embracing the teeming inhabitants of the Valley and all those scattered over the three million-square-mile expanse of the Sahara Desert, then dropping them and entering his vehicle.

"Here, I say," I said, genuinely alarmed at the thought of being left alone in such a spot. "What time's dawn, actually?"

"Dawn, Sir, actually? About dawn, Sir, actually, I do not know. Will that be all, Sir? Thank *you*, Sir, Madam!" receiving from me a generous helping of closely folded baksheesh which a lifetime of experience told him was an ample sufficiency without actually counting it. And he drove away.

It was now 5:15 A.M. and bloody cold with the wind that was raising the sand around us coming off the snowbound High Atlas in Morocco, 2,500 miles to the west, with nothing in between to slow it down as it droned over the debased "weruins" up to which we climbed. Underfoot they felt like what they were (I had forgotten to bring a torch), a bulldozed brick barrack block with sheaves of those metal rods that are used to keep reinforced concrete together protruding from them, and lots of broken glass, all of which made it impossible to walk or even run about in order to keep warm. We tried running on the spot but it was exhausting. Then we tried slapping one another, but I did it too hard and we had a row.

Then, around 6:15 A.M., the terrible wind suddenly ceased, as if whoever was in charge had switched it off at the main, the sand fell back to earth where it belonged, the sky over the Gulf of Suez and Sinai turned an improbable shade of mauve, overhead the morning star shone down brilliantly out of a sky that had suddenly become deep indigo, and the Pyramids of Giza—two huge ones, of King Cheops and King Chephren, a lesser one of King Mykerinos, and three little ones, one behind the other—appeared to rise up out of the ground with the rapidity of mushrooms in a slow-motion film, the only Wonders of the Seven Wonders of the ancient world—first designated by Antipater of Sidon in the second century B.C., six of which were on the shores of the Mediterranean (the other, which was not, was the Hanging Gardens of Babylon)—to survive more or less intact.

Looking at them, under a sky that was now rapidly turning from mauve to apple green and lower down was the color of honey, with the lights of Cairo glimpsed shining between them until they were either switched off or made invisible by the strengthening light of day, there was no doubt that these were among a select body of man-made wonders of any date which in spite of having all the attributes of follies and having suffered severely from overexposure, actually came up to expectations, if for nothing else, for their shapeliness.

The Great Pyramid was built by King Cheops, Kheops or Khufu, who is thought to have begun his reign in about 2690 B.C. It is the first of the three Pyramids built at Giza by the kings of the Fourth Dynasty, which lasted from 2720 to 2560 B.C. The Great Pyramid was known to the Egyptians by the enigmatic name Ekhet Khufu, the Horizon of Khufu. The other two have more prosaic names.

The Second Pyramid, called Wer-Khefré (Great is Khefré), was built by the king of that name (Herodotus called him Chephren as do most people today), who reigned from about 2650 to 2600 B.C. The Third Pyramid, Neter Menkewré (Divine is Menkewré), was built by the son of Chephren, referred to by Herodotus as Mykerinos, and according to Herodotus its construction was inspired by the Greek courtesan, Rhodopis.

The Great Pyramid is the most famous, the largest, the highest, the most visited, the most written about, the most scrupulously measured, and the one that has attracted more crackpots than all the other pyramids put together.

The limestone plateau on which it and the other Giza Pyramids are built is roughly a mile square, about forty acres, of which the Great Pyramid covers thirteen acres, the equivalent, according to an American source, of seven New

York midtown blocks. An area large enough, according to an even more assiduous calculator, to contain the Houses of Parliament and St. Paul's Cathedral, or the cathedrals at Florence, Milan, St. Peter's at Rome, Westminster Abbey, and St. Paul's.

Napoleon, in a rapid calculation made after he had defeated the Mamelukes at the Battle of the Pyramids, while his generals and savants were on top of the Pyramid admiring the view, worked out that the amount of stone in the Three Pyramids of Giza—what another of his savants, Baron Denon, described as "the final link between the colossi of art and the colossal works of nature"—was sufficient to build a wall ten feet high and one foot thick round the whole of France (the effect of which would have been incalculable), and this did not include the casing stones.

The Pyramids of Giza remained undamaged externally until 1196, when Malik el-Kamil, a nephew of Saladin, who later became ruler of Egypt, made, for what was otherwise a prudent man, a mad attempt to demolish the Pyramid of Mykerinos. But after months of frenetic activity his demolition workers had only succeeded in stripping part of the casing, which was of granite in the lower courses, limestone in the upper ones, from one of the sides.

In 1356 Sultan Hasan began work on the great mosque which was to bear his name and stone quarried from the Pyramids was used to build what is accepted to be, if not the most beautiful, the finest example of Mameluke architecture in Cairo. Forty years later the Seigneur d'Anglure, on a pilgrimage to the Holy Land, reported "that of these stones are built, and have been built these many years, the finest constructions to be seen in Cairo and Babylon."

In a century or so the Arabs succeeded in removing the entire twenty-two acres of limestone casing, eight feet four inches thick, from the Great Pyramid, apart from a few courses at the base which escaped their attentions because they were covered with rubble, and used it not only to build architectural masterpieces but to construct bridges over irrigation canals, walls, dwelling houses, and for other mundane purposes.

The last serious plan to destroy the Great Pyramid, some say all three, was made by Mohammed Ali, the viceroy of Egypt, in 1833. He issued an order that the proposed Nile barrages, north of Cairo, which were to control the flow of water through the delta, should be built with stone from this source. This meant, now that the casing stones had all been used up, removing the backing stones which made up the four faces, and attacking the core, which would have turned it from a pyramid into a shapeless heap of rubble. It was Linant de Bellefonds, the French engineer who initiated the construction of the barrages, who persuaded the viceroy that it would be less expensive to quarry fresh stone than to dismantle a pyramid.

*   *   *

And now, across the mist-filled Valley of the Nile, the sun came roaring up from behind a black rampart of cloud that was resting on top of the escarpment of the Mukattam Hills, turning what is a seven-hundred-foot limestone escarpment into what looked like a colossal mountain range. It shone palely at first on the southern faces of the three big pyramids, but diagonally so that the countless thousands or millions of stones that composed them stood out in such a way that each individual one was distinct from its immediate neighbor and one had the crazy feeling that with enough patience one could have counted them.

As the sun rose it shone down into the thick white mist that filled the valley and illuminated the tops of what must have been some immensely tall palm trees which rose up through it, producing an unearthly effect, as it would be, I imagined, to look across the Styx.

It also illuminated the hideous "weruins" in which we were imbrangled, and for a few moments it filled the whole of this vast landscape, in which, apart from ourselves, there was not a living thing to be seen, with a vinous, purply light. Then everything turned suddenly golden. It was like the spring-time of the world and we set off downhill into the eye of this golden orb for what must be, for no one has so far come up with a scheme to make you pay for looking at them, the greatest free show on earth.

Then, just as the Pyramids had seemed to rise out of the earth, so when we were at last among them, did a picturesque, elderly, shifty-looking Bedouin, mounted on a camel and with a donkey in tow, close in to the Pyramid of Chephren. Perhaps he had spent the night in one of the innumerable, lesser tombs with which the plateau is riddled.

"Good morning, King Solomon," he said, dismounting from the camel, which made a noise like a punctured airbed as it sank down, "I kiss your hand," seizing it and doing so before I could stop him. "Good morning, Queen of Sheba, I kiss your hand also."

"Oh no you jolly well don't!" said the newly elevated Queen, dexterously avoiding this attention. "You kiss your own."

To tell the truth, he was a distinctly smelly old Bedouin. If he had come out of a Fourth Dynasty rock tomb then he needed a re-embalming service. He was a Nagama, one of a highly sophisticated tribe of Bedouin who for uncountable centuries (they may have commissioned the Pyramids as a tourist attraction) have descended like swarms of gadflies on visitors in order to suck them dry of life-giving baksheesh, in return offering their victims camel, horse, and donkey rides and, until recently, when some killjoy forbade the practice, assisting them up the outside of the Great Pyramid, at the same time contriving to maneuver female ones wearing skirts into positions of peculiar indelicacy, not all of them fortuitous.

Now he offered us a selection of these various services, including the opportunity to take his photograph in one of the stylized poses the Nagamas permit themselves in this traffic with the infidel. To all of which, not wishing to hurt his feelings but enjoying being called "King Solomon" as much as I enjoy being addressed as "Squire" by London taximen, I replied, "Later, later!"

"Laters, laters! See you laters, alligators! In a whiles, crocodiles!" said the Son of the Desert, getting the message finally that we were a no-show, fishing a transistor designed to look like a military transmitter out of his saddle bag, plugging in to Radio Cairo, and departing in a blast of harem music round the southwest corner of the Pyramid of Chephren, which was now the color of Kerrygold butter but with added coloring, with his donkey in tow.

Close in under the cold, sunless north face of the Great Pyramid, looking up its fifty-one degree slope to a summit eighty-five feet higher than the cross on top of St. Paul's, I had the impression that a petrified seventh wave to overtop all seventh waves was about to fall on us and rub us out. Outside the original entrance and another forced entry made the Caliph al-Mamun in A.D. 820, which made it look as if it had been gnawed by giant mice, there were two notices: NO SMOKING IN THE PYRAMID and NO CLIMBING THE PYRAMID. Across the way from these holes in the Pyramid two young Japanese, a man and a pretty girl, and an elderly American couple were hovering indecisively outside an office advertising trips to the interior at £2 ($2.80) a head. *'O-nayo-gozaimasu!'* the Japanese said, bowing as if welcoming us to a tea ceremony, baring what looked like a couple of upper and lower sets of silicon chips.

"They don't open till ten," said the American gentleman whose name, he told us, was Henry Haythorn. "Can you beat it? Rosie and I got up specially to be here before the coaches. I guess now we'd better go on back down to the Mena House, grab breakfast and come back up again."

Guarding the entrance to the still-locked interior was a Tourist Policeman, member of an admirable force specially recruited to protect visitors to Egypt from being defrauded and other forms of molestation.

"Gom on," said this resourceful representative of law and order. "No need of a ticket. You go now. Many peoples later. Give me one half pound each. Gom on!"

We went in through al-Mamun's forced entry to the Great Pyramid. Abdulla al-Mamun was Caliph of Baghdad, the highly cultivated son of Harun el-Rashid. In A.D. 820, while on an expedition to Egypt to subdue the Copts and Bedouin, he initiated a search for a secret chamber in the great Pyramid reputed to contain maps and spheres, long-forgotten information about the earth and heavens, rustproof weapons and glass that would bend without breaking. At that time the glittering white limestone casing that must have made it a truly wondrous sight in sun and moonlight was still in position, as it had been in the time of Herodotus in the fifth century, B.C., Siodorus Siculus of Agyrium in the first century B.C. and Strabo, who visited it on a trip up the Nile in 24 B.C. Strabo had described a hinged door in the north face which when closed was indistinguishable from the rest of the casing and which led into a low, narrow passage which descended into a vermin-infested pit a hundred and fifty feet below the level of the plateau, on the ceiling of which Greek and Roman trippers had used the smoke of torches to write their names.

Unable to discover the door, which had presumably once more become a secret with the passing of nearly eight and a half centuries, al-Mamun ordered great fires to be banked against the casing stones at the seventh course, which eventually proved to be ten courses lower than the actual entrance. Then, when the stones were red-hot, vinegar was poured on them and they shattered. What he and his men found within was remarkable enough architecturally, but they appear to have found no treasure, and the Arab workers employed on the project were extremely displeased.

Inside, the Pyramid was surprisingly hot. The smell was not what we had steeled ourselves to support, what someone had described as being like the inside of a public telephone box. Instead it was the stench of the deodorants with which mad humanity now sprays its nooks and crannies in order to suppress more natural, feral odors. The going was hard. Anything that isn't horizontal in the Pyramid has a gradient of twenty-five degrees, one in two, and I was carrying a suitcase which contained cameras, quantities of baksheesh, passports, and some great tomes about pyramids, everything I felt we might need in a pyramid and which I was reluctant to entrust to a policeman, even a Tourist Policeman, as I had no key with which to lock it.

One belief held by some pyramidologists is that the Great Pyramid is an enormous allegory in stone, built under the influence of Divine Revelation, and that every part of it that can be measured has some particular significance.

What is perhaps the finest flowering of this belief was produced by David Davidson, a structural engineer from Leeds. An agnostic when he began his researches in the 1900s, he soon took off more or less completely and published an enormous book, *The Great Pyramid: Its Divine Message*, which was one of the volumes inside my suitcase. A bestseller, it is nevertheless one of the most difficult books to read, which is not to denigrate it, as indeed it must have been to write and print. (In case the reader was not getting the message, the author paraphrased whole paragraphs and had them printed in small type in the margin.)

"The Great Pyramid of Giza," Davidson wrote, "is a building well and truly laid, perfect in its orientation and built within five points symbolizing the five points of the fullness of the stature of Christ . . . four define the corners of the base square—symbolizing the foundations of Apostles and Prophets—the fifth point of the Apex of the Pyramid . . . the Headstone and Chief Corner Stone, Jesus himself as the Head of the Body; the Stone rejected by the Builders."

Because we had entered the Pryamid by al-Mamun's forced entrance we had failed to travel down the Descending Passage as far as the First Ascending Passage, a stretch which for Davidson symbolized "The Period of Initiation into the Elements of the Mysteries of the Universe in a Spiritually Degenerate Age, from the time of the Pyramid's construction to the time of the

Exodus of Israel," which he dated 2625 to 1486 B.C. By doing so we had avoided one of the worst fates in Davidson's Pyramid Game, which was getting into the dead-end of the Descending Passage. This passage began below the First Ascending Passage and, once into it, any member of the human race descended irrevocably towards Ignorance and Evil. We had missed it because al-Mamun's forced entrance had carried us across the Entrance Passage on what was the equivalent of a spiritual flyover.

However, by missing the way down to Eternal Damnation, we had also missed the entrance to the First Ascending Passage which begins at the date of the Exodus, 1486 B.C., ends at the Crucifixion and is symbolized by the granite plug which blocks its lower end, "sealing up all the Treasures of Light, Wisdom and Understanding." It was also the "Hall of Truth in Darkness" up which "Nation Israel progressed under the Yoke of the Law towards the True Light, the coming of which was to lighten the Darkness of the World."

There was no doubt about the fate of those who rejected the Messiah. It was awful. Borne swiftly along the horizontal passage leading off from the top of the Hall of Truth in Darkness, symbolizing "The Epoch of Spiritual Rebirth," they found themselves in the Queen's Chamber, otherwise the "Chamber of Jewish destiny" and, the way Davidson interpreted it, a spiritual dead-end.

But by now we were no longer engaged in what had been beginning to resemble a game of snakes and ladders, with rules invented by Davidson, played out on an evolutionary, spiritual plane. Instead we were plodding on foot what seemed interminably upwards in al-Mamun's most awesome discovery, the Great Gallery, which leads into the heart of the Pyramid. Nearly thirty feet high, a hundred and sixty feet long, its walls of polished granite seven feet apart at their widest point but diminishing in width towards the ceiling, and so finely jointed that it is impossible to insinuate a hair between them, it is a place of nightmare.

It was also Davidson's "Hall of Truth," a direct route, symbolizing the Christian Dispensation, up which we were climbing at the rate of one pyramid-inch a year, with no chance of taking a wrong turn, from the Crucifixion (7 April A.D. 30 according to the Old Style, Julian Calendar), to the first day of the Great War (4–5 August 1914, according to the Gregorian, new one). It was rather like being on a moving staircase in a chic department store which normally takes you to the restaurant on the roof without stop-offs but has ceased to function so that you have to foot it.

At the top, having hauled ourselves over a monolith known as the Great Step, which symbolized "The Great Epoch of Science for the Consummation of the Age," we passed, bent double, through "The First Passage of Tribulation" which led from 4 August 1914 to 11 November 1918. From there, after the Armistice, we successfully negotiated "The Chamber of the Triple Veil" which would have been a continuous period of woe and tribulation, lasting until 1936, if Divine intervention had not shortened it so that it ended 29 May 1928.

With the goal almost in sight we passed through "The Passage of Final Tribulation," which extended from 1928 to 1936—a period (was it a coincidence?) that almost entirely covered my schooldays—after which came the end of all toil and pain and the end of human chronology in "The Chamber of the Mystery of the Open Tomb," better known as "The King's Chamber" to non-pyramidologists.

It was a tense moment, the one before entering it. In theory it should have disappeared on the night of 15–16 September 1936, and everything else with it, but it was still there, an astonishing construction at the heart of an edifice in which the epithet loses force from sheer overuse.

In it is what archaeologists believe to be the empty, lidless tomb chest of King Cheops, cut from granite so hard that saws nine feet long with jewelled teeth and drills tipped with diamonds or corundum had to be used to cut it and hollow it out; what some pyramidologists believe to be a symbol of the Resurrection in a chamber in which "The Cleansing of the Nations in the Presence of the Master of Death and the Grave" should have taken place back in 1936, a happening I would have dearly liked to witness from a safe distance, and judging by the smell inside it something of which they still stood in need. Others believe that it embodies a standard of cubic measure left for posterity to do what it will with.

And above this chamber, which is entirely sheathed in polished granite, unvisitable, are five more chambers, one above the other, with floors and ceilings each composed of forty-three granite monoliths and two enormous limestone ones at the very top, each of the granite ones—many of them badly cracked by an earthquake thought to have taken place soon after the presumed burial of the King (those in the King's Chamber, including walls and ceilings, are all cracked)—weighing between forty and seventy tons. Here, three hundred feet or so below the apex of the Pyramid, two hundred feet from the nearest open air (the King's Chamber is connected with the open air by two long ducts), and with the ever-present possibility that another earth tremor might bring down something like four thousand tons of assorted limestone and granite monoliths on our heads, I felt as if I was already buried alive.

There was a sudden flash, brighter than a thousand suns as it bounced off the polished walls, caused by the Japanese gentleman letting off a fully thyristorized, dedicated AF 200-type flash on top of a Pentax fitted with a lens that seemed more suitable for photographing what lay on the floor at our feet than the actual chamber. Perhaps this was what he was photographing, this unsuitable human offering on the floor.

"Holy hat!" said a fine hard voice that I recognized as that of Rosie, the Girl from the Middle West. "Who in hell laid that? Don't say it was the cop. They got a sign outside, 'No Smoking,' What they want's one saying, 'No Crapping.'"

"Well, it wasn't one of us," I said, beginning to suspect that Rosie must have had some more lively incarnation before settling down to life entomb-ment with Haythorn in Peoria, or wherever.

"Let's get out of here," Wanda said, who in some ways is disappointingly sensitive for one who prefers to travel rough. "I think I'm going to be sick."

Whatever the reason, she was not the only visitor to find the King's Chamber too much for her. In it, or on the way to or from it, Abd el-Latif, the chronicler of al-Mamun's excavations, who taught medicine and history at Baghdad, had fainted away. Napoleon, left alone in it on 12 August 1799, at his own request, as Alexander the Great is said to have been, refused to speak of what happened while he was in it, and said that he never wanted the incident referred to again. "What's the use. You would never believe me," were his last words on the subject to Count Las Cases on St. Helena, shortly before his death.

"I'm with you all the way, honey!" said Rosie. And to me, "Lead on, Macduff!"

Having set Henry and Rosie safely on course, toddling down the road towards the Mena House, we went to visit the Nagamas, down at the place below the plateau where they relaxed and fed their animals bright green forage. There they didn't try to sell you anything. They sat looking noble by their dung fires, surrounded by couched camels, donkeys which occasionally let loose volleys of hysterical, spine-chilling shrieks,and hobbled horses, bellyaching about the state of the nation and particularly of the tourist trade. It was like being in the worst sort of London club.

"No more Yumbos," they said, which was all Sadat's fault, getting himself assassinated. "No more English! No more Germans! No more Americans! No more French!" one elder intoned. It sounded like a dirge, or an end-of-term hymn. We tried to persuade them that it was a world recession that was keeping people at home and the jumbo jets half empty and shouldn't they be thinking of putting a few of their fellow Nagamas in mothballs until things looked up, but it was no good and we left them listening to their soothsayer and nodding in gloomy acquiescence.

> The *Ascent* of the Pyramid though fatiguing is perfectly safe. The traveler selects two or three of the Bedouin. With one holding each hand, and the third pushing behind, he begins the ascent of the steps. The ascent can be made in ten to fifteen minutes but, in hot weather especially, the traveler is recommended to take nearly double the time . . .
>
> *Egypt and the Sudan*, Karl Baedeker, Eighth edition

Later that afternoon I climbed the Great Pyramid from the northwest corner in Baedeker's ten minutes without any Bedouin to push, pull, and support me. The easiest way is from the northeast corner, but as it is now forbidden to climb it from any corner I wanted to be out of sight of the

Pyramids police station, which is situated in what used to be one of King Farouk's pleasure houses on the edge of the plateau below the east face. The top, truncated by the removal of the limestone, is about twelve yards square, and I was the only one on it.

The view could scarcely have been more extensive. To the west, the northwest and the south, where the stepped Pyramid of Sakhara, prototype of the Giza Pyramids, stood on the edge of the plateau above the valley, was the Libyan desert, which in the late afternoon sunshine looked as if melted chocolate had been poured over it. Across the river, below the cliffs of the Mokattam Hills, from which so much of the six million tons of stone used to build this single pyramid was quarried, were the mosques and spectacular minarets of Muslim Cairo, the largest city in Africa, and the great labyrinthine cemeteries, now also occupied by the poor. And the other cities: the secretive remnants of Old Coptic Cairo, which also conceals within it the first known city on this site; the Roman, pre-Christian fortress called Babylon, and out beyond it, lapped by smoking rubbish dumps that may soon engulf them, the burnt brick and stone remains of El Fustat, the oldest Arab settlement, established in A.D. 641. And down towards the Nile, to the north of Old Cairo, was the modern city with the high buildings rising above it, not enough of them, as in Manhattan, to form groves and forests which give them an air of majesty, but as they are in London, in melancholy twos and threes, or completely isolated.

And out beyond the road to the Pyramids which we had traversed what now seemed a long time ago, lined with rickety-looking apartment blocks and nightclubs and hoardings advertising enormous belly dancers, was rural Egypt, full of fields of dark Nile silt intersected by canals with the tall palm trees soaring overhead. Fields in which the *fellahin*, the peasants, who still make up some eighty percent of the population, men with big bones, yellowish complexions, wide mouths full of excellent, intensely white teeth, rather thick noses, and dense black eyelashes shielding brilliant almond eyes, use wooden plows drawn by bullocks and raise water from one level to another using the *shâdûf*, a bucket suspended by a rope from a swinging beam suspended between two uprights with a counterpoise weight at the other end, just as their ancestors are shown doing on the walls of the ancient tombs. Men who for working in the fields wear nothing but skullcap, cotton drawers, and a sort of apron. Their women wear the *burko*, or face veil of black crepe, which conceals everything except the eyes, beautified with *kohl*, made with smoke-black which is produced by burning a sort of aromatic resin. In some cases the *burko* reaches almost to the feet which, like the hands, are stained with henna. Some have tattoo marks in blue or greenish colors tattooed on their foreheads, hands, and feet. They live in single-story houses that are simple rectangles of Nile mud thatched with straw in which the hens roost. By nature home-loving, despising persons of every other faith as children of perdition, submissive yet obstinate, cheerful, hospitable, temperate yet licentious, quarrelsome, terrible liars (falsehood was commended by the Prophet when it tended to reconcile persons at variance with one another and in order to please one's wife, and in Eygpt has long since reached a point of development that entitles it to be regarded as an art form), and hard-working by necessity rather than nature.

Long ago their ancestors migrated from western Asia to the Valley of the Nile, which they called Atur. There they settled on its banks and mingled their blood with that of the indigenous Africans and, by the construction of a complex system of irrigation works which relied on the *shâdûf* or on long lines of men simply passing buckets from one to another, they succeeded in winning from the deserts which hemmed the river in closely on either side, a thin green line of oasis which extended downstream to the point below the present city of Cairo where the waters of the Nile expand to water a fan-shaped area of constantly replenished alluvium, the Delta, which together with the region between the Tigris and the Euphrates, was the richest farm land in the whole of the ancient world.

They were the first recorded people to sail the waters of the Mediterranean, but not the first to do so. In about 2600 B.C. the Pharaoh Seneferu, the immediate predecessor of Cheops, the builder of the Great Pyramid, ordered the cutting of a hieroglyphic inscription at Medum on the left bank of the Nile in Lower Egypt, where he was subsequently interred in a great, stepped pyramid. It announced the bringing of forty ships of one hundred cubits with cedar wood from Byblos on the coast of Lebanon, the oldest known city, for the furnishing of temples and palaces, the first recorded sea voyage in the history of the world, although by that time men had already been sailing in the Mediterranean for at least four thousand years.

The Egyptian ships were little more than scaled-up river boats with punt-shaped hulls. They were equipped with a single sail and were propelled by a dozen or so oarsmen on either side and they were steered with oars lashed to upright posts.

By the time the voyage to Byblos took place Egyptian civilization was highly developed and extremely sophisticated. The Egyptians had the advantage of living on the banks of the Nile, the only really navigable river that debouched into the Mediterranean; but in spite of this they were basically freshwater rather than deepwater sailors, using river boats, the smaller ones made of papyrus reed, for internal communication and depending for their prosperity on intensive farming rather than on external trade.

But in spite of knowing these things, and in spite of what someone in London before we left on this trip had said about the top of the Pyramid being a good place to collect my thoughts about the Mediterranean, it was no good at all. For one thing I couldn't see it. For another, however fine the view and what it conjured up, for me it was the Pyramids themselves, and particularly the one I was at present standing on, that dominated everything. In the mind's eye it was the embodiment of what can only be described as an insane and misplaced expenditure of human effort which for the protagonists, except those of the ruling and priestly caste who initiated it, can have had little or no religious significance and have given little hope of personal salvation, or even of an afterlife.

According to what seems a more or less generally accepted opinion based on the writings of Herodotus, the only author of ancient times to have left an account of their construction, 100,000 men were employed each year for three months from July to the end of October (the period when the Nile flooded and the mass of the population would have been idle) on the building of the Great Pyramid for a period of twenty years. In addition there would have been a large force of quarrymen and stonemasons, estimated at some 40,000, who would have worked all the year round. It has also been estimated that a further 150,000 women and children, dependents of the workers, would have encamped around the site, and that a large proportion of the 400,000-strong standing army would have had to be deployed as guards.

The number of stones transported was approximately 2.3 million, including 115,000 glittering white limestone casing stones, with an average weight of two and a half tons. About 115,000 blocks a year which, if each one was handled, as they are thought to have been, by gangs of eight men—inscriptions recording the names of individual members of such gangs have been discovered—would have meant each gang moving ten or twelve blocks every twelve days, from the Mokattam quarries to the right bank of the Nile on a causeway, then across the river by boat, and up to the plateau on another causeway. Ten years alone may have been devoted to the construction of this colossal causeway on the left bank, and if this is so then the figures given may be completely wrong.

If they are not wrong (the figures are Sir Flinders Petrie's) and are not a gross underestimate, this meant, assuming 7,300 workdays, delivering 315 stones a day, 26 stones an hour, working twelve hours a day. However this does not take into account the granite monoliths used in the construction of the King's Chamber and the others above it, some of which weighed seventy tons, the weight of a locomotive. They were cut in the quarries of Syene, near Aswan, 500 miles upstream, and transported to the site in reed boats. To drag such blocks, and there were limestone blocks used for the same purpose of commensurable size, up a simple incline of one in twenty-five, the gradient of the Giza causeway, would have required at least 900 men for each block, disposed in double ranks and hauling on four ropes to raise them 120 vertical feet to the plateau. Once they reached the plateau the stones had to be lifted into position, and some experts suggest that a simple, straight, inclined ramp, of the sort referred to by Herodotus, would have been impracticable as it would have had to be increased in height constantly as the building progressed, with a consequent increase in gradient. To carry a one in ten ramp to the top of the Pryamid would have meant starting it more than 3,000 yards from the foot of it, down in the river valley, and this would have required more than seventy-five million cubic feet of mud bricks, four times the number of cubic feet of stone in the entire Pyramid. Various suggestions have been made as to how it was done: by the use of tapering ramps or with ramps with slanting sides which wound up around the Pyramid, encompassing it on all four sides. The refuse from the cutting of the stone at the site, which was thrown down over the escarpment, amounted to half the bulk of the entire Pyramid, and this was only one of three.

So far as is known all that has ever been found in the Great Pyramid is the single, empty tomb chest, vermin, and huge bats. It may have been pillaged as early as the Twelfth Dynasty, 2000–1790 B.C., the most prosperous period in the history of Ancient Egypt.

What was it, if it was not a tomb, or besides being a tomb? Our suitcase also contained a giant paperback version of a book entitled *Secrets of the Great Pyramid,* written by an American, Peter Tompkins, who first visited it in 1941. His book sums up more or less everything known about it. Without Sir Flinders Petrie, Tompkins, and Davidson, none of whose books are really suitable for reading in the field, to me the Pyramid would have been a pyramid built that way because the builders liked the shape.

Is it, Tompkins asked, to quote him, pure chance that its structure incorporates a value for *pi* (the ratio of the circumference of a circle to its diameter) accurate to several places of decimals; that the King's Chamber incorporates the sacred triangles which Pythagoras embodied in his theorem, triangles which Plato said were "the building blocks of the Cosmos"? Does its shape incorporate the fundamental proportions of what is known as the golden section (the proportion of the two divisions of a straight line, or the two divisions of a plane figure, such that the smaller is to the larger as the larger is to the sum of the two, known by the Greek letter *phi*)? On the other hand were *pi*, Pythagoras's Theorem, and *phi* known about at the time the Pyramid was built?

Was it built as an almanac, by means of which the length of the year could be measured accurately; a giant theodolite, used for surveying the Delta and the Nile Valley; an accurately adjusted compass; a geodetic marker from which the geography of the world could be extended; a celestial observatory from which maps and tables of the stellar hemisphere could be accurately reproduced; a depository of an ancient system of weights and measures, left for posterity; a scale model of the northern hemisphere, incorporating the geographical degrees of latitude and longitude; or a building constructed under the influence of Divine Revelation, an allegory in stone?

All the various and almost innumerable theories seem to depend on the meaning attributed to such terms as "accurate" and "precise," and whether the various sorts of measures used, such as "British inches," "sacred inches," "pyramid inches," "sacred cubits," "profane cubits," and other variations, have been manipulated to achieve a desired result.

As one American coarsely put it: "If a suitable measurement is found—say versts, hands, or cables—an exact equivalent to the distance to Timbuctu is certain to be found in the roof girder of the Crystal Palace, or in the number of Street Lamps in Bond Street, or in the Specific Gravity of Mud . . ."

I was now joined by a host of little Nagamas, fiends in nightshirts who had seen me climb the Pyramid and now, with their insatiable demands for baksheesh and their constant tugging at my clothing, very nearly succeeded in driving me round the bend.

Before retreating I took one more look over the edge. It was a Friday, the Muslim day of rest, and the lower courses of the Great Pyramid and to a lesser extent that of King Chephren were filled, although the sun was setting now, with happy bands of modern Egyptians, couples and families and bands of students, most of whom had come out from Cairo or Giza by bus, car, shared taxi, or on motorcycles to spend the day picnicking, singing, sometimes to the accompaniment of musical instruments, or listening to transistors, while others played football on the level expanses at the foot of it. Almost all, without exception, if we passed close enough to them, had welcomed us to Egypt, had asked us if we liked the country, if we liked them, and, if they were eating or drinking, had invited us to join them. The proximity of these Egyptians also ensured in some mysterious way freedom from the attentions of the Nagamas. What a difference, I thought, it made in one's relations with them, to be no longer a member of an occupying army, as I had been, who referred to them one and all collectively as "wogs."

When I reached the bottom I was met by the same Tourist Policeman who had admitted us to the Pyramid.

"No climbing of the Great Pyramid," he said severely. It was as if we had never met before. "Fine is fifteen Egyptian pounds."

"I haven't got fifteen Egyptian pounds," I said. It was true. I imagined he wouldn't want a check on American Express.

"Okay," he said. "You give me one Egyptian pound."

"Okay," I said. I liked this policeman. He reduced justice to a level of extreme simplicity, if not absurdity.

"Okay," he said, pocketing the money, saluting smartly and moving off, having successfully solved yet another problem for a foreign tourist in distress.

Florence Nightingale

At Ipsamboul

One does not think of "The Lady with the Lamp" as a travel writer, but in the autumn of 1849, when she was nearly thirty years old, she ventured to Egypt with her friends Charles and Selma Bracebridge. (At the same time, unknown to her, Gustave Flaubert was departing France for *his* Egyptian tour.) She wrote long, lovely letters to her family, which were not published until 1987; these form her only published writing not on nursing, and they are formidable. "One wonders," she wrote, "that people come back from Egypt and live lives as they did before." Florence Nightingale certainly did not; within five years, the Crimean War would make her a legend. *Ipsamboul*, by the way, is the nineteenth-century spelling for what we know as "Abu-Simbel."

My Dearest People,
Here we are arrived at the last and greatest point of our voyage—greatest it is in all respects—I can fancy nothing greater. All that I have imagined has fallen short of Ipsamboul (of the great temple of the Osirides), and thank God that we have come here. I can conceive nothing in Thebes to equal this, and am well satisfied to turn back now, for we are to go no farther. We arrived here on the fifteenth, about nine o'clock, and climbed the bank immediately to the lesser temple to see that first. There is no effect about the exterior at all, you don't know where the rock ends, and the temple begins, the slanting lines of the face of the temple (none of them parallel) are ugly, and the six colossal figures between the slants impossible to see, as the bank slopes straight down from the temple door to the river. Yet I have a love for the place; it is so innocent, so childish, so simple, so like the Athor, "the Lady of Aboccis" (the old name of Aboo Simbil) whom it represents. *Athor* means the habitation of Horus, and *Horus* means God; therefore Athor is nature, the world, in which God dwells, and which reveals Him. Her inscription calls her the "nurse, who fills heaven and earth with her beneficent acts." As such, she is identical with Isis. And her temple is so like nature, cheerful and simple, and to me at least, not very interesting, with her great broad innocent face and childlike expression, for it would not do if nature always kept us in a state of excitement.

She is the same as the Grecian Aphrodite, yet how different—her simple, almost infantine, beauty to the more intellectual, yet at the same time more sensual, conscious beauty of the Greek Venus. It is the difference between Aspasia and Desdemona. She is also the goddess of joy, the lady of the dance and mirth, a sort of joy like that of children playing at daisy chains, not that of the feast of Epicurus. She is a secondary goddess, and her connection with the earth is more intimate than that of the real goddesses—her expression shows none of their supernatural serenity, but a simple enjoyment of her flowers and creatures.

The temple is small, the first chamber hewn in the rock and supported by six pillars, with the Athor head upon each; then a vestibule or pro sekos; then the sekos or sacred place, with her image in it. It was built by the Great Rameses, of the nineteenth dynasty, who reigned thirteen centuries and a half before Christ. The conqueror and Sesostris of the Greeks, and his figure, with those of his two queens, both evidently portraits, and one a most beautiful woman, are in "intaglio rilevato," all over the walls. Everywhere Rameses' queens occupy as conspicuous a place as himself. One only of the representations interested me much. It was the Great Rameses crowned by the good and the evil principle on either side. What a deep philosophy!—what theory of the world has ever gone further than this? The evil is not the opposer of the good, but its *collaborateur*—the left hand of God, as the good is His right. I don't think I ever saw anything which affected me much more than this (three thousand years ago)—the king at his entrance into life is initiated into the belief that what *we* call the evil was the giver of life and power as well as the good. Tell Aunt M. I thought of her when I looked at him, and of all she had taught me, and rejoiced to think how the same light dawns upon the wise from the two ends of space and of time.

The old Egyptians believed that out of good came forth evil, and out of evil came forth good; or as I should translate it, out of the well ordered comes forth the inharmonious, the passionate; and out of disorder again order; and both are a benefit. The Romans, who were a more literal people, and we their descendants, never understood this, and have set our faces against evil, like the later Egyptians, and scratched his nose.

Some people have seen a portrait of Joseph in the ass-headed god with square ears, Ombte. I myself incline to this opinion, considering him under the later idea; as I never could bear Joseph for making all the free property of Egypt into king's property, the fee simple of all Egypt into leasehold, the cause of half the evil at this present day.

But I am in a hurry to get on to the great temple, the Temple of the Sun, as he stands side by side with the modest little temple of his daughter, the mistress of the West, the lady of evening, of the morning star (Athor), who receives him every night at the end of his course behind her mountain, when he sets into her resting place.

*   *   *

We clambered and slid through the avalanche of sand, which now separates the two temples. There they sit, the four mighty colossi, seventy feet high, facing the East, with the image of the sun between them, the sandhill sloping up to the chin of the northernmost colossus.

Sublime in the highest style of intellectual beauty; intellect without effort, without suffering. I would not call it intellectual either, it is so entirely opposed to that of the Jupiter Capitolinus; it is more the beauty of the soul— not a feature is correct—but the whole effect is more expressive of spiritual grandeur than anything I could have imagined. It makes the impression upon one that thousands of voices do, uniting in one unanimous simultaneous feeling of enthusiasm or emotion, which is said to overcome the strongest man. Yet the figures are anything but beautiful; no anatomy, no proportion; it is a new language to learn, and we have no language to express it. Here I have the advantage; for being equally ignorant of the language of any art, I was as open to impression from them as from Greek or any other art. The part of the rock smoothed for the temple face is about 100 feet to the highest row of ornament. Over the door is the image of the sun, and on either side an intaglio figure of the Great Rameses, offering, not burnt sacrifices, not even flowers, nor fruit, but a figure of *Justice* in his right hand. "Sacrifices and burnt offering thou hast not desired, else would I give it." "For what does the Lord require of thee, but to do justly."

What more refined idea of sacrifice could you have than this? Yet inside I was still more struck by the king offering justice to the God who gives him *in return life* and *purity* in either hand.

The door, which is about twenty feet high, does not reach nearly up to the knee of the colossus. Alas! the sand is now as high as three feet below the top of the door, and into this magnificent temple you have to crawl on all fours. But I am not sure that the effect is not increased by it. When you have slipped down an inclined plane of sand twenty feet high, which is like entering into the bowels of the earth, you find yourself in a gigantic hall, wrapped in eternal twilight, and you see nothing but eight colossal figures of Osiris standing against as many square pillars which support the rocky roof, their arms crossed upon their breast, the shepherd's crook and the flagellum in either hand, for he is here in his character of judge of the dead, lord of Amenti, or the lower world of departed souls; and truly it looks like the lower world, the region of spirits; no light irritates your eyes, no sound annoys your ear, no breath of wind sets your teeth on edge; the atmosphere is much warmer than the outer air; this atmosphere, which is never stirred by anything but the beetle, the only creature light enough to tread this sand without being buried in it.

"Full of grace and truth," as his inscription bears, indeed he looks. I waited for him to speak; but he did not. Through two other halls I passed, till at last I found myself in a chamber in the rock, where sat, in the silence of an eternal night, four figures against the farther end. I could see nothing more;

yet I did not feel afraid as I did at Karnak, though I was quite alone in these subterraneous halls, for the sublime expression of that judge of the dead had looked down upon me, the incarnation of the goodness of the deity, as Osiris is; and I thought how beautiful the idea which placed him in the foremost hall, and then led the worshiper gradually on to the more awful attributes of the deity; for here, as I could dimly see through the darkness, sat the creative powers of the eternal mind, Neph, "the intellect," Amun, the "concealed god," Phthah, "the creator of the visible world," and Ra, "the sustainer," Ra, "the sun," to whom the temple is dedicated. The heat was intense, it was as if this were the focus of the vivifying power of those attributes; and before them stood an altar, the first and last we shall see—the real old altar upon which stood the sacred ark. As to having had sacrifices here, it is physically impossible in any part of the temple; the door of the Osiris hall is the only outlet, and there is no possibility of any others.

I turned to go out, and saw at the farther end the golden sand glittering in the sunshine outside the top of the door; and the long sandhill, sloping down from it to the feet of the innermost Osirides, which are left quite free, all but their pedestals, looked like the waves of time, gradually flowing in and covering up these imperishable genii, who have seen three thousand years pass over their heads, and heed them not. In the holiest place, there where no sound ever reaches, it is as if you felt the sensible progress of time, not by the tick of a clock, as we measure time, but by some spiritual pulse which marks to you its onward march, not by its second, nor its minute, nor its hour-hand, but by its century-hand. I thought of the worshipers of three thousand years ago; how they by this time have reached the goal of spiritual ambition, have brought all their thoughts to serve God or the ideal of goodness; how we stand there with the same goal before us, only as distant as the star, which, a little later, I saw rising exactly over that same sandhill in the center of the top of the doorway—how to them all other thoughts are now as nothing, and the ideal we all pursue of happiness is won; not because they have not probably sufferings, like ours, but because they no longer suggest any other thought but of doing God's will, which is happiness. I thought how, three thousand years hence, we might perhaps have attained—and others would stand here, and still those old gods would be sitting in the eternal twilight. Silent they sat and stern—and never moved; and I left them.

We shall never enjoy another place like Ipsamboul; the absolute solitude of it—the absence of a present, of any of one's fellow creatures who contrast the past with that horrible Egyptian present. You look abroad and see no tokens of habitation; the power of leaving the boat and running up to the temple at any hour of the day or night, without a whole escort at your heels; the silence and stillness and freedom of it were what we shall never have again. At Luxor the present was such as to annihilate all pleasure in anything; and at Derr, where we stopped on the thirteenth for an hour, the cries and crowd were so insupportable that we saw the temple as quickly as we could, and I have no more idea of it at this moment than you have.

I came out of the penetralia and looked again upon the glorious colossi. I wish all my friends could see them once in their lives, if only for a moment; or that I could describe to anyone the look of intense repose in those faces. I think Europeans are perhaps better able to judge of them than any others, to Europeans they must be always more peculiarly affecting, the revelation of an entirely new kind of life. To us toil and excitement and restless anxiety are so familiar, that we have even consecrated them in Christianity. To the Greeks intellectual activity seemed the highest god they could frame. To the Egyptians calm of soul was the characteristic of a Divine Being. Their Osiris is never represented (at least nowhere that I have seen him) as sharing in the agitations of humanity, though he took upon him their nature.

It is so touching to come thus to the "ashes of their fathers and the temples of their gods," and even "to the tender mother that dandled them to rest," for here is Rameses' Queen—that beautiful tender face—to descend into the bowels of the earth and find this revelation fresh and new, of a nation three thousand years passed away, that at first one is quite overwhelmed, and I assure you one is surprised to find oneself thinking of nothing at all, mechanically reading the names, which are alas scrawled over every statue, or counting the footsteps of the Scarabus as he leaves his track upon the sand. It is like what one reads of people doing under a great blow, counting the fringe on the rug, or some such thing, instead of thinking of the event.

We went up to the top of the rock under which the temple is quarried, to look up the Nile. It is separated from the next cliff by a sand slip. I sighed for a walk in the Alps, the tropical Alps, and I walked round the valley and to the next mountain, and took a long last look south into Abyssinia, for farther we were not to go. I saw nothing, met nothing, that had life, or *had had* life, but the whitened bones of a poor camel. And I reached the top of the next cliff. Oh, would I could describe that, my last real African view!—the golden sand, north, south, east, and west, except where the blue Nile flowed, strewn with bright purple granite stones, the black ridges of mountains, east and west, volcanic rocks, gigantic jet-black wigwam-looking hills. If you can imagine the largest glaciers you ever saw, the Mer de Glace at Chamouni, with all the avalanches golden sand, and all the ridges purple granite, not one blade of green anywhere, except where a sunk fence, for I can call it nothing else, bounds the river, and is cultivated with lupins, that is Nubia. It reminded me perpetually of the philosopher's stone. The people tried to make gold, and prayed to the Deity that he would turn all their soil to gold, and this must be the consequence. The banks of the rivers look like a beetle's back, green and gold, the rest of the country like one vast vein of metal ore.

They sent our Nubian steersman after their "wild ass of the wilderness," but he found a nice bank of sand in the sun, and lay down on his face to sleep. I thought he had had an apoplectic stroke (for you can see figures miles off, as large as life in this atmosphere), and hastened to his assistance; whereupon he got up, and carried me down the next sand avalanche like a child. They help you so beautifully, these Nubians, that your feet hardly seem to touch the ground; the sand is so fine and soft that you sink at every step almost to your knees.

We came back to the dahabieh for candles and went all over the great temple. Every inch of it is covered with sculptures, perfectly uninjured except the coloring, which is gone, but the outlines are as sharp as ever. But what is the good of attempting to describe that which is now as sharply cut in my memory as in the stone, but of which I shall give no idea to you? It seems to me as if I had never seen sculpture before, as if the Elgin marbles were tame beside them! as if I had now begun to live in heroic times. The great Rameses holds by the hair of the head eleven captives kneeling before him, in the presence of the god Ra, who decrees their destiny. Everything is done here in the presence of the gods. Rameses receives life and power from his patron Ra (after whom he is named), dedicates to him his victories, receives from him commands how his defeated nations are to be disposed of. It reminds one of another nation and another leader, whose name only differs by the omission of the first syllable from Rameses. But the most curious part of the thing is the sublime expression of this Rameses—I never saw so beautiful a countenance. It is not a man murdering other men; it is the type of power. The captives too are not bound, but with their hands free, and some even holding daggers, so that indeed everybody has seen in it only an allegory expressive of dominion over the enemies of his country.

Three types of face in the captives are quite distinct; a negro, an Ethiopian and an Eastern, showing that, at this early period of Rameses' reign, his conquests had extended into Asia and south Africa. If it is really a portrait of Rameses, he must have been a noble creature. His name means "tried," or "regenerated by Ra," as Thothmosis means "regenerate by Thoth." The last two syllables Mss (for, in the old Egyptian, as in Arabic and Hebrew, there are no vowels) immediately recall another name—and Moses does mean "saved," "regenerate," "initiated."

The two long sides of the Osiris hall are taken up by the battle scenes, which make even a heroic age run round in a peaceful brain like mine. Rameses in his chariot, hurried along by his galloping horses, the reins twisted round his waist, drawing his bow upon the foe, in full career, preceded by his constant lion. Rameses dismounted and killing a chief whom he holds by the arm, in the exact attitude of the Pætus and Arria, so that one would think the artist of that must have seen this. Rameses in his chariot commanding. These below, and a row of Rameses in conference with different gods above, occupy all the south wall, while the north is a series of small battle-chariots standing on their heads, on their tails, in every possible position, while Rameses sitting is receiving a deputation of conquered nations. One king dismounts from his chariot and holds the reins with one hand, while he makes an obeisance to Rameses with the other. All this north wall relates to the first year of his reign; and the temple appears to have been finished early in his reign, as an inscription relating to the thirty-fifth on the south wall was evidently added afterwards. He reigned from 1388 to 1322 B.C.

and Egypt is covered with his monuments—the Augustan age of Egyptian art.

All these figures are in "intaglio rilevato," very like Flaxman's outlines; the Rameses about ten feet high. But spirited as they are, I, for one, am very soon tired of them. I never made much hand of chivalry or Homer, and I returned back to my beloved adytum.

In Ipsamboul you first know what solitude is. In England, the utmost solitude you can obtain is surrounded by human beings; but there in the depths of the rock, in eternal darkness, where no sound ever reaches, solitude is no longer a name, it is a presence. In the evening we made a great fire upon the altar, and while our turbaned crew fed it, we sat in the entrance on the top of our hillock, and enjoyed the sight and feeling of the ancient worship restored. But then I knew that I liked, yes, and appreciated the Egyptian worship much more now in its desolate grandeur than then in its pomp and show. I felt as if the temple was profaned, and the solitude of the "Unutterable God" broken in upon—and I was glad when the blaze and glare were over.

Before sunrise the next day Σ and I were sitting on the soft warm fine sand, watching for the first rays of his own bright Egyptian sun to illuminate that glorious colossus. It was very cold; but oh! the luxury of that soft warm bed, without creatures, without damp, without dirt, which shakes off directly. When you are cold you bury your feet in it, and it warms them; when you are tired, you lie down upon it; when your head aches with staring, you sit and watch the scarabei with their pretty tracks; no cries for "Baksheesh," and "La Hawagee" (you merchant) pester you, and you are as happy as the day is long. But the day broke; the top of the rock became golden—the golden rays crept down—one colossus gave a radiant smile, as his own glorious sun reached him—he was bathed in living light—yes, really living, for it made him live, while the other, still gray, shadowy and stern as a ghost was unreached by the "Revealer of Life." We watched him till he too was lighted up, and then sat down over against the temple doors and looked in.

The Marys could hardly have been more surprised when they saw the angel whose countenance was bright as snow, and knew that He whom they sought was risen, than we were when we saw the resurrection which had taken place there. One spot of golden light on the third Osiris spread and spread till it lighted up the cheek of the second and first. They smiled in their solemn beauty, but did not speak—a flush came over their faces for a moment—it was an awful moment—it was only a blast of sand stirring outside in the golden sunlight, but the reflection had lighted them up, and in this morning eastern light I could go over all the sculptures in the temple, and see them quite plain; but still my heart yearned for the solitary four in the holy place, whom no light ever approaches. I was surprised to find them still sitting there—they are so living—yet there they have sat for three thousand years, for three thousand years the Osiridæ have seen the sun rise as they saw it that morning, and will for thousands of years more.

In the afternoon it was announced, to my unspeakable delight, that we were to stay another day at Aboo Simbil, another sun to see rise there, another evening to watch the stars, the only thing we wanted was a moon-light.

I climbed up into the lap of one of the colossi, the southermost, who is quite uncovered, his knee is considerably above the doorway top.

To please them, I measured his middle finger, four feet. But to see my Hall of the Genii, my beloved Temple of Ipsamboul, all upon paper, with rule and line, brings it down to the level of Chatsworth in my imagination; and I won't give you the measurement of one of the colossi, I am afraid of getting like Dante. What does it matter whether Rameses' ear is two or three feet long? Champollion has dreadfully spoilt one of the colossi by whitewashing its face. I never look at that one. Imagine painting one of the pinnacles of Westminster Abbey red. It is a dissight from afar off. All that day I spent wandering about within the temple, and in the evening the new moon, like a silver boat, rested on the surface of the cliff for a moment, and then set, leaving behind it the old moon, plainly visible upon the top of the rock, after the silver thread was gone, for some moments. I never saw that sight before.

The next morning we were there again at dawn, and again saw the wonderful light, the resurrection of those colossi, their own eastern sun saluting them. In what their beauty consists it requires a wiser eye than mine to tell you—their faces are rounded, their foreheads are low, their lips thick, nothing which generally gives expression or saves from monotony, is there. The figures are clumsy, the shoulders unmodeled, the hands resting on knees like flounders, excessively short from thigh to knee, the legs like posts. Yet no one would say that those faces were expressionless, no one that has seen them, but they will live in his memory as the sublimest expression of spiritual and intellectual repose he has ever seen.

The ceiling of the great Osiris hall came out in the morning light—huge overshadowing wings crossed it from side to side. "He shall cover thee with his feathers, and under the shadow of his wings shalt thou trust." I never understood the Bible till I came to Egypt. "The Almighty shall overshadow thee"; and, "as a mother will I nurture thee." The vulture, whose shadowy wings are here portrayed, is the Egyptian symbol for a mother, and in this position, as protectress of men, she becomes a sublime representation. The king never goes out to battle, or "runs" into the presence of the gods, without this beautiful Eilethyia hovering over his head to protect him (though in a somewhat different form, with wings folded round her, instead of outspread). When she is the protectress of the country, Eilethyia spreads her glorious wings and holds two ostrich feathers in her claws, as in this ceiling. She is the beautiful headdress of Rameses' queen, whose portrait is all over the temple, and who stands behind him in the captive picture, the most lovely countenance, her black hair gathered together with a golden fibula on the side of her forehead, and then falling on her shoulders. The second queen, a somewhat pugnosed female, is offering to Athor in her temple, where the first also appears. Everywhere she occupies the place which the most advanced

Christian civilization gives to woman—always the one wife, nowhere the face veiled, often the regent, the sovereign, or the co-ruler with a brother. Woman may be quite satisfied with her *Christian* position in old Egypt. The tricolor border of red, blue, and white runs round the ceiling, the sacred colors of light, wisdom, and purity.

Egypt is beginning to speak a language to me, even in the ugliest symbols of her gods; and I find there such pleasant talk—philosophy for the curious, comfort for the weary, amusement for the innocent.

The sovereign of Egypt really deserved to be a sovereign; for he appears to have been chief in every act, just as the superior of a religious order was, at first, intended to be the superior only in every act of difficulty, self-denial, or active benevolence; the king hardly ever appears carried by his fellowmen on an ignoble throne, but driving his own chariot, fighting the enemies of his country, or running full tilt on his own feet into the presence of the assemblies of the gods. This is how one oftenest sees him.

But a little representation of him there is on the side of one of the great Osiris pillars in Ipsamboul, which pleased me more than any. He is offering Truth to Mau, the son of the sun, who expresses the insight, light, or pure intellect of God, and sometimes the world, the "true image of God," but always "the highest property of God in nature as well as man." He is that property, if we may so speak, "which proves the reality of God's attributes by the truth," or definiteness of the manifestations he makes of himself in nature.

It is a beautiful idea—is it not?—this offering Thmei (Truth) to the god, but more peculiarly interesting to us from its being the original of the "Urim and Thummim." The Egyptian judges, who were all high priests, wore a breastplate with Ra and Thmei, both in the dual (*lights* and *truths*), upon it; Ra in his double capacity of physical and intellectual light; Thmei perhaps as subjective and objective truth—i.e. truth as it appeared to the witness, and truth in an absolute sense. Now Urim and Thummim mean light and truth, the two lights and the two truths.

The judge gave judgment by touching one of the litigants with the figure as a token of the justice of his cause. I shall bring one home for Baron Rolfe. Dear Judge Coltman is gone where truths are no longer two (but all is one), and does not want it.

The king is represented so often with truth (or justice) as a fit offering for the gods; because, said the old Egyptians, this benefits your neighbors, while those pitiful other three cardinal virtues, prudence, temperance, fortitude, benefit only yourself. They knew a thing or two, those old Egyptians, don't you think so? When they spoke of a dead friend, they did not say, as we do, the "lost," or the "deceased," which is not true, as we all acknowledge in the Prayer Book, nor "poor so and so"; but the "justified" (matu); for the dead, who were found worthy, bore on their heads the feather of Truth or Justice, and took her hieroglyph.

I wish I could tell one-half their philosophic ways. I must not forget the sacred boat in which people have seen Noah and his Ark, the Arkite worship, and all sorts of things, but which seems to be only a very natural emblem for a country which lived by its inundations, whose god Neph, "the Spirit of God which moved upon the face of the waters," was called "Lord of the Inundations," and was very likely, with the Egyptian want of imagination, to do this in a boat.

There are eight little chambers hewn in the rock, opening out of the Osiris hall, and covered with sculptures of offerings; but as these must be gone through with a candle, and it is impossible to enjoy anything in that way, I do not describe them. Some of them are left unfinished, as the workmen left them three thousand years ago—the line drawn but not cut.

The temple of Ipsamboul is the only thing which has ever made an impression upon me like that of St. Peter's, yet how different. We bade him adieu at nine o'clock that morning. I never thought I should have made a friend and a home for life of an Egyptian temple, nor been so sorry to look for the last time on that holiest place.

We bade him goodbye, and turned our prow northwards, for we were to go no farther. Our poor yard had been already taken down, and laid along from end to end. Our proud *Parthenope* no longer floated in the Nile breeze, and we, our eyes full of sand and tears (which made mud), very hungry, very sorry, very tired, watched from the deck the last of the colossi.

Redmond O'Hanlon

Into the Heart of Borneo

In 1983 Redmond O'Hanlon—natural history reviewer for *The Times Literary Supplement*—and poet James Fenton launched their expedition into Borneo. The result is one of the great travel books of recent years. The B-movie title of O'Hanlon's book is apt, reflecting the slapstick spirit of the book, with Fenton and O'Hanlon playing the parts of Abbott and Costello.

The first real sight of the Borneo kingfishers was . . . startling. Brighter than any illustration could ever be, apparently radiating blue and orange from its back and stomach all around itself into the background of green until it seemed to be a bird four times its size, its large bill translucent, carmine-red in the sun, the Black-capped kingfisher (in fact an eater of insects) was often so tame it never bothered to fly from us at all, but sat bobbing on its bough, *chick-chicking* loud and shrill, furious to be disturbed. The Stork-billed kingfisher, however, much bigger, its front end built like the nosecone of a missile, always flew off, screaming as it went, the silky light blue of its rump disappearing fast and low upriver to a hiding-perch in some habitual tree.

A small heron, the Little green heron, slate-gray and furtive, skulked about the river margins, or the island shingle banks, or amongst the beached driftwood; and our own Common sandpiper, always solitary (except at dusk when we might see three or four come skimming past just above the water) seemed to like riding on drifting logs, hopping off to run about the mud or the shingle.

Looking at one, as small and brown, as agile and elegant and friendly as if I had been watching it in Poole Harbor, I thought of Beccari's record of one of its feeding habits: "When crocodiles lie thus with open jaws, small shore birds, especially waders of the sandpiper kind, which are always running about on the banks in search of food, enter the huge reptiles' mouths to capture any such small fry as may have sought refuge among the teeth or in the folds of the mucus membrane of the mouth or pharynx. Indeed, if I remember right, I have witnessed the thing myself; but now as I write I cannot feel quite sure that it was not one of many stories told me by my men."

James, his huge head laid back on the hump of our kit under the tarpaulin, was having one of his five-minute snoozes. The vein on his right temple was distended with blood, a sure sign that his cerebellum was awash with extra dissolved oxygen, and that some piece of programming, vital to the production of a future poem, was in progress.

"James!"

An eye opened.

"What is it?"

"Just this—if you *do* see a log floating *upriver,* let me know."

"Crocodiles?"

"Well, not the estuarine one that reallly goes for you. Not up here. But Tweedie and Harrison think we might see the freshwater Gharial. The fifteen-foot one with the five-foot snout and all those teeth."

"Really, Redmond," said James, raising himself up on an elbow and looking about, "you're absurd. You live in the nineteenth century. Every-thing's changed, although you don't appear to notice. Nowadays you will have no difficulty whatever in recognizing a crocodile. Everyone knows—they come with an outboard motor at the back and a Kenwood mixer at the front."

I sat back in the boat. When the temperature is 110° and the humidity ninety-eight percent, when you're soaking wet and rotting a bit in the crotch, then even weak jokes like that, in the worst possible taste, seem extraor-dinarily funny.

At five o'clock in the afternoon we entered a wider stretch of river where a tributary joined the main stream and a low ridge of shingle had formed down the center of the water course. Dana decided to make camp.

"Good fishing. Very good," said Leon, looking at the swirling white water, the fallen trees and the eddies by the far bank.

We pulled the canoe well out of the water and tied its bow-rope high up the trunk of a tree, in case of floods in the night, and then stretched out on the sand for a rest. Butterflies began to gather. Hundreds of butterflies, flying at different heights and speeds, floating, flapping awkwardly in small bursts, gliding, fluttering like bats, winnowing, some flying fast and direct like a wren in trouble, made their way toward us and settled on our boots and trousers, clustered on our shirts, sucked the sweat from our arms. There were Whites, Yellows and Blues; Swallowtails, black, banded or spotted with blue-greens; and, just outside the clustering circle of small butterflies, the magnificent species which Alfred Russel Wallace named after James Brooke, *Troides brookiana,* the Rajah Brooke's birdwing.

Sucking our clothes and skin with their thread-like proboscides at one end, the butterflies exuded a white goo over us from their anal vents at the other. Getting up, brushing them off as gently as possible, I walked away from my companion the mandatory few yards and took a pee myself. Whilst my patch of urine was still steaming slightly on the muddy sand, the males of Rajah Brooke's birdwing (the females, fully employed laying eggs in the jungle trees, are seldom seen) flew over and crowded down on it, elbowing each other with the joints on their legs, pushing and shoving to get at the liquid, the brilliant green feather-shaped marks on their black wings trembling slightly as they fed. I began, prematurely, to feel a part of things.

In fact, having run to the canoe to fetch the shockproof, waterproof, more-or-less-everything-proof (but, sadly, fixed-lens) heavy-duty Fuji cameras, I began to feel, as I crawled on my stomach toward the pullulating insects, more than a passing pride in the quality of my offering. After all, some thirteen inches from my own nose and closing, was the very butterfly which Wallace described in 1855:

> the Ornithoptera Brookeana, one of the most elegant species known. This beautiful creature has very long and pointed wings, almost resembling a sphinx moth in shape. It is deep velvety black, with a curved band of spots of a brilliant metallic-green color extending across the wings from tip to tip, each spot being shaped exactly like a small triangular feather, and having very much the effect of a row of the Wing Coverts of the Mexican trojon laid upon black velvet. The only other marks are a broad neck-collar of vivid crimson, and a few delicate white touches on the outer margins of the hind wings. This species, which was then quite new and which I named after Sir James Brooke, was very rare. It was seen occasionally flying swiftly in the clearings, and now and then settling for an instant at puddles and muddy places, so that I only succeeded in capturing two or three specimens.

While photographing this butterfly (with a fixed wide-angle lens which I knew would produce a hopeless picture), which later proved to be very common all the way up the Baleh to its source, I felt the excitement that Wallace himself describes, on capturing its close cousin *Ornithoptera croesus:* "Fine specimens of the male are more than seven inches across the wings, which are velvety black and fiery orange, the latter color replacing the green of the allied species. The beauty and brilliancy of this insect are indescribable, and none but a naturalist can understand the intense excitement I experienced when I at length captured it . . . my heart began to beat violently, the blood rushed to my head, and I felt much more like fainting than I have done when in apprehension of immediate death. I had a headache the rest of the day, so great was the excitement produced by what will appear to most people a very inadequate cause."

I, too, had a headache for the rest of the day, but then perhaps it was the sun, or the mere thought of our fishing equipment. For after a burning swig all round from the arak rice-brandy five-gallon converted petrol can, Dana, Leon and Inghai, drawing their parangs from their carved wooden scabbards, set off to cut down the saplings for our pole-beds; and I decided it was time that James and I taught them how to fish to maximum effect, like Englishmen. But first a little practice would be necessary.

Withdrawing quietly behind a massive jumble of boulders, well out of sight, I unpacked our precious cargo. Two new extendable rods, the toughest in town. A hundred yards of heavy line. A heavy bag of assorted lead weights. A termite's nest of swivels. A thornbush of hooks. Fifty different spinners, their spoons flashing in the sun, all shapes and all sizes for every kind of fish in every sort of inland water.

"The trouble is," said James, flicking a rod handle and watching the sections telescope out into the blue beyond, "my elder brother was the fisherman. That was his thing, you see, he filled that role. So I had to pretend it was a bore; and I never learned."

"What? You never fished?"

"No. Never. What about you?"

"Well, *my* elder brother went fishing."

"So you can't either?"

"Not exactly. Not with a rod. I used to go mackerel fishing with a line. All over the place."

"Mackerel fishing! Now you tell me!" said James, looking really quite agitated and frightening a bright orange damsel fly off his hat. "Still," he said, calming down, "if *they* could do it it can't be that diffy, can it?"

"Of course not—you just stick the spinner and swivels and weights on that end and swing it through the air."

The heat was unbearable. The fiddling was insupportable. The gut got tangled; the hooks stuck in our fingers; the knot diagram would have given Baden-Powell a blood clot in the brain. We did it all and forgot the nasty little weights. But eventually we were ready to kill fish.

"The SAS say it's simpler to stick in a hand grenade."

"They're right," said James.

"But the Major said all you had to do was hang your dick in the river and pull it out with fish on it."

"Why don't you stick your dick in the river?" said James.

Standing firm and straight, James cast the spinner into the river. It landed in the water straight down at the end of the rod. Clunk. James pulled. The line snapped. We went through the whole nasty rigmarole again, with fresh swivels, weights and spinner.

"Try again. Throw it a little farther."

James reached right back and then swung the rod forwards and sideways as if he was axing a tree.

At that very moment, it seemed, the Borneo banded hornet, *Vesta tropica,* sunk its sting into my right buttock.

"Jesus!" I said.

It was huge and jointed, this hornet, flashing red and silver in the sun.

"You are hooked up," said James, matter-of-factly. "You have a spinner in your bum."

There was a weird, gurgling, jungle sound behind us. Dana, Leon, and Inghai were leaning against the boulders. The Iban, when they decide that something is really funny, and know that they are going to laugh for a long time, lie down first.

Dana, Leon, and Inghai lay down.

"You should try it with harpoon!" shrieked Leon, helpless.

Jonathan Raban

The River

In *Old Glory*—in many ways the aquatic equivalent of *Blue Highways*—Englishman Jonathan Raban travels down the Mississippi from Minneapolis to New Orleans in a sixteen-foot boat. Inspired by Huckleberry Finn, Raban lets the current take his boat and his story where it will, from Red Wing to Natchez, from Des Moines to Baton Rouge, from the sublime to the ridiculous. "Everything would be left to chance," he decided. "There would be no advance reservations, no letters of introduction. One would try to be as much like a piece of driftwood as one could manage."

I had crossed and recrossed the Mississippi. There were eighteen bridges over it in as many miles, and it seemed that already I had been on most of them. Yet I was having almost as much trouble as De Soto or La Salle in actually reaching the riverbank. Once, the Mississippi had provided Minneapolis and St. Paul with the reason for their existence. Later, it had turned into an impediment to their joint commercial life, to be spanned at every possible point. Now it wasn't even an impediment. The Twin Cities went about their business as if the river didn't exist. No road that I could see led down to it. From a gloomy little bar on First Street, I could smell the Mississippi, but didn't know how to reach it. Feeling foolish, I called the bartender over.

"How exactly do I get down to the Mississippi?"

"The river? She's on the far side of the tracks." The *wrong* side of the tracks. The river had been consigned to the part of town classically set aside for the American poor. It belonged to the same category as vandalized public housing projects, junked automobiles, and dead cats. I was appalled. No one would have dared do such a thing to the river in my head.

I left my beer untouched. Across the street, there was a potter's field of ancient railroads. Most had died. Others were in that geriatric state where

270

death is just a whisker away. It was a sorry strip, half a mile wide, of dingy grass, cracked ties, and crumbling rails. The rolling stock looked as if it had rusted solid on its tracks. I couldn't see any locomotives, only the names of the surviving railroad companies, painted in flaky lettering on the sides of the cars. BURLINGTON NORTHERN. CHICAGO AND NORTH WESTERN. MINNESOTA TRANSFER. THE SOO LINE. CHICAGO, MILWAUKEE, ST. PAUL AND PACIFIC. Crickets wheezed and scraped at my feet as I crossed from track to track. The soggy holiday air smelled of diesel oil, rotting wood, and river.

I clambered between two standing chains of freight cars, slid down a culvert of cinders, and there was the Mississippi. All that I could see at first was what it was not. It was not a great glassy sweep of water, big enough to make the civilization on its banks look small. It wasn't the amazing blue of the cover of my old copy of *Huckleberry Finn.* Nor was it the terrible chocolate flood of Charles Dickens and Frances Trollope.

It was just a river. From where I stood, the far bank was no more than a couple of hundred yards away. Its color was much the same as that of my domestic Thames: a pale dun, like iced tea with a lot of mosquito larvae wriggling in the glass. I squatted moodily on a bleached rock, looking across at the dead smokestacks of a Victorian mill and listening to the rumble of a weir upstream. I lit a cigarette to frighten off the gnats buzzing in a thick cloud around my head, and flipped the empty pack into the river. The surface of the water was scrolled with slowly moving eddies. My cigarette pack drifted for a moment, slipped into the crease of an eddy, and was taken crabwise off across the stream. How long, I wondered, would it take to reach the Gulf of Mexico? Two thousand miles at . . . what—four, five miles an hour? A month? Six weeks? At any rate, it would arrive long before I did. I watched its red flip-top slowly circling in the tepid water until it was carried out of sight.

I realized that I'd seen this bit of river before, in a dozen or so bad nineteenth-century engravings, most of them by untalented but adventurous Germans who had traveled up and down the Mississippi with sketchbooks. The rock on which I sat was exactly where they must have set up their equipment to draw the Falls of St. Anthony. Then the river spilled over a succession of steep limestone steps. It was famously picturesque. The Germans represented the waterfalls by taking a pen and a ruler and making a hatchwork of parallel vertical lines. It must have been a very orderly way of passing an afternoon. They then colored them in with a fierce mat white. The general impression was that at this point the Mississippi was a cascade of toothpaste; one could almost see the army of hired hands squeezing the giant tubes behind the falls. The kindest thing that one could say about the engravings was that they were a vivid illustration of the sheer bewilderment of the European imagination when it tried to confront the raw wilderness of the American West.

For even in 1800, this place had been utterly wild—far wilder than the Alps, or the Upper Rhine, or the English Lake District, or any of the other places to which romantic pilgrims went in search of wilderness. Fort Snelling, just downstream, was the last outpost of white America against the Sioux. In 1805, Colonel Zebulon Montgomery Pike led an expedition to the headwaters of the Mississippi and camped beside the Falls of St. Anthony. A Sioux warrior stole the Colonel's American flag while Pike was out hunting for geese, swans, ducks, and deer. In his notebook, he was very hard on the local savages and wrote that he had shot "a remarkably large raccoon" on the riverbank.

Then the falls had been harnessed to turn millwheels. The remains of the mills still lined the far shore, their brickwork fallen in, their paddles long gone. They'd ground corn and sawed up forestfuls of timber. The falls had blocked any further navigation of the river to steamboats, and Minneapolis had been the natural place to join the railroad system to the waterway.

In 1861, Anthony Trollope came to Minneapolis by train, but couldn't make up his mind about whether the place, whose name he found delightfully ridiculous, ought properly to be called a village or a town. Mark Twain came here in 1880 and found a city that had swollen to the size of St. Paul, its "Siamese twin." The two cities were the Ronny and Donny of the Northwest, joined at the breastbone and the abdomen, facing each other for every second of their lives, interesting to visit, alive, real, and living. By then, sixteen different railroads met up in the desolate sidings at my back, and they were knocking the heart out of the commercial life of the river. In 1904, the Baedeker Guide to the United States, rather at a loss to find nice remarks to make about Minneapolis, was at least able to describe it as "the flour-milling capital of the world."

And the river . . . poor, schooled, shriveled river. All this piling up of one technology on top of another—railroad on steamboat, interstate highway on railroad, hydroelectric dam on watermill—had reduced the Mississippi from a wonder of nature to this sluggish canal on the wrong side of the tracks. Bridged, dammed, locked, piered, she was safe now. Minneapolis had no need to bother with her. It had turned its back on the water, and only odd foreigners like me with dreams in their heads came here to brood over what had happened to her.

Out in the stream, the grubby current humped against the giant steel mooring bitts to which no barges were tethered. I thought I saw a dead fish, but it turned out to be a condom. I remembered the old spelling bee, the voices of little girls chanting in a primary-school classroom:

> Mrs. M., Mrs. I., Mrs. S.S.I.
> Mrs. P., Mrs. P., Mrs. Ippi, Ippi, aye!

The condom went off in pursuit of my cigarette pack—a "French tickler" with a nasty semblance of swimming life. I suppose that some indigent peasant in Yucatán might find a use for it when it finally washed up on his beach.

It was a forlorn walk upriver, through the chunky, honey-colored arches of the old Burlington Northern railroad bridge. I had not expected to feel quite so elegiac about the Mississippi quite so soon. That was supposed to happen later on in the plot.

Beyond the bridge, I came on the last of the fetters that Minneapolis had built around the river in order to cramp its style, the new lock and dam at the top end of what had once been the Falls of St. Anthony. It had been finished only sixteen years before, in 1963, and it had turned what remained of the rapids into a watery equivalent of a split-level putting green.

It wasn't picturesque at all. No romantic German would have wanted to set up his sketchbook in front of it. Yet one had to admit that the thing was a wonder of sorts in its own right. I was used to the tiny, pretty wooden locks on England's eighteenth-century canals—dripping little chambers seven feet wide and sixty or seventy feet long. This was a monster. Two city blocks could have been comfortably sunk in its basin. Its fifty-foot drop looked more, a dizzying black pit in the river. The lockmen were talking to each other over walkie-talkie radios. With a hundred yards or more of bald concrete between each man, the place felt more like an international airport than a device for ordering a river. Why, too, on this empty afternoon when the only things stirring were the crickets in the overgrown railroad tracks, was all this Oscar-Lima-Charleying going on over the short waves? The lock was a gigantic toy. The lockmen were playing at being lockmen; gates and valves and sluices were being opened and shut for the simple boyish pleasure of watching that staggering quantity of rancid Mississippi water boil up in the basin.

I found the lockmaster, captaining this pointless operation from an upper deck, his handset squawking incomprehensibly. He had the contentedly abstracted look of a man listening to a favorite piece of music. I felt I had a useful hold over him, having caught him out tinkering with several million gallons of river just for the hell of it.

"Just fillin' her up," he said, gazing happily down into his private maelstrom. It didn't sound like much of an explanation to me. If I'd come along fifteen minutes later, I suppose he would have said that he was "just emptying her out" in exactly the same tone of voice.

"She's real quiet today, real quiet. . . ." The entire building thrummed under my feet as water from the river raced through the tunnels to fill the chamber. "Feel it?" the lockmaster said. "That's twenty-three thousand gallons a second coming in down there." He stood at the window, alternately shouting into his radio and waving his arms at the men below: Bernstein conjuring the *Dies Irae* through its fortissimo climax. There were the giant bass drums, there the massed choir, there the trumpets, there the trombones. He was a maestro of water. I found the performance splendidly exciting, but from a practical point of view, I didn't like the look of it at all. A sixteen-foot boat would be . . . I tried to measure sixteen feet against the lock wall. Hardly more significant than an empty Budweiser can or a fallen leaf.

"I'm going to take a sixteen-foot boat down the river to New Orleans and the Gulf of Mexico," I said. "At least, that's what I *was* going to do."

"Sixteen feet? That's a pretty good size of boat. You won't have too much trouble at all. I seen guys go down the Mississippi in all kinds of things. Twelve-foot jonboats . . . canoes . . . why, just a month or two back, we had two crazies go through here in a pedal boat like they have in parks. They thought they was going to New Orleans."

The thought of the two men in the pedal boat took the glory out of my own trip at a stroke.

"Did they make it?"

"I never heard nothing of them since."

I had, after all, dreamed of disappearing from the world, WENT DOWN THE MISSISSIPPI, NEVER HEARD OF SINCE, would at least make a tantalizing line on a modest memorial slab somewhere.

"Oh, you'll have problems. You get down in some of the big pools, like the Dubuque pool—that's one of the worst pools, is the Dubuque pool. She's wide open: four, five miles, as far as you can see. There's stump lines. . . . When you're out there . . . boy, when it gets rough it can really get rough in a hurry. Then you'll get wakes. When some of them big tows get down in the flats, they're pushing along at ten, twelve miles an hour, and they'll turn the whole river to a rooster tail."

"What do I do then?"

"You stay right inshore and ride those waves out. If you're in the channel, you'll be running into waves that are seven feet tall. Even up here, we've had boats tipped over, just from wakes. We get drownings every day. You going to ride the Mississippi, you better respect her or she'll do you in."

His lock basin had filled. It had the absolute stillness of the moment after the last note of the finale before the applause begins. He ran his eye along the brimming surface. I felt that the lockmaster was a kindred spirit, a man who simply loved water. He softened every time he looked at his pet element, his long, chipped hatchet face taking on a moony otherworldliness.

"But you've got to watch that sky. You ever see anything queer about it, if the clouds look wrong somehow, you get off the river. Oh, you'll see thunder and lightning. Hell, you could run into a hurricane. There's storms on the Mississippi so bad even the big tows get lost sometimes. There's tows gone down there, just sucked under in a storm on the river. She can be meaner than the ocean. But you'll be okay. Just remember, if there's something in the air that don't feel right, *get off the river.* You'll get to know her. You'll learn the signs. The time you got to start worrying is when she goes dead quiet. That's when she means to get up to something, and that's when you get off that river."

He had put me back in touch with the dream. The lockmaster's river and mine were, thank God, the same beautiful, treacherous place. He had grown up right beside it in the little river town of Lansing, Iowa. When he left school, he had become a commercial fisherman and trapper. Then he'd got a job as a construction worker, building levees to contain the floodwaters of the Mississippi. From there he had gone on to work as a bargeman and had graduated to being a full-fledged river pilot, ferrying barge fleets between Minneapolis and St. Louis.

"In 1960, I got married. Hell, I wanted to stay on the river, but my wife was mad. You know the way women change you? My wife . . . she don't care for the Mississippi too much."

So he had settled on his lock. I asked him how much he still missed being a pilot.

"Every time a tow goes through here, I think I'm up there in that wheelhouse."

Upstream of us, a tow was swinging round the bend of Nicollet Island. It looked as if someone had turned several tall apartment buildings on their faces and set them afloat. It was not a "tow" at all, in fact: It was a push. Somewhere far at the back of the fleet of barges, now lost behind the island, now printing blots of smoke on the sky, was a boat that wasn't a boat, but a blunt white four-story house, all balconies and verandas, mounted over the top of an enormous engine. This displaced housing project filled the river. Its wake shook the trees on the banks and sent a curling wave far into the shore.

"Three by three," the lockmaster said. "A little one. A single. You should see a double come through here."

"Uh-huh," I said, as noncommittally as possible. I didn't want to be too soft a touch for Minnesota comedians. "So what's a double, and what do you do with it?"

"A double, she could be fifteen barges, three wide, five long. You push nine of 'em in. Break the couplings. Boat backs out with six barges. Then they lock 'em, raise 'em up, drag a cable on 'em, snake 'em up the wall. Drop back. Pick up the second half. Then they make up the fleet and away they go."

"I think I lost about six barges somewhere."

"You'll see how they lock-through. There's twenty-nine locks between here and St. Louis. After that it's open river. Then you'll see the real big tows. Fifty, sixty barges. That'd be around eight acres. And that's something else."

Looking at the wake of the baby tow ahead of us, I felt an apprehensive surge in my guts, seeing waves as high as houses breaking on my cockleshell.

"That trip you're making . . . now, that's something I'd like to do. You a married man?"

"Not exactly."

"If you was married . . . Boy, if I told my wife I was going to ride the river down through New Orleans . . . reckon she'd be around at her attorney's, filing for divorce."

The huge gates at the head of the lock swung open on hydraulic winches.

"All those river towns . . . they're different than the inland towns—looser, more wild. A few years back, they were really wild, those river towns." He seemed to be thinking of his own past and his present compromises. "Yeah," he said a little sadly, "they were wild."

He locked the tow through. Thirteen thousand tons of grain bound for

Baton Rouge, Louisiana. When the pilot's voice came through on the radio, he spoke in the singsong whiffle of the very deep South.

"Well, Cap—wish I was goin' with you," said the lockmaster into his handset. I supposed that he said that to everyone.

On Tuesday, I drove out to see my boat. I had firm ideas about what a boat should be. One of the river books over which I'd pored during the summer had been Henry Thoreau's *A Week on the Concord and Merrimack Rivers.* Thoreau had made his inland voyage in a green-and-blue dory, "a creature of two elements, related by one half of its structure to some swift and shapely fish, and by the other to some strong and graceful bird." I had been tempted to send this lovely specification on an airmail postcard to Crystal Marine.

The boatyard lay far out of town, away from the river, at the end of a dismal suburban boulevard. In the lot at the back, a hundred boats were tipped up on trailers, identifiable only by their numbers. Mine was WS 1368 DD. It was just a mustard-colored shell of aluminum. Blunt-backed, broad in the beam, this bare piece of riveted alloy did not look like a craft in which one might float at all easily into an idyll. It was related to neither fish nor bird, but to some new, efficient brand of nonstick saucepan.

Herb Heichert, the joint owner of the yard, stood by while I walked in a slow circle around this unalluring object, trying to think of something polite to say about it.

"How do you like it?" His voice had the rusty remains of German in it.

"It looks . . . strong," I said. "Would it be easy to sink?"

"No, you got plenty of flotation there. See those seats? That's where you got your flotation."

I was glad that I had flotation. I thought of it more as a moral quality than as a physical property. I'd always wanted to have flotation.

"Now we got to fix you up with the right rig for the river." He leaned on the transom. The boat boomed like a dull gong. Mr. Heichert pointed at the blank metallic space.

"All these hulls, they come in the same, and every one she goes out different. You got to build it around the customer, right? No one's the same. Everybody's different. That's America. That's the American Way. We're in the customization business here. You take a plain old hull and you build a guy's whole identity into it. Look, I'll show you—"

He led me to his showroom. Boats hung on ropes from the ceiling, stood on trailers, and were rooted by their keels to the walls. My mind boggled at the identities of the guys for whom they had been customized. One was carpeted from bow to stern in blood-red polystyrene fur; another, in the kind of artificial grass which undertakers spread over fresh graves.

"When a fella gets a boat, he gets real sore if he sees some other fella riding round the lake in a boat just like the one he's got himself. Round here, everyone's an *individualist.*"

So it appeared. I tried to focus my eyes on a boat on which every last inch had been covered with swirling rainbows of acrylic paint. The effect was roughly comparable to taking a heavy overdose of lysergic acid. A little dinghy had a ship's wheel that might have been salvaged from the wreck of the *Golden Hind.* I peered into cocktail cabinets and freezers and rang the great brass bell that was mounted over a chubby day boat.

"Know what this is?" Herb was playing with a bit of fun technology that had been screwed to the thwart of a red-and-white-striped skiff. Fifty stars were painted on its stern. "Electronic fish locator. Like radar. See here— switch it on, it finds your fish for you, shows you what size it is, what the depth of water is there . . . all you got to do is put your pole over the side and catch it."

It struck me as immoral.

"We like our gizmos here."

"Will the fish locator tell you what bait to use as well?"

"They must be working on that, I guess."

When we returned to the lot, I saw WS 1368 DD through rather different eyes, as an empty canvas on which Herb Heichert was going to paint a gaudy extravaganza. I had certainly come to the right person: He was the works manager of a dream factory. I was bothered, though, by the fact that the dreams he dealt in bore no resemblance at all to mine.

"So what do you think?"

"I'll need somewhere to put my charts. A chart stand."

Oddly, a chart stand turned out to be the only gizmo that Herb had never been asked to fit to a boat. We set about designing one: a foldaway wooden frame with a button-down front of transparent plastic.

"The guys here stick to the lakes mostly. They don't use charts."

We settled on navigation lights, a steering wheel, an electric pump, and a swivel seat. Herb seemed disappointed with my parsimony.

"Fish locator?"

"No, thanks."

"We could run you up a paint job."

"No, it's fine as it is."

With oars, anchor, and the engine that was now running in a tank at the workshop, I would have the vessel I needed to sail into my Cockaigne. Aesthetically, it might not be a patch on Thoreau's dory or Huck's raft, but it would be fast enough to run from trouble. And I had plenty of flotation.

I needed to lay in some provisions. Thoreau had taken a supply of melons and potatoes on his trip. Huck and Jim had loaded up with traps, setlines for catfish, a lantern, a gun, and a Barlow knife. I went shopping in the city, hoping that if I acquired a few symbols of pioneer self-sufficiency it would bring about a transformation of my character and turn me into a proper outdoor adventurer.

Minneapolis itself, though, had gone indoors. When it had done all it could to tinker with the Mississippi; when the bridges, mills, power plants, locks, and dams had been finished; then the city had turned its back on the river and focused inward on itself. Now it was engaged in yet another exercise in utopian gadgetry; building a city within a city, a perfumed maze of artificial streets and plazas set in midair, four stories above the ground.

No wonder the streets had seemed so empty. The city had gone somewhere else and cunningly hidden itself inside its own facade. To go shopping, one had to take the elevator up to this other Minneapolis. It was completely synthetic urban space. Glassed-in "skyways" vaulted from block to block, and the shopping plazas had been quarried out of the middles of existing buildings like so many chambers, grottoes, and tunnels in a mountain of rock.

Here, fountains trickled in carpeted parks. The conditioned air smelled of cologne and was thickened with a faint, colorless spray of Muzak. The stores were open-fronted, like the stalls of a covered Arab souk. Like all the best utopias, this one was only half-built. It was the nucleus of a dream city designed to stretch out and farther out until Minneapolis-in-the-air would be suspended like an aureole over deserted ruins of Minneapolis-on-the-ground. If one put one's ear to the walls, one might hear the distant reverberation of workmen with pneumatic drills tunneling out more corridors and plazas in the wider reaches of the city.

The skyway system was as vividly expressive of the peculiar genius of Minneapolis as the rollercoasting freeways are of Los Angeles or the glass-and-cement cliffs of New York. Only a city with really horrible weather could have arrived at such a thing. Here people had left their local nature behind altogether. It was something nasty down below, and the skyways floated serenely over the top of it. "Nature" here was of the chic and expensive kind that comes only from the most superior of florists: ornamental palms and ferns, rooted not in soil but in coppery chips of synthetic petroleum extract.

Voices melted into the musical syrup of André Kostelanetz that trickled from hidden speakers in the palm fronds. Footsteps expired on the carpeted halls. At a mock-Parisian street café, the shoppers sat out at gingham tables, drinking Sanka with nonsaccharine sugar substitutes. Skyway-city turned one into an escapee. It was a place where everyone was on the run—from the brutish climate, from carcinogens, from muggers, rapists, automobile horns. Even one's own body was being discreetly disinfected and homogenized by the deodorant air. Up here, everything was *real nice:* We were nice people who smelled nice, looked nice, and did nice things in nice places.

Four floors below, we could see the nasty world we'd left behind. Hennepin Avenue was stretched out in front of us, famous for the Original Sin in which it wallowed. Beneath the skyway, a crummy little store sold rubber wear and shackles. Posters for the blue-movie houses showed nipples and pudenda so imaginatively colored and airbrushed that they'd ceased to look human in origin. A wino pissed in a doorway, watched by his dog. It was a pregnant bitch, and looked vaguely ashamed of its owner.

Looking down on that fallen world from the standpoint of this temporary synthetic Eden, I thought that perhaps Minneapolis and I were really on much the same track, traveling hopefully, never arriving. I loved the audacity of that American principle which says, When life gets tainted or goes stale, junk it! Leave it behind! Go West. Go up. Move on. Minneapolis had lit out from its river. Now it was trying to wave goodbye to its own streets. The skyways were just the latest stage in its long voyage out and away. "Where ya goin?" said the truckdriver to the hitchhiker at the end of *Manhattan Transfer.* "I dunno. Purdy far." It was the same answer that I'd given to the drunk in Moby Dick's, and on the skyways the whole city seemed to be echoing that classic traveler's statement of intent.

Our voyages, though, led in separate directions, and I seemed to have made yet another knight's move away from the river; so I was cheered to see a rack of corncob pipes in a cigar store. They weren't called corncob pipes—that would have been too straightforward for this realm of artifice and invention. They were advertised as "Missouri Meerschaum," and I bought two of them, along with a tin of Captain Black Smoking Tobacco, which sounded suitably swarthy, and a Zippo windproof lighter. Drifting idly through more chambers of glass and ferns and tea-garden rumbas, I picked up a corkscrew, a thermos flask, and a khaki rain hat. I reached my hotel room half a mile away without ever touching ground.

I sat in front of the mirror and tried to construct the man who was going to ride the river. I packed a corncob with Captain Black, lit it with my Zippo, jammed my new hat over my ears and looked in the glass, hoping to see the beginnings of a true voyager. The effect was not good. The face reflected there belonged to a grinning scoutmaster.

Half the luggage in my room was books. For months I'd been collecting them in London. I had found more in New York. They were the stuff out of which I had been making my imagined river, and as the Mississippi grew more real, I would have to start dumping them overboard.

The one I liked best was titled *The Navigator.* Set in cheap, jerky type, it had been published in Pittsburgh in 1814, and it had been written by Zadok Cramer as a pocket guide for immigrants and traders who wanted to travel on the Western rivers. It had detailed maps of the Ohio and the Mississippi, and it was full of notes about where one could find lodgings, where the best places were to tie up one's boat, which were the most dangerous bits of the river, what to do in storms, and how to test sandbars for safety. When I had first looked at it, I had thought it a charming curio; now its cracked pages were beginning to take on a riveting up-to-dateness. Cramer's first remarks about the Mississippi were standard pietistic twaddle:

> This noble and celebrated stream, this Nile of North America, commands the wonder of the old world, while it attracts the admiration of the new. . . .

Within a paragraph, though, Cramer was scoring direct hits.

> To a stranger, the first view of the Mississippi conveys not that idea of
> grandeur which he may have pictured to himself: His first judgment
> will rest upon the appearance of its breadth, in which respect it is
> inferior to many rivers of much less note.

Exactly. Cramer knew only the lower river, below its junction with the Ohio at
Cairo, Illinois; I wished he'd been able to see it from the railroad tracks at
Minneapolis. Flicking through, I went back to his section of general hints for
intending voyagers.

> The first thing to be attended to by emigrants or traders wanting to
> descend the river, is to procure a boat, to be ready so as to take
> advantage of the times of flood, and to be careful that the boat be a
> good one.

Well, I had attended to that, all right. Right now, Herb Heichert should be
fixing the steering gear to the motor and putting in the circuitry for my
navigation lights. Cramer's tone grew sharply monitory. This business of
going down the river must not be done impetuously. There were, he said, too
many "young and inexperienced" navigators who,

> being flushed with the idea of a fortune before them, hastily buy a
> boat, load, jump into it themselves, fly to the steering oar, and halloo
> to the hands to *pull out.* Now swimming in good water, and unap-
> prehensive of the bad, they think themselves safe, until alarmed by
> the rumbling of the boat on a ripple, or shoving herself into the mud
> on a sandbar.

In Cramer's day, no one thought of going down the river without a copy of *The
Navigator.* It was a much-reprinted bestseller—and ironically enough, it became a hazard to navigation in its own right.

At least, that is what it was for Timothy Flint, a Presbyterian minister
from Boston who went west with his family, taking the river route, intending
to do some evangelizing among the rednecks on the shores. He had a dreadful
time of it. His book, *Recollections of the Last Ten Years Passed in Occasional
Residences and Journeyings in the Valley of the Mississippi* (1826), was a
wonderful inventory of terrors and disasters. The Flint family had innumerable brushes with death on the river, and *The Navigator* was directly responsible for the first of these catastrophes.

> On a sudden the roar of the river admonished us that we were near a
> ripple. We had with us that famous book "The Navigator" as it is
> called. The boat began to exchange its gentle and imperceptible

advance for a furious progress. Soon after, it gave a violent bounce against a rock on one side, which threatened to capsize it. On recovering her level, she immediately bounded on the opposite side, and that in its turn was keeled up. Instead of running to the oar, we ran to look in "The Navigator." The owner was pale. The children shrieked. The hardware came tumbling upon us from the shelves, and Mrs. Flint was almost literally buried amidst locks, latches, knives, and pieces of domestic cotton.

There was a moral for me here somewhere. Like the Reverend Timothy Flint, I was an incorrigibly bookish man. The river in my books was one thing; that sludgy beast beyond the tracks was quite another—and I had better start getting the distinction between the two clear in my head. If I didn't, I was going to run dangerously, perhaps finally, aground.

Herb Heichert was too much of an artist to take much notice of my dull and utilitarian specifications. When I arrived at the boatyard the next day, everything was fixed: the wheel, the lights, the pump that would drain the boat at the flick of a switch, a swivel seat of imitation pigskin and a neatly carpentered chart stand. What I had not bargained for was the canopy that now fluttered over it, a candy-striped sheet rigged up on a folding aluminum frame. Nor was I prepared for the fact that the boat was no longer just called WS 1368 DD. The words RABAN'S NEST had been painted in enormous black letters on both sides.

"Like your canopy?" Herb said. "Now you got a surrey with a fringe on the top."

"The canopy looks fine, but what's this 'Raban's Nest' stuff?"

"Couldn't resist it. Thought it up in the night. Just came to me. Don't you like it?"

We trailed it down to the river at Camden to try it out. The afternoon was rank and sweaty, and the Mississippi here drifted in a listless sweep between two bridges, a mile north of the end of commercial navigation. It looked as tame as a fishpond in a civic park. Root beer cans bobbed in the scum at its edge, and more condoms dangled from the branches of the trees like a freak show of spring blossoms.

We pushed the boat out from a concrete slip overhung by willows. In the water, it suddenly looked tiny, its canopy riffling in the feeble wind, its broken reflection a scatter of chips of yellow, white, and scarlet.

"Floats, anyhow," Herb said.

Swinging there on the current, it abruptly changed sex. It switched from an *it* to a *her.* She looked just right, and I felt a new rush of excitement at the prospect of my voyage.

I sat up in the bow while Herb started the motor and aimed the boat at the bridge downstream. She was alarmingly fast. As Herb pushed the throttle forward, she lifted her sharp nose clean out of the water and settled on her rump, her wake fanning in a wide V to both shores. Herb sent her into a careening series of figure-eights, with the boat heeling over until the river sluiced by the top of her gunwales. As she cut into her own wake, the aluminum hull clanged as if it had hit rock. Clinging on up front, I was high over Herb's head down in the stern.

"You got to see the limits of what she can do!" Herb called over the yakking chatter of the outboard. He spun the wheel and the boat flipped its head, jumped violently on its wake, and headed off on another diagonal.

"Floating log! You got to watch for floating logs! You hit a log, it'll rip the lower unit out!" Not knowing what a lower unit was, I searched the river for floating logs and saw that we were in the middle of an archipelago of the things. Herb was zigzagging at speed between sodden tree trunks whose only indications were a few innocent-looking twigs sticking out above the greasy water.

He turned the boat around on the current, where it slowed, pointing upstream, the motor just ticking over. My turn. I joined Herb in the stern and started off by muddling up the throttle lever and the gear-change stick. Gingerly I set it in forward gear and gave it a cautious dribble of gas.

For me, the boat would hardly steer at all. Its nose wobbled this way and that, and we corkscrewed slowly in the vague direction of the bank from which we'd come.

"Keep to the main channel!" Herb reached for the wheel. "Watch for the buoys! You get out of the channel, you'll run on a wing dam!"

"*Wing* dam?"

"Yeah. The wing dams, they run out twenty, thirty yards into the river. You can't see them when she's high as this, but they're there. Maybe six inches underwater. Maybe a couple of feet. They're real *rascals*. They built them out of riprap . . . rocks and stuff. You run into a wing dam, you'll be real lucky if your motor's the only thing you lose—it can take the bottom clean out of the boat. Hey, don't get too close to them buoys, now! See that log? Watch the piles of the bridge!"

This was probably the safest little stretch on the whole river. Even here, though, there seemed to be more snags and hazards than I would ever be able to comfortably keep in my head at once.

"Those moored barges over there? You keep well clear of them. When the current runs up against them it makes for one hell of a big undertow. Not so much up here, but lower on down the river when the current gets to be stronger, it can suck you right under if your motor stalls ahead of a line of barges. You don't often hear of guys going in at one end of a barge fleet and coming up alive at the other."

"And people do go under?"

"Happens every year." Herb looked pleased with this piece of information. "I don't know nothing much about the river. The only times I go boating is on the lakes. I wouldn't mess with the Mississippi. I guess I'm kind of sweet on the idea of staying alive."

The boat maundered downstream, going hardly quicker than the current. Every time I touched the wheel, its head whipped sideways and threatened to take us straight into a wing dam, a log, a buoy, or the piling of a bridge. I found it impossible to keep a steady course.

"You'll get used to it. After three, four days of riding the river it'll be no different than driving a car. You'll be okay. Watch your charts, keep in the channel, look out for them towboats. . . . Remember, you don't have to do *nothing* fast. Think about it. Do it slow. You run into any kind of trouble, think slow and you'll make out okay. Hey! Remember what I said about logs?"

I thought fast, panicked, and we smashed into the log broadside. The hull shuddered and clanged.

"You have to do that a few times. It's the only way you'll learn."

"I'm just frightened that the next mistake I make will be the fatal one."

"We'll rig you out with a life vest."

We were getting into the start of the commercial river. There were more lines of moored barge fleets parked in front of wharves and grain stores. A shovel-fronted tug was crossing the stream ahead of us, throwing up a wake that looked too high for me to handle. I turned the boat around and headed back for the bridge.

"You know how to take a wake? Never get caught sideways to it. Steer into the wave. If they're big and close together, you'll have to ride them out on a diagonal."

He took over the wheel from me and steered for the tug. Close to, its stern waves were running in steep ridges, four feet high and less than twenty feet apart. Herb drove squarely into them, and the boat see-sawed from crest to crest, plunging down, then tilting sharply upward to the oily sky. As each new wave hit the bow, the metal rang out in a melancholy boom.

"Never take it too fast. You don't want to pop a rivet."

My stomach was leading a private yo-yo life of its own.

"See? She hain't taken on a spoonful. You take a wake right, you won't have no problem at all. You let her swing you round broadside, though, she'll roll you right over. Then you'll have to swim down to New Orleans. Guy even tried *that* once. He made, oh, I guess a coupla hundred miles. Then had to climb out. His skin was all boils and sores . . . looked like he had leprosy, they said."

Driving the boat on farther downstream, I went very quiet indeed. Scared by the wake, I'd forgotten my difficulties in steering the boat and was surprised to notice that she was now keeping to a reasonably steady path. I dodged a floating log. I kept to the main channel, watching the twin unfolding lines of red and black buoys. Red to port and black to starboard. This had nothing to do with daydreams and boyhood memories; it was the serious business of learning to ride the river. For the next two hours I crammed myself with everything that Herb could teach me. I rode out the wake of two small tows. I practiced holding the bow into the face of a wave while the wave itself took hold of the boat's nose and tried to swing it around and lay it in its trough. I began to read the surface of the river, hunting for the telltale riffs in the current where the submerged wing dams ran out from the shore. I got accustomed to spinning the boat around, throttling it back and putting it hard into reverse gear. As the traffic on the river thickened, with tugs swinging whole fleets of barges around on the current, I did my best to think slow, feeling childishly dependent on Herb, who stood at my side saying very little except *Easy* and *Okay* and *Watch it*, as if he were gentling a nervous horse. I thought a lot about the warning that I'd been given by the lockmaster. *You better respect her, or she'll do you in.*

Back in the evening inside Minneapolis-in-the-air, I was the one lone diner in a restaurant full of families and couples. I picked at an omelet which had been cooked to the texture of chamois leather and drank, rather more enthusiastically, a bottle of California chablis, feeling my solitude as a conspicuous caste mark.

Most travel involves the reassuring presence of other travelers: One joins that easygoing society of professional solitaries who are themselves just passing through—the salesmen, homesick U.N. peacekeepers, drifters in search of jobs, political scientists pretending to be agricultural advisers, anthropologists who haven't had a bath for weeks, and the rest of that roving crew who prop up bars in foreign places and make for poker schools and conversation. On this trip, though, I was traveling through someone else's domestic interior; a stranger in the American living room. Here, if one didn't have a family one was at least supposed to be a delegate to a visiting convention, with a lapel badge and a light hound's-tooth suit to prove it. Lacking both, I felt that Minneapolis was condemning me to the grim demimonde of Hennepin Avenue.

Trying to look, at least, like an occupied man, I spread out my navigation charts conspicuously on the restaurant table and set to studying them. I had only the volume of charts for the "upper river," the 860-mile stretch from Minneapolis down to the junction with the Ohio at Cairo. It was a huge, ring-bound book, broad and thick enough to stun a sheep with, handsomely produced by the U.S. Army Corps of Engineers. By an act of Congress in 1917, the management of the river had been put into the hands of the Secretary of War, and it was still military territory. In a country where really good maps are curiously hard to find, these charts were a cartographer's masterpiece. Brilliantly particular in their details, severe in their exclusion of irrelevant bits of landscape, they gave a practical soldier's-eye view of the Mississippi, breaking it down into a clean summary of all the logistical problems involved in its mile-by-mile navigation. Weeks later, when I got hold of the charts for the "lower river," from Cairo down to the Gulf of Mexico, I was disappointed to find that they were hopelessly inferior—so small in scale, so careless in their inclusion of a distracting mass of surrounding countryside, that the Mississippi wasn't the hero of the book at all, but a minor character following its wriggly career somewhere out on the obscure edge of things.

These, though, were everything that charts should be. At a scale of two inches to the mile, they gave the river a decently heroic size. Turning the sheets, I watched it growing from less than half an inch wide in Minneapolis to sweeps of four and five inches as it suddenly swelled out just a few miles south of the city. Here it became a pale blue tesselation of lakes, islands, "sloughs," chutes, "towheads," "stump fields," bars, and creeks. The red vein of the main channel tacked from shore to shore, hedged in by the dotted outlines of "submerged features" that I was going to have to learn to steer clear of—the wing dams, hidden bank supports, pipes, cables, wrecks, and stumps.

I was enjoyably lost in the difficulties of getting from Mile 818 to Mile 816 (all distances were numbered from Mile 0 at Cairo). Running close to the Minnesota shore past Boulanger Slough, I'd pass the light and the government daymark on the bank, then begin a long eastward swing out across the river to Wisconsin, keeping on a narrow track between a stump field to my left and a serrated line of wing dams on my right. Buck Island wasn't an island at all, but a miniature Caribbean, backed by another stump field. Past the head of Nininger Slough, I'd graze the Wisconsin shore, following the railroad tracks as they ran along the water's edge, then swing out again, to position-up to enter Lock No. 2 at Hastings.

"Excuse me, sir, but are you the gentleman from England that's going down the river?"

In the electric-candle dusk of the restaurant, all I could see was a stooping business suit. It was pearl gray and filled to capacity.

"That's right. I'm just looking at where I hope I'll be tomorrow on the charts." I pointed to the bloody hairline.

"Lois?" the business suit called to a table somewhere behind him. "Yeah, I was right. It's him. It's the guy I said it was. He's got maps." In an afterthought he said to me, "Read about you in the paper. I was telling Lois—that's my wife—I was saying, 'There's that guy, at that table.' Recognized you from your picture in the paper."

I took this as a prelude to a relationship of some kind, but when I started to reply, his back was already turned to me and he was on his way to finish his dinner across the restaurant. I would have been glad to talk to anybody at that moment, and I found his abrupt departure unsettling. What *was* he doing? I supposed that he must have been settling a bet. I found it saddening that the business suit might have won a dollar by establishing my identity. I would not have risked a bet on it myself.

The charts had lost their vividness. After Lock 2, the river narrowed sharply between Lake Isabelle and Lake Conley. There was a marina on the Minnesota bank, just south of Hastings. After that, I couldn't be bothered to follow it further. The chablis bottle was empty. The waiting check looked rapacious. I saw the face of the business suit turned momentarily toward my table. It was meaty, and it was laughing.

I slept thinly. High wakes from towboats came rolling at me through my dreams. There were floating logs, and the propeller screamed on the rocks of a wing dam, and the boat pitched and clanged, and I tried to remember why on earth I was here, out of character in a Boy Scout hat. Later, with the curtains drawn against the sun, jittery and unshaven, I ordered up breakfast from Room Service and packed my bag.

The waiter who brought my eggs and coffee looked as if he had already done some growing that morning since he had put on his tuxedo. His forearms stuck out of his cuffs, and his collar was popping around his Adam's apple.

"I saw the article about you in the paper. The trip you're making . . . I really envy you."

"Really?"

"That's something *I'd* like to do, go down the river. St. Louis, New Orleans." He named them as I used to name them to myself.

"Why don't you go?"

"I'm buying time. Working through the summer. Most days, when I can, I go down to the lock and dam and look at the river. You're taking a boat, right? I want to build a raft."

"I thought of that too. I think it could be hellishly dangerous."

"People nowadays, nobody does nothing. Everyone plays safe and stays home. I'm going to save myself some bread and get out of this city. I'd like to work on the towboats . . . get a start as a barge hand. . . . But that river . . . shit! I love it, you know?"

I showed him my charts. He pored over them, saying, "Hey! . . . Hey! . . . Hey!" and clicking his tongue noisily against his front teeth. "Just looking at these, man . . . I *am* going to build that raft. There's a place up above the lock, a friend and me, we were talking about putting it together up there."

"On a raft you're going to have a lot of trouble keeping out of the way of the tows, aren't you?"

"Yeah . . . I guess so. . . ."

I had intruded a ponderous detail that had no place in the waiter's vision. He shook out his forelock of Swedish-colored hair.

"I better get back. Hey, have a *fantastic* ride, will you?"

"You too," I said.

"Yeah . . . well . . ." He laughed. "Wouldn't that be something else?"

It had faded into the conditional. Every time the waiter looked at the river he thought of lighting out, and the thought was sufficient in itself—more sustaining, even, than any real journey could be.

* * *

I found it harder to leave the city than I'd planned. Herb's partner had been doing some heavy public relations, and by the time I reached the river a crowd was waiting. Two television crews had turned out, and a gang of passersby had thickened around the television crews. No one seemed to know why anyone was here. But whatever it was, it was going to be on TV. There were rumors of a drowning, a rare bird, the arrival of the *Delta Queen* steamboat, and various other wonders. I was introduced to a spruce old man with an Instamatic camera and a basset hound. He was announced as the King of Camden, and very kindly took my picture. As he put away his camera he said, "I got an album of photos of people who've been on TV."

The boat went growling from its trailer into the water. I sprinkled a few drops of five-dollar champagne over her bow and shared the rest of the bottle with Herb, the King, and the basset hound. I heaved my case into the front of the boat and was about to take off when the TV crews intervened.

I've always enjoyed slow-motion action replays on television. I now found myself living in one. Acting under instructions, I held the neck of the champagne bottle over the bow of the boat. I shook hands with Herb. I climbed into the boat. I pushed off with an oar. I started the motor with a jerk of the cord. I waved to the King (who was by this time happily engaged in photographing the cameramen). I steered for the railroad bridge downstream. As soon as I had passed under its arches and was out of sight, I returned to the slip, got out of the boat, picked up the empty bottle, held it over the bow, shook hands with Herb, got into the boat, and went through the rest of the mime until I reached the bridge, then turned back to repeat the whole sequence one more time. With each new performance, these movements stiffened until they took on the ritual grotesquerie of a scene from Kabuki theatre. I became a star at taking my leave of Minneapolis: now christening my boat, now waving, now setting my face southward with, I thought, a becoming expression of jowly determination. The twin violet eyes of the cameras followed me with the same indifferent gaze that I'd noticed in the cow at the state fair. My head rattled with a conundrum: If my going away didn't happen on TV, it wouldn't be real; if it did happen on TV, it couldn't be real.

There was one problem with a sound boom; two hairs in the camera gate; one time when my motor wouldn't start; and a hitch involving a small boy and a basset hound. After the sixth rerun, I got back to find the crowd dissolving and the TV crews packing their equipment back into their vans. I turned around. No one remarked my last departure. I slipped into the main channel and let the boat take root in the river.

At last I had the Mississippi to myself, and it seemed that Minneapolis had conspired to make a gift of it to me for the afternoon. Nothing was moving. Barges and towboats were moored at the wharves, but no one was about on them. Cranes and derricks were frozen on the sky, caught at odd angles, as if their operators had been suddenly called away. The air was inert, and the surface of the river was as finely patterned as a fingerprint. Every twist and eddy of the current showed up as a black-pencil curlicue on the water. One day, I'd learn to interpret every squiggle—at least, I'd try to. For now, it was enough to be moving just for moving's sake, like Baudelaire's lost balloon.

A factory went by; an empty dock; a lone man with a paintbrush on the deck of a tug, who looked up for a moment from his work and waved; then summer-dusty trees, massed and entangled on a shore of powdery sand. Rising fish left circles on the water here, and the current squeezed them into narrow ovals, before they faded into the scratched wax polish of the top of the river. It was lovely to be afloat at last, part of the drift of things. All I needed was a pet fox from a Bingham painting to throw his black reflection on the water.

Beyond the riverbank, the city blocks wobbled and tapered in the afternoon haze. They looked so insubstantial that a cooling wind might have wiped them away altogether. Pity the typists, doormen, cleaners, clerks, executive vice-presidents locked in those trembling columns of gas! I had the natural superiority of the truant; out of it all, on my own limb, at a happy angle to the rest of society. The motor chirruped smoothly behind me, the boat kept up an unwavering line between the buoys, and in this still water I could see the floating logs fifty yards ahead and swing casually around them.

The upper lock at the Falls of St. Anthony was already open for me when I rounded Nicollet Island. Up on the platform, Herb, the lockmaster, and the King were leaning over the railing. I crashed into the chamber wall, overshot the ropes that had been lowered for me to hang on to, reversed furiously, crashed again, and just managed to grab one of the lines before the steel gates at the back of the lock closed with a hiss and a clunk.

"Okay," said Herb. "You'll learn."

"Wish I was going with you," said the lockmaster.

The lock had seemed huge when I'd stood above it four days ago. Inside the chamber, it felt twice as big. I clung to my pair of ropes. The water began to bubble and boil as the lock emptied. The boat edged down the slimy wall, and the faces above my head grew smaller and vaguer. As I dropped to thirty, then forty, then fifty feet down, it was like entering a new element in which the air was dank and cellarlike; I was far out of earshot of the people I had left back up there in the city daylight, their voices lost in the gurgling and sluicing of Mississippi water. The boat tugged and swung on the ropes, and even in a sweater I was shivering. Looking up at the pale pink blotches of Herb, the King, and the lockmaster, I felt that this descent was a kind of symbolic induction, a rite of passage into my new state as a river traveler.

I couldn't hear what they were calling. The front gates of the lock opened on a blinding rectangle of day, and I was out, past the railroad sidings, into another chamber, another drop, more clammy half-darkness, and another wide-open afternoon.

In that sudden alarm which sets in an hour or so after one has started any journey, I ran through the inventory of what I'd packed. My Hostmaster soda siphon with its box of bulbs for putting bubbles into tap water . . . chapstick . . . aerogrammes . . . the ineffective electrical gadget that was supposed to put instant creases in my trousers . . . surely I had left my hotel room quite bare. Then I remembered. On the lower shelf of the bedside table, a fatal place to put anything, I had left my copy of *Huckleberry Finn*, open face down at the bit where Huck plays the mean trick on Jim with the sloughed rattlesnake skin. Damn, damn, damn. Slowing on the current, I thought that perhaps my loss wasn't such a bad augury after all. This was a voyage I was going to have to make alone.

Phillip Roth

The Wall

Thousands of Jews each year journey to Israel to come in touch with their history as a people and to take their places as links in that long chain. But author Nathan Zuckerman, the protagonist in Philip Roth's novel *The Counterlife,* has come to Israel not in search of himself but to find his brother. At the Wailing Wall he finds *tsouris,* in the person of Jimmy Ben-Joseph.

When I'd visited Israel back in 1960, the Old City was still on the other side of the border. Across the narrow valley opening out behind this same hotel, I'd been able to watch the armed Jordanian soldiers posted as guards atop the Wall but of course I'd never got to visit the Temple remnant known as the Western or Wailing Wall. I was curious now to see if anything like what had happened to my brother in Mea She'arim would surprise and overtake me while standing at this, the most hallowed of all Jewish places. When I asked at the desk, the hotel clerk had assured me that I wouldn't find myself alone there, not at any hour. "Every Jew should go at night," he told me, "you'll remember it for the rest of your life." With nothing to do until I left the next morning for Agor, I got a cab to drive me over.

It *was* more impressive than I'd anticipated, perhaps because the floodlights dramatizing the massive weight of the ancient stones seemed simultaneously to be illuminating the most poignant of history's themes: Transience, Endurance, Destruction, Hope. The Wall was asymmetrically framed by a pair of minarets jutting up from the holy Arab compound just beyond, and by two mosque domes there, the grand one of gold and a smaller one of silver, placed as though subtly to unbalance the picturesque composition. Even the full moon, hoisted to an unobtrusive height so as to avoid the suggestion of superfluous kitsch, seemed, beside those domes silhouetting the sky, decorative ingenuity in a very minor mode. This gorgeous Oriental nighttime backdrop made of the Wailing Wall square an enormous outdoor theater, the stage for some lavish, epic, operatic production whose extras one could watch walking casually about, a handful already got up in their religious costumes and the rest, unbearded, still in street clothes.

Approaching the Wall from the old Jewish quarter, I had to pass through a security barrier at the top of a long flight of stairs. A middle-aged Sephardic soldier, scruffily dressed in army fatigues, fumbled through the tourists' shopping bags and purses before letting them pass on. At the foot of the stairs, lounging back on their elbows, as oblivious to the Divine Presence as to the crowd milling about, were four more Israeli soldiers, all quite young, any one of whom, I thought, could have been Shuki's son, out not practicing his piano. Like the guard up by the barrier, each appeared to have improvised a uniform from a heap of old clothes at an army surplus store. They reminded me of the hippies I used to see around Bethesda Fountain in Central Park during the Vietnam War years, except that slung across these Israeli khaki rags were automatic weapons.

A stone divider insulated those who'd come to pray piously at the Wall from the people circulating in the square. There was a small table at one end of the barrier and on it a box of cardboard yarmulkes for hatless male visitors—women prayed by themselves down at their own partitioned segment of the Wall. Two of the Orthodox were stationed—or had decided to situate themselves—just beside the table. The older one, a slight, bent figure with a storybook white beard and a cane, was seated on the stone bench running parallel to the Wall; the other, who was probably younger than I, was a bulky man in a long black coat, with a heavy face and a stiff beard shaped like a coal scoop or a shovel. He stood above the man with the cane, talking with great intensity; however, no sooner had I placed a yarmulke on my head than abruptly he turned his attention on me. "*Shalom. Shalom aleichem.*"

"*Shalom,*" I replied.

"I collect. Charity."

"Me too," the old man chimed in.

"Yes? Charity for what?"

"Poor families," answered the one with the black shovel beard.

I reached into my pocket and came up with all my change, Israeli and English. To me this seemed a generous enough donation given the nebulous quality of the philanthropy he claimed to represent. He offered in return, however, a just perceptible look that I had to admire for its fine expressive blend of incredulity and contempt. "You don't have paper money?" he asked. "A couple of dollars?"

Because my meticulous concern for his "credentials" suddenly struck me as pretty funny in the circumstances, and also because old-fashioned shnorring is so much more humanly appealing than authorized, respectable, humanitarian "fund-raising," I began to laugh. "Gentlemen," I said, "fellows—" but the shovel-beard was already showing me, rather like a curtain dropping when the act is over, the back of his extensive black coat, and had already resumed firing his Yiddish at the seated old man. It hadn't taken all day for him to decide not to waste time on a cheap Jew like me.

Standing singly at the Wall, some rapidly swaying and rhythmically bobbing as they recited their prayers, others motionless but for the lightning flutter of their mouths, were seventeen of the world's twelve million Jews communing with the King of the Universe. To me it looked as though they were communing solely with the stones in whose crevices pigeons were roosting some twenty feet above their heads. I thought (as I am predisposed to think), "If there is a God who plays a role in our world, I will eat every hat in this town"—nonetheless, I couldn't help but be gripped by the sight of this rock-worship, exemplifying as it did to me the most awesomely retarded aspect of the human mind. Rock is just right, I thought: What on earth could be less responsive? Even the cloud drifting by overhead, Shuki's late father's "Jewish cloud," appeared less indifferent to our encompassed and uncertain existence. I think that I would have felt less detached from seventeen Jews who openly admitted that they *were* talking to rock than from these seventeen who imagined themselves telexing the Creator directly; had I known for sure it was rock and rock alone that they knew they were addressing, I might even have joined in. Kissing God's ass, Shuki had called it, with more distaste than I could muster. I was simply reminded of my lifelong disaffection from such rites.

I edged up to the Wall to get a better look, and from only a few feet away watched a man in an ordinary business suit, a middle-aged man with a monogrammed briefcase at his feet, conclude his prayers by placing two soft kisses upon the stone, kisses such as my own mother would lay upon my brow when I was a child home in bed with a fever. The fingertips of one hand remained in gentlest conjunction with the Wall even after he had lifted his lips from the last lingering kiss.

Of course, to be as tenderized by a block of stone as a mother is by her ailing child needn't really mean a thing. You can go around kissing all the walls in the world, and all the crosses, and the femurs and tibias of all the holy blessed martyrs ever butchered by the infidel, and back in your office be a son of a bitch to the staff and at home a perfect prick to your family. Local history hardly argued that transcendence over ordinary human failings, let alone the really vicious proclivities, is likely to be expedited by pious deeds committed in Jerusalem. Nonetheless, at that moment, even I got a little carried away, and would have been willing to concede that what had just been enacted before me with such affecting sweetness might not be *entirely* inane. Then again I could have been wrong.

Nearby, an archway opened into a large cavernous vault where, through a floodlit grate in the stone floor, you could see that there was even more Wailing Wall below the ground than above—way back then was way down there. A hundred or so square feet, the entry to this chamber, were partitioned off into a smallish makeshift room that, except for the fire-blackened, roughly vaulted ceiling and the stones of the Second Temple Wall, looked something like the unprepossessing neighborhood synagogue where I had been enrolled for late-afternoon Hebrew classes at the age of ten. The large Torah ark might have been built as a woodwork project by a first-year shop class in vocational school—it was as unholy-looking as it could possibly be. Rows of storage shelves along the wall facing the ark were piled unevenly with a couple of hundred worn prayer books, and, randomly scattered about, were a dozen battered plastic chairs. But what reminded me most of my old Talmud Torah wasn't so much the similarity of the decor as the congregation. A chazan stood off in one corner, flanked by two very thin teenagers in Chasidic garb who chanted intermittently with great fervor while he intoned in a rough baritone wail—otherwise the worshipers seemed only marginally engaged by the liturgy. It was very much as I remembered things back on Schley Street in Newark: Some of them kept turning around to see if anything of more piquancy might be developing elsewhere, while others looked every which way, as though for friends they were expecting to arrive. The remaining few, in a desultory way, seemed to be counting the house.

I was just easing myself in beside the bookshelves—so as to look on unobtrusively from the sidelines—when I was approached by a young Chasid, distinguished in this assemblage by the elegant fit of his long satin coat and the unblemished black sheen of a new velvet hat with a low crown and an imposing brim. His pallor was alarming, however, a skin tone a breath away from the morgue. The elongated fingers with which he was tapping my shoulder suggested something erotically creepy at one extreme and excruciatingly delicate at the other, the hand of the helpless maiden *and* of the lurid ghoul. He was inviting me, worldlessly, to take a book and join the minyan. When I whispered no, he replied, in hollow, accented English, "Come. We need you, mister."

I shook my head again just as the chazan, with a raw, wrenching wail that could well have been some terrible reprimand, pronounced "Adonoi," the name of the Lord.

Unfazed, the young Chasid repeated, "Come," and pointed beyond the partition to what looked more like an empty warehouse than a house of prayer, the sort of space that a smart New York entrepreneur would jump to convert to sauna, tennis courts, steam room, and swimming pool: The Wailing Wall Health and Racquet Club.

In there too were pious worshipers, seated with their prayer books only inches from the Wall. Leaning forward, their elbows on their knees, they reminded me of poor souls who'd been waiting all day in a welfare office or on an unemployment line. Low lozenge-like floodlights did not serve to make the place any cozier or more congenial. Religion couldn't come less adorned than this. These Jews needed nothing but that wall.

Collectively they emitted a faint murmur that sounded like bees at work—the bees genetically commandeered to pray for the hive.

Still patiently waiting at my side was the elegant young Chasid.

"I can't help you out," I whispered.

"Only a minute, mister."

You couldn't say he was insisting. In a way he didn't even seem to care. From the fixed look in his eye and the flat, forceless voice, I might even have concluded, in another context, that he was mentally a little deficient, but I was trying hard here to be a generous, tolerant cultural relativist—trying a hell of a lot harder than he was.

"Sorry," I said. "That's it."

"Where are you from? The States? You were bar mitzvah?"

I looked away.

"Come," he said.

"Please—enough."

"But you are a Jew who was bar mitzvah."

Here we go. One Jew is about to explain to another Jew that he is not the same kind of Jew that the first Jew is—the source, this situation, of several hundred thousand jokes, not to mention all the works of fiction. "I am not observant," I said. "I don't participate in prayer."

"Why do you come here?" But it was again as though he wasn't asking because he really cared. I was beginning to doubt that he fully understood his own English, let alone mine.

"To see the Old Temple Wall," I replied. "To see Jews who *do* participate in prayer. I'm a tourist."

"You had religious education?"

"None that you could take seriously."

"I pity you." So flatly stated that he might as well have been telling me the time.

"Yes, you feel sorry for me?"

"Secular don't know what they are living for."

"I can see how to you it might look that way."

"Secular are coming back. Jews worse than you."

"Really? How much worse?"

"I don't like to say even."

"What is it? Drugs? Sex? Money?"

"Worse. Come, mister. It'll be mitzvah, mister."

If I was correctly reading his persistence, my secularism represented to him nothing more than a slightly ridiculous mistake. It wasn't even worth getting excited about. That I wasn't pious was the result of some misunderstanding.

Even while I was making a stab at surmising what he thought, I realized that of course I could have no more idea of what was going on in his mind than he could have of what was going on in mine. I doubt that he even tried to figure out what was in mine.

"Leave me alone, okay?"

"Come," he said.

"Please, what's it to you whether I pray or not?" I didn't bother to tell him—because I didn't think it was my place to—that frankly I consider praying beneath my dignity. "Let me just stand quietly out of the way here and watch."

"Where in the States? Brooklyn? California?"

"Where are *you* from?"

"From? I am a Jew. Come."

"Look, I'm not criticizing your observance or your outfit or your appearance, I don't even mind your insinuations about my shortcomings—so why are you so offended by me?" Not that he appeared in the least offended, but I was trying to place our discussion on a higher plane.

"Mister, you are circumcised?"

"Do you want me to draw you a picture?"

"Your wife is a shiksa," he suddenly announced.

"That wasn't as hard to figure out as you like to make it seem," I said, but in the bloodless face there was neither amusement nor fellow-feeling—only a pair of unfazed eyes focused blandly on my ridiculous resistance. "All four of my wives have been shiksas," I told him.

"Why, mister?"

"That's the sort of Jew I am, Mac."

"Come," he said, motioning to indicate that it was time for me to stop being silly and to do as I was told.

"Look, get yourself another boy, all right?"

But because he couldn't completely follow what I was saying, or because he wanted to harass me and drive my sinfulness from this holy place, or because he wished to correct the little mistake of my having left the fold, or maybe because he simply needed another pious Jew in the world the way someone who is thirsty needs a glass of water, he wouldn't let me be. He just stood there saying "Come," and just as stubbornly I remained where I was. I wasn't committing any infraction of religious law, and refused either to do as he wished or to take flight as an intruder. I wondered if, in fact, I hadn't been right at the outset, and if he wasn't perhaps a little defective, though on further reflection, I saw it could well appear that the man without all his marbles had to be the one with four Gentile wives.

I was out of the cavern no more than a minute, taking a last look around the square at the minarets, the moon, the domes, the Wall, when someone was shouting at me, "It's you!"

Standing in my path was a tall young man with a thin, scraggly growth of beard who looked as though he had all he could do not to give me an enormous hug. He was panting hard, whether from excitement or from having run to catch me. I couldn't tell. And he was laughing, gusts of jubilant, euphoric laughter. I don't think I've ever before come across anyone so tickled to see me.

"It's really you! Here! Great! I've read all your books! You wrote about my family! The Lustigs of West Orange! In *Higher Education*! That's them! I'm your biggest admirer in the world! *Mixed Emotions* is your best book, better than *Carnovsky*! How come you're wearing a cardboard yarmulke? You should be wearing a beautiful, embroidered *kipa* like mine!"

He showed me the skullcap—held by a hair-clip to the top of his head—as though it had been designed for him by a Paris milliner. He was in his mid-twenties, a very tall, dark-haired, boyishly handsome young American in a gray cotton jogging suit, red running shoes, and the embroidered *kipa*. He danced in place even as he spoke, bounding up on his toes, his arms jiggling like a boxer's before the bell to round one. I didn't know what to make of him.

"So you're a West Orange Lustig," I said.

"I'm Jimmy Ben-Joseph, Nathan! You look great! Those pictures on your books don't do you justice! You're a good-looking guy! You just got married! You have a new wife! Numero four! Let's hope this time it works!"

I began laughing myself. "Why do you know all this?"

"I'm your greatest fan. I know everything about you. I write too. I wrote the Five Books of Jimmy!"

"Haven't read them."

"They haven't been published yet. What are you doing here, Nathan?"

"Seeing the sights. What are *you* doing?"

"I was praying for you to come! I've been here at the Wailing Wall praying for you to come—and you came!"

"Okay, calm down, Jim."

I still couldn't tell whether he was half-crazy or completely crazy or just seething with energy, a manicky kid far away from home clowning around and having a good time. But since I was beginning to suspect that he might be a little of all three, I started back toward the low stone barrier and the table where I'd picked up my yarmulke. Beyond a gate across the square I could see several taxis waiting. I'd catch one back to the hotel. Intriguing as people like Jimmy can sometimes be, you usually get the best of them in the first three minutes. I've attracted them before.

He didn't exactly walk *with* me as I started off but, springing on the toes of his running shoes, proceeded backwards away from the Wall a couple of steps in front of me. "I'm a student at the Diaspora Yeshivah," he explained.

"Is there such a place?"

"You never heard of the Diaspora Yeshivah? It's over there on top of Mount Zion! On top of King David's mountain! You should come and visit! You should come and stay! The Diaspora Yeshivah is made for guys like you! You've been away from the Jewish people too long!"

"So they tell me. And how long do you plan to stay?"

"In Eretz Yisrael? The rest of my life!"

"And how long have you been here?"

"Twelve days!"

In the setting of his surprisingly small, delicately boned face, which was miniaturized further by a narrow frame of new whiskers, his eyes looked to be still in the throes of creation, precariously trembling bubbles at the tip of a fiery eruption.

"You're in quite a hyped-up state, Jimmy."

"You bet! I'm high as a kite on Jewish commitment!"

"Jimmy the Luftyid, the High-Flying Jew."

"And you? What are you, Nathan? Do you even know?"

"Me? From the look of things, a grounded Jew. Where'd you go to college, Jim?"

"Lafayette College. Easton, PA. Habitat of Larry Holmes. I studied acting and journalism. But now I'm back with the Jewish people! You shouldn't be estranged, Nathan! You'd make a great Jew!"

I was laughing again—so was he. "Tell me," I said, "are you here alone or with a girlfriend?"

"No, no girlfriend—Rabbi Greenspan is going to find me a wife. I want eight kids. Only a girl here will understand. I want a religious girl. Multiply and be fruitful!"

"Well, you've got a new name, a start on a new beard, Rabbi Greenspan is out looking for the right girl—and you're even living on top of King David's mountain. Sounds like you've got it made."

At the table by the barrier, where there was nobody any longer collecting for the poor, if there ever had been, I placed my yarmulke on top of the others piled in the box. When I extended my hand Jimmy took it, not to shake but to hold affectionately between the two of his.

"But where are you going? I'll walk you. I'll show you Mount Zion, Nathan. You can meet Rabbi Greenspan."

"I've already got my wife—numero four. I have to be off," I said, breaking away from him. *"Shalom."*

"But," he called after me, having resumed that vigorous, athletic bounding about on his toes, "do you even understand why I love and respect you the way I do?"

"Not really."

"Because of the way you write about baseball! Because of all you feel about baseball! That's the thing that's missing here. How can there be Jews without baseball? I ask Rabbi Greenspan but he don't comprendo. Not until there is baseball in Israel will Messiah come! Nathan, I want to play center field for the Jerusalem Giants!"

Waving goodbye—and thinking how relieved the Lustigs must be back in West Orange now that Jimmy is here in Eretz Yisrael and Rabbi Greenspan's to worry about—I called, "Go right ahead!"

"I will, I will if you say so, Nate!" and beneath the bright floodlights, he suddenly broke away and began to run—back-pedaling first, then turning to his right, and with his delicate, freshly bearded face cocked as though to follow the flight of a ball struck off a Louisville Slugger from somewhere up in the old Jewish quarter, he was racing back toward the Wailing Wall without any regard for who or what might be in his way. And in a piercing voice that must have made him something of a find for the Lafayette College Drama Society, he began to shout, "Ben-Joseph is going back, back—it could be gone, it may be gone, this could be curtains for Jerusalem!" Then, with no more than three feet between him and the stones of the Wall—and the worshipers at the Wall—Jimmy leaped, sailing recklessly into the air, his long left arm extended high across his body and far above his embroidered *kipa*. "Ben-Joseph catches it!" he screamed, as along the length of the Wall a few of the worshipers turned indignantly to see what the disturbance was. Most, however, were so rapt in prayer that they didn't even bother looking up. "Ben-Joseph catches it!" he cried again, holding the imaginary ball in the pocket of his imaginary glove and jumping up and down in the very spot where he had marvelously brought it in. "The game is over!" Jimmy was shouting. "The season is over! The Jerusalem Giants win the pennant! The Jerusalem Giants win the pennant! Messiah is on his way!"

Israel Shenker

A Bookworm's Holiday in Wales

Alphabetical serendipity brings us from Israel to Israel Shenker, and by his words to Wales. This article appeared in the New York Times Sunday Travel Section, in June 1985, and we clipped the piece then, thinking one day we too would go to the tin tabernacle at St. Deiniol's. If this is your idea of a splendid vacation, you might consider writing the booking secretary at St. Deiniol's Library, Hawarden Deeside, Clwyd CH5 3DE, North Wales, Great Britain.

The welcome mat was out for me at St. Deiniol's, as long as I was not deliberately working to undermine the Anglican religion. It seemed so little to ask. I dismissed every subversive impulse and applied for admission.

St. Deiniol's is probably the world's only residential library, and William E. Gladstone (1809–1898) founded it and set the rules. Having served the nation four times as Prime Minister, he was used to getting his way—and getting out of the way when Disraeli had more votes.

Year after year, Gladstone spent about six months at Hawarden (pronounced HAR-den) Castle, seven miles from Chester, just across the Welsh border. There he raised a large family, felled hundreds of trees for relaxation, and spent the toiling hours in his library-study, known as the temple of peace.

Near the end of his life he founded the temple's annex at St. Deiniol's, setting it up near the castle in a ramshackle structure and endowing it with thirty thousand pounds and thirty thousand books. At age eighty he trundled many of the volumes over himself in a wheelbarrow, helped to shelve them, and was chagrined to find that three percent of his purchased books were duplicates.

"The tin tabernacle," is how Peter Jagger, the Anglican minister who serves as warden (boss) and chief librarian of St. Deiniol's, describes the old

299

place. Gladstone believed in spending money on books, not buildings, but after his death a stately sandstone building was erected as a gift to the nation and to those admitted to St. Deiniol's.

There is room for forty-six guests in single-, twin-, and double-bedded rooms, each with desk as well as hot and cold running water—not quite as austere as monks' cells, but hardly the stuff of Helmsley, Hilton, or Hyatt. On the other hand, do *they* have a stately oak library with about one hundred thirty thousand books (great oaks from thirty thousand little acorns grown), including fifty thousand from the Victorian era, a thorough representation of English literature down to the close of the nineteenth century, a huge collection on theology from the seventeenth century onward? Can any of *them* boast of having the Gladstone family papers—a quarter of a million items—and even the 107 volumes of notes, on some 5,130 English churches, by Sir Stephen Glynne, Gladstone's brother-in-law? Do they have thirty-eight volumes of Gladstone speeches, or books with Gladstone's annotations? And what about the pamphlet collection—about forty thousand separate loads of invective—including the one by Gladstone on the Vatican and civil allegiance that sold over one hundred fifty thousand copies and earned him two thousand pounds? Pope Pius IX himself helped with sales, by calling Gladstone "a viper attacking the barque of St. Peter."

"So you wish to undertake some research?" the library brochure asks. "Are you writing a book? Would you like to catch up on your reading? Must you get away to prepare for an examination [or] need free access to a wide-ranging library?" I dismissed all such suggestions. All I wanted to do was satisfy my curiosity about a place that would not rent me an austere lodging before receiving a testimonial from "a person holding public office, e.g., a university or college appointment, a clergyman, doctor, or an already established Reader at St. Deiniol's."

And how about the rates for room and board—including three nourishing meals, morning coffee, afternoon tea, and bedtime tea or coffee—ranging from £8 (about $10) a day for full-time students and unemployed postgraduates, up to £17.83 (including tax) for those whose expenses are being paid or subsidized by nonchurch sources? "Many pay eight pounds a day and it costs us fifteen," said Mr. Jagger. "At our prices we could fill our beds with people who want cheap holidays."

He is not a rosewater cleric out of P. G. Wodehouse. This is a sturdy Yorkshire go-getter who not only studied theology for seven years, and history after that, but also burrowed deep into the techniques of business management. He welcomes conference groups, and he has performed miracles in getting tough business people to contribute services and odd bits of paving to St. Deiniol's. If he had just a little bit more loose change he would be delighted to upgrade the accommodations, and he also wants to build a quadrangle on the ground level for handicapped guests. "If there's a Carnegie we'll call it the Carnegie wing," he said, fixing me with a stern eye, as though I knew where the Carnegies spent their summer holidays.

Mr. Jagger is nonetheless a soft touch for hardship cases, or at least prepared to make the best of them. He gave some students room and board in exchange for their painting a back corridor. When the government cut off grants for library assistants, he kept several on as volunteers—again in exchange for room and board.

St. Deiniol's fills up at Easter, and is busy from June through September. There are fewer guests during the academic year, and the annual occupancy rate is about 60 percent. Rank has no privilege here—the Archbishop of Canterbury, a member of parliament, and a secondary school student get identical accommodations. Michael Ramsay, who was to be Archbishop of Canterbury, wrote his first book here. Harold Wilson, one of Gladstone's successors as Prime Minister, wrote part of his Gladstone Prize Essay here. "The great scholars get on with their work," said Mr. Jagger. "Some of the pretentious ones immediately let you know how important they are."

I may or may not have rubbed shoulders at meals—served by waitresses—with a future prime minister, but I did meet a woman who was turning out a conscientious spot of homework. Dr. Ivy Oates, a sixty-nine-year-old general practitioner from Sheffield, came to St. Deiniol's for the first time ten years ago, and has been coming back regularly a week before her Open University exams, or for long weekends to prepare written assignments. "At home you've got meals to get, and the house looks at you and the telephone goes," she explained. "Here it was quiet, it was beautiful, and the library has got the atmosphere conducive to study. You could work in peace and settle down without any trouble."

In 1982 her course was the history of mathematics, in 1983 evolution, and last year "Science and Belief from Darwin to Einstein." "You meet such nice people here," Dr. Oates said. "There was once an American lady here who got ill and called me in the night."

Malcolm Lambert, who teaches medieval history at the University of Bristol, arrived for the first time in 1965, as a research student. "I liked it because it was so cheap," he said. "It was three pounds a week, all found [room and board], and if you had a good feed once a week it was all right." He stayed once for eighteen months, purchasing rare books he needed for his research that St. Deiniol's happened not to have, and he felt he was still coming out ahead.

Until thirty years ago women were not admitted as residents. Once they were, Professor Lambert met his wife-to-be at St. Deiniol's and they eventually celebrated their silver wedding anniversary there. They now come to the library with their friends the Jarmans. Thomas Jarmon wrote *The Rise and Fall of Nazi Germany.* "Perhaps St. Deiniol's is a bit of a Shangri-La," he said. "You want to stay on. You don't want to leave."

"In the old days they couldn't heat the place—didn't have enough money," said Professor Lambert. "It was a vicious circle—no money, no heating, no guests, and no money."

There is now effective central heating, and Professor Lambert had brought sixteen students—all paying their own way—who had just been admitted to Bristol to study history. The students were given assignments to prepare at St. Deiniol's, for example: "Explain why the Kings of England were able to conquer Wales, but not Scotland." One seminar on medieval history was going to be held in the keep of Hawarden's old castle. While I was at St. Deiniol's there was to be an after-dinner lecture on Franklin D. Roosevelt, by John Kentleton, who teaches American history at the University of Liverpool. "We have some of our lectures in the pub," Professor Lambert told me, and his wife added: "We thought we'd publish 'The Fox & Grapes Papers.'"

The Fox & Grapes is one of the three local pubs. At St. Deiniol's, going to the pub is known as "choir practice." Thus far Mr. Jagger has resisted pleas for a bar at the library, and for wine at meals.

We all pressed our way to the pub bar for our drinks, and took them along into the small private room for the lecture. Having lived in the States during most of the years of the F.D.R. presidency, I arrogantly doubted whether I would learn much and expected a dry evening, but the lecture was informative and even gripping.

My neighbor and drinking partner at the talk, John Buchanan, is an Episcopal minister in Mount Pleasant, a suburb of Charleston, South Carolina. He was spending a six-month sabbatical at St. Deiniol's, along with his wife and two daughters, who were attending Hawarden's secondary school. Mr. Buchanan's bishop, FitzSimons Allison, formerly of Grace Church in Manhattan, had stayed at St. Deiniol's, and recommended it. Mr. Buchanan was spending much of his time reading books on contemporary Christian spirituality.

Gladstone spoke of the purpose of St. Deiniol's as "divine learning"—in which he included the classics. He wanted "a house of study for the glory of God and the culture of man," an "intellectual hospice." But he insisted that the hospitality "should as far as possible be made available for persons beyond the pale of the Anglican Church or even of the Christian Religion."

One of Mr. Jagger's predecessors tried to turn the library into a theological college, which was not the founder's intention, nor is it Mr. Jagger's. But the staff still prepares ordinands—over thirty years of age—for unpaid church service. "We've trained lawyers, headmasters, schoolmasters, bank managers, doctors, and engineers," said Mr. Jagger, who acts as principal of the course.

The statutes require the warden-librarian to be a clerk in holy orders of the Anglican Communion, and he must abide by "the rule of clerical subscription"—abstaining from diocesan or parish work. The first warden was Gladstone's son-in-law, and the cult of personality is still going strong: Mr. Jagger is working hard on a two-volume study of Gladstone as politician and Christian.

St. Deiniol's lives very much under the shadow of the great man. There are Gladstone portraits and statues, large and small, in halls, dining room, common room, floor hall, stairwell, gallery window, and library proper. On the front lawn stands a huge Gladstone statue refused by Dublin, though Gladstone supported home rule for Ireland.

The very divisions that Gladstone imposed in the library still hold sway; A is prolegomena, B bible, C patristics, D philosophy, E doctrine, F spirituality, G godly worship, and so on, omitting H (hell?) and I (infidels? idolatry?), proceeding all the way to W—topography and travel. The library has open shelves, and readers can take books back to their rooms. There are no keys to bedroom doors, and there has never been a theft reported by any resident.

But this is not paradise. Gladstone's official correspondence—with the help of his secretaries Gladstone wrote twenty-five thousand a year while Prime Minister—has been carted off to the British Museum, in 750 volumes. Most of the correspondence with the royal family is likewise in London, but that may be just as well. Gladstone was not precisely Victoria's favorite, nor she his—he called the Queen "Her Infallibility."

Sir William Gladstone, great-grandson of the founder, former Chief Scout of Britain, now lives in Hawarden Castle, acts as chairman of the library's management committee, and provides the library with passes admitting guests to his grounds. St. Deiniol himself was not a Gladstone, but a sixth-century Celtic saint. Despite all his miracles, he, too, would have had to submit a testimonial to get into this bookworm's heaven.

Applications and further information are available from the Booking Secretary, St. Deiniol's Library, Hawarden Deeside, Clwyd CH5 3DF, North Wales, Great Britain; telephone Hawarden 532350.

Walter Sullivan

Getting the Lay of the Land—From the Air

Unlike trains or ships, airplanes are conveyances without community,
dead time between destinations. How does one have a memorable
transcontinental journey on a plane other than having a meal tray land
in your lap, losing your luggage, or landing at the wrong airport?
Walter Sullivan, science writer for the *New York Times*, has found a way
to make life at thirty thousand feet interesting—provided you don't, as
experienced fliers are accustomed to do, reserve an aisle seat.

Y ou can't see anything from 30,000 feet. Get an aisle seat, order a drink,
lean back, and go to sleep." So goes the refrain that denies to countless air
travelers what, on a transcontinental flight, can be an exciting visual experience.

On a clear day the panorama passing below unfolds a history of colliding
continents, ice sheet invasions, floods, meteorite impacts, and volcanic eruptions of great magnitude. One can trace the evolution of those most intriguing of land forms—river meanders of strikingly uniform sinuousity. One can
follow the westward march of the pioneers and the dynamic, continuing
evolution of cities and suburbs. Only from earth orbit is the perspective
grander.

After heading west from New York, for example, one does not have to be a
geologist to marvel at the incredibly uniform folds of the Appalachians,
vestiges of the great collision of Europe and Africa with North America several
hundred million years ago.

NEW YORK
TO LOS ANGELES

The standard route to Los Angeles crosses the Susquehanna River near
the ill-fated nuclear power plant at Three Mile Island. To the left, contour strip

304

farming, designed to curb erosion, has imprinted on the landscape patterns like those of an abstract painter. To the right, at Harrisburg, the river has cut multiple water gaps through the ridges. Beyond, on the left, are the Chambersburg and Gettysburg battlefields.

In Ohio, after crossing the Ohio River at Wheeling, West Virginia, one begins to see the rectangular divisions that become far more striking farther west. These are products of the National Survey, inaugurated largely on the initiative of Thomas Jefferson when the young republic emerged from the Revolution deeply in debt. Selling land to colonizers was a way to liquidate at least part of it, and the plan devised by Jefferson and his colleagues ended by dividing most of the United States into counties six miles on a side subdivided into square mile sections.

Nowhere else on earth is geometry so dramatically imposed on the landscape. Because the meridians, or north south lines, converge toward the north (they all meet at the North Pole), they must be offset periodically to maintain the six-mile spacing of counties. Such offsets can often be seen in north south county roads.

Some areas are watered by center-pivot irrigation systems, resulting in panoramas of circular fields, each exactly filling one quarter-of-a-mile-square section. Other patterns have been imposed on the landscape by terracing for soil conservation or strip-cropping in which alternate strips of land are farmed or left fallow to reduce wind losses and allow restoration of soil moisture.

While pilots may digress to avoid storms or for other reasons, the standard route to Los Angeles crosses the Mississippi south of Mark Twain's hometown of Hannibal, Missouri, and follows the Missouri River to Kansas City. At many points one can see where back-and-forth migrations of a meandering river have left a multitude of concentric arcs delineating its former loops. The curves are preserved in rows of trees, intervening fields and swampy areas, forming repetitive patterns only visible from on high. Beneath the flight path west of Kansas City, the Oregon and Santa Fe trails diverged, but in only a few stretches are the wagon tracks still visible from aloft.

One of the greatest thrills of the transcontinental traveler, be it by Conestoga wagon, automobile, or plane, is the first glimpse of the Rocky Mountain Front Range. On the Los Angeles route it rises as the glittering, snow-clad peaks of the Sangre de Cristo, a 220-mile arc of mountains that was said to have been named by a Spanish priest who, on first seeing them, exclaimed: "Sangre de Christo!" ("Blood of Christ!").

The route crosses the range in southern Colorado south of 14,363-foot Blanca Peak, the range's highest. Beyond, in the San Luis Valley, the flight passes south of Great Sand Dunes National Monument and then over Shiprock in the northwest corner of New Mexico, a volcanic spire rising 1,400 feet above the desert plain in the Navajo Indian Reservation. It was originally the underground throat of a great volcano, but the surrounding landscape has eroded away.

In northeast Arizona the path crosses coal-rich Black Mesa, scarred by a strip mine of the Peabody Coal Company. Beyond and to the north stretches an extraordinary feature—the Echo Cliffs Monocline—formed where many sedimentary layers were draped over a steplike break in the landscape. The layers have been eroded away, exposing the edges of each as a multitude of parallel ridges.

In this arid region canyon walls and freestanding towers document millions of years of sediment accumulation—periods of desert winds, tropical landscapes, and changing climate. Over the south rim of the Grand Canyon such a history is exposed in as magnificent a fashion as anywhere on earth. The final stretch crosses Lake Mojave on the Colorado River and then follows the San Bernardino and San Gabriel Mountains into Los Angeles.

LOS ANGELES
TO NEW YORK

The standard Los Angeles–New York route lies farther south and crosses other wonders of the American landscape, including the world's freshest meteorite impact crater. Initially, the route passes over the luxurious resort of Palm Springs and Joshua Tree National Monument. Most flights then follow the route across the desert of the Colorado Aqueduct, which, by delivering water from the Colorado River, helped make Los Angeles possible. That river is crossed where Parker Dam has impounded long, narrow Lake Havasu.

Across Arizona the route follows the scenic south margin of the Colorado Plateau, a region of Arizona, Utah, Colorado, and New Mexico that has been raised a mile above the surrounding landscape, yet has remained largely flat, like the floor of a rising freight elevator. Its southern edge is a 300-mile series of escarpments known as the Mogollon Rim.

Here, near Sedona, towering outcroppings of the plateau are layered in countless shades of red, yellow, and brown. Volcanic eruptions on the plateau have poured lava over the rim, producing ramps such as the one that carries Interstate 17 up onto the plateau between Phoenix and Flagstaff. Eruptions near the San Francisco Peaks, prominent remnant of a shattered volcano north of the flight path, have occurred as recently as 1064, two years before the Norman invasion of England.

A short distance to the east, the route passes over Meteor Crater, gouged out twenty-five thousand years ago by the explosive impact of a meteorite thought to have been 140 feet in diameter traveling at forty-five thousand miles an hour. The crater is three miles in circumference, forming a natural stadium so vast that on its floor twenty football games could be played simultaneously before two million onlookers.

The Rio Grande Rift Valley is crossed near Taos pueblo, north of Santa Fe and south of a large open-pit molybdenum mine in the Sangre de Cristo

Mountains. Beyond the mountains the Santa Fe Trail is followed across the Oklahoma Panhandle. In the Flint Hills of southeast Kansas, past Wichita, there are striking chevron patterns on the landscape where rivers have cut through alternate layers of white, flinty sandstone and gray shale.

The Mississippi and Missouri Rivers are creased at their junction above St. Louis, and the Ohio River is passed in southern Indiana. Beyond that, strip mines cut into the coal-rich mountains near Charleston, West Virginia. After traversing the strikingly uniform Appalachian Ridges and the Blue Ridge at the south end of Skyline Drive, the route passes south of Washington and northeast toward New York.

NEW YORK
TO SAN FRANCISCO

One gets an entirely different view of the continent—its glacial scars, mountain-building masterpieces, and history of catastrophic floods—on the route from New York to San Francisco. It passes south of Niagara Falls, across the Great Lakes to Green Bay, Wisconsin, and then over regions of Wisconsin and Minnesota whose landscape was radically altered by flowing ice.

Elsewhere water has carved the landscape into central and tributary valleys resembling the trunk and branches of a tree. But here the ice rubbed out those patterns, leaving kettle-hole ponds where large chunks of the glacier lingered as the melting ice deposited rocks and soil around them. This is ideal dairying land—the source of Wisconsin's famous cheeses.

The Mississippi River is crossed at Minneapolis and, beyond it, the Missouri River where it is impounded to form Lake Oahe, extending across half of South Dakota. The Black Hills of Indian-fighting lore are to the left and to the right is Devils Tower, a landmark that figured in the film *Close Encounters of the Third Kind.*

Before reaching the Big Horn Mountain the route crosses an area of eastern Wyoming where vast, shallow coal deposits are being strip-mined. The largely unspoiled wilderness of the Wind River Range is crossed near 13,800-foot Gannett Peak, Wyoming's highest. From the air few features of the Western landscape are as striking as the eroded domes of western Wyoming. Their tops, worn away by millennia of wind and rain, display their many layers like those of an onion cut in cross section.

Along the Idaho-Utah border north of Great Salt Lake the path lies over Red Rock Pass, the collapse of which led to one of the greatest floods on record. During the last ice age Great Salt Lake swelled to become more than a thousand feet deeper than it is today. It spread from Utah into Nevada on the west and reached Red Rock Pass in Idaho to the north.

When it overflowed, the racing waters in a matter of hours lowered the pass by 344 feet, allowing a wall of water to race north into the valley of the

Snake River, scouring its walls in a manner no geologist could explain until the scope of this flood was recognized. The torrent flowed down Hells Canyon into the state of Washington and on to the sea.

The route crosses successive ranges of the Basin and Range Province, likened by the nineteenth-century geologist Clarence Edward Dutton to "an army of caterpillars crawling northward out of Mexico." It reaches the towering east wall of the Sierra Nevada, two miles high, just north of circular Mono Lake and its associated volcanic craters.

Earthquakes and other ominous signs have led geologists to fear renewed eruptions near Mammoth Lakes, to the south, where an eruption seven hundred thousand years ago threw up an estimated 140 cubic miles of ash—600 times more than the Mount St. Helens eruption in 1980. The telltale ash of this event has been found as far away as Arkansas, Louisiana, and Mexico.

As the Sierras are crossed the traveler can enjoy a magnificent view of Yosemite before crossing the Central Valley of California and the patchwork quilt of salt ponds on the east side of San Francisco Bay. Each pond, because of its algal inhabitants, is a brilliant hue of red, pink, yellow, or brown.

SAN FRANCISCO
TO NEW YORK

Across California the route lies north of that on the westbound flights, crossing rice-growing areas along the lower Sacramento River, the city of Sacramento, and areas of placer-mining for gold where the landscape has been overturned into gravel ridges.

The Sierras are crossed north of Lake Tahoe at Donner Pass, where forty-seven members of the Donner party died in the winter of 1846–47. Past Reno, Nevada, Walker Lake, a relic of ice age flooding, lies to the north. The path lies over Carson Sink, which is sometimes flooded. Then, until it veers southeast at the Black Hills of South Dakota, the route is almost the same as the westbound.

The Missouri River is crossed at Fort Randall Reservoir, as the plane heads toward Sioux Falls, South Dakota, and the landscape begins to show effects of the great ice sheet that once lay upon it. After passing over the Mississippi on the Iowa-Wisconsin border, however, a small region is crossed whose branching, water-carved valley systems show that it was bypassed by the ice.

After crossing Lake Michigan and Detroit the route passes over Lake Erie, northern Pennsylvania, and northern New Jersey.

Experiencing the wonders of such a journey depends, of course, on the weather. One should also make a point of asking for a window seat not over the wing and on the side away from solar glare, which will depend on one's direction and the time. With luck the journey can be memorable.

Paul Theroux

The Train to Mallaig

In 1977 the Massachusetts-born author moved with his family to Great Britain, which in time would become the subject of *The Kingdom by the Sea*, the source of this excerpt. Theroux took as his mission the circumnavigation on foot and by train of the whole of Great Britain, and he fell in with strangers as gifted travel writers do. As an American commenting often acidly on the manners of his cousins, Theroux did a turn on Trollope and Dickens that did not universally amuse. Still, it was undeniably a first-rate book, as Theroux had given readers of *The Great Railway Bazaar* and *The Old Patagonian Express* reason to expect.

After my days of being menaced by Belfast's ugly face I went by boat and train to Glasgow and found it peaceful, even pretty. It had a bad name. "Gleska," people said, and mocked the toothless population and spoke of razor fights in the Gorbals, and made haggis jokes. Yet Glasgow was pleasant—not broken but eroded. The slums were gone, the buildings washed of their soot; the city looked dignified—no barricades, no scorchings. Well, I had just struggled ashore from that island of antiquated passions. In Ireland I had felt as though I had been walking blindly into the dark. But Scotland made me hopeful. This sunny day stretched all the way to Oban, where I was headed.

On my way from Glasgow Central to Queen Street Station, I fell in with two postmen. They asked me where I had come from. I told them Ulster. They said, "Och!"

"It's full of broken windows," I said.

"Aye. And broken *hids!*" one said.

The other man said, "We got our Catholics. Ha' ye nae heard of the Rangers and Celtics fitba matches? They play each other a guid sux tames a year, but there's nae *always* a riot."

No alphabet exists for the Glaswegian accent—phonetic symbols are no good either without a glottal stop, a snort, or a wheeze. I met rural-dwelling Scots who told me they could not understand anyone in Glasgow. The Ulster accent took a moment to turn from noise to language: I heard someone speak and then in the echo of the voice there was a meaning. But this did not always happen in Scotland: The echo was meaningless, and in Glasgow it was a strangled peevish hiccup, sudden and untranslatable.

I rode in an empty railway car up the Clyde, past tenements. I wondered about their age. They were striking in their size and their darkness—six stories of stone, looking like prisons or lunatic asylums. Had the Scots originated the tenement? Their word for these old blocks was "lands" and they had been using the word since the fifteenth century.

We went past Dumbarton (Dun Bretane, "Hill of the Britons"), along the muddy rockstrewn shore, the Firth of Clyde. Across the firth was the busy port of Greenock ("birthplace of Captain Kidd, the pirate"). There were hills behind it. I always had trouble with hills. These were not so much risen loaves as smooth and sloping and lightly upholstered . . .

A big old man came through the connecting door, and though there was not another person in the whole railway car, he sat beside me. I put my notebook into my pocket.

"I hope you're not embarrassed," he said.

Not embarrassed but something—perhaps startled.

"I'm going to Oban," I said.

"Good," he said. "We can talk." He was also going the hundred miles.

But he did most of the talking. He was very old and even sitting next to me he was a foot higher. He looked like a pope. He had a fat nose and big baggy-fleshed hands. He wore a long black overcoat and carried a small parcel of books tied with twine: detective stories. His name was John L. Davidson and he had been born in Lanarkshire in 1895. He said that occasionally he did feel eighty-seven years old. How long had he lived in Dumbarton? "Only fifty years," he said. He lived in the Dumbarton Home for Aged Gentlefolks now. Everyone he had ever known was dead.

He said, "I'm only seven years younger than John Logie Baird. Have you not heard of him? He invented the tellyvision. He was born here in Helensburgh."

I looked out of the window.

"Over there somewhere," Mr. Davidson said. "His teachers at school didnae think he was very bright. They thought he was a head case. One day he decided to invent a tellyphone. He put a wire across the road, a tellyphone instrument at either end, one in his house and one in his friend's. A man was riding a horse down the road, didnae see the wire—and strangled! Hanged himself on the wire of John Logie Baird's tellyphone! That's a true story."

We came to Garelochhead, we traveled past Loch Long. The mountains above it were dark and rough, like enormous pieces of dusty coal. They were surrounded by pinewoods. The loch was blue-black and looked depthless.

"This loch is so long, so deep, and so straight they test torpedoes in it," Mr. Davidson said. "You can shoot a torpedo from one end to the other— thirteen miles or more. Want to see something interesting?"

He stood up and beckoned me to the window, and slid it down and said, "Watch."

We were coming to a junction, more tracks, and an isolated signal box. There were woods and hills all around. I expected the train to stop, but it did not even slow down. Mr. Davidson stuck his parcel of books out of the window and dangled it. A railwayman was standing on a small raised platform near the signal box. He snatched the books and yelled, "Thank you!"

"I've come this way before. The trains don't stop. I heard that the signalman here likes to read a good book. There's no shops here, no library, so I brought those books for him."

Mr. Davidson had no idea who the signalman was, nor did he know his name. He only knew that the man liked to read a good book.

"There used to be ever so many wee houses on this line, but now there's not many. It's out of touch. You see people on the train—after they've finished with their newspaper they throw it out the window to someone on the line to read."

Then Mr. Davidson screamed. He erupted in anger, just like that, without any warning.

"But some of them make me cross! People who travel through Scotland on the train, doing the crossword puzzle! Why do they bother to come!"

And, just as suddenly, he was calm: "They call that mountain 'The Cobbler.' There's an open trough just behind it"—he pronounced it *troch*, to rhyme with loch.

At flat, mirror-still Loch Lomond, white as ice under a white sky, Mr. Davidson began talking about printing unions. I had told him I was in publishing.

"You're not one of these bloody Fleet Street buggers!" he roared. It was another of his angry eruptions. "The printing unions are bloody! They're just protecting their own interests. They show up drunk and they get paid! 'Pay up!' 'But he's drunk!' 'Och, aye, but you cannae bag Wully!' 'I'll bag him!' 'Bag him and we'll all go out!' It's bloody stupid!"

Mr. Davidson was roaring at the window, at the creamy clouds reflected in the loch, not at me.

"I'm not a Queen Anne Tory," he said. "I'm a moderate Labour man. Aye, Jimmy, I was a trade unionist in 1912!"

He said he had been in the retail trade all his life—the grocery trade, another man's shop. He worked long hours. Eight in the morning until eight in the evening. A half-hour for lunch, a half-hour for tea.

The hills were bare from their mid-section upwards, and below this line were small pine trees. Mr. Davidson was very silent and then he leaned towards me and whispered sadly, "Everything you read's nae true."

He exploded again.

"They went daft with afforestation! It takes forty years for a tree to be useful. You could have forty years of lambs here, and instead they have trees!"

But there were not many trees. Three hundred years ago this district was full of hardwood forests—oak and beech. They were cut down and made into charcoal for the iron smelters at Taynuilt, up the line, famous for its cannon balls—Lord Nelson had fired them at the Battle of Trafalgar. Now the trees were wispy pines, and the hills were rocky and bare and black-streaked with falling water. The dark clouds were like another range of mountains, another foreign land, and the sun on some stones gave them a pale boney gleam.

I suppressed a shiver and said that it seemed rather bleak around here.

"Aye," Mr. Davidson said. "That's where its beauty comes from."

And he went to sleep. His mouth dropped open and he slept so soundly I thought he had died.

Later, Mr. Davidson awoke and gulped, seeming to swallow what remained of his fatigue. He recognized Kilchurn Castle. He said there had been a crazy old woman living in the ruin until very recently. She had thought she was the last of the Campbells. But he had also known hard times, he said. He had had "three spells of poverty"—no work and nothing to eat.

"And I couldn't join the army. I wore spectacles, you see. If you wore spectacles a gas-mask was useless."

Then he was talking about the Somme.

"This country has no friends"—he meant Britain—"only enemies, and debts. We spent years paying off the Boer War debt. And we're still in debt."

He hugged his heavy coat around himself and frowned. When he did this he looked shaggy and bearish. He was thinking.

"But there's nae debt for the Third World War. There'll be naebody left. Naebody can pay naebody! I blame"—he was erupting again—"I blame the poultices in the House of Commons! They'll start the next war and then there'll be naebody!"

We came to Oban. The railway station was white, with a blue trim, and had a clocktower showing the right time. There were seals in the harbor. On a hill above town was a full-sized replica of the Roman Colosseum, started in 1897 by a banker who thought something so ambitious would solve the unemployment problem. It was never finished; it was lovely and skeletal, symmetrical, purposeless. McCaig's Folly, they called it.

Even in Oban Mr. Davidson stayed by my side as he had in the empty railway car. He said the folly had a window for every day of the year.

"I'm a bachelor," he then explained. "I never married."

"No woman at all in eighty-seven years?"

"Nothing. And no drinking."

"Never had a drink?"

"Maybe a toddy or two," he said. "And I never smoked."

"A blameless life," I said.

"I've been sick, though," he said. "But nothing as far as sexual, drinking, or smoking."

Oban was made of stone. It was Scottish and solid, no honky-tonk, no spivs. It was a town of cold bright rooms, with rosy-cheeked people in sweaters sitting inside and rubbing their hands; it had fresh air and freezing water. If you were cold you went for a walk and swung your arms to get the circulation up—no hearth fires until October. In Oban it struck me that most Scottish buildings looked as durable as banks. Here the dull clean town was on a coast of wild water and islands.

Some of these Scottish coastal towns looked as if they had been thrown out of the ground. They were fine polished versions of the same rocks they were on, but cut square and higher—not brought and built there by bricklayers but carved out of these granite cliffs.

I saw Mr. Davidson my second day in Oban. He looked dead on a George Street bench, facing the harbor. His big hands were folded across his stomach, his mouth hung open. He had no suitcase—nothing but a rail ticket. Where had he slept? But I resisted asking questions, because I feared his answers.

He opened his yellow eyes on me.

I said, "I'm thinking of going to Fort William."

"There's a train in an hour," he said. "Where's your knapsack, Jimmy?"

He called everyone Jimmy.

I said, "At the bus shelter. I'm taking a bus up the coast."

He said, "I wasn't planning to do that."

"I'm sticking to the coast."

"Aye, Jimmy, stick to the coast." And he closed his eyes.

But there was a wild-eyed man on the bus. His name was Whitelaw, he chewed a pipe-stem, he watched the window and shouted.

There were cages in the sea.

He cried, "Fish farm!"

There was dark and frothy water under the Connel Bridge.

He cried, "Falls of Lora!"

I saw boggy fields.

He cried, "That's where they cut peat!"

He was animated by the landscape. I wondered whether it was a Scottish trait. I had never seen an English person behave like this.

He cried, "The tide's out!"

It was. Eventually he got off the bus, at Portnacroish, on the Sound of Shuna.

It was a complicated coastline of hills and bays, lochs and rushing burns. It could not have been anything but the Scottish coast—so much water, so much steepness, such rocks. Ballachulish was like an alpine valley that had been scoured of all its softness—the feathery trees and chalets and brown cows whirled off its slopes, and all the gentle angles scraped away, until it lay bare and rugged, a naked landscape awaiting turf and forest.

Most of this western coastline in Scotland looked elemental in that way— as if it had been whipped clean, and was waiting completion. It was hard and plain, most of it. It was very cold. I imagined sheep dying on it. Fort William was powerfully craggy. I began to think that this was the most spectacular coastline I had seen so far in Britain—huger than Cornwall, darker than Wales, wilder than Antrim. I stared at it and decided that it was ferocious rather than pretty, with a size and a texture that was surprisingly unfinished. It changed with the light as coastal cliffs always did; it was always massive, but in certain pale light it seemed murderous.

I was anonymous in Fort William. The other visitors had knapsacks, too, and oily shoes and binoculars. With Ben Nevis above it, and all the campsites of the highlands just behind it, Fort William was full of hikers and fresh-air fiends all frantically interrogating each other about footpaths. The town was crowded and unpleasant-looking, heaving with campers, so after lunch I wiped my mouth and walked north and west along the railway line to the coast. Once again I thought: Some travel is a fantasy of running away.

Three miles away I came to the lower end of the Caledonian Canal. I wanted to see a boat passing through, but there was nothing on it except ducks. It was a sunny day and I was glad to be alone in the empty glen.

Then a wheezing voice said, "Hae ye got a match?" and I almost jumped out of my skin.

It was Jock MacDougall, with red eyes and a filthy face, trembling next to a tree. He had a scabby wound on his forehead and his clothes were rags.

"I just want a match," he said. "I'm nae being cheeky."

He was trying to reassure me: He knew he was filthy and dangerous-looking. I gave him my matches and he slowly lit an inch-long cigarette butt that was flat, as if it had been stepped on. What an odd person to meet in a green glen.

He said, "I was never had up for assault or bodily harm or a breach of the peace in me whole life."

I stared at him. I did not know what to say.

"Only for being drunk and incapable," he said.

He had a little camp nearby—a nest of rags, some bottles, a smoky fire, and two comrades. There was a frightened woman named Alice and a man named Crawford, who was even filthier than MacDougall. Crawford called himself Tex. He was from Aberdeen.

"But I'm a Glasgow man," Jock said. "A Glasgow man will stick by you."

Alice looked wildly at him, but said nothing. She looked injured and was very silent.

Jock sang a song.

Coom doon the stairs.
Tie up your bonny hairs!

This seemed to frighten Alice even more.

He sang a song about a place called Fyvie. He said, "At Fyvie there's a statue of a cow!"

"What's your trade?" Crawford said. He had a dewdrop at the end of his nose and smelled of dead leaves.

I told them I was in publishing.

"Ha!" Jock said. "I'm a tramp! I'm a man of the road!"

Crawford said, "Do much traveling?"

"A certain amount," I said.

Crawford said, "I've been everywhere in the world."

"New Jersey? Argentina? Fiji?" I asked.

"Everywhere," he said.

I asked him to describe for me some of the more colorful spots he had seen.

"That would be too hard. There were so many."

Five feet away Jock was crouching with his arm around Alice. Then he thrust his hand under her green sweater and she squawked.

"I have three passports," Crawford said. "A woman in Perth once said to me, 'I'd like to have twenty-four hours with you.'"

This amazed me. He stank, his teeth were black, he had blades of grass in his beard.

"She said, 'Know what you should do? You should write a travel book.'"

"Why don't you?" I asked. Now I was sorry I had told him I was in publishing. But what would he write, under this tree?

"There's too many bloody travel books," he said, and faced me, as if challenging me to deny it.

I did not deny it.

"Why are you here in Scotland?" Jock shouted to me. "People in Scotland are rubbish!"

I said I had to go, but they stood on the path blocking my way.

"Give me some money," Jock said.

"Which way to Corpach?" I asked, still walking.

"I'm not telling any secrets unless you pay me!"

"All right, I'll pay."

He pointed. "Down there on the road."

I gave him a ten pence coin.

He said, "Give me sixty or seventy."

"That was only worth ten," I said. "Now step aside."

The train was the 16:30 to Mallaig. I looked back and saw the hump of Ben Nevis, with streaks and splashes of snow in some of its hollows. It was a huge gray forehead of rock, with a green bare dome in front of it, and three more on the south side. All the mountains here had the contours of hogs.

Mrs. Gordon in the next seat said, "Taking the train, to me, is like going to the cinema."

It was a splendid ride to Mallaig—one of the most scenic railway journeys in the world. But the train itself was dull and the passengers watchful and reverent, intimidated by all this scenery.

Scotland had a paradoxical beauty—its landscape was both lovely and severe; it was a monotonous extravaganza. The towns were as dull as any I had even seen in my life, and the surrounding mountains very wild. I liked what I saw but I kept wanting to leave. And the Scots had a nervous way with a joke. Their wit was aggressive and unsmiling. I kept wondering: Was that meant to be funny? When they were forthright they could become personal, especially on the subject of money. A Scot I met in Oban had accused me of wasting money when I told him that I had been planning to take a first-class sleeper to London—regarded it as wasteful and selfish that I should want to be alone. And here on this Mallaig train a man wanted to know why, if there was no Youth Hostel in Mallaig, I planned to stay the night there? And why hadn't I bought a round-trip ticket—didn't I know it was cheaper than the one-way fare on a weekend? This was Mr. Buckie, who saved rubber bands— he had fourteen on his wrist—and had been wearing the same tweed cap since 1953, Coronation Year. He was not trying to be helpful. Penny-pinching had made him abusive, obstructive, and cross. He ended up by disliking me, as if I was wasting *his* money.

But I thought: In travel you meet people who try to lay hold of you, who take charge like parents, and criticize. Another of travel's pleasures was turning your back on them and leaving and never having to explain.

I changed my seat as we passed along the shore of Loch Eil. There were high mountains rising in the west, and more lochs. Some of the mountains were three thousand feet high and some lochs a thousand feet deep (Loch Morar a few miles away was even deeper). We crossed the Glenfinnian Via- duct—it was curved and long and had romanesque arches, and it stood at the north end of the shiny black water of Loch Shiel, which lay beneath more rugged mountains.

There was great emptiness here. The train stayed high on the hillsides and did not descend into the valleys. There were ferns and bracken in the foreground, and some trees growing in narrow sheltered gullies out of the wind, but no human beings. The westerly gales had torn the soil from most hillsides. It was hard and lovely. The beauty was only part of it; you had to be tough to live here.

The landscape widened after Loch Ailort Station, and we were heading west where the bright sun was setting, making the water blaze on Loch Nan Uamh, which was also the sea, and making the green grass luminous and vibrant, as if the pasture were trembling a foot from the ground. The light was perfect, because there was nothing in the way: The mountains stood separate and all the sea lochs were long and stretched westward, so that the last of the sun shone uninterruptedly down their length.

The train bucked and turned north at Arisaig. The bays were like crater crusts filled with water. The offshore islands—Rhum, Eigg, Muck and

Canna—had names like items from a misspelt menu. The Scour of Eigg was a hatchet shape against the sky. And now beneath the train there was a basin of green fields for three miles to the Sound of Sleat—and above the train were mountains of cracked rock, and swatches of purple heather. Suddenly a horse was silhouetted in the sun, cropping grass beside the sea.

The train stopped at the level crossing at Morar—the opening and closing of gates, the latching and unlatching, clunk, clunk; and then chugged into Mallaig, where people were swimming in the freezing water, the foaming waves making lace caps for their bobbing heads.

That night I stared out of the window at the freakish mountains on Skye. They were sharp-pointed, fantastic, and high, like peaks in dragon stories. They were the Cuillins, and their strange shape made them look unclimbable. Although it was after eleven there was enough light for me to see them, and then near midnight they were ghostlier still: It was like winter light, a February afternoon in Boston, with the grayness of a gathering shadow.

In all my coastal travel I never met a fisherman who said he was satisfied. They hated the life, they said. The prices were bad, the competition was tough, the waters were overfished. Foreign fishermen were to blame—the Russians, the Japanese, the Danes. Foreigners scooped up everything— sprats, fry, undersized fish—and beat them into fishmeal on their factory ships.

Captain Cameron on his fishing boat *Lord Roberts* at Mallaig said, "Anyone here would sell his boat if he could get a fair price for it. The fishing business is dead. I should have sold mine when I could, a few years ago. Now I'm fifty-seven, and I have to work as long as I can. I won't be able to retire— haven't got the money. I'll work until I'm too weak to go on and then my kids will be cursed with this bloody boat."

He was taking seventeen crates of prawns' tails ashore, about a thousand pounds' worth, but his fuel bill for this trip was five hundred and he had a crew of five. There was hardly any profit in it. They had been at sea for nearly a week.

"Some day there'll be no fishing at all," Captain Cameron said. "It'll pass into ancient history."

On my second morning at Mallaig, Mrs. Fleming's daughter served me my breakfast and said, "Princess Diana's had a baby boy."

Everyone was pleased: an heir to the throne. It was another national event in an eventful period. The Falklands War had started and finished as I had been traveling. The pope had come and gone. The Royal Baby was born— Prince William. A railway strike was threatened. Three million people were unemployed—13 percent of the workforce—and one person out of six in Scotland was without a job. There was a deranged murderer loose in Yorkshire. They were public events and they had the effect of making people unusually talkative. "This Falklands business—" And then the American president visited and went horseback riding with the Queen. He made a speech. People smiled a little when they heard my accent. "I just saw your president on television—" It was supposed to be a kingdom of tight-lipped people, but the war and the strife and the pope and now the birth of a future king had brought about a relentless garrulity. I needed a little air.

I took the road north out of the town. The road ended; a track began. It was a rough stony path which circled a gray hill above the sea. I walked along the shore of Loch Nevis. Just over the hill at Loch Morar people sometimes searched for underwater monsters. I walked to Inverie, which was a house on a road that went nowhere. I wondered how much farther I should go. The coast was in-and-out for hundreds of miles. I liked walking, but I was no snorting rambler with plus-fours and a pick-axe. If I saw a sheep on the path I stopped and stared at it. I sat down and sketched a tall thistle at Inverie—the Scottish thistles seemed to me magical, and as complicated as crystals. I looked at birds. I tried to think of descriptions for these unusual islands—they were less like islands than old bare mountains in the sea. I was distracted by all the water and rock, the great heights of cloud, the ruined stone cottages along the coastal paths, the lived-in cottages in remote places which looked as though they were growing more remote—places only reachable in small boats.

It would have taken more than a week to walk from Mallaig to the Kyle of Lochalsh, up the coast. So I sailed there in the ferry *Lochmorar,* twenty-three miles along the Sound of Sleat. The boat passed more of these remote cottages. It said something about Scottish self-reliance and toughness that people willingly lived in such difficult places. In the whole of Britain there could not have been houses more inaccessible than these scattered over the shores of the Western Isles. The Scots here chose a distant ledge or a remote shore, and put up a stone house, and slammed their door on the world.

The coast had deep inlets and high cliffs, and it was so steep it had the effect of concentrating travelers in specific places. On this boat, for example. Or on certain valley roads. In Fort William and Oban and Mallaig. In England and Wales people were quickly absorbed by the countryside, and the coastal towns could seem very empty. But here in Scotland the countryside and the coastal steepness was forbidding, and so everyone traveled on a few routes; and they had always traveled on those routes. The traveler to Mull had to go to Oban, just like Doctor Johnson and Boswell in 1773.

At the Kyle of Lochalsh I crossed to Skye, on the ferry to Kyleakin ("from Hakon, King of Norway, who sailed through here in 1263") and walked the empty roads to Broadford, eight miles. I stayed and climbed partway up a red mountain merely to have another glimpse at the Cuillins. I did not go any closer. I wanted to save them for another time. I had seen so much on the British coast that I never wanted to see again that it was a surprise and a pleasure to find a place I wished to return to. It gave me hope, because I knew I would not come back alone. I wanted to come here again with someone I loved and say, "Look."

The sun on Skye warmed the pines and the flowers and gave it the fragrance of Nantucket.

The way between the huge simple mountains and cold lochs, from the Kyle of Lochalsh to Dingwall, was one of the great railway routes of Britain. It took me off the coast, but what else could I do? The northerly shore was broken and labyrinthine. It would only be a stunt to follow every mile of it, just to report on Loch Snizort and Trotternish. And the train was a greater temptation. Anyway, many of these lochs were also notches on the coast. Loch Carron, for example: The south bank, on which this train was traveling, was sixteen miles of coast.

Nothing looked to me colder than a Scottish loch, and they seemed to become colder still as the clouds piled up and night deepened. But these were short nights—a few cloudy hours of wintry light, and then morning. It was eight o'clock and every landscape feature was clearly visible: the water, the hills, the trees and farms, the long valley floor of Glen Carron that seemed to be covered with grassy mounds—tombs and tumuli.

"Ach, some of these villages have been here since the year dot," a man named Macnab said to me. Yes, they had a mossy, buried look. But many looked bleakly exposed, plopped down and untidy with no hedges, no bushes. The bushiest thing in Achnasheen was the stationmaster's beard.

We were delayed at Garve. I thought: I'll give it an hour and if we're still here I'll get off and walk up the Black Water or hitch to Ullapool. (Delays always sent me to my map for an escape route.)

Malcolm Biles asked for a look at my map. He was twenty-three, a post office clerk from Inverness, who was on a cheap day-return. I had wanted to meet a post office worker, I told him. British post office workers did much more than sell stamps. They processed car licenses, television licenses, Family Allowances, pensions, Inland Telegram Postal Orders, all the tasks required by the Post Office Savings Bank, and a hundred other things. They had seven weeks' training and the rest had to be learned on the job, in full view of the impatient public. It was Malcolm who spoke of the impatience. People were much ruder than they used to be and some of them stood there and ticked you off!

"What about dog licenses?" I asked.

Dog licenses! It was Malcolm Biles's favorite subject. The price of a dog licence was thirty-seven-and-a-half pence, because in 1880 it had been fixed at seven shillings and sixpence. The fee had never been changed. Wasn't that silly? I agreed it was. There were six million dogs in Britain, and only half of them were licensed. But the amazing thing was that it cost four pounds (almost seven dollars) to collect the dog license—the time, paperwork, and so forth.

"Why not abolish the fee?" I asked.

Malcolm said, "That would be giving up."

"Why not increase it to something realistic—say, five quid?"

"That would be unpopular," he said. "No government would dare try it."

"How long do you figure you'll be staying in the post office?"

"For the rest of my life, I hope," he said. The train jolted. "Ah, we're away."

I tried to imagine a whole lifetime in a post office. I could not imagine it. I got to the end of a few years and then nothing would come—a blur, fatigue, bewilderment, indifference. It was easier to imagine the life of that crofter talking gently to his dog at Strathpeffer.

Still, we discussed the post office and debated the issue of dog licenses until we came to Dingwall ("birthplace of Macbeth").

Colin Thubron

Where Nights Are Longest

Colin Thubron, author of the highly regarded travel book *Mirror to Damascus*, set out on a ten-thousand-mile journey between the Baltic and the Caucasus that covered two and a half months, staying in campsites and occasional hotels, frequently trailed by the KGB—a less glamorous trip one cannot imagine. But Thubron's gift is to transmute the ordinary into the extraordinary, as he does in this passage from his account of his travels by car through Western Russia, published in Britain as *Among the Russians* in 1983, and as *Where Nights Are Longest* in the United States one year later.

A hundred miles later the first mountains appeared. Huge but insubstantial, they shifted and overlapped like shadows thrown on the sky. At dusk, when I arrived in the campsite at Pyatigorsk, it was to find these outworks of the Caucasus hovering all around in black, refractory silhouettes. The camp was half empty. I carried my bedding to my sleeping hut under a sky already flashing with stars. But somebody had arrived before me.

"You will please excuse me, sir"—I saw a dark man with a smooth-skinned, ingratiating face. "May I petition your kindness to call me Misha? I was appointed here as your guide by the authorities because they consider you particularly honorable."

I wasn't anxious to be noticed by the nameless authorities, but his whimsical English dismissed a faint disquiet. He was small and slight, with an ambivalent face: a forty-year-old boy. His head looked perfectly circular, and was muffled in short black hair incongruously flecked by gray. From time to time his quaint, phrasebook speech was pocked by unintentional slang.

"Tomorrow we will visit the beauties of Pyatigorsk spa. But first may I lavish with you some booze on the occasion of your successful arrival?" In either hand he held a bottle of Georgian champagne, and all the time he spoke his forehead shot up and down in comical spasms and his eyes popped, as if he were trying to keep awake.

"It is not allowed to guides to tipple along with foreigners, nevertheless," he said, then uncorked the champagne and gurgled it into two glasses plucked from his pockets. We sat at the table in my hut, with the curtains drawn. Misha stretched back in his chair with self-conscious hedonism, cigarette in one hand, champagne glass poised in the other, his face crossed by a sybaritic grin. I could not make him out. "To tell you the truth, there's nothing to do in Pyatigorsk spa at all," he said, "unless you have a stomach complaint. As for me, my own origins, sir, are not in Pyatigorsk. According to the anthropology, I believe I have Tartar blood. I am from the Volga. But sometimes people mistake me for a mountain Jew, or an Italian, perhaps, because I talk too much."

He spoke unlaughing. Sometimes his alternate pedantry and vulgarisms gave me the fleeting illusion of a Dickensian gentleman fallen on evil days. He had studied English, he said, at the pedagogical institute in Moscow. Now he was a schoolmaster and part-time guide in Pyatigorsk. "And what is your profession?" he suddenly asked.

I launched into an outdated story about a company directorship. He poured out more champagne.

"You were today a long time arriving here. I have been waiting for you since three o'clock—propping up the bar, if thus I may put it." His forehead performed a mazurka of spasms. I thought he was slightly drunk. "I feared something had befallen you."

No, I said, nothing. He uncorked the second bottle of champagne with a celebratory flourish. "This is Black Label Georgian. The best! Now this company directorship of yours . . ."

The drink seemed to be seeping into my eyes, clouding them. I was watching Misha through a muslin curtain. His forehead was shooting about in self-conscious imbecility now. I wondered momentarily if he were retarded. But his questions had become more searching. Somewhere, far back in my mind, a warning bell was sounding.

"Tomorrow," he was saying, "we will go into the mountains. There is a game reserve where I have a certain buddy. I do not wish to press my insistences upon you, but you are a sportsman are you not? I love hunting. Do you love hunting? It is forbidden there, but nevertheless."

The second bottle was draining fast. Misha refilled the glasses with remorseless devotion, grinning at nothing. I reckoned he was drunker than I, but my head was already swaying feebly, and to refuse the last champagne was to insult his hospitality.

He began talking politics. He was a member of the Communist Party, he said, and certainly he seemed modestly privileged: He had worked as an interpreter with Russian groups abroad; he had also read the best-known Western exposés of the Soviet way of life. "Those books are right," he said. "Politics here are a farce." He burped. "Just propaganda. Nobody can find out anything serious except through the Party grapevine. Do you know there are strikes going on in Poland at this moment . . . serious strikes . . . almost nobody in this country knows about them?" And what were my politics, he asked?

I mumbled some British complacencies, gauging my own drunkenness, feeling unhappy. When he next refilled my glass, I surreptitiously emptied it into an ashtray. I did not take his news on Poland seriously; I had heard nothing.

A distant, slurring voice (my own) asked: "How can you be a Party member when you think it's all a farce?"

He smiled, and misunderstood. "I deserve my place in the Party. In the early sixties I was with Soviet troops in Somalia, shooting members of the Somalia resistance and so forth. Then the country's allegiances, if thus I may put it, unfortunately changed to the British, and we were chucked out." He said the word *British* as if it had nothing to do with me (and his history was badly garbled).

"You shot Somalis . . . but you think your politics . . ."

In my champagne-sodden mind the idea of Misha was by now hypnotic. I foraged for some hidden rationale to his self-canceling beliefs, but he intimated none. One moment he let drop that the whole Soviet Union was rife with corruption. The next he asked me to send him a postcard of Britain congratulating him on his country's glorious October Socialist Revolution. His talk was an obscene chiaroscuro of ideology and cynicism. It was as if his integrity had rotted away long ago, or never existed.

Suddenly he said: "You will not refer on me to the authorities?"

"I don't know any authorities."

He dropped his cigarette into the ashtray. It fizzed in my discarded champagne. "Why have you poured it away?" He stood up. "We'll go to the camp restaurant. I have friends waiting there. We'll have a party."

From this later, drink-fuddled celebration, which drowsed and gabbled far into the night, I retrieve only random glimpses. A gallery of inebriate faces glows in my memory, severed from time and place; their remarks surface in meaningless isolation, and whole conversations lie stranded without starts or ends. But the faces, I recall, encapsuled in miniature the Soviet empire. Opposite me a Slav suet-pudding physiognomy proposed cumbersome toasts and cracked into smiles with the slowness of a geological fault, while beside him a citron-skinned architect might have sprung from the pages of Russian folklore. On my right Misha's low brows and Tartar cheeks surrounded bright but indecipherable eyes; to my left a long-faced Armenian barman, with the creamy skin and voice of his people, offered me seductive sums for my Morris.

The architect, I thought, looked restrained, ill at ease. He talked to me ruefully. His teenage children, he said, were besotted by pop music; as for him, he wondered if I had any records of Victor Sylvester with me—he loved those. He shared the Russian passion for the countryside, and would often vanish on two-day fishing expeditions, although this upset his wife.

"Actually he fishes for women," said the suet pudding, fracturing into a grin. "There aren't any in Pyatigorsk, only sanatoria."

One by one we declaimed portentous toasts, groping to our feet with teetering solemnity. Wine, vodka, and Armenian three-star brandy slopped down our throats in ceremonial debauch. With each toast the little glasses of vodka were tossed back at a gulp, so that drunkenness advanced in dazed leaps and bounds, and faculties were amputated at a stroke. On one side of me the Armenian's car-prices spiraled into fantasy, on the other Misha kept clinking his glass against mine, chirruping "Quite sincerely!" and spoke of himself in the third person. "Misha needs a holiday. . . . Misha is quite fed up with being a schoolmaster. . . . Tomorrow, or perhaps the day after, we will go into the mountains and see the eternal snows. Misha loves beauty. Do you love beauty?"—glasses clashed—"Quite sincerely! . . . Misha should have been a lawyer. . . . What did your father make you do? . . . He didn't? Your fathers in the West, they're very lenient. . . . Quite sincerely! I was only seventeen, and I wanted to do law. . . ." Snatches of pop songs droned inconsequently in his speech, then he would change the subject without warning or ask sudden questions.

"It's true there are no girls in Pyatigorsk . . . not after Moscow. Misha enjoyed himself in Moscow. But it's not a good city for the personal relationships. . . . *Bye-bye, baby, bye-bye.* . . . Russian girls, let me tell you, sir, make very good wives, excellent in the home, very tender and not very sexually experienced. . . . What is your father's job?"

It struck me that Misha was not only drunk but pretending, perhaps enjoying the idea of drunkenness, I didn't know. His forehead and eyes wrinkled and popped in unison. "Let me tell you, sir, there was a Belgian girl on the language course in Moscow . . . lovely wide hips, very womanlike . . . oh Misha! *Save all your kisses for me.* . . . How is it you are allowed on such a tour by your authorities? You must be an important person. . . ."

But a tiny, watchful fragment of myself was refusing to get drunk. I remembered a sixteenth-century ambassador to Moscow writing that he could only avoid stupor by feigning it already, otherwise he was forced to continue drinking. Feigning wasn't difficult. My head had become a hydrogen balloon tethered among empty bottles and dismembered expressions. The architect, as it happened, resembled a French schoolmaster from my childhood, so that in my drugged vision the two men—the present and the imagined—nudged each other bifocally and occasionally overlapped. For all I know I began calling him "sir" and conjugating irregular verbs.

Then the suet pudding lumbered to his feet for yet another toast. We had already pledged eternal friendship, the beauty of women, the peoples of our two countries, our families and much else, and had now entered a realm of flowery, maudlin libations which threatened to drop me senseless. "We come like many rivers from different sources," he intoned, "yet we meet in the same sea, under the same sky, so let us drink. . . ."

Two or three more vodkas, I calculated, and I'd be insensible. I proposed my return toast in a babble of goodwill and mixed metaphors, and spilled my glass unseen into a vase of plastic flowers.

Soon afterwards the restaurant closed, and we were stumbling out under the stars. The air was soft and warm. Goodnights sounded in the dark. I walked gingerly to the camp gates. My feet felt numb on the path. Misha kept blundering against me. "You can't drive home in your state," I said.

"It doesn't matter," he slurred. "The police won't do . . . anything to me."

"Why not?"

"Because I work. . . ." He floundered again, recovered; but I suddenly knew what he was going to say. "Because I work . . . for the KGB."

My voice sounded flat. "What's that like?"

"Mostly rather . . . boring."

We were approaching the gates, where porters loitered. I had time, I estimated, for one more question. "I don't imagine they're interested in me, are they?"

An ugly silence fell. "In you . . . especially." Then he disappeared through the gates and into the dark.

Mark Twain

Roughing It in Paradise

The lines below are taken from *Roughing It,* Mark Twain's 1872 follow-up to the roaring success of *Innocents Abroad.* In 1880 came another great book of travel, *A Tramp Abroad.* The following years brought him fortune and fame, but by 1894 some disastrous business decisions had thrown him into bankruptcy. Compelled to repay hundreds of thousands of dollars, he embarked upon a lecture tour (reported in his final book of travel, *Following the Equator,* 1897) that took him once again to the Hawaii he had described in *Roughing It.* But in 1895, when his spirits were at lowest ebb and he might well have sought permanent sanctuary in that "paradise for an indolent man," as he had once called Hawaii, he and his fellow passengers were not permitted to land.

On Sunday morning, March 18, 1866, the steamer *Ajax* sailed into Honolulu Harbor while the bells of six different mission churches called the freshly converted faithful to worship. Among the passengers most eager to go ashore was a thirty-one-year-old knockabout journalist named Samuel Clemens, on assignment for the Sacramento *Union.* Mark Twain would later make the Mississippi immortal, but first Hawaii would make him famous. He spent four months and a day exploring the islands and sent back twenty-five dispatches (at twenty dollars each), recounting all that he had seen and heard. Fresh from the grime and clamor of the California mining camps, he was enraptured by the lush, silent Hawaiian landscape and was alternately amused and fascinated by the native Hawaiians and the missionaries, planters, whalers, and hangers-on already seeking to displace them. Compared with his later works, the letters from the Sandwich Islands are crude, repetitive, and overwritten, but they are also filled with his inexhaustible love of the absurd and his sharp eye for detail, and—polished up and tightly edited—they form a major part of his first book, *Roughing It,* published six years after his return to the mainland. By that time he had delivered a humorous lecture on Hawaii—sometimes billed as "Our Fellow Savages of the

Sandwich Islands"—before packed houses from San Francisco to Keokuk to Manhattan. Most of the selections [below] are from *Roughing It.*

The chief pride of Maui is her dead volcano of Haleakala—which means translated, "The House of the Sun." We climbed a thousand feet up the side of this isolated colossus one afternoon; then camped, and next day climbed the remaining nine thousand feet, and anchored on the summit, where we built a fire and froze and roasted by turns all night. With the first pallor of dawn we got up and saw things that were new to us. Mounted on a commanding pinnacle, we watched Nature work her silent wonders. The sea was spread abroad on every hand, its tumbled surface seeming only wrinkled and dimpled in the distance. A broad valley below appeared like an ample checkerboard, its velvety-green sugar plantations alternating with dun squares of barrenness and groves of trees diminished to mossy tufts. Beyond the valley were mountains picturesquely grouped together; but bear in mind, we fancied that we were looking *up* at these things—not down. We seemed to sit in the bottom of a symmetrical bowl ten thousand feet deep, with the valley and the skirting sea lifted away into the sky above us! It was curious; and not only curious, but aggravating; for it was having our trouble all for nothing, to climb ten thousand feet toward heaven and then have to look *up* at our scenery. However, we had to be content with it and made the best of it; for all we could do we could not coax our landscape down out of the clouds. . . .

I have spoken of the outside view—but we had an inside one, too. That was the yawning dead crater, into which we now and then tumbled rocks, half as large as a barrel, from our perch, and saw them go careering down the almost perpendicular sides, bounding three hundred feet at a jump; kicking up dust clouds wherever they stuck; diminishing to our view as they sped farther into distance; growing invisible, finally, and only betraying their course by faint little puffs of dust; and coming to a halt at last in the bottom of the abyss, two thousand five hundred feet down from where they started! It was magnificent sport. We wore ourselves out at it. . . . Presently vagrant white clouds came drifting along, high over the sea and the valley; then they came in couples and groups, then in imposing squadrons; gradually joining their forces, they banked themselves solidly together, a thousand feet under us, and *totally shut out land and ocean*—not a vestige of *anything* was left in view but just a little of the rim of the crater, circling away from the pinnacle whereon we sat (for a ghostly procession of wanderers from the filmy hosts without had drifted through a chasm in the crater wall and filed round and round, and gathered and sunk and blended together till the abyss was stored to the brim with a fleecy fog). Thus banked, motion ceased, and silence reigned. Clear to the horizon, league on league, the snowy floor stretched without a break—not level, but in rounded folds, with shallow creases between, and with here and there stately piles of vapory architecture lifting themselves aloft out of the common plain—some near at hand, some in the

middle distances, and others relieving the monotony of the remote solitudes. . . . I felt like the Last Man, neglected of the judgment, and left pin-
nacled in mid-heaven, a forgotten relic of a vanished world. . . .

While I was in Honolulu I witnessed the ceremonious funeral of the king's
sister, Her Royal Highness the Princess Victoria. According to the royal
custom, the remains had lain in state at the palace *thirty days,* watched day
and night by a guard of honor. And during all that time a great multitude of
natives from the several islands had kept the palace grounds well crowded
and had made the place a pandemonium every night with their howlings and
wailings, beating of tom-toms, and dancing of the (at other times) forbidden
hula-hula by half-clad maidens to the music of songs of questionable decency
chanted in honor of the deceased. . . .

As the procession filed through the gate, the military deployed handsomely to the right and left and formed an avenue through which the long
column of mourners passed to the tomb. The coffin was borne through the
door of the mausoleum, followed by the king and his chiefs, the great officers
of the kingdom, foreign consuls, ambassadors, and distinguished
guests. . . . At this point of the proceedings the multitude set up such a
heartbroken wailing as I hope never to hear again. The soldiers fired three
volleys of musketry—the wailing being previously silenced to permit of the
guns being heard. His Highness Prince William, in a showy military uniform
(the "true prince," this—scion of the house overthrown by the present dynasty—he was formerly betrothed to the princess but was not allowed to
marry her), stood guard and paced back and forth within the door. The
privileged few who followed the coffin into the mausoleum remained some
time, but the king soon came out and stood in the door and near one side of
it. A stranger could have guessed his rank (although he was so simply and
unpretentiously dressed) by the profound deference paid him by all persons
in his vicinity; by seeing his high officers receive his quiet orders and
suggestions with bowed and uncovered heads; and by observing how careful
those persons who came out of the mausoleum were to avoid "crowding" him
(although there was room enough in the doorway for a wagon to pass, for that
matter); how respectfully they edged out sideways, scraping their back
against the wall and always presenting a front view of their persons to His
Majesty, and never putting their hats on until they were well out of the royal
presence.

He was dressed entirely in black—dress coat and silk hat—and looked
rather democratic in the midst of the showy uniforms about him. On his
breast he wore a large gold star, which was half-hidden by the lapel of his
coat. He remained at the door a half hour. Finally he entered his carriage and
drove away, and the populace shortly began to drop into his wake. While he
was in view there was but one man who attracted more attention than

himself, and that was Harris (the Yankee prime minister). This feeble person-age had crape enough around his hat to express the grief of an entire nation, and as usual he neglected no opportunity of making himself conspicuous and exciting the admiration of the simple Kanakas.

     The farther I traveled through the town the better I liked it. Every step revealed a new contrast—disclosed something I was unaccustomed to. In place of the grand mud-colored brown fronts of San Francisco, I saw dwellings built of straw, adobes, and cream-colored pebble-and-shell-conglomerated coral, cut into oblong blocks and laid in cement; also a great number of neat white cottages, with green window shutters; in place of front yards like billiard tables with iron fences around them, I saw these homes surrounded by ample yards, thickly clad with green grass, and shaded by tall trees, through whose dense foliage the sun could scarcely penetrate. . . .

     I looked on a multitude of people, some white, in white coats, vests, pantaloons, even white cloth shoes, made snowy with chalk duly laid on every morning; but the majority of the people were almost as dark as Negroes—women with comely features, fine black eyes, rounded forms, inclining to the voluptuous, clad in a single bright red or white garment that fell free and unconfined from shoulder to heel, long black hair falling loose, gypsy hats, encircled with wreaths of natural flowers of a brilliant carmine tint; plenty of dark men in various costumes, and some with nothing on but a battered stovepipe hat tilted on the nose, and a very scant breechclout; certain smoke-dried children were clothed in nothing but sunshine—a very neat-fitting and picturesque apparel indeed. . . .

     The missionaries have Christianized and educated all the natives. They all belong to the church, and there is not one of them, above the age of eight years, but can read and write with facility in the native tongue. It is the most universally educated race of people outside of China. They have any quantity of books, printed in the Kanaka language, and all the natives are fond of reading. They are inveterate churchgoers—nothing can keep them away. All this ameliorating cultivation has at last built up in the native women a profound respect for chastity—in other people. Perhaps that is enough to say on that head. The national sin will die out when the race does, but perhaps not earlier. But doubtless this purifying is not far off, when we reflect that contact with civilization and the whites has reduced the native population from *four hundred thousand* (Captain Cook's estimate) to *fifty-five thousand* in something over eight years!

     Society is a queer medley in this notable missionary, whaling, and gov-ernmental center. If you get into conversation with a stranger and experience that natural desire to know what sort of ground you are treading on by finding out what manner of man your stranger is, strike out boldly and address him as "Captain." Watch him narrowly and if you see by his counte-

nance that you are on the wrong tack, ask him where he preaches. It is a safe
bet that he is either a missionary or captain of a whaler. I am now personally
acquainted with seventy-two captains and ninety-six missionaries. The captains and ministers form one-half of the population; the third fourth is
composed of common Kanakas and mercantile foreigners and their families,
and the final fourth is made up of high officers of the Hawaiian government.
And there are just about cats enough for three apiece all around.

        In the rural districts of any of the Islands, the traveler hourly comes upon
parties of dusky maidens bathing in the streams or in the sea without any
clothing on and exhibiting no very intemperate zeal in the matter of hiding
their nakedness. When the missionaries first took up their residence in
Honolulu, the native women would pay their families frequent friendly visits,
day by day, not even clothed with a blush. It was found a hard matter to
convince them that this was rather indelicate. Finally the missionaries provided them with long, loose calico robes, and that ended the difficulty—for
the women would troop through the town, stark naked, with their robes
folded under their arms, march to the missionary houses, and then proceed
to dress! The natives soon manifested a strong proclivity for clothing, but it
was shortly apparent that they only wanted it for grandeur. The missionaries
imported a quantity of hats, bonnets, and other male and female wearing
apparel, instituted a general distribution, and begged the people not to come
to church naked, next Sunday, as usual. And they did not; but the national
spirit of unselfishness led them to divide up with neighbors who were not at
the distribution, and next Sabbath the poor preachers could hardly keep
countenance before their vast congregations. In the midst of the reading of a
hymn a brown, stately dame would sweep up the aisle with a world of airs,
with nothing in the world on but a stovepipe hat and a pair of cheap gloves;
another dame would follow, tricked out in a man's shirt, and nothing else;
another one would enter with a flourish, with simply the sleeves of a bright
calico dress tied around her waist and the rest of the garment dragging
behind like a peacock's tail off duty; a stately . . . Kanaka would stalk in with a
woman's bonnet on, wrong side before—only this, and nothing more; after
him would stride his fellow, with the legs of a pair of pantaloons tied around
his neck, the rest of his person untrammeled; in his rear would come another
gentleman simply gotten up in a fiery necktie and a striped vest. The poor
creatures were beaming with complacency and wholly unconscious of any
absurdity in their appearance. They gazed at each other with happy admiration, and it was plain to see that the young girls were taking note of what each
other had on, as naturally as if they had always lived in a land of Bibles and
knew what churches were made for; here was the evidence of a dawning
civilization. The spectacle which the congregation presented was so extraordinary and withal so moving that the missionaries found it difficult to

keep to the text and go on with the services; and by and by when the simple children of the sun began a general swapping of garments in open meeting and produced some irresistibly grotesque effects in the course of redressing, there was nothing for it but to cut the thing short with the benediction and dismiss the fantastic assemblage.

Though Mark Twain never managed to revisit his beloved islands, he came close. He returned to Honolulu Harbor in 1895, but cholera was raging in the city, and none of the passengers aboard his ship was allowed to disembark. "If I might I would go ashore," he wrote in his journal, "and never leave." But he could not arrange it. His "dream of twenty-nine years" was shattered. Nonetheless, he was consulted as a Hawaiian expert for the rest of his life. In 1873, as the United States debated annexation, he wrote:

We *must* annex those people. We can afflict them with our wise and beneficent governments. We can introduce the novelty of thieves, all the way up from street-car pickpockets to municipal robbers and Government defaulters, and show them how amusing it is to arrest them and try them and then turn them loose—some for cash and some for 'political influence.' We can make them ashamed of their simple and primitive justice. . . . We can give them juries composed entirely of the most simple and charming leatherheads. We can give them railway corporations who will buy their Legislature like old clothes, and run over their best citizens and complain of the corpses for smearing their unpleasant juices on the track . . . we can furnish them some Jay Goulds who will do away with their old-time notion that stealing is not respectable. . . . We can give them lectures! I will go myself.

We can make that little bunch of sleepy islands the hottest corner on earth, and array it in the moral splendor of our high and holy civilization. Annexation is what the poor islanders need. "Shall we to men benighted, the lamp of life deny?"

He expressed his devotion to the islands in a very different way in 1889. At a dinner held in honor of a baseball team about to embark for Hawaii on a world tour, he recalled the place as he'd first seen it.

No alien land in all the world has any deep strong charm for me but that one, no other land could so longingly and so beseechingly haunt me, sleeping and waking, through half a lifetime, as that one has done. Other things leave me, but it abides; other things change, but it remains the same. For me its balmy airs are always blowing, its summer seas flashing in the sun, the pulsing of its surfbeat is in my ear; I can see its garlanded crags, its leaping cascades, its plumy palms drowsing by the shore, its remote summits floating like islands above the cloud rack; I can feel the spirit of its woodland solitudes, I can hear the plash of its brooks, in my nostrils still lives the breath of flowers that perished twenty years ago.

Evelyn Waugh

Pompeian Dances

"From 1928 until 1937," Waugh wrote, "I had no fixed home and no possessions which could not conveniently go on a porter's barrow. I traveled continuously, in England and abroad." His first travel book was *Labels*, issued in 1929 and so called because "All the places I visited on this trip are already fully labeled." He went from the Mediterranean in that book to less predictable spots in Arabia, South America, and Africa in his next three (all four books were collapsed into one valedictory to travel in 1945, *When the Going Was Good*).

The arrival of the *Stella Polaris* caused excitement. She came in late in the evening, having encountered some very heavy weather on her way from Barcelona. I saw her lights across the harbor and heard her band faintly playing dance music, but it was not until next morning that I went to look closely at her. She was certainly a very pretty ship, standing rather high in the water, with the tall, pointed prow of a sailing yacht, white all over except for her single yellow funnel.

Every Englishman abroad, until it is proved to the contrary, likes to consider himself a traveler and not a tourist. As I watched my luggage being lifted on to the *Stella* I knew that it was no use keeping up the pretense any longer. My fellow passengers and I were tourists, without any compromise or extenuation.

The *Stella Polaris* is a Norwegian-owned six-thousand-ton motor yacht, carrying, when full, about two hundred passengers. As one would expect from her origin, she exhibited a Nordic and almost glacial cleanliness. I have never seen anything outside a hospital so much scrubbed and polished. She carried an English doctor and nurse; otherwise the officers and crew, hairdresser, photographer, and other miscellaneous officials were all Norwegian. The stewards came of that cosmopolitan and polyglot race, Norwegian, Swiss,

British, Italian, which supply the servants of the world. They maintained a Jeeves-like standard of courtesy and efficiency which was a particular delight to the English passengers, many of whom had been driven abroad by the problem of servants in their own homes. The passengers, too, were of all nationalities, but British strongly predominated, and English was the official language of the ship. The officers seemed to speak all languages with equal ease; several of them had first gone to sea in windjammers; sitting out between dances after dinner, while the ship ran on smoothly at fifteen knots into the warm darkness, they used to tell hair-raising stories of their early days, of typhoons and calms and privations; I think that when they were getting a little bored by their sheltered lives they found these reminiscences consoling.

I soon found my fellow passengers and their behavior in the different places we visited a far more absorbing study than the places themselves.

One type which abounds on cruising ships is the middle-aged widow of comfortable means; their children are safely stored away at trustworthy boarding schools; their servants are troublesome; they find themselves in control of more money than they have been used to; their eyes stray to the advertisements of shipping companies and find there just that assembly of phrases—half-poetic, just perceptibly aphrodisiac—which can produce at will in the unsophisticated a state of mild unreality and glamor. "Mystery, History, Leisure, Pleasure." There is no directly defined sexual appeal. That rosy sequence of association, desert moon, pyramids, palms, sphinx, camels, oasis, priest in high minaret chanting the evening prayer, Allah, Hichens, Mrs. Sheridan, all delicately point the way to sheik, rape, and harem—but the happily dilatory mind does not follow them to this forbidding conclusion; it sees the direction and admires the view from afar.

I do not think these happier travelers are ever disappointed in anything they see. They come back to the ship from each expedition with their eyes glowing; they have been initiated into strange mysteries, and their speech is rich with the words of the travel bureau's advertising manager; their arms are full of purchases. It is quite extraordinary to see what they will buy. I suppose it is the housekeeping habit run riot after twenty years of buying electric lightbulbs and tinned apricots and children's winter underwear. They become adept in bargaining, and may be seen in the lounge over their evening coffee, lying prodigiously to each other, like the fishermen of comic magazines, comparing prices and passing their acquisitions from hand to hand amid a buzz of admiration and competitive anecdote. I wonder what happens to all this trash. When it reaches England and is finally unpacked in the gray light of some provincial morning, has it lost some of its glamor? Does it look at all like the other bric-à-brac displayed in the fancy goods emporium down the street? Is it distributed among relatives and friends to show that they are not forgotten during the voyage?—or is it treasured, every bit of it, hung upon walls and displayed on occasional tables, a bane to the house-parlor-maid but a continual reminder of those magical evenings under a wider sky, of dance music and the handsome figures of the officers, of temple bells heard across the water, of the inscrutable half-light in the bazaars, of Allah, Hichens, and Mrs. Sheridan?

But there were many kinds of passenger on board. I made friends with a young couple named Geoffrey and Juliet.

There was a series of land excursions organized on board the *Stella* by a patient and very charming Norwegian ex-sea-captain in a little office on the promenade deck, and one of the questions most exhaustively discussed among the passengers was whether these were worthwhile. At Naples, where I set out entirely alone with a very little knowledge of Italian, I wished very much that I had joined one of the parties.

We ran into the bay early on Sunday morning, and moored alongside the quay. There was a German-owned tourist ship in the harbor, which we were to see several times during the next few weeks, as she was following practically the same course as ourselves. She was built on much the same lines as the *Stella*, but the officers spoke contemptuously of her seaworthiness. She had capsized, they said, on the day she was launched, and was now ballasted with concrete. She carried a small black airplane on her deck, and the passengers paid about five guineas a time to fly over the harbor. At night her name appeared on the boat deck in illuminated letters. She had two bands which played almost incessantly. Her passengers were all middle-aged Germans, unbelievably ugly but dressed with courage and enterprise. One man wore a morning coat, white trousers, and a beret. Everyone in the *Stella* felt great contempt for this vulgar ship.

By the time that we had finished breakfast, all the formalities of passport and quarantine offices were over, and we were free to go on shore when we liked. A number of English ladies went off in a body, carrying prayerbooks, in search of the Protestant church. They were outrageously cheated by their cab driver, they complained later, who drove them circuitously and charged them eighty-five lire. He had also suggested that instead of going to matins they should visit some Pompeian dances. I, too, was persecuted in a precisely similar way. As soon as I landed a small man in a straw hat ran to greet me, with evident cordiality. He had a brown, very cheerful face, and an engaging smile.

"Hullo, yes, you sir. Good morning," he cried. "You wanta one nice woman."

I said, no, not quite as early in the day as that.

"Well then, you wanta see Pompeian dances. Glass house. All-a-girls naked. Vair artistic, vair smutty, vair French."

I still said no, and he went on to suggest other diversions rarely associated with Sunday morning. In this way we walked the length of the quay as far as the cab rank at the harbor entrance. Here I took a small carriage. The pimp attempted to climb on to the box, but was roughly repulsed by the driver. I told him to drive me to the cathedral, but he took me instead to a house of evil character.

"In there," said the driver, "Pompeian dances."

"No," I said, "the cathedral."

The driver shrugged his shoulders. When we reached the cathedral the fare was eight lire, but the supplement showed thirty-five. I was out of practice in traveling, and after an altercation in which I tried to make all the wrong points, I paid him and went into the cathedral. It was full of worshipers. One of them detached himself from his prayers and came over to where I was standing.

"After the Mass. You wanta come see Pompeian dances?"

I shook my head in Protestant aloofness.

"Fine girls?"

I looked away. He shrugged his shoulders, crossed himself, and relapsed into devotion. . . .

At dinner that evening at the Captain's table the lady next to me said, "Oh, Mr. Waugh, the custodian at the museum was telling me about some very interesting old Pompeian dances which are still performed, apparently. I couldn't quite follow all he said, but they sounded well worth seeing. I was wondering whether you would care to—"

Donald E. Westlake and Abby Adams

Discovering Belize

Belize is the Cayman Islands of the 1960s: The former British Honduras offers friendliness, beaches, mountains, Mayan ruins—and no
threat, as yet, of the touristic hordes that have descended upon Mexico
and the Bahamas. The prolific mystery writer and his journalist wife
provide a model of practical, terse travel writing that, when published
in 1984, made Belize seem absolutely the best place on Earth.

Here's what we did one day in Belize. We got up late for breakfast on
Ambergris Cay, a sandy island twenty miles offshore, out by the barrier reef.
After a farewell swim in the sapphire-blue Caribbean, we packed, were driven
the half-mile to the airport, and took the twenty-minute flight to Belize's
Municipal Airport, where Gerald Garbutt of Royal Rentals waited for us with
our rented car. We had a Lebanese-and-Caribbean lunch at the villa (one
serving of hummus, another of lobster), drove due west from the city out
along the road leading to Guatemala, turned off onto a terrible rock road up
into the hills and drove sixteen miles to Blancaneaux Lodge in Pine Mountain
Ridge. After unpacking in our thatched-roof cabin on the slope above Prevas-
sion Creek, surrounded by the pine-covered tallest mountains in the country,
we put on our swimsuits, rock-scrambled for a quarter-mile along the creek
past foamy rapids and deep green pools, and went skinnydipping under the
afternoon sun.

Much of what we like about Belize was encapsulated in that single day. It
is so small and yet so varied that you can swim in the ocean in the morning
and in a mountain stream in the afternoon. Its tourist industry is so tiny and
new that the owner of the car rental company delivers your car, and yet the
country is so modern that there are half a dozen scheduled and charter

336

airlines operating within it. And while the country is small, its population is even smaller; a scant one hundred fifty thousand people from every race and every continent in a nation the size and shape of New Jersey (which holds seven million).

Most people, when we say we're going to Belize, ask, "Where in Africa is that?" Nowhere in Africa. The former British Honduras, which became the independent land of Belize only three years ago, is at the northeast corner of Central America, tucked in just under Mexico's Yucatan peninsula, with 170 miles of coastline along the western edge of the Caribbean Sea. You could think of it as a Caribbean island unaccountably attached to the shoulder of Central America.

But if Belize, for all its Caribbean coastline, is a Central American country, isn't it dangerous there? Absolutely not. The only English-speaking nation in Central America, and the only former British colony there, it is stable and democratic and welcoming. The police don't even carry guns. A sign we saw on a waterfront warehouse in Belize City captures the flavor: "Anyone found pilfering cargo will be severely dealt with." This is a nation whose authority figure is the nanny, not the death squad.

Being not quite an island, and not quite Central America, and not quite a regular tourist stop, gives Belize certain charms and advantages. Pre-Columbian Mayan temples and cities are an afternoon's drive from white sand Caribbean beaches. Dense mysterious rain forest and jungle gives way to flat farmland—sugar in the north, citrus crops in the south—and pastures where little white birds stand proudly on the backs of the grazing cattle. Decent accommodations can be found in most of the country, but you will never be in a tourist ghetto, cut off from the life around you, lost in a mob of sightseers.

And then there's the barrier reef, second longest in the world. Averaging about twenty miles offshore, the reef extends the entire length of the coast, protecting it from the main force of the sea and making Belize one of the finest places in the world for sailing enthusiasts; with the reef to cut the swells and a steady offshore breeze, you never want to tack toward home.

The reef itself, dotted with hundreds of islands, is a magnet for snorkelers and divers, with intricate coral structures that house a staggering variety of animal and plant life. For the angler, such game fish as bonefish, tarpon, snook, and grouper abound; the local commercial fishermen harvest these, as well as lobster, shrimp, conch, and crab.

Inland, there are the ruined cities and temples of the Maya. Until recently, the civilizations of pre-Columbian Mesoamerica have been best known through digs in neighboring Mexico and Guatemala, but in the last decade or so a great number of ancient Mayan sites have been found and mapped in Belize. One, Caracol, as yet completely unexplored, is estimated by archaeologists to be even larger than Tikul in Guatemala, long considered the largest of all Mayan settlements. Unfortunately, Caracol is deep in rain forest without even an access road at this point, so only the hardiest visitor can get there. But other sites, such as Altun Ha and Xunantunich, with its 130-foot high temple, still the tallest man-made structure in the nation, have been cleared. They are being maintained against the encroaching jungle and are easily reached. A middle range is found in such sites as Lubantuum or Nim Li Punit or Lamanai, where archaeological work has been done in the past or continues to some extent today. In such places, where access is not quite impossible, the buildings and statues and bas reliefs are for the most part still in the jungle's green grip. (Lamanai was occupied more or less continuously from about 1600 B.C. to almost A.D. 1600—longer than Rome.) It is in sites like this, and not in the tidied-up temples with little signs and guideposts, that you feel the weight of time and come to believe in the reality of those ancient people. Their spirit is present also in the flesh and blood of their descendants, present-day Maya Indians who work their farms and build their thatched-roof cottages in the shadows of the ruined temples.

For the traveler, Belize begins with Belize City. All flights to the country land at Belize International Airport, while internal flights use Belize Municipal Airport, right in town. The former capital, built virtually at sea level on the coast at the mouth of Haulover Creek, it was devastated by Hurricane Hattie in 1961. Since then a new capital, called Belmopan after the Maya Mopan tribe, has been built fifty miles inland, but to date only four thousand inhabitants occupy Belmopan's "planned" city, while ten times that number still crowd into Belize City's dilapidated frame structures.

Belize City is a lively, untidy town, whose charm can be found in its bustling polyglot people; in the ramshackle remains of carpenter-Gothic villas from more prosperous colonial times; in the glimpse of the blue Caribbean at the end of a bougainvillea-festooned alleyway. (It's a low skyline; in the whole country, there isn't one elevator.)

There are a total of three roads in all of Belize, none of them very good. About the best is the newly completed Northern Highway between Belize City and the Mexican border. It passes so close to Altun Ha that several years ago the archaeologists were appalled to find a road repair crew using thousand-year-old blocks for roadfill. Farther north, around Orange Walk Town, you pass through the neat domain of the German Mennonite farmers who, in the last quarter of a century, have become the heart of Belize's small dairy industry. Sugar is also very important here, and on the right day you'll suddenly find yourself passing miles of parked trucks and wagons piled high with sugarcane. They are in line for the big sugar mill, and entire short-term communities form while they wait. We have passed card games, meals in preparation, passionate discussion groups, and even more passionate couples.

The Western Highway connects Belize City with the Guatemalan border. About thirty miles out is Hattieville, populated by former Belize City residents; driven here by Hurricane Hattie in 1961, they chose to stay and with rare amiability named the new place after the disaster that had occasioned it. Farther on you pass the new capital, Belmopan, and beyond that the landscape changes; marsh and savannah are replaced by dense jungle and hills. Farther on again, jungle gives way to tropical pine forest. This is Mountain Pine Ridge, a land of rushing streams, wild orchids, puma and ocelot, and great fantastic limestone caves, some of which are treasure troves of Mayan artifacts. Out near the Guatemalan border is San Ignacio, a colorful Spanish-speaking town, perched high above a deep river gorge. The San Ignacio Hotel makes a good base for a visit to Xunantunich.

The third road heads south from Belmopan, is called the Hummingbird Highway, and is highly treacherous. Belizean friends looked at us with new respect when we told them we'd driven the whole thing, then decided we must be merely insane when we admitted we'd done it with an ordinary car and not something with four-wheel drive. Twenty-seven miles south of Belmopan is a lovely and surprising wayside restaurant called Jungle Gardens, owned by a young American woman, Mary Cariddi, and managed by a Canadian named Louise Lines, whose architect husband, Ron, is an unassuming fount of knowledge. Simple but good food and drink, fine conversation, and a menagerie including a deer and a coatimundi in addition to the dog and cat.

About seventy miles south of Belize City sits the small coastal town of Dandriga, settled in the early nineteenth century by Garifuna, a mix of African blacks and Carib Indians who migrated here from the island of St. Vincent. They retain their language and customs, which include colorful dances that derive directly from Africa. The Pelican Beach Hotel, just outside town on the coast, is a good jumping-off point for nature or archæological expeditions into the bush, including canoe trips down Stann Creek, or for trips out to the reef. The hotel is popular with biologists doing field work in the area, and its guests often include entire class groups from American colleges, complete with field assignments and accompanying chaperone-teacher.

Belize's largest offshore island and its most popular tourist destination is Ambergris Cay. The most developed part of the island is the fishing village of San Pedro at its southern end, although "developed" is an odd term for a place almost empty of cars, where the one-room bank is open three mornings a week and placid dogs sleep at high noon on the white sand of the main street. The reef lies half a mile out, but for the less ambitious the beaches are clean and white, the sun shines three hundred days a year and there are just enough bars to make for a pleasant evening's pub crawl. (Go to Fido's and buy a rum and grapefruit juice for Rick the piano player. Everybody goes to Rick's place.)

Belizeans who feel Ambergris Cay is becoming too commercial go to Placentia, a tiny fishing village at the tip of a narrow peninsula of the same name, 130 miles down the coast from Belize City. There is no actual road in Placentia, only a two-foot wide sidewalk meandering past the shabby little houses built high on stilts.

Others of the smaller cays, with very limited service, attract yachts-people and fishing enthusiasts. About the largest of these, Cay Caulker, is charmingly described in one local publication as having "a fishing community of about four hundred people, including several permanent tourists." Where do we sign up?

Now how long can it last? Belize, with all its natural amenities, is a vacation spot of rare variety and pleasures, and there's no way it can avoid becoming increasingly popular. In years to come, Kentucky Fried Chicken shops and mass-produced "native handicrafts" will undoubtedly become part of the scene, but not yet. Happily, very happily, not yet.

Ben Yagoda

Unfolding the Nation

Perhaps this piece in *The Armchair Traveler* should have been the first—just as at a ballgame you can't tell the players without a score-card, you don't know where you are about to travel without a road map. But then Ben Yagoda would have had to change his name to Agoda; oh well. Here's all you ever wanted to know about American road maps but were afraid to ask.

On Thanksgiving Day in 1895 the Chicago *Times-Herald* sponsored a fifty-four-mile road race from Jackson Park to Waukegan and on to Lincoln Park. The prize was $5,000. The eventual winner, a man by the name of Frank Duryea, had at least two advantages over his competitors. First, unlike some of them, he was driving a car propelled by gasoline. Second, Duryea had noticed that the paper had published a rough plotting of the course, and he'd had the good sense to rip it out and use it. He thus made not only money but history. By virtue of his action the *Times-Herald* illustration transcended newspaper graphics to become the first American automobile road map.

The distinction is significant only in retrospect; at the time its effects were nil. After all, what need was there for road maps when, even in 1900, there were a mere eight thousand registered automobiles in the entire country? But as the century shifted into gear, things changed. By 1910 almost a million cars had been registered; by 1915 more than two million. With this new popularity came innovations in the superstructure of motoring, innovations that, considering their improvised character, proved to be surprisingly durable. In 1908 came the first concrete road, a mile-long stretch of Detroit's Woodward Avenue. Almost immediately motorists from hundreds of miles around made pilgrimages to drive on it. This was a year after the first pedestrian safety island, in San Francisco, and three years before the first painted dividing line, in Michigan. In 1914 Cleveland introduced the first electric traffic signal, and Buffalo put up the first no-left-turn sign in 1916.

Previously motoring had been a form of on-the-edge recreation, something like hang-gliding today. Now it was transportation, and motorists needed guidance on how to get where they wanted to go. The roads in a good many urban areas were already mapped, thanks to the bicycle craze of the 1880s and 1890s. But bicycle maps were next to useless to motorists. Cyclists could negotiate mountain trails, pedal their way through alleys or, in an emergency, carry their vehicles across streams; motorists could not. Something new was needed.

As it happened, that something did not—at least at first—turn out to be the road map. Starting not long after the turn of the century, various concerns—tire companies, automobile associations, newspapers, car manufacturers, and resorts—began issuing road guides, in bound, folded, or pamphlet form, each spelling out one or more specific routes. For every turn along the way there was a precise mileage reading, which the motorist was to find on his odometer. In a book put out in 1898 by the White Company, for example, Route 56 is a 110-mile journey from South Bend to Chicago; the driver is told to get ready at mile 80.3, and "at the next corner turn left passing 'Mike's Place' on the right." Publishing the guide was hardly a civic-minded gesture on the part of White, a manufacturer of steam cars. Not only is the book filled with advertisements, but almost every route in it ends at a branch of the firm.

These early road guides generally included a map or two, but they were not to be relied on. As the Hartford Rubber Works, a tire concern, admitted in its *Automobile Good Roads and Tours,* published in 1905, "A very thorough preliminary search showed that there were no maps which could be used as a basis for this work. . . . Much has been willingly left to geographical sense, and the tourist's own constructive faculty."

There was considerable variation in the books. In one or another you could find promotional claims ("That the White raises less dust than any other car was proven beyond question in the 'Dust competition' held last year by the Royal Automobile Club of England on the Brooklands race-track"); useful advice ("Look out for auto-trap [speed trap], especially in the thinly settled part of town"); and even navigational tips that suggest the precarious nature of motoring early in the century. One book gives detailed instructions, complete with a sketch of the Big Dipper, on how to find "true north."

A major innovation in the guidebooks was the use of photographs of key points along the route; some included a picture of every turn. (Early examples show a car making the maneuver in question, while later ones, their authors having learned an important lesson, showed the turn from the perspective of the driver.) An obvious problem for the compilers of photo guides was that if the enterprise wasn't to take an intolerable amount of time, at least two researchers were needed: one to drive, and one to take odometer readings, pictures, and notes. Andrew McNally II, son of the founding partner of Rand McNally & Company, solved this problem by enlisting his bride; the *Rand McNally Chicago to Milwaukee Photo-Auto Guide* of 1909 is a record of their honeymoon trip.

Another difficulty with the guidebooks was that landmarks on the order of Mike's Place were not permanent. So, in the 1910s, a number of guidebook makers took the sensible step of making their *own* landmarks. In the middle of the decade, the Goodrich tire company began putting up guideposts, described as follows in one of their books: "Erected for the express purpose of guiding motor travel. This sign is made of porcelain enamel in three colors, erected on four-inch oak posts, ten feet long. Each post is thoroughly creosoted and planted three feet into the ground." The company's guidebooks then supplied directions keyed to the markers.

The guides were useful, but they could not hold sway for very long. As new roads were built, the books, which had gotten more unwieldy every year, simply could not cover all the possible routes. It was time for the road map.

Maps designed exclusively for autos had been produced at least as early as 1900, the date of a series of pocket maps put out by George Walker of Boston, which can be found in the map collection of the New York Public Library. His maps are in perfect condition, printed in delicate colors and handsome typography, beautifully bound and backed with stiff gauze covers, and—miraculously, considering the legendary difficulties later generations of drivers have had with the task—effortless to fold.

There was no shortage of other maps produced in the following years, many of them published by the American Automobile Association, founded in 1902. (In the early teens the AAA began putting out what later became known as Trip-Tiks, elongated, horizontal strip maps customized to guide members on their travels. It provides the same service today.) But there was one drawback in using maps for directional guidance at this time: Roads had no names or at best had local, unofficial ones (Lincoln Highway, Dixie Highway, Post Road) that changed as you went from one town to another. How were these roads to be identified on maps?

A solution to this problem was hit on by John Brink, a draftsman on the staff of Rand McNally. In 1916 the company ran a contest, offering $100 to the employee who suggested the best new map product. Brink suggested road maps specifically designed for motorists. To deal with the route-naming difficulty, he proposed that Rand McNally take the Goodrich trail markers one step better and put up posts that *numbered* major routes, which would then be correlated with the maps. Brink, named head of Rand McNally's new Blazed Trails Department, put his scheme into practice in 1917, when his Illinois *Auto Trails* map was published. The next year Brink used his summer vacation to blaze the route from Kalamazoo, Michigan, to Cincinnati.

In his diary he recorded his method: "I started out for the field with my car loaded with 400 cardboard signs (coated to resist the weather), ten pounds of broadhead tacks, and a magnetic hammer, not to mention a pair of overalls. Commencing at Kalamazoo, I worked south, and in nine working days, reached Richmond, Ind. I had blazed 180 miles of road, tacking up 355 signs that consumed 22 pounds of tack."

Brink's idea might have been too good. It so clearly made sense that now dozens of civic organizations, auto clubs, state road departments, and map companies began blazing trails, with the confusing result that some roads were marked by as many as a dozen contradictory signposts. Clearly, government intervention was called for. It started to arrive in 1920, when Wisconsin became the first state to number its roads; by 1924 twenty-one other states had followed its lead. By the end of the decade, 75,884 miles of "U.S. Routes" were in place, the precursor to the Interstate Highway System of the 1950s.

A map innovator perhaps the equal of John Brink was an advertising man named William B. Akin. In 1913 the Gulf Refining Company erected, on a Pittsburgh street corner, the nation's very first drive-in gasoline service station. In the fall of 1913, Akin suggested that Gulf print up some maps of the country's roads and give them away to customers as promotional tools.

The idea caught on. By 1920 Gulf was giving away sixteen million Eastern states maps a year, and before long, with every other gasoline company following its lead, free road maps were the way virtually every American motorist figured out how to get from one place to another. From the thirties on, these folded maps of cities, states, and regions changed very little in form, except for occasional experiments like a 1955 map Esso put out of the route from New York to Florida. It is a cartographic fact of life that some people find it hard to use a map to proceed south, when a line veering off to the right represents a left turn. In an attempt to rectify the situation, Esso put Florida on the top. The break with convention proved to be too great, and after ten years the experiment was abandoned.

By this time free road maps had come to seem an American institution, something of an inalienable right. In the fifties, a publication of the General Drafting Company, one of the companies that, along with Rand McNally, designed and sold the road maps to the oil companies, mused: "It seems to us that there is a close parallel between maps and television. Both are free to the public, both have mass appeal. Both depend on high quality to produce low-cost results for advertisers. Both call for human interest, novelty, attractiveness, and good taste in their commercials. There is one big plus for maps. They have retention value. Their 'commercials' live on for months, even years."

Such pride would not go unpunished. In 1972, two hundred and fifty million free maps were produced for the oil companies, more than ever before. The very next autumn the Arab oil embargo struck, an event that proved to be the death knell for the free road map. Shortages and gas lines did away with the intense competition that had spawned promotional giveaways. By 1978 the free road map had gone the way of the Packard, Ebbets Field, and the fifteen-cent cup of coffee. Today maps are available at gas stations and bookstores, but they can cost up to three dollars.

Still, free road maps left their mark. For one thing, they taught several generations of Americans a skill that had once been the esoteric province of yachtsmen, surveyors, and generals. Indeed, officers who served in both world wars found that in the Second their men could read reconnaissance maps more proficiently than they could in the First. The reason was road maps.

By definition realistic, road maps have also touched a lyrical vein in the American sensibility, offering an image of the country that is almost poetic. Unfolding a state map and following a crooked line to a town called, say, Clarion, is a potent imaginative experience; it makes you ponder.

To Jack Kerouac the open road was "one long red line called Route 6 that led from Cape Cod clear to Ely, Nevada, and then dipped down to Los Angeles." A more recent writer, William Least Heat Moon, also sees the road map as a metaphor of sorts. In the preface to his book *Blue Highways,* he writes: "On the old highway maps of America, the main routes were red and the back roads blue. Now even the colors are changing. But in those brevities just before dawn and a little after dusk—times neither day nor night—the old roads return to the sky some of its color. Then, in truth, they carry a mysterious cast of blue, and it's that time when the pull of the blue highway is strongest, when the open road is a beckoning, a strangeness, a place where a man can lose himself."

Chiang Yee

On Bedloe's Island

There are tourists who plod up the stairs of Lady Liberty just so they can get to the top and say they did it, and there are travelers who approach the statue with a sense of pilgrimage. We daresay that those in the second camp are overwhelmingly the foreign-born who, in times not so distant, might have first apprehended the reality of America here as their ship steamed on to Ellis Island, where immigrants were received. These were the most adventurous travelers—the ones who turned their backs on home and history and bet all on tomorrow. *The Silent Traveler in New York*, from which this passage is excerpted, is but one of the author/painter's many books of shimmering prose and delicate watercolors.

I take the advice of the Roman poet Martial:

So, Posthumus, you'll live tomorrow, you say:
Too late, too late, the wise lived yesterday!

Though not particularly wise, I certainly "lived yesterday." I do not know how I shall live today or tomorrow, because planning my day seems to impose a restriction on my spirit. I find it more satisfying to recall my past activities. I take real pleasure in recalling the happy time I spent at Liberty, by which of course I mean the Statue of Liberty on Bedloe's Island, southwest of Manhattan. I heard of Liberty before I sailed for New York, watched it from afar while approaching the City, and finally became on intimate terms with it, for I actually went through its body right up to the head!

It was a sunny, hazy afternoon, typical of early spring in New York, when I took a subway train to Bowling Green and thence went to Battery Place for a return ticket to the Statue of Liberty. The steamer was just about to leave and I mounted to the upper deck. Most of the space along the railings was already occupied, most of the seats too, and everyone was talking hard. Youngsters were violently running round the decks and shouting their heads off. Young

346

couples were laughing and even wrestling without restraint; I suppose because they were on their way to Liberty.

I seemed to be the only person on the steamer without a companion, but I had perhaps a different motive from the rest in visiting Liberty. I watched the wharf slowly recede and the downtown skyscrapers diminish as we moved away. The sunbeams caught and gilded their windows through the bluish haze, and touched the shiny silvery wings of seagulls swooping astern.

The haze was not unlike that of the Thames estuary, but without its damp cold. For a considerable time I could not see the Statue, the steamer was still too far away. Gradually a brightly lit vertical tube peered through the haze and I recognized the Statue. The general effect reminded me of Cleopatra's Needle in Central Park lit by flood-lighting. The color turned out to be an illusion created by distance. The Statue was not now emerald green at all.

Passing a cheerful group of people waiting on the landing stage to be taken back to New York, I followed my fellow passengers through the gate in the base of the pedestal. We walked in line between thick ropes and entered a lift on payment of a fee. Someone gave a fifty-cent piece for change and the white-haired attendant remarked that he had not seen a silver piece like that for years. As soon as the lift began to go up, a mysterious voice began telling the story of the Statue; its remarks were conveniently timed to conclude before we reached the top. It gave a great deal of information in a very short time, most of which I could not hear. The "top" turned out to be only the top of the pedestal, whence we had to climb flight after flight of stairs, each narrower than the last. Though we knew we had started from the foot of the Statue, there was nothing to indicate our progress through the body. Inside were huge metal beams and machinery, awe-inspiring to my unmechanical eye. Breath began to be short and legs to ache as we mounted, but no one was daunted, and we all reached the head. At least twenty of us were able to move about freely inside the head. We looked through the apertures round the crown. There were maps above each hole, but I could see very little through the thick haze. Many expressed disappointment, but I knew I had chosen the right day. I had wanted to see Liberty in the original meaning of the word and here I was—in space! Suddenly I overheard someone say triumphantly, "It's reducing anyway. It's reducing. I think I've lost five pounds!" Another use for Liberty!

The descent was easier and I got out of the building quickly. Before I did so, I glanced at the photographs of the Statue on the wall and read the long poem entitled *The New Colossus* by Emma Lazarus. I liked its last stanza:

> Give me your tired, your poor,
> Your huddled masses, yearning to be free.
> The wretched refuse of your teeming shore.
> Send these, the homeless, tempest-tossed to me.
> I lift the lamp beside the golden door.

From a paper giving the dimensions of the Statue the detail which struck me was that the length of the finernail is thirteen inches. It reminded me how, in bygone days in China, some gentlefolk of both sexes used to wear very long fingernails as a sign of gentility, an indication that they did no manual work. Those were the days! No Chinese of today can afford such an affectation. My young compatriots probably do not even know that there were ever such people. But I, with one foot in that bygone age, saw one or two of them in my youth, and it pleased me now to fancy that the Statue of Liberty was a Chinese lady of great virtue and purity, chosen as a symbol because she possessed a strong free will of her own, despite the bondage laid on her by tradition.

I went into the island café for a Coca-Cola. A few tables were spread outside under yellow sunshades, and many people were having meals. Others were busy writing postcards and buying souvenirs. Later I strolled round the star-shaped base and then aproached the water. A few small fir trees are grouped here and there, and the whole island is well laid-out with cement bricks and green lawns. The water's edge is as straight as if cut with a knife.

I was surprised at the lack of natural features. I had never come across before a piece of land *entirely* remade by man. The architectural achievements of New York fill me with wonder, but give me no feeling of stability. New Yorkers—and probably other Westerners—seem ever eager to alter the whole face of a landscape. I should not be astonished to hear one day that the little islands round Manhattan had been removed altogether. To me, the smallest Pacific atoll has the permanent look of all natural things, whereas Bedloe's Island I should suppose to have been *built* in the sea by Americans had I not been told the truth. Aerial photographs of Ellis Island, Governor's Island, Welfare Island, and Bedloe's Island make these whims of Nature look like marvelously well-made, scale-model toys. They suggest, too, the house-rafts of bamboo or logs which float down the Yangtse River from Chungking, occasionally remaining stationary in the middle of the river for a while, with the local folk taking no notice of them, and presently drifting silently on their way. I often saw them outside my native city Kiukiang. The "sailors" lived just like people in the city. If the upright hand of the Statue of Liberty held a long pole instead of a torch, I should expect Bedloe's Island to move gently away one day like a raft. But I dare say it is more likely to be towed away by tugs to "a more convenient site". . . .

A certain man of Ch'i one day, some twenty-three hundred years ago, began to dread the fall of Heaven. As he knew no way to prevent this calamity, he worried over it day and night, forgetting to eat and to sleep. But Heaven did not fall. And probably Bedloe's Island will remain very much where it is today.

I confess I never understood how Frederic Auguste Bartholdi, the originator and sculptor of the Statue of Liberty, came to conceive such a fantastic scheme. It is a piece of *Occidental* inscrutability to me. None of the many lovers of liberty before Bartholdi thought of such a way to proclaim their faith. In addition to his artistic ability and technical achievement, Bartholdi's powers of imagination must have been exceptionally great. Visitors to the Statue of Liberty should remember not only its name and colossal size but also the man who made it.

The poem, *The New Colossus*, expresses the effect of the Statue on a poet's mind. So far I have not found anything dealing with its artistic merits, which I doubt if we can judge adequately from the small reproductions in metal or pottery which are on sale as souvenirs. Perhaps its gigantic dimensions prevent it being judged at all from the artistic point of view. Size alone can impress but can also minimize artistic effect. Too-small dimensions will tend to confuse the spectator, while too-big ones are beyond his grasp. For instance, I admire Frank Brangwyn's mural paintings inside the RCA buildings, but I prefer to look at postcard reproductions of them rather than at the originals, which are so high upon the huge walls that my eyes cannot take them all in at once. Similarly I find it difficult to appreciate the artistic merit of the enormous sculpture of Atlas outside RCA Building. Pressed by the crowds moving along the pavement I have to stand too close to it to see it properly. The placing of an outsize work of art presents serious difficulties. Bartholdi's choice of Bedloe's Island for his Statue of Liberty was perhaps the happiest part of his work. He wanted it to be, above all, *impressive,* and it impresses every visitor to New York. I read somewhere that Bartholdi began work on the Statue in 1879. The building of skyscrapers was a much later development. I am no student of the history of architecture and have no urge to trace the origin of skyscrapers, but clearly the impulse which made Bartholdi build his 305-foot statue must have been the same which later prompted the solving of the technical problems involved in building skyscrapers three times that height.

Possibly the Temple of Isis by King Nekhtnebf about 350 B.C. on the Island of Philae in the Nile, Egypt, which was protected by a stone quay all round with the necessary staircases, etc., had something to do with Bartholdi's thought on his gigantic project at first. Or he had in mind the Egyptian Pyramids and Sphinx, and the colossal monuments and statues of the Greco-Roman world; but to me his Statue seems more akin to the early Chinese colossal sculpture of Buddha on the rocks of the Yun-kan and Tun-huang caves. These huge stone representations of Buddha still rouse onlookers to veneration and faith. I regard the Statue of Liberty not merely as a Statue but as a symbol of a faith, and meditating in front of it I tried to visualize what Liberty has meant for mankind. There have been grand words uttered about it by the great thinkers of the past, but the following poem by William Lloyd Garrison (1805–1879) appeals particularly to me:

> High walls and huge the body may confine,
> And iron gates obstruct the prisoner's gaze,

And massive bolts may baffle his design,
   And vigilant keepers watch his devious ways;
But scorns the immortal mind such base control;
   No chains can bind it, and no cell inclose.
Swifter than light it flies from pole to pole,
   And in a flash from earth to heaven it goes.
It leaps from mount to mount; from vale to vale
   It wanders, plucking honeyed fruits and flowers;
It visits home to hear the fireside tale
   And in sweet converse pass the joyous hours;
'Tis up before the sun, roaming afar,
   And in its watches wearies every star.

Though no actual word or term for Liberty is to be found in the ancient Chinese Classics, "to be one's absolute true self" is the principal Confucian teaching, and "to keep one's soul free" the chief point of the rhythm of life advocated by Lao Tzŭ, who originated Taoism. Chuang Tzŭ, the sage and disciple of Lao Tzŭ, was once angling in the river P'u. When messengers came from the King of Ch'u asking him to take up a high administrative position, he replied that he had heard that a holy tortoise which had died three thousand years before was kept by the king in a golden casket in the great hall of his ancestral shrine. Supposing that when this tortoise was caught it had been allowed to choose between dying and having its bones preserved and venerated for centuries, and keeping itself alive with its tail dragging in the mud, he inquired of the Court messengers which fate they would have preferred. Their answer being the latter, Chuang Tzŭ told them to go away and let him drag his tail in the mud. And he was at once left alone, for, fortunately, his regard for liberty was appreciated by the messengers.

But the idea of liberty has not always been so well understood. In modern life its meaning has become more and more obscured. I do not refer to politics, which I cannot pretend to understand; what I deplore is that we human beings seem to have lost the sense of liberty in our daily life. We "tighten our belt" to order; we follow every fashion; we listen to what we are told; we are bound by convention. I know that there are many who are happily married, but I am inclined to think that in every country there are some husbands like the one in the following Chinese story:

One night a much-henpecked husband began to smile in his sleep. The wife gave him a punch to wake him up and asked what had made him so happy in his dream. The answer was that he dreamed he had taken a small wife (concubine). This made the wife furious, and adopting her usual method, she punished him by making him kneel beside the bed and giving him a good beating. The husband begged her not to take it seriously, saying, "Dreams are only illusions." She retorted that he could dream on any subject but this one. He promised to do so. However, the wife was not sure how she could know what he was dreaming about. "It will be easy," replied the husband, "I shall be safe from temptation if you let me sleep quietly until I wake in the morning."

The poor man was not even accorded liberty in his dreams. But can we really declare that any one of us today possesses the *feeling* of liberty? To regain this priceless sense and preserve ourselves from further degeneration, what could be better than to use the Statue of Liberty as a center of pilgrimage? New Yorkers seem to be fond of notable processions: Why should there not be an annual procession to the Statue? Husbands like the one in the story, anyhow, would gladly participate!